# BACKLASH Against the ADA

**Corporealities:** Discourses of Disability

David T. Mitchell and Sharon L. Snyder, editors

# BACKLASH
## Against the ADA

## REINTERPRETING DISABILITY RIGHTS

*Edited by Linda Hamilton Krieger*

THE UNIVERSITY OF MICHIGAN PRESS

Ann Arbor

To Vicki

Copyright © by the University of Michigan 2003
All rights reserved
Published in the United States of America by
The University of Michigan Press
Manufactured in the United States of America
⊗ Printed on acid-free paper

2006   2005   2004   2003      4   3   2   1

A CIP catalog record for this book is available from the British Library.

Library of Congress Cataloging-in-Publication Data

Backlash against the ADA : reinterpreting disability rights / edited
    by Linda Hamilton Krieger.
        p.   cm. — (Corporealities)
    Includes index.
    ISBN 0-472-09825-X (cloth : alk. paper) — ISBN 0-472-06825-3
    (pbk. : alk. paper)
        1. People with disabilities—Legal status, laws, etc.—United
    States—History.   2. People with disabilities—United States—
    History.   I. Krieger, Linda Hamilton, 1954–   II. Series.
    KF480 .B33   2003
    342.73'087—dc21                                    2002010531

# Acknowledgments

Many of the articles in this collection were published in earlier form by the *Berkeley Journal of Employment and Labor Law,* a student-edited law review at the University of California at Berkeley, School of Law (Boalt Hall). Grateful acknowledgment is made to the journal for permission to republish these materials here in revised form.

Early drafts of the articles, along with other papers and responsive commentaries, were presented at a two-day symposium entitled "Backlash Against the ADA: Interdisciplinary Perspectives and Implications for Social Justice Strategies," held at Berkeley in March 1999. I would like to thank the journal's 1998–99 members and editorial board, the many students, lawyers, activists, and disability community members who attended and participated in the symposium, and the event's major financial sponsors. These included Disability Rights Advocates, World Institute on Disability, Disability Rights Education and Defense Fund, San Francisco Foundation's Disability Rights Advocates Fund, Pacific Bell, Lexis-Nexis, Van Loben Sels Foundation, Ladder Fund of the Tides Foundation, Corporation on Disabilities and Telecommunication, Sunrise Medical, Issue Dynamics, Inc., U.C. Berkeley School of Law (Boalt Hall), Boalt Hall Students Association, and Boalt Hall Center for Social Justice.

Acknowledgment is made to Larry Wright for permission to reprint a cartoon originally appearing in the *Detroit News* and to Gary Brookins for permission to reprint a cartoon originally appearing in the *Richmond Times-Dispatch.*

Linda Hamilton Krieger

# Contents

*Linda Hamilton Krieger*

# Introduction

For civil rights lawyers who had toiled through the 1980s in the increasingly barren fields of race and sex discrimination law, the charmed passage of the Americans with Disabilities Act through the U.S. House and Senate and across a Republican president's desk must have seemed vaguely surreal. The strongly bipartisan House vote in the summer of 1990 was a remarkable 377 to 28, the vote in the Senate an equally overwhelming 91 to 6.[1] Rising to speak in favor of the bill, Republican cosponsor Orrin Hatch—not known for impassioned endorsements of new civil rights protections—had cried on the Senate floor.[2] Senator Tom Harkin, who had earlier delivered his floor remarks in American Sign Language, said of bill following the Senate vote, "It will change the way we live forever."[3]

Signing the bill into law, President Bush was equally effusive. Describing the nation's historical treatment of the disabled as a "shameful wall of exclusion," President Bush compared passage of the ADA to the destruction of the Berlin Wall:

> Now I am signing legislation that takes a sledgehammer to another wall, one that has for too many generations separated Americans with disabilities from the freedom they could glimpse but not grasp. And once again we rejoice as this barrier falls, proclaiming together we will not accept, we will not excuse, we will not tolerate discrimination in America. . . . Let the shameful wall of exclusion finally come tumbling down.[4]

At the July 27 signing ceremony, held on the White House South Lawn to accommodate the large crowd of activists in attendance, President Bush cavalierly dismissed predictions that the law would prove too costly or loose an avalanche of lawsuits.[5] Republican senator Bob Dole, a strong ADA supporter, admitted that the new law would place "some burden" on business, but found that burden justified because the act would "make it much easier" for America's disabled.[6]

For traditional civil rights lawyers, this was incongruous fare. For the previous two months, Senators Dole and Hatch, along with Vice President Quayle, President Bush, and others in his administration, had been sharply denouncing the Civil Rights Act of 1990,[7] pejoratively labeling it a "quota bill."[8] The soon-to-be-vetoed legislation, which in much-diluted form eventually became the Civil Rights Act of 1991,[9] sought to countermand a series of Supreme Court cases that, among other things, had virtually erased disparate impact theory,[10] an accepted feature of Title VII jurisprudence since the early 1970s. The veto, which the Senate failed to override by one vote, represented a dispiriting defeat for traditional civil rights constituencies and their lawyers.

The Civil Rights Act of 1990 was not the only employment rights casualty of President Bush's veto power. Just a year before he signed the ADA into law, the president had vetoed a bill that would have raised the minimum wage from $3.35 an hour to $4.55.[11] Stunning the congressional leadership, the veto came a mere fifty-one minutes after the bill had reached the president's desk. On June 29, 1990, only two days after the ADA's festive South Lawn signing ceremony, President Bush vetoed the Family and Medical Leave Act, which would have required covered employers to accommodate workers by providing up to twelve weeks of unpaid leave in cases of family illness or childbirth. In defense of the veto, Bush stated that such practices should not be mandated by the government, but should rather be "crafted at the workplace by employers and employees."[12] Neither the minimum wage hike nor the FMLA, which Bush vetoed again in 1992, would become law until passed by the next Congress and signed into law in 1993 by newly inaugurated President William Jefferson Clinton.

It must have been difficult for traditional civil rights lawyers, reeling from these many setbacks, to comprehend the triumphal enthusiasm with which Republican senators and administration officials celebrated the passage of the ADA. How could such a transformative statute, requiring not only formal equality, as the nondiscrimination concept had traditionally been understood, but also structural equality—the accommodation of difference—have passed by such lopsided margins? How could it have garnered so much support from Republicans in the House and Senate, or from a Republican president who had in other contexts so vigorously resisted the expansion of civil rights protections? How could the president and the Republican congressional leadership embrace the disparate impact provisions of the ADA so readily, while at the same time sharply decrying them in the doomed Civil Rights Act of 1990?

There was incredulity in the traditional civil rights community, but there was also hope—hope not only that the ADA would transform the lives of disabled Americans, but also that the theoretical breakthrough represented by reasonable accommodation theory would eventually play a role in solving other equality problems, which the more broadly accepted equal treatment principle had proven inadequate to address.

The Americans with Disabilities Act, and the administrative regulations that followed it, seemed to hold enormous practical and theoretical potential. The act's definition of disability had been drawn broadly, to cover not only the "traditional disabled," such as individuals who were blind, deaf, or used wheelchairs, but also people who had stigmatizing medical conditions such as diabetes, epilepsy, or morbid obesity. It covered not only people who were actually disabled, but those who had a record of a disability, such as cancer survivors, whom employers might be unwilling to hire for fear of increased medical insurance costs or future incapacity. The statute covered people who were not disabled at all, but were simply perceived as such, like people with asymptomatic HIV or a genetic predisposition toward a particular illness. It covered not only physical disabilities, but mental disabilities as well, arguably the most stigmatizing medical conditions in American society.

The ADA incorporated a profoundly different model of equality from that associated with traditional nondiscrimination statutes like Title VII of the Civil Rights Act of 1964.[13] As a practical matter, those statutes, for the most part, required only *formal* equality: equal treatment of similarly situated individuals.[14] As numerous legal scholars had observed, the equal treatment principle had not proven tremendously effective in addressing problems of equality and difference.[15] The ADA required not only that disabled individuals be treated no worse than nondisabled individuals with whom they were similarly situated, but also that in certain contexts they be treated differently, arguably better, to achieve an equal effect.[16]

In this regard, the statute and its implementing regulations required covered employers to do something that no federal employment rights statute had required before: engage with a disabled employee or applicant in a good faith interactive process to find ways to accommodate the employee's disability and enable him or her to work.[17] This "duty to bargain in good faith" represented a dramatic shift in the ordinary power relationship between employers and employees on such issues as shift assignments, hours of work, physical plant, or the division of job duties among employees. At least in the nonunion context, these had previously been aspects of the employer-employee relationship over which employers had exercised exclusive control, subject of course to the basic nondiscrimination principle that no applicant or employee could be treated less favorably for a reason specifically proscribed by law.

When enacted in the summer of 1990, the ADA was the only employment-related federal civil rights statute that centrally featured a structural theory of equality. Title VII's disparate impact theory, which had been under attack throughout the 1980s, had been all but obliterated by the Supreme Court's decision in *Wards Cove Packing Company v. Atonio,*[18] and by the president's veto of the Civil Rights Act of 1990. Other Supreme Court cases had years before either strongly implied or explicitly precluded the assertion of disparate impact claims in Title VII pay equity cases,[19] or in cases seeking to enforce constitutionally based protections against discrimination on the basis of race, sex, or national origin.[20] And, in *Trans World Airlines, Inc. v. Hardison,*[21] the Court had so severely limited Title VII's religious accommodation principle as to render it virtually useless.

The ADA's embrace of structural equality seemed clear and unambiguous. Qualification standards, employment tests, or other selection devices having an unjustified disparate impact on disabled applicants or employees were clearly defined as discriminatory,[22] as were standards, criteria, or methods of administration that had discriminatory effects.[23] The nondiscrimination principle unambiguously included a duty of reasonable accommodation, with which employers were required to comply even if the accommodation lowered an employee's net marginal productivity, so long as the expense incurred did not rise to the level of "undue hardship."[24]

The ADA and its implementing regulations had yet another remarkable feature: they limited an employer's prerogative to exclude a disabled person from a particular job based on a scientifically unsound assessment of the risks to health and safety posed by the person's disability. Under the new law, an employer could exclude a disabled individual from a particular job on safety grounds only if the person presented a "direct threat"[25] to the health or safety of others in the workplace, as that term had been narrowly interpreted under the Rehabilitation Act of 1973.[26] Specifically, under the direct threat defense an employer could exclude a disabled individual from a particular job only upon a "reasonable medical judgment that relies on the most current medical knowledge and/or the best available objective evidence," taking into account the duration of the alleged risk, the nature and severity of the potential harm, the imminence and actual likelihood that the potential harm would occur.[27]

Because stigmatizing conditions are so often associated with irrational perceptions of danger,[28] and because risk assessment in any context is more often based on popular myths and stereotypes than on sound scientific analysis,[29] the ADA's direct threat defense was potentially transformative. No longer, it seemed, could a disabled person be excluded from a particular job because his or her presence was in good faith viewed as presenting an elevated health or safety risk. In making any such assessment, the ADA seemed to require that an employer replace an "intuitive" or "popular" approach to risk assessment with more scientific methods and standards.

In short, the Americans with Disabilities Act appeared to be a "second generation"[30] civil rights statute, advancing formal and structural models of equality by imposing both a duty of accommodation and a duty of formal nondiscrimination, regulating health and safety risk analysis in situations involving disabled employees or applicants, and extending these protections to an apparently wide class—a class ranging far beyond those traditionally viewed as disabled in legal and popular culture. Supporters hailed it as a triumph of a new "civil rights" or "social" model of disability over an older and outmoded "impairment" or "public benefits" model.[31] The ADA promised to revive the concept of stigma as a powerful hermeneutic for the elaboration and judicial application of American civil rights law.[32] Supporters and detractors alike predicted that the structural approach to equality advanced by the ADA might eventually diffuse into other areas of the law, eroding the entrenched understanding that equality always—and only—requires equal treatment under rules and practices assumed to be neutral.

The employment discrimination provisions of the ADA were phased in gradually between 1990 and 1994. The act, although passed in 1990, did not become effective until 1992,[33] at which point Title I, which prohibits discrimination in employment, covered employers with twenty-five or more employees.[34] In 1994, coverage was extended to employers with fifteen or more employees.[35] Within the disability activist community, expectations for the statute ran high. Within the employer community, so did concerns. Across the country, large law firms began running training sessions for their employer clients and strategy development workshops for employment defense lawyers, who would soon busy themselves preventing and defending cases brought under the new law.[36]

Relatively quickly, as judicial opinions in Title I cases began to accumulate, it became clear that the act was not being interpreted as its drafters and supporters within the disability rights movement had planned. Indeed, by 1996 many in the disability community were speaking of an emerging judicial backlash against the ADA. Law review articles written by many of the statute's drafters described a powerful narrowing trend in the federal judiciary, especially on the foundational question of who was a "person with a disability," entitled to protection under the act. These articles, which told a consistent and to disability activists troubling story, bore titles such as

> The Incredible Shrinking Protected Class: Redefining the Scope of Disability Under the Americans with Disabilities Act[37]

> "Substantially Limited" Protection from Disability Discrimination: The Special Treatment Model and Misconstructions of the Definition of Disability[38]

> Restoring Regard for the "Regarded as" Prong: Giving Effect to Congressional Intent[39]

and, more recently,

> Delusions of Rights: Americans with Psychiatric Disabilities, Employment Discrimination, and the Americans with Disabilities Act[40]

> The Supreme Court's Definition of Disability under the ADA: A Return to the Dark Ages.[41]

Early on, one might have discounted these alarmist accounts on the grounds that partisans on one or another side of a disputed social issue often overestimate the strength of a hostile trend. But, as time went on, various developments suggested that something worthy of note was, in fact, happening with respect to judicial interpretation and application of the ADA. Systematic studies of ADA Title I cases published in 1998 and 1999 lent the first sound empirical support to the more impressionistic accounts of ADA advocates. In fact, as these studies showed, the overwhelming majority of ADA employment discrimination plaintiffs were losing their cases, and the federal judiciary was interpreting the law in consistently narrowing ways.

A study of federal district court decisions conducted by the American Bar Association reported in 1998 that, in a data set including all published ADA Title I cases that had gone to judgment either before or after trial, plaintiffs had lost 92 percent of the time.[42] In the Fifth Circuit, the figure was a startling 95 percent.[43]

Less than a year later, Ohio State law professor Ruth Colker published an even more comprehensive study of outcomes in federal district and appellate ADA Title I decisions.[44] Professor Colker's two-part data set included not only the cases analyzed in the American Bar Association study, but also published and unpublished federal circuit court decisions available through Westlaw or other electronic reporting services.[45] Before analyzing these data, Professor Colker excluded cases that could readily be identified as "frivolous," including cases filed against a noncovered entity, cases challenging conduct that occurred before the act's effective date, and cases otherwise asserting claims that could not possibly be covered by the ADA.[46]

Colker's results reinforced the American Bar Association findings. With respect to cases included in the appeals court data set, defendants had prevailed at the trial court level 94 percent of the time. As to that 94 percent, where plaintiffs were appealing an adverse district court judgment, defendants prevailed on appeal 84 percent of the time.[47] Of the 6 percent of circuit court cases in which plaintiffs had prevailed in the district court, almost half, or 48 percent, were reversed in defendants' favor on appeal.[48] Colker's reanalysis of the ABA data set largely confirmed the studies' original conclusions; she found that defendants had prevailed 92.7 percent of the time.[49]

Colker's content analysis of courts' opinions in these cases proved equally unsettling for disability rights advocates. Closely reviewing the decisions contained in the district and appellate court data sets, she demonstrated that courts were systematically deploying two strategies in ruling against plaintiffs. First, district courts were granting and appellate courts were confirming summary judgments against plaintiffs even in situations where material issues of fact were clearly present, thereby keeping cases from proceeding to jury trial.[50] Second, Colker showed, in construing the ADA's many ambiguous provisions, courts were consistently refusing to follow either the act's extensive legislative history or the administrative regulations and other interpretive guidance issued by the Equal Employment Opportunity Commission.[51]

Of course, one might attribute these results to the fact that, during the 1990s, the ADA was a new and complicated statute, with many ambiguous provisions. Accordingly, one might speculate, the pattern of negative outcomes might simply reflect the conditions of judicial uncertainty in which ADA claims were being adjudicated. However, in a more recent study, Colker disconfirmed this hypothesis, demonstrating that levels of judicial uncertainty did not significantly predict ADA appellate outcomes.[52] Moreover, noted Colker, during the late 1960s and early 1970s, Title VII of the Civil Rights Act of 1964 was also a new and complex statute. However, Colker's data showed that appellate outcomes in the early years of Title VII enforcement were decidedly proplaintiff, not prodefendant.[53]

One might also attempt to explain these statistics by positing an adverse selection effect, caused by the more meritorious cases being resolved before any judicial complaint is filed. But as Steven Percy's essay later in this volume suggests, one finds little support for this view in statistics maintained by the EEOC.

Between 1992 and 1998, the Equal Employment Opportunity Commission resolved a total of 106,988 charges of discrimination under the ADA. Of these, only 4,027, or 3.8 percent, resulted in reasonable cause determinations, and only 14,729, or 13.8 percent, resulted in "merit resolutions" of any kind, including settlements, withdrawal with benefits, or determinations of reasonable cause.[54] The largest category of administrative dispositions consisted of "no cause" determinations, which accounted for 51.4 percent of all dispositions, followed by "administrative closures," at 34.9 percent, many of which result from a charging party obtaining a right to sue and commencing his or her own legal action before the EEOC has completed its investigation.[55] Although more detailed study and analysis would certainly aid our understanding of how ADA cases proceed from initial dispute to litigation, there is little in the EEOC data to support the theory that a disproportionate share of nonmeritorious cases were reaching the federal courts.

Oddly, during the years in which the cases analyzed in the Colker and ABA studies were accumulating, one could never have gleaned from popular media coverage of the ADA that the administrative and judicial tide was flowing so powerfully against ADA plaintiffs. The picture being painted in the media was in fact precisely the opposite—of a law and an administrative agency run wildly amuck, granting windfalls to unworthy plaintiffs and forcing employers to "bend over backwards"[56] to accommodate preposterous claims. Articles and commentary in the nation's leading newspapers bore headlines such as these:

The Disabilities Act's Parade of Absurdities[57]

Disabilities Law Protects Bad Doctors[58]

Disabilities Act Abused? Law's Use Sparks Debate[59]

Negative media commentary crested after publication of the EEOC *Guidance on the Americans with Disabilities Act and Psychiatric Disabilities* in March 1997.[60] Intended to help employers understand what the act did and did not require, the *Guidance* unleashed a torrent of rhetorical attacks on both the ADA and the EEOC. Leading newspapers in major metropolitan areas ran stories and commentary with headlines like, "Late for Work: Plead

Reprinted courtesy of Larry Wright and the *Detroit News*.

Insanity,"[61] "Protection for the Personality-Impaired,"[62] and "Gray Matter; Breaks for Mental Illness: Just What the Government Ordered."[63] Cartoonists had a field day, as the above selection from the *Detroit News*[64] exemplifies.

The ADA's "image problem" was not confined to the print media. The act was pilloried in television news and sitcom programming as well.[65] In all likelihood, many Americans' understanding of the ADA was shaped by a *Simpsons* episode entitled "King Sized Homer," in which Bart Simpson's father attempted to eat himself to a weight of three hundred pounds, so that he could be diagnosed as "hyperobese" and use the ADA to avoid participation in an otherwise mandatory workplace exercise program. Others may have learned about the law while watching a *King of the Hill* episode entitled "Junkie Business," in which a drooling, near catatonic addict-employee, who spent much of the work day in a fetal position, claimed protection of the ADA to avoid being fired. His "rights" to come in late, to have the lights dimmed, and to do little productive work are championed by a social worker, who, sporting a wrist brace for carpal tunnel syndrome, refers to himself and his addict-client as the "truly disabled." One by one, other employees at the business follow suit, until no one but the beleaguered manager is doing any work. Everyone else is claiming to be disabled and, under the sheltering wings of the ADA, immune from discipline or discharge.

Hopes that the United States Supreme Court might reverse the hostile judicial tide were temporarily buoyed in 1998, with the Court's decision in *Bragdon v. Abbott*,[66] which held that asymptomatic HIV infection constituted a disability within the meaning of the ADA from the moment of infection. But the hopes buoyed by *Bragdon* were dashed a year later, when in a trilogy of ADA Title I cases[67] the Court interpreted the act's definition of disability in the same crabbed manner as had the lower-court decisions so vehemently criticized by disability activists and advocates. The Court's decisions in *Sutton, Murphy,* and *Kirkingburg,* in a very real sense, gutted the ADA, leaving in a catch-22 vast numbers of disabled people whose impairments were sufficiently mitigated by medication and other assistive devices as to enable them to work: if mitigating measures or their own determination enabled disabled people to function without substantial limitation, they were considered "not disabled" within the meaning of the ADA and lost their federal statutory protection from discrimination. If their impairments, without mitigation, resulted in a functional limitation, they would in all likelihood be deemed "not qualified," and thus, not entitled to ADA protection either.

If the Court's decisions in the *Sutton* trilogy dashed ADA plaintiff advocates' hopes, the Court's next move swept up and tossed out the scattered pieces. In *Trustees of the University of Alabama v. Garrett*,[68] the Supreme Court held that by providing a disabled individual with a right to sue a state employer for damages resulting from employment discrimination based on disability, Congress, in enacting Title I of the ADA, had exceeded its authority under Section 5 of the Fourteenth Amendment[69] and had improperly attempted to abrogate the rights of the states as sovereign entities under the Constitution's Eleventh Amendment. More simply stated, in *Garrett* the Court held that, as applied to private actions for damages against the states, Title I of the ADA was unconstitutional.

In fairness, *Garrett* was about far more than the Americans with Disabilities Act. The Court's decision in that case was but one small part of a much larger political struggle between Congress and the Supreme Court, a struggle that extends far beyond any disagreement the two branches might have over the ADA. Throughout the 1990s, by a narrow five-to-four majority,[70] the most conservative justices on the Rehnquist Court had been systematically expanding state immunity from suit under the Eleventh Amendment and, in corresponding fashion, limiting Congress's authority to enact civil rights laws protecting from state discrimination groups that, in the Court's view, were not entitled to heightened protection under the Fourteenth Amendment's Equal Protection Clause.[71]

The *Garrett* Court held that Congress could enact antidiscrimination legislation enforceable against the states in private suits for money damages only if, in passing the legislation, it was acting pursuant to its powers under Section 5 of the Fourteenth Amendment. Section 5 authorizes Congress to enforce, by "appropriate legislation," the provisions of Section 1, which includes the Equal Protection Clause. Following its earlier decision in *Kimel v. Florida Board of Regents*[72] holding the Age Discrimination in Employment Act unconstitutional as applied against the states, the *Garrett* majority declared that only the Court, and not Congress, had the constitutional power to determine what Section 1 of the Fourteenth Amendment meant and what rights it conferred on members of the groups it protected.

This is what makes *Garrett* important from a disability studies perspective. The degree of protection against state-sponsored discrimination conferred on members of a particular social group depends on whether that group is deemed to constitute a "suspect" or "quasi-suspect" class for equal protection purposes. Unless a class is deemed "suspect" or "quasi-suspect," the Equal Protection Clause of the Fourteenth Amendment provides its members with little protection indeed. So long as discriminatory state treatment of a nonsuspect or non-quasi-suspect class has a "rational basis," the Equal Protection Clause is not violated.

Race has long been considered a "suspect classification" for equal protection purposes.[73] To pass constitutional muster, a racial classification must be narrowly tailored to achieve a compelling state interest.[74] Sex has long (although less long than race) been considered a "quasi-suspect" classification.[75] To survive equal protection scrutiny, a sex-based classification must be "substantially related" to the achievement of an "important state objective."[76] In 1985, in *City of Cleburne v. Cleburne Living Center*,[77] the Supreme Court held that mentally retarded persons did not constitute a "suspect" or "quasi-suspect" class for equal protection purposes. So long as discriminatory state action toward the mentally retarded had a "rational basis," held the *Cleburne* Court, the discriminatory treatment was permissible under the Equal Protection Clause.

In the years following *Cleburne Living Center*, disability studies scholars and disability rights activists advocated a minority group model of disability. The minority group model frames the problem of disablement as a product not of impairment per se, but of discrimination against persons with impairments. As Harlan Hahn, Matthew Diller, Kay Schriner, and Richard Scotch later in this volume explain, the minority group model of disability galvanized communities of disabled people, sparked a period of political activism, and ultimately informed the contours of disability discrimination legislation and administrative regulations.

Congress wrote the minority group model of disability into the ADA's preamble, making abundantly clear its position that, *Cleburne Living Center* notwithstanding, people with disabilities should be viewed as a suspect class entitled to the highest level of Fourteenth Amendment protection. Specifically, in the preamble, Congress wrote that people with disabilities constituted "a discrete and insular minority," historically subjected to isolation, segregation, and "purposeful unequal treatment" that relegates them to a position of "political powerlessness in our society."[78] To anyone familiar with the Court's equal protection jurisprudence, this language unmistakably signals suspect classification status. In Congress's view, unambiguously expressed in the language of the ADA, discriminatory state treatment of disabled people should be subjected to the highest level of scrutiny under the Equal Protection Clause.[79] So, on the eve of the Court's decision in *Garrett*, Congress has taken the position, stated in the ADA's preamble, that people with disabilities should be viewed, for Equal Protection purposes, as a subordinated minority group. The Court, in *Cleburne*, had stated that they should not. *Garrett*, then, like *Kimel* before it, represented a high stakes political struggle between Congress and the Supreme Court over who would have the authority to determine who was entitled to protection from "rational" discrimination under the Equal Protection Clause, and who was not.

In *Garrett*, the Court arrogated this constitutional authority to itself, and itself alone. Congressional findings that people with disabilities were a discrete and insular minority, subject to a history of purposeful discriminatory treatment by the states did not matter, stated the *Garrett* majority. The Court, and the Court alone, had the constitutional authority to determine who is a member of a subordinated minority, and who is not. And disabled people are not. Accordingly, since Section 1 of the Fourteenth Amendment does not protect disabled people from "rational" discrimination, including failure to make reasonable accommodations (which, after all, cost money) or the use of disability as a statistically useful proxy (no matter how over- or underinclusive) for some other trait, Congress could not, under its Section 5 powers, enact legislation prohibiting the states from doing something they would otherwise be permitted to do under the Fourteenth Amendment. *Garrett*, in short, represents a clear, judicial rejection of, one might say a judicial backlash against, the minority group model of disability.

The Supreme Court's 2001–2002 term brought further setbacks for disability rights activists. Maintaining its crabbed approach to the definition of disability displayed in the *Sutton* trilogy, in January 2002, the Court ruled in *Toyota Motor Manufacturing v. Williams,* that an ADA plaintiff with severe carpal tunnel syndrome and other musculoskeletal disorders, which limited her ability to perform manual tasks involved in playing with her children, shopping, doing housework and gardening, and working, had not established that she was a "person with a disability" within the meaning of the ADA.[80]

Three and a half months later, in *US Airways v. Barnett,* the Supreme Court held that absent special circumstances, accommodation in the form of reassignment to a vacant position is *per se* unreasonable within the meaning of the ADA if another employee would otherwise be entitled to the position under the terms of a seniority system.[81] Although not unexpected, the Court's decision in *Barnett* seemed plainly wrong as a matter of statutory interpretation. Unlike other federal employment discrimination statutes, the ADA contains no defense for seniority systems, and the act's legislative history makes abundantly clear that this legislative omission was deliberate. That the Court would decide against the ADA plaintiff in the face of the statute's text and legislative history provided additional support for the backlash thesis.

Predictions that a public and judicial backlash against the ADA might occur emerged as early as 1994. Perhaps the first such concern was voiced that year by Joseph Shapiro. In an article that troubled many ADA activists, Shapiro cautioned that, because passage of the ADA was not preceded by a well-publicized social movement, the act, along with the people who mobilized or enforced it, might be particularly vulnerable to misinterpretation, hostility, resentment, and other backlash effects.[82] Shapiro reiterated these concerns the same year, in his landmark book about the modern American disability rights movement.[83]

Additional predictions of backlash followed in the law review literature. The first surfaced in 1995, in an article by Professor Deborah Calloway on the potential implications of new structural theories of equality.[84] Calloway's prediction was soon followed by claims that a judicial and media backlash against the ADA was in fact already under way.[85] By the time the American Bar Association study was released, many within the disability advocacy community were speaking openly of a growing backlash against the ADA.

Most of us involved in this or other social justice struggles have at one time or another referred to resistance to civil rights initiatives as a "backlash." Whether working to advance the rights of women, to win basic civil rights for lesbians and gay men, to defend affirmative action, or to bring about the full integration of people with disabilities into every facet of economic, political, cultural, and social life, referring to resistance as backlash is, among other things, a good way to blow off steam. Of course, it is one thing to blow off steam and quite another to think systematically about precisely what backlash might be, what causes it to occur, and how it might be prevented or reckoned with if and when it emerges.

The articles collected in this book represent an attempt to encourage this sort of systematic thinking. The book brings together the reflections of a distinguished group of disability activists, lawyers, and scholars from the fields of law, sociology, psychology, political science, economics, history, and English literature, whose work has centered on disability rights issues. The book attempts to address, from a variety of perspectives, the following issues and questions, among others:

> What is "backlash?" Can it meaningfully be distinguished from other forms of retrenchment or resistance to social change initiatives?

> Is there in fact an ongoing backlash against the ADA and related disability rights initiatives?

> If so, how is that backlash manifest in the media, in judicial decision making, and in academic or other social commentary?

> Assuming some discrete phenomenon that could be called a backlash exists, to what factors might it reasonably be attributed? How can our efforts to understand this phenomenon be informed by insights from legal studies and from other disciplines, such as sociology, psychology, political science, economics, history, or disability studies?

> What are the implications of public, media, and judicial responses to the ADA for future strategies in disability advocacy and policymaking, or for strategy in social justice movements generally?

Three of the papers explore patterns of judicial response to the ADA from a legal studies perspective. In "Judicial Backlash, the ADA, and the Civil Rights Model of Disability," Matthew Diller provides a broad overview of these patterns and suggests two partial explanations for them. First, in interpreting the ADA, judges are continuing to rely on an outdated impairment model of disability, rather than a civil rights or sociopolitical model. This old impairment model of disability, Diller suggests, leads to a highly restrictive approach to statutory coverage. Second, by advancing a structural rather than merely formal model of equality, the ADA stands beside affirmative action on the front lines of a cultural war about the meaning of equality in a diverse society and about the legal interventions properly taken to effectuate it.

In her contribution, law professor and ADA lawyer Wendy Parmet[86] continues the inquiry with an examination of the "mitigating measures" controversy culminating in the Supreme Court's decisions in the *Sutton* trilogy, and shows how the mitigating measures issue operated to narrow the scope of ADA coverage. Parmet's investigation reveals a consistent pattern of judicial refusal to utilize either the Act's legislative history or the administrative regulations promulgated by the EEOC in defining disability for ADA coverage purposes. She explores this pattern's connection with the "new textualist"[87] school of statutory interpretation championed by conservative Supreme Court associate justice Antonin Scalia, and concludes that, in focusing on the purported "plain meaning" of statutory terms, textualist methodology necessarily enmeshes the interpreter in the same stereotypic understandings of relevant constructs that a transformative statute like the ADA was designed to destabilize and displace.

Broadening the legal lens to incorporate a political science perspective, Professor Anita Silvers, a philosopher, and Michael Stein, a legal historian, focus on the Supreme Court's decision in *Trustees of the University of Alabama v. Garrett*. They trace the logic of the *Garrett* majority's decision back into the retrogressive ideological framework and empirically unsound assumptions supporting such now discredited equal protection cases as *Plessy v. Ferguson*, which ushered in the "separate but equal" doctrine ultimately rejected in *Brown v. Board of Education*, and *Goesart v. Cleary*, which justified discriminatory state classification by sex under the "separate spheres" rationale rejected in cases like *Reed v. Reed*[88] and *Frontiero v. Richardson*.[89]

Professors Diller, Parmet, Silvers, and Stein all describe a startling disconnect between the understanding of the ADA shared by the activists and legislative aides who drafted the statute and that of the private lawyers and judges who eventually shaped its interpretation. Insights into the various factors contributing to this conceptual disconnect are developed in another set of papers, which includes contributions by political scientist Harlan Hahn, psychologist Kay Schriner and sociologist Richard Scotch, and English literature scholar Lennard Davis.

In "Accommodations and the ADA: Unreasonable Bias or Biased Reasoning?" Professor Hahn argues that the crabbed judicial interpretations of the ADA described by Professors Diller, Parmet, Silvers, and Stein stem from three fundamental sources: (1) widespread judicial confusion over the relationship between impairment and disability; (2) the failure or refusal of judges to adopt a sociopolitical conception of disability; and (3) judicial resistance to the "minority group" approach to disability policy issues. He traces the enduring influence of paternalism and covert hostility toward the disabled on judicial responses to disability discrimination claims, and proposes a principle of "equal environmental adaptations" as a tool for slicing through attitudinal and conceptual barriers to full implementation of the policy goals underlying the ADA.

Professor Davis continues this excavation of judicial attitudes toward people with disabilities in his intellectually playful and engaging essay, "Bending Over Backwards: Disability, Narcissism, and the Law." Bringing Freud and Shakespeare to bear on the reading of ADA cases as narrative texts, Davis demonstrates that ADA plaintiffs are being portrayed in federal case law in much the same way as people with disabilities have been depicted in English literature and Freudian theory—as narcissistic, self-concerned, and overly demanding. Davis's observations echo Harlan Hahn's claim that popular and legal discourse on disability remains heavily freighted with covert hostility and resentment directed toward the disabled.

Readers unfamiliar with the social model of disability will appreciate the concise and accessible overview of that subject provided by Kay Schriner and Richard Scotch's "The ADA and the Meaning of Disability." As Schriner and Scotch explain, under an older "impairment" or "rehabilitation" model, disability is discursively located within the disabled individual. Under this approach, an impairment is seen as causing disability if it prevents the disabled person from functioning effectively in the world as it is. If the individual can be retrained or cured, he or she is no longer considered disabled. If neither retraining nor cure is possible, social welfare benefits provide the disabled person with a subsistence income. Under this older model, which still underlies the federal Social Security disability system, a certification of disability operates as a kind of ticket into the system of rehabilitation or support, and signals to both the disabled individual and to members of the surrounding polity that the individual is neither expected nor entitled to function fully in the larger socioeconomic world.

The model of disability reflected in the ADA represents a fundamentally different theoretical framework. Under the social model, disability is seen as resulting not from impairment per se, but from an interaction between the impairment and the surrounding structural and attitudinal environment. Under this approach, *environments,* not simply *impairments,* cause disability.

Two consequences flow from this conceptual understanding, one implicated in the definition of disability and the other in ascertaining society's proper response to it. First, under a social approach to disability, determining whether a particular condition is disabling requires an examination of the attitudinal and structural environment in which a person functions, not merely an examination of the person him- or herself. Accordingly, an impairment may be disabling in one structural and attitudinal environment but not in another. Second, once disability is no longer located entirely within the impaired individual, but in the environment as well, the presence of an impairment can be seen as triggering societal obligation to *change* the environment, so that a disabled individual can function despite his or her impairment. As the articles by Professors Hahn, Davis, and Schriner and Scotch demonstrate, appreciating the differences between the impairment and social models of disability is central to understanding the Americans with Disabilities Act.

"Psychiatric Disabilities, the Americans with Disabilities Act, and the New Workplace Violence Account," by Vicki Laden and Gregory Schwartz, excavates the depiction of psychiatric disability in the media and then traces those depictions into ADA jurisprudence and human resource management discourse. Specifically, they explore the impact of one particular discursive frame on judicial and public responses to the ADA. Identifying a rhetorical construct they refer to as the *new workplace violence account,* Laden and Schwartz examine its use in attempts to delegitimate the ADA. They argue that the account's depiction of the volatile, psychotic employee, poised to explode in lethal violence, is used by media critics who claim that the ADA has deprived employers of the ability to protect employees from a potent workplace threat. They go on to describe a new violence prevention industry, composed of defense-side employment lawyers, security experts, and consultants, who counsel employers on "how to identify and remove potentially violent workers in the hands-tied era of the ADA." This rapidly expanding industry, Laden and Schwartz contend, advances bold claims about the enormity and severity of the problem, reinforcing a key premise of ADA critics, that the act unreasonably subordinates interests in public safety to the "special rights" of the mentally ill. Through a close examination of judicial decisions and defense firms' training materials on the one hand, and a review of relevant, current social science research on the other, Laden and Schwartz both expose the flawed empirical basis undergirding claims relating to prediction of dangerousness and explore the implications of current scientific knowledge for compliance with the ADA and for administrative and judicial interpretation of its direct threat defense.

Laden and Schwartz's observations about the impact of media depictions on public attitudes toward the ADA are profoundly important. Popular attitudes toward legal rights and obligations are likely influenced more by people's *beliefs* about what legal and regulatory schemes require, how they are enforced, and the effects of enforcement on individuals and society than by actual legal doctrine, enforcement activities, or (to the extent they can be accurately measured) practical effects. Popular beliefs about law are shaped by many factors, including media coverage, through which a particular set of scripts, symbols, and condensing themes is transmitted to the reading and viewing public.

To the extent that a particular law or regulatory regime is politically controversial, that controversy will be enacted in the print and broadcast media, as positive and negative scripts, symbols, and condensing themes compete for audience attention. The particular condensing themes that prevail in this contest become the dominant cognitive and attitudinal frames through which people assign meaning to the law and construe efforts to mobilize or enforce it. These *media frames*[90] organize the relevant discourse, both for the journalists who create the coverage and for the public, which reads, hears, or views it. Eventually, sociocultural dissemination of particular media representations proceeds to the point that it becomes meaningful to refer to these representations not only as media frames, but also as broader *discursive frames,* which influence popular attitudes toward the law, its enforcers, and its beneficiaries.

Bringing radical theory to bear on the ADA backlash problem, Marta Russell argues in "Backlash, the Political Economy, and Structural Exclusion" that public hostility toward the ADA is driven in large measure by the high levels of job instability and worker displacement characterizing American labor markets. These conditions, she contends, breed insecurity, fear, and resentment toward employment protections extended to members of disadvantaged groups. Russell suggests that hostility toward identity group–based employment protections will persist until employment at a living wage and access to health care are treated as fundamental rights attending membership in society, rather than as incidents of increasingly unstable employment status.

The next two papers extend the investigation to areas beyond Title I of the ADA. Political scientist Stephen Percy opens with an analysis of administrative enforcement activities by the EEOC and the Department of Justice, identifying key areas of dispute or analytical difficulty. Professor Percy's exploration raises a number of intriguing questions about the problems associated with the use of indeterminate legal standards in complex regulatory regimes. Both the Rehabilitation Act and the ADA incorporate standards that might reasonably be described as "complex," or "tempering." Figuring out how to comply with these standards, which include "reasonable accommodation," "undue hardship," even "disability" as defined in the ADA and the Rehabilitation Act, often requires a complex, situation-specific balancing of underspecified factors by unsophisticated legal actors.

Professor Percy's investigation suggests that, even setting aside the tug-of-war often associated with implementation of a new regulatory regime, hostility toward the ADA may reflect, at least in part, the negative affective response generated by a regulatory combination of normative uncertainty and potential liability. When one crafts laws utilizing complex tempering principles, how do they work? Do indeterminate standards function effectively in guiding statutory compliance, enforcement, or judicial interpretation? What strains do underspecified legal standards place on courts and administrative agencies, whose legitimacy often depends on perceptions that they are "applying" rather than "making" the law?

These questions bring us full circle to the project's central questions. In the specific context of disability rights, and also more generally, what is the relationship between law and social change? When are legal strategies relatively more effective in moving social justice movements forward, and when relatively less so? What is the significance of backlash in this context? Is it a meaningful construct, or merely an epithet used by social change activists to describe the arguments and activities of their opponents? If it is a meaningful construct, how and why does it emerge? And finally, how do these questions relate to public, judicial, and media responses to the Americans with Disabilities Act?

In closing the volume, law professor Linda Hamilton Krieger offers a theoretical framework for addressing these questions, and for applying it to various observations and insights offered by the book's other contributors. Her central premise is simple: to understand the role of law in effecting social change, one must consider the relationship between formal legal rules and constructs on the one hand, and informal social norms and institutionalized practices on the other. At its root, backlash, whether directed against the ADA or against any other transformative legal regime, is about this relationship and can be avoided or addressed only through careful attention to the complex processes that mediate it.

NOTES

1. Pub. L. No. 101–336, 104 Stat. 327 (1990); *see also* Fred Pelka, The ABC-CLIO Companion to the Disability Rights Movement 20 (1997).

2. Elaine S. Povich, *Senate OK's Bill Fixing Rights of the Disabled,* Chi. Trib., July 14, 1990, at 1.

3. *Bush Eager to Sign Bill Opening Doors for 43 Million Disabled,* Orlando Sentinel Trib., July 14, 1990, at A1.

4. *Knocking Down a Barrier,* Newsday (Nassau and Suffolk Edition), July 27, 1990, at 7.

5. President Bush was quoted in the Boston Globe as stating, "We've all been determined to ensure that it gives flexibility, particularly in terms of the timetable of implementation, and we've been committed to containing the costs that may be incurred." John W. Mashek, *To Cheers, Bush Signs Rights Law for Disabled,* Boston Globe, July 27, 1990, at 4.

6. *Id.*

7. *See, e.g.* 136 Cong. Rec. S10287–01 (statement of Senator Metzenbaum, citing *A Red Herring in Black and White,* N.Y. Times, July 23, 1990 at 14); 136 Cong. Rec. S9809, S9814; 136 Cong. Rec. S10321.

8. On July 19, 1990, Vice President Dan Quayle said of the act, "[T]he Administration is not going to have a quota bill crammed down its throat disguised as a civil rights bill." Steven A. Holmes, *Accord Is Sought on Rights Measure to Avert a Veto,* N.Y. Times, July 20, 1990, at A1. Quayle's comments followed upon those of White House chief of staff John Sununu, who on July 17, stated, "The bill, as crafted right now, is a quota bill . . ." Steve Gerstel, *Senate Limits Debate on Civil Rights Bill; Veto Threatened,* United Press Int'l, July 17, 1990. Senator Hatch referred to the bill as "terrible," even "heinous," and predicted that it would "create a litigation bonanza." Concluded Hatch in one interview, "Even a cursory review reveals that (the bill) is simply and unalterably a quota bill." In his veto statement, delivered on October 20, 1990, President Bush justified his action by stating, "I will not sign a quota bill." George Archibald, *Special Report: The Bush Record,* Wash. Times, September 13, 1992, at A8.

9. Pub. L. No. 102–166, 105 Stat. 1071 (1991).

10. The disparate impact case was *Wards Cove Packing Company v. Atonio,* 490 U.S. 642 (1989).

11. President Bush vetoed the minimum wage bill on June 13, 1989. *See* 135 Cong. Rec. H2498–03 (1989).

12. *See* 136 Cong. Rec. H24451–02 (1990).

13. 42 U.S.C. § 2000e (1994) (as amended).

14. Title VII's disparate impact theory does represent a structural model of equality. However, that theory can be applied only in very narrow circumstances. For a discussion of this issue, see Linda Hamilton Krieger, *The Content of Our Categories: A Cognitive Bias Approach to Discrimination and Equal Employment Opportunity,* 47 Stan. L. Rev. 1161, 1162 n.3 (1995).

15. *See, e.g.,* Martha Minow, Making All the Difference: Inclusion, Exclusion, and American Law (1990); Christine A. Littleton, *Reconstructing Sexual Equality,* 75 Cal. L. Rev. 1279 (1987) (exploring problems of gender equality and

difference); Linda J. Krieger & Patricia Cooney, *The Miller Wohl Controversy: Equal Treatment, Positive Action, and the Meaning of Women's Equality, in* D. KELLY WEISBERG, FEMINIST LEGAL THEORY: FOUNDATIONS 156 (1993).

16. The term "discriminate," which was not defined at all in the Civil Rights Act of 1964, is defined in a highly detailed and multifaceted way in § 102 of the ADA. With respect to reasonable accommodation, § 102 provides that the term "discriminate" includes "not making reasonable accommodations to the known physical or mental limitations of an otherwise qualified individual with a disability who is an applicant or employee, unless such covered entity can demonstrate that the accommodation would impose an undue hardship on the operation of the business of such covered entity." 42 U.S.C. § 12112(b)(5)(A). The meaning of "undue hardship" is defined in the statutes implementing regulations at 29 C.F.R. § 1630.2(p).

17. The "interactive process duty" is described at 29 C.F.R. § 1630(o)(3):

> To determine the appropriate reasonable accommodation it may be necessary for the covered entity to initiate an informal, interactive process with the qualified individual with a disability in need of the accommodation. This process should identify the precise limitations resulting from the disability and potential reasonable accommodations that could overcome those limitations.

18. 490 U.S. 642 (1989).

19. Although the issue was not directly before it, the Supreme Court in *County of Washington v. Gunther,* 452 U.S. 161, 170 (1981) suggested that Title VII's Bennett Amendment, 42 U.S.C. § 2000e-2(h), which incorporated into the statute the affirmative defenses contained in the Equal Pay Act of 1963, would in all likelihood preclude the use of disparate impact theory in Title VII pay equity cases. This has been, and continues to be, the approach taken in a majority of the circuits. *See, e g ,* Auto Workers v. Michigan, 886 F.2d 766, 769 (6th Cir. 1989); State, County, & Municipal Employees v. Washington, 770 F.2d 1401, 1405, 1408 (9th Cir. 1985).

20. Washington v. Davis, 426 U.S. 229 (1976) (holding that disparate impact theory unavailable in cases asserting rights under the equal protection clause of the Fifth and Fourteenth Amendments).

21. 432 U.S. 63 (1977).

22. 42 U.S.C. § 12112(b)(6).

23. 42 U.S.C. § 12112(b)(3)(A).

24. 42 U.S.C. § 12112(b)(5). The meaning of "undue hardship" is spelled out in the ADA's implementing regulations at 29 C.F.R. § 1603.2(p)(1).

25. The direct threat defense is found in § 103 of the Americans with Disabilities Act, 29 U.S.C. § 12113(b).

26. Section 501 of the ADA provides: "Except as otherwise provided in this Act, nothing in this Act shall be construed to apply a lesser standard than the standards applied under title V of the Rehabilitation Act of 1973; (29 U.S.C. 790 et seq.) or the regulations issued by Federal agencies pursuant to such title." The direct threat defense had been defined for § 504 purposes in terms virtually identical to those incorporated into the ADA Regulations in *School Board v. Arline,* 480 U.S. 273, 288 (1987).

27. 29 C.F.R. § 1630.2(r).

28.  In connection with this aspect of stigma, see generally, ERVING GOFFMAN, STIGMA: NOTES ON THE MANAGEMENT OF SPOILED IDENTITY (1963). This point is developed later in this volume in Vicki A. Laden & Gregory Schwartz, *Psychiatric Disabilities, the Americans with Disabilities Act, and the New Workplace Violence Account.*

29.  For an interesting exploration of this phenomenon and its broader implications for governmental risk regulation, see Timur Kuran & Cass Sunstein, *Availability Cascades and Risk Regulation,* 51 STAN. L. REV. 683 (1999) (describing the threats to rational regulatory activity posed by popular dynamics of risk perception).

30.  I borrow here from Robert Burgdorf, *The Americans with Disabilities Act: Analysis and Implications of a Second-Generation Civil Rights Statute,* 26 HARV. C.R.-C.L. L. REV. 413 (1991).

31.  *See, e.g.,* Jonathan C. Drimmer, *Cripples, Overcomers, and Civil Rights: Tracing the Evolution of Federal Legislation and Social Policy for People with Disabilities,* 40 UCLA L. REV. 1341, 1357–58 (1993); Richard K. Scotch & Kay Schriner, *Disability, Civil Rights, and Public Policy: The Politics of Implementation,* 22 J. POL'Y STUD. 170 (1994). For a thorough treatment of the development of the civil rights and social models of disability within the disability rights movement, see RICHARD K. SCOTCH, FROM GOOD WILL TO CIVIL RIGHTS: TRANSFORMING FEDERAL DISABILITY POLICY (1984) (focusing on events connected with the passage and implementation of § 504 of the Rehabilitation Act of 1973). In this volume, see Harlan Hahn, *Accommodations and the ADA: Unreasonable Bias or Biased Reasoning?*

32.  *See, e.g.,* Jonathan Drimmer, *Cripples, Overcomers, and Civil Rights, supra* note 31, at 1349–51 (discussing concept of stigma in relation to disability rights law and policy); *see generally* Harlan Hahn, *The Appearance of Physical Difference: A New Agenda for Political Research,* J. HEALTH & HUM. RESOURCES ADMIN. 391 (1991) (discussing stigma and other aspects of the attitudinal environment in relation to the concept of discrimination).

33.  P.L. 101–336, Title I, § 108, 104 Stat. 337 (1990) ("This Title [42 U.S.C. §§ 12111–12117] shall become effective 24 months after the date of enactment").

34.  42 U.S.C. § 12111(5).

35.  *Id.*

36.  For further discussion of these developments, see Chai Feldblum, *The Definition of Disability Under Federal Anti-discrimination Law: What Happened? Why? And What Can We Do About It?* 21 BERKELEY J. EMP. & LAB. L. 91 (2000).

37.  Steven S. Locke, *The Incredible Shrinking Protected Class: Redefining the Scope of Disability Under the Americans with Disabilities Act,* 68 COLO. L. REV. 107 (1997).

38.  Robert Burgdorf, *"Substantially Limited" Protection from Disability Discrimination: The Special Treatment Model and Misconstructions of the Definition of Disability,* 42 VILL. L. REV. 409 (1997).

39.  Arlene Mayerson, *Restoring Regard for the "Regarded as" Prong: Giving Effect to Congressional Intent,* 42 VILL. L. REV. 587 (1998).

40.  Susan Stefan, *Delusions of Rights: Americans with Psychiatric Disabilities, Employment Discrimination, and the Americans with Disabilities Act,* 52 ALA. L. REV. 271 (2000).

41. Bonnie Poitras Tucker, *The Supreme Court's Definition of Disability Under the ADA: A Return to the Dark Ages,* 52 ALA. L. REV. 321 (2000).

42. American Bar Association Commission on Mental and Physical Disability, *Study Finds Employers Win Most ADA Title I Judicial and Administrative Complaints,* 22 MENTAL AND PHYSICAL DISABILITY L. REP. 403.

43. *Id.*

44. Ruth Colker, *The Americans with Disabilities Act: A Windfall for Defendants,* 34 HARV. C.R.-C.L. L. REV. 99 (1999).

45. *Id.* at 103.

46. *Id.* at 106 n.39.

47. *Id.* at 108.

48. *Id.*

49. *Id.* at 109. For a variety of reasons, these results probably *overestimate* plaintiffs' rates of success. While a discussion of these reasons is beyond the scope of this paper, interested readers are referred to Colker's discussion at pp. 104–5 and 108–9. Her reasoning in this regard parallels earlier observations in Peter Siegelman & John J. Donohue III, *Studying the Iceberg from Its Tip: A Comparison of Published and Unpublished Employment Discrimination Cases,* 24 L. & SOC'Y REV. 1133 (1990).

50. *Id.* at 101.

51. *Id.* at 102.

52. Ruth Colker, *Winning and Losing Under the ADA,* 62 OHIO ST. L. J. 240 (2001).

53. *Id.* at 260.

54. United States Equal Employment Opportunity Commission, *Americans with Disabilities Act of 1990 (ADA) Charges FY 1992–1998* (EEOC 1999), available at http://www.eeoc.gov/stats/ada.html.

55. *Id.*

56. I nod here to Lennard Davis, later in this volume, *Bending Over Backwards: Disability, Narcissism and the Law.*

57. James Bovard, *The Disabilities Act's Parade of Absurdities,* WALL ST. J., June 22, 1995, at A6.

58. Walter Olson, *Disabilities Law Protects Bad Doctors,* N.Y. TIMES, November 28, 1997, at A39.

59. Stephanie Armour, *Disabilities Act Abused? Law's Use Sparks Debate,* USA TODAY, September 25, 1998, at 1B.

60. United States Equal Employment Opportunity Commission, *Enforcement Guidance on the Americans with Disabilities Act and Psychiatric Disabilities* (EEOC 1997), available at http://www.eeoc.gov/docs/psych.html.

61. Dennis Byrne, *Late for Work? Plead Insanity,* CHI. SUN-TIMES, May 8, 1997, at 39.

62. George Will, *Protection for the Personality-Impaired,* WASH. POST, Apr. 4, 1996, at A31.

63. Sheryl Gay Stolberg, Week in Review Desk: *Gray Matter; Breaks for Mental Illness: Just What the Government Ordered,* N.Y. TIMES, May 4, 1997, at A1 (Week in Review, § 4).

64. Larry Wright, ©DETROIT NEWS, 1997. Reprinted with permission.

65. Cary LaCheen, *Achy Breaky Pelvis, Lumber Lung, and Juggler's Despair: The Portrayal of the Americans with Disabilities Act on Television*, 21 BERKELEY J. EMP. & LAB. L. 223 (2000).

66. Bragdon v. Abbott, 524 U.S. 624, 639 (1998).

67. Sutton v. United Airlines, Inc., 527 U.S. 471(1999) (severe myopia); Murphy v. United Parcel Serv. Inc., 527 U.S. 516 (1999) (hypertension); and Albertson's v. Kirkingburg, 527 U.S. 555 (1999) (monocular vision).

68. 531 U.S. 356 (2001).

69. Section 5 of the Fourteenth Amendment provides:
The Congress shall have power to enforce, by appropriate legislation, the provisions of this article [the Fourteenth Amendment].
U.S. CONST. amend. XIV, § 5.

70. The conservative majority, familiar to anyone who followed the fall 2000 presidential recount controversy culminating in *Bush v. Gore*, 531 U.S. 98 (2000), consists of Justices Rehnquist, Scalia, Thomas, O'Connor, and Kennedy, opposed by a minority including Justices Souter, Breyer, Stevens, and Ginsburg.

71. Section 1 of the Fourteenth Amendment provides, in relevant part:
No State shall make or enforce any law which shall abridge the privileges or immunities of citizens of the United States; nor shall any State deprive any person of life, liberty, or property, without due process of law; nor deny to any person within its jurisdiction the equal protection of the laws.
U.S. CONST. amend. XIV, § 1.
For an excellent analysis of the nature and profound significance of this line of Supreme Court cases, interested readers are referred to Robert C. Post and Reva B. Siegel, *Equal Protection by Law: Federal Antidiscrimination Legislation After Morrison and Kimel*, 110 YALE L.J. 441 (2000).

72. 528 U.S. 62 (2000).

73. City of Richmond v. J.A. Croson Co., 488 U.S. 469, 500.

74. Palmore v. Sidoti, 466 U.S. 429, 432–33 (1984) (phrasing the test as requiring a "compelling governmental interest" that "must be 'necessary . . . to the accomplishment' of their legitimate purpose'") (quoting McLaughlin v. Florida, 379 U.S. 184, 186 (1964)).

75. Craig v. Boren, 429 U.S. 190, 197 (1976).

76. *Id.*

77. 473 U.S. 432 (1985).

78. 42 U.S.C. § 12117 (1994).

79. United States v. Carolene Prod. Co., 304 U.S. 144, 153 n.4 (1937).

80. 112 U.S. 681 (2002).

81. 112 U.S. 1516 (2002).

82. Joseph P. Shapiro, *Disability Policy and the Media: A Stealth Civil Rights Movement Bypasses the Press and Defies Conventional Wisdom*, 22 POL'Y STUD. J. 123 (1994).

83. Joseph P. Shapiro, NO PITY: PEOPLE WITH DISABILITIES FORGING A CIVIL RIGHTS MOVEMENT 70–73, 328 (1994) (discussing potential for backlash against disability rights advocacy).

84. Deborah A. Calloway, *Dealing with Diversity: Changing Theories of Discrimination*, 10 ST. JOHN'S J. LEG. COMMENTARY 481, 492 ("Expansive reading of the

ADA definition of disability combined with demands for equal employment opportunity through workplace accommodation for individuals currently outside of ADA coverage may create a backlash against the rights granted under the ADA similar to the backlash against affirmative action"). For later references to potential ADA backlash, see, e.g., Wendy E. Parmet, Mark A. Gottleib, and Richard A Daynard, *Accommodating Vulnerabilities to Environmental Tobacco Smoke: A Prism for Understanding the ADA*, 12 J. L. & HEALTH 1, 3–4, 21 (1997–98) (discussing the connection between an expansive definition of disability and attacks on the ADA); Christopher Aaron Jones, *Legislative Subterfuge? Failing to Insure Persons with Mental Illness Under the Mental Health Parity Act and the Americans with Disabilities Act*, 50 VAND. L. REV. 753, 785 (1997) (noting that by failing to define key statutory terms and provisions with sufficient specificity, Congress gives lip service to broad social ideals, but foists key controversial decisions and the hostility those decisions generate onto courts and administrative agencies).

85. For examples of these claims, see, e.g., Ruth Colker, *Hypercapitalism: Affirmative Protections for People with Disabilities: Illness and Parenting Responsibilities Under United States Law*, YALE J.L. & FEMINISM 213 (1997) ("The backlash against the Americans with Disabilities Act . . . has been immediate and strong"); Paul Steven Miller, *The Americans with Disabilities Act in Texas: The EEOC's Continuing Efforts in Enforcement*, 34 HOUS. L. REV. 777, 779 (1997) (citing Kathi Wolf, *Bashing the Disabled: The New Hate Crime*, THE PROGRESSIVE, Nov. 1995, at 24); Paul Steven Miller, *The EEOC's Enforcement of the Americans with Disabilities Act in the Sixth Circuit*, 48 CASE W. RES. 217, 218 (1998).

86. Wendy Parmet, *Plain Meaning and Mitigating Measures: Judicial Interpretations of the Meaning of Disability*.

87. I nod here to William Eskridge Jr., *The New Textualism*, 37 UCLA L. REV. 621 (1990).

88. 404 U.S. 71 (1971).

89. 411 U.S. 677 (1973).

90. This term is taken from TODD GITLIN, THE WHOLE WORLD IS WATCHING: MASS MEDIA IN THE MAKING AND UNMAKING OF THE NEW LEFT (1980). Gitlin defines media frames as "persistent patterns of cognition, interpretation, and presentation, of selection, emphasis, and exclusion, by which symbol-handlers routinely organize discourse, whether verbal or visual." *Id.* at 7. Gitlin's construction draws on the earlier work of Erving Goffman, who in more general terms described frames as implicit theories about the nature of reality, used heuristically to comprehend, manage, and respond to it. *See* Erving Goffman, FRAME ANALYSIS: AN ESSAY ON THE ORGANIZATION OF EXPERIENCE, 10–11 (1974).

*Harlan Hahn*

# Accommodations and the ADA
## Unreasonable Bias or Biased Reasoning?

Among the cleavages marked by gender, age, race or ethnicity, and sexual orientation that divide members of modern society, perhaps few schisms have produced more superficial agreement—and more covert conflict— than the faint, wavering, but ineluctable line that separates self-identified persons with disabilities and the dominant or supposedly nondisabled majority. Many of the latter claim to be sympathetic and even supportive regarding the aspirations of disabled citizens. Some experts expound at length on the benefits of the latest treatments or assistive devices for the disabled person. Only a few have expressed open criticism or opposition to the principle of equal rights for Americans with disabilities. Nonetheless, many activists in the disability rights movement may react with a knowing glance, a meaningful smile, a slight shake of the head, and a muttered aside: "They just don't get it, do they?"

This lack of understanding has also been evident in the failure to reach a consensus about the meaning of concepts and terms that are crucial to an interpretation of the Americans with Disabilities Act (ADA).[1] Disabled and nondisabled persons frequently seem to be "talking past each other." The superficial discussion of issues that appear to evoke agreement, but are actually the source of deep-seated conflict, has delayed an accurate appreciation of public, judicial, and other reactions to the ADA. The distinction between impairment and disability has been obscured. Legal definitions have emphasized functional attributes instead of stigma and unfavorable attitudes as major sources of discrimination. And lawyers and judges have displayed a strong resistance to research based on the "minority group" model of disability. As a result, controversies about the ADA have been shaped by a "disabling discourse" rather than by discourse about disability.

An important part of this miscommunication probably can be ascribed to nondisabled domination of the interpretation of the ADA. Citizens with disabilities have been largely excluded from this process. Whereas few analysts would contend that laws prohibiting discrimination on the basis of gender and race or ethnicity should be implemented without consulting the experience of women or African Americans, respectively, a similar recognition has not been extended to the disabled minority. Furthermore, the nondisabled monopoly over major decisions about the ADA can be accurately characterized by the concept of paternalism. These circumstances not only legitimate patterns of subjugation between nondisabled and disabled portions of the population, but they also simultaneously deny the existence of such subordination. Major Supreme Court decisions about disability rights, therefore, have been decidedly unfavorable to the interests of this segment of society. Such judgments have ignored the many advantages conferred on the nondisabled and the disadvantages imposed on people with disabilities by features of the environment that are virtually invisible or taken for granted. In fact, judicial opinions have increasingly suggested that the protection granted Americans with disabilities constitutes a kind of unreasonable bias that extends beyond the guarantees bestowed on other individuals. No attention is devoted to the *biased reasoning* produced by the failure to consider the benefits bequeathed to the nondisabled or the penalties inflicted on disabled citizens by the existing milieu.

The covert hostility and paternalism that permeates public and judicial perspectives has, of course, perpetuated the unequal status of disabled persons. One means of redressing this oppression might be achieved through adherence to the principle of *equal environmental adaptations,* which would seek to "level the playing field" by permitting disabled citizens to enjoy benefits commensurate with the advantages given the nondisabled in an unaccommodating environment. Perhaps the most essential prerequisite for this change would be the development of a new dialogue about disability based on candid opposition rather than paternalistic sentiments. In the absence of such debate, ameliorating the problems of disabled Americans through the ADA is more difficult.

## Disabling Discourse

Misunderstandings about social issues seldom emerge in a vacuum. Any attempt to comprehend the nature and origins of divided views about disability rights, therefore, must be founded on an enhanced appreciation of the radically different hermeneutics through which nondisabled and disabled people frame the pertinent questions. Much of this discord has revolved around the definition of disability.

*Disability and Impairment*

One of the most fundamental differences between disabled and nondisabled groups involves the description of the principal problem encountered by people with disabilities. While dominant segments of the population tend to believe that these difficulties stem primarily from internal traits, an increasing proportion of disabled persons feel that their main impediments are located in the external environment. This dichotomy seems to parallel the distinction between impairments—which are equated with physiological, anatomical, or mental abnormality or loss—and disabilities, which frequently involve an admixture of bodily and environmental attributes.[2] For those who have never had any experience with disability, blame for threatened interference with favorite or essential activities is usually concentrated on an organic impairment. People who live with disability, however, are preoccupied by the challenge posed by environmental barriers to increased social participation. Most nondisabled persons do not appear to understand the powerful influence upon their consideration of disability that is exerted by the traditional model of impairments, which also contributes to the continued subordination of disabled individuals.

The imprint of a fear of impairment is evident in the widespread tendency to view disability as a medical or an economic problem. Perhaps the earliest and most widely adopted understanding of disability in public policy is related to the definition of an inability to earn a livelihood, which has been used in social welfare legislation in America since a law passed by the Continental Congress during the Revolutionary War.[3] Perhaps the most popular perception of disability, however, is derived from a medical model that equates impairments with diagnostic classifications labeled by etiological considerations or by parts of the body.[4] Ironically, this conceptual framework, which developed from the need for professional intervention to treat acute maladies, is of relatively little value either in finding cures for many impairments (which often reduce the physician to the passive role of monitoring or evaluating the progress of chronic difficulties) or in permitting public agencies to discover an empirical correlation between various types of impairments and the ability to work.[5] Both medical and work definitions, however, assess impairments almost exclusively as a functional concern; both regard disability as a limitation or loss. According to this view, by definition, disabled people suffer from a deprivation of occupational as well as physical or mental capacities, which deprivation reduces their status and worth as human beings.

The only remedies that have been developed to address disability as an impairment or functional problem are embodied in the concepts of medical and vocational rehabilitation.[6] Neither solution has been particularly satisfactory even for the most ardent proponents of these disciplines. Despite the best efforts of physicians and a host of other health professionals, for example, most chronic impairments are permanent; they cannot be "fixed" or repaired completely. Until the advent of bionic sales catalogs, therefore, the average disabled person will never approximate the standards of ordinary or "normal," let alone optimal, functioning. Similarly, much of the success of the federal-state vocational rehabilitation program can be attributed to a process of "creaming," through which job placement services were devoted primarily to the most cooperative, the least needy, and the least disabled clients,[7] at least prior to the reversal of priorities mandated by the Rehabilitation Act of 1973.[8] The unemployment rate for adults with enduring impairments, most of whom are anxious and able to work, has remained at an extraordinarily high level (approximating two-thirds) in the United States as well as in other advanced industrial nations.

Medical personnel and rehabilitation counselors have sought to alleviate the functional burdens of impairment primarily through private or public charities. Many people with disabilities have been especially critical of "telethons" and similar events, often hosted by nondisabled celebrities such as Jerry Lewis, that not only depict an image of disabled children and adults as helpless or pathetic creatures but that also raise funds almost exclusively for medical research or "cures," thereby reinforcing the presumption that the elimination of the impairment (or the disabled individual?) is the sole appropriate solution to this problem. Yet politicians and professional interest groups have never endorsed a program comparable to Medicare for Americans with disabilities. In fact, since disabled persons seldom can secure entry-level employment that pays a sufficiently high salary or that offers group insurance covering "preexisting conditions," many disabled citizens can only meet their continuing medical expenses by qualifying for programs such as Supplemental Security Insurance (SSI) or Social Security Disability Insurance (SSDI) that create "disincentives" by providing health care needed to survive in exchange for the promise of unending joblessness.[9] As a result, the disabled minority has become one of the few groups in the "deserving poor" that can use enforced idleness to become culturally legitimate recipients of donations either through welfare benefits or through begging.

Finally, most plans to ameliorate functional impairments devised by medical and vocational rehabilitation have depended on individual rather than collective action. The reliance of professionals upon clinical methods is clearly indicated by the fact that rehabilitation specialists borrowed from psychiatry and psychology instead of the social sciences to promote an assumption that the socially and economically marginal status of disabled persons stemmed from a lack of motivation and emotional adjustment.[10] One of the few medical approaches to disability that extended beyond the boundaries of the human body imposed by clinical techniques was the pernicious doctrine of eugenics that resulted in tragedies such as the Supreme Court decision upholding the constitutionality of involuntary sterilization in *Buck v. Bell*,[11] as well as scientific concepts justifying the extermination of millions of disabled persons in the Holocaust.[12] Ironically, public health has displayed more concern about the prevention of impairments than about the fate of disabled people. Similarly, even though the growth of disability roles has been influenced less by the prevalence of impairments than by broad trends in the labor force that might be altered through changes in employment programs,[13] economic approaches to rehabilitation have tended to focus primarily on individual counseling and on vocational interest and aptitude instead of public policy.

Most judicial decisions about disability rights in the ADA and related measures have steadfastly clung to the dubious proposition that the problems of disabled citizens are a direct result of their impairments. One major source of this confusion of disability and impairments probably can be ascribed to the failure of disabled people to surmount an initial hurdle to their social and political recognition, namely, they have frequently been unsuccessful in refuting implicit or explicit allegations of biological inferiority. Hence, by definition, people with disabilities are inherently unequal because they are functionally impaired. Both the dictates of meritocratic principles and the nature of their limitations often form the foundations of assumptions that support arguments to prevent disabled citizens from claiming rights equivalent to their nondisabled counterparts.

The struggle to rebut accusations of organic inferiority is a process that other minority groups have had to sustain in order to secure eventual legal protection. Since the nineteenth century, even the most advanced scientific thinking and research has been molded by debates about the alleged intellectual inferiority of African Americans and other minorities,[14] and Supreme Court opinions were infused with extraordinarily patriarchal and paternalistic stereotypes about women.[15] The history of classic judicial opinions that bear the imprint of the dominant conceptual paradigms of the era in which these cases were decided underscores the realization that information or conclusions that appear to be neutral or impartial actually are based on knowledge that is socially and culturally determined. In fact, the tendency to treat impairment and disability as synonymous probably can be traced, in part, to the overwhelming power that has been vested in scientific interpretations of physical traits in Western society since the eighteenth century. There are, of course, many other theoretical perspectives on disability.[16] There is reason to believe, therefore, that courts can disentangle the concepts of impairment and disability as readily as they became intertwined in earlier analysis.

Part of the difficulty of unraveling the concepts of impairment and disability, however, probably can be attributed to the misunderstanding provoked by the three-pronged definition of disability in the ADA.[17] By stressing limits on "major life activities" to the neglect of other elements of the ADA definition, courts have virtually folded the latter two prongs into the first spur, so that the question of defining whether or not a plaintiff has a disability is determined almost exclusively by disputes about the loss of a major life activity.[18] Apparently reflecting the confusion of impairment and disability, judges have tended to ignore the prongs of the definition that can be construed to prohibit discrimination against someone who is "regarded as having such an impairment" or who has "a record of such impairment."[19] In 1987, the Supreme Court held that a teacher who had been forced to bear the stigma of an earlier diagnosis of tuberculosis was entitled to protection from discrimination based on disability.[20] In *Bragdon v. Abbott*,[21] however, the Court returned to a strictly functional understanding of disability by deciding that an asymptomatic person infected with HIV could bring suit under the ADA because her impairment interfered with her capacity for reproduction, which was, for her, a major life activity. As a result of this confusion over the various ADA prongs, legal conflict about the ADA ban against discrimination has degenerated into rather mundane disputes about whether a worker can be fired for wearing eyeglasses, for taking medication for hypertension, or for a vision impairment in one eye.[22]

Subsequently, the Supreme Court has also invoked rather arcane legal concepts to invalidate the rights of disabled persons. In *University of Alabama v. Garrett*, for example, the Eleventh Amendment concerning lawsuits against the states was used to strike down efforts by two disabled employees of a state institution to enforce the ban on discrimination in Title I of the ADA.[23] Ironically, while early civil rights litigation frequently depended upon indications of "state action" to attack discriminatory behavior, the holding in *Garrett* seemed to imply that private businesses might be more vulnerable to ADA claims than public employers. Although some observers interpreted the case as merely another round in a continuing dispute about federalism,[24] the decision failed to prevent discrimination against a nurse who had cancer and a security guard who requested work in a nonsmoking area.

The tendency to equate disability and impairment has done much to undermine the effectiveness of the ADA. There is little evidence that the statute has ended the long-standing practice of using disability as a means of permitting personnel officers to sort out job applications and to exclude unwanted candidates for employment. In addition, weakness in the courts' implementation of the ADA has been ascribed to the disproportionate selection of cases involving relatively minor or insignificant disabilities.[25] The effort to resolve questions about the hypothetical link between types of impairments and judicial outcomes, however, might require the use of techniques such as detailed interviewing and narrative analysis[26] that extend beyond simply quantitative studies. One in-depth analysis of the accounts of employment discrimination cases launched by ten workers with mobility impairments, most of whom were eventually defeated in court and fired from their jobs, disclosed that they were left with little more than the hope that the ADA might bring increased justice to other citizens with disabilities in the future.[27] These findings lend at least some credence to the speculation that the characteristics of the plaintiffs may have been a less important determinant of the litigation than the social, political, and legal values of nondisabled employers, attorneys, and judges who have scant personal awareness or education concerning the prejudice and discrimination encountered by disabled Americans. Efforts to expand public knowledge and to improve judicial decisions regarding the ADA, therefore, could be facilitated by the development of a new understanding of the nature and meaning of disability.

## A New Definition of Disability

Judicial interpretations of ADA definitions have not established a foundation for major advances in disability rights. On the contrary, the conceptual confusion that permeates this issue has sometimes been exploited to defeat the goals of disabled citizens. Perhaps the clearest examples of these machinations are the cases in which employers have urged courts to invoke the doctrine of estoppel to dismiss the ADA suits of disabled workers who had previously received Supplemental Security Income or payments from Social Security Disability Insurance.[28] Decisions upholding this viewpoint have relied upon the discrepancy between the definition of "work disability" that permits individuals to secure SSI or SSDI benefits if they are

unable to engage in substantial gainful activity or to qualify for employment, and the ADA definition of impairments limiting "major life activities" that allows persons to seek "reasonable accommodations."[29] This contention is clearly inconsistent with the intent of the ADA to reduce
unemployment among people with disabilities and to encourage them to
return to the productive workforce. The application of the notion of estoppel to the tension between SSI or SSDI definitions and the meaning of disability in the ADA also subverts several specific provisions of social welfare
laws that are designed to promote remunerative work for disabled people,
such as vocational counseling, "trial work periods," and PASS (Plan to
Achieve Self-Sufficiency) programs. Perhaps most importantly, these contradictions have been created by public policy rather than individual motivation; and citizens with disabilities should not be penalized for paradoxes
that can only be rectified by legislators.

There appears to be a pressing need to seek judicial attention and acceptance for a sociopolitical definition of disability as the product of interaction between individuals and the environment.[30] From this perspective, the
major problems confronted by people with disabilities can be traced to the
restraints imposed by a disabling environment instead of personal defects
or deficiencies. This conceptualization can be applied to the architectural
barriers that impede the activities of persons with mobility impairments
and to the communication barriers that restrict people with sensory
impairments. In a world adapted to the needs and interests of everyone,
functional limitations (or impairments) would be virtually nonexistent. In
surroundings adapted to an increasing range of human capabilities, such
restrictions would be diminished. Obstacles exist, therefore, because the
present environment was basically designed for "the average person plus or
minus half a standard deviation."[31] The configurations of the existing environment confer significant rewards on the nondisabled and corresponding
penalties on citizens with disabilities. This sociopolitical definition, which
became the foundation for legislation such as the ADA, has allowed a
recognition that disabled people comprise a disadvantaged group subjected
to discrimination and entitled to legal and constitutional protection.

Perhaps the principal explanation for the continued tendency by the
courts to muddle the assessment of discrimination under the ADA by treating disability as little more than impairment can be traced to the failure of
the judiciary to adopt, or even to acknowledge, the sociopolitical perspective.[32] Features of the human-made environment that segregate disabled
citizens from the rest of the population have not been decreed by
immutable natural laws, nor were they produced by historical happen-

stance or coincidence. They represent conscious choices that had the effect of including some groups, such as the dominant segments of society, and excluding others who were "different" or disabled. Disability thus is essentially similar and certainly analogous to other physical characteristics such as skin color, ethnic features, and sex that are perceived either through casual observation or close inspection. These bodily traits have been used by humans as bases for differentiating and discriminating against other people; they form the foundation for prejudices derived from cultural meanings that have evolved through centuries.[33] In the case of people with disabilities, bigotry or bias is evoked either by visible bodily differences or by stigmatizing labels attached to physiological attributes. Through the process of labeling,[34] people with so-called hidden as well as obvious disabilities become the targets of discrimination. As a result, visibility and labeling might be identified as the key elements in a sociopolitical definition of disability that is not dependent on the concept of impairment.[35]

The sociopolitical definition also focuses on the attitudinal environment as the principal source of the barriers confronting people with disabilities. Ironically, this phenomenon, which often seems to escape the attention of nondisabled researchers,[36] has been a major concern of disabled persons. "When groups of disabled people are asked about the greatest obstacle they confront, the reply usually comes back in a single chorus: 'attitudes.'"[37] The apparent neglect by the judiciary of attitudes that produce discrimination against citizens with disabilities is somewhat remarkable especially in view of the enormous accumulation of evidence revealing that visible or labeled differences frequently provoke feelings of antipathy and avoidance. Some researchers have identified such a propensity in infants, a phenomenon known as "stranger anxiety" that may originate in the first year of life.[38] Another taxonomy has suggested that the origins of discrimination on the basis of disability could be attributed either to "existential anxiety"—the dread that such a phenomenon might affect an observer especially in the process of aging—or to "aesthetic anxiety"—the fear of the alien, strange, displeasing, unattractive, or "different."[39] Adverse reactions to people with disabilities appear to be elicited largely by visible or labeled traits, which appear to transform the disabled individual into the unfamiliar "Other."[40]

A classic study of social interactions revealed that disabled adults usually felt obliged to reduce the unspoken discomfort of nondisabled individuals,[41] which was also disclosed in experimental settings by detectable physiological responses.[42] Perhaps the most compelling documentation of the displeasure and uneasiness aroused by the visible signs of disability, however, was provided by the unfavorable reactions of nondisabled children and adults to a series of drawings of young people with obvious disabilities.[43] These studies appeared to yield more clear and convincing proof of bias and aversion than the famous Clark and Clark study of doll preferences[44] cited by the Supreme Court in footnote 11 of the *Brown v. Board of Education*[45] opinion. Perhaps the most important point to be made about these attitudes, however, is that they are usually held by nondisabled people. Thus the divisions between African Americans and whites, men and women, and Latinos and Anglos are replicated by the distinction created by visible and labeled disabilities. This unavoidable fact not only belies the allegation that nondisabled people are not opposed to the goals of the disabled minority, but it also indicates the powerful vested interests that underlie the relationship of dominance and subordination between these segments of the population.

Disability also has played the predominant role in the development of the concept of stigma, which was probably best explained by Goffman when he wrote, "By definition, of course, we believe the person with a stigma is not quite human."[46] Through the process of stigmatizing, individuals are deprived of their humanity, which can be regarded as an even more severe loss than the denial of legal rights imposed on citizens who become the victims of intolerance or bigotry. In fact, disability has been described as "the most severely stigmatized" of all physical differences.[47] Even though notions of stigma and difference have been elaborated in subsequent studies,[48] these ideas have never been effectively integrated into legal battles concerning prejudice and discrimination. Contentions about attitudinal discrimination against people with disabilities, however, seem to be as firmly supported by empirical evidence as arguments that have been made on behalf of other minority groups.[49]

*The Minority Group Model*

The sociopolitical definition is the foundation of the minority group model of disability, which contends that disabled Americans are entitled to the same legal and constitutional protection as other disadvantaged groups.[50] This concept actually has an extensive history. In 1953, a major study published by the Social Science Research Council endorsed "the very general assumption that in American culture physically disabled persons, like Negroes and children, for example, have the position of an underprivileged minority."[51] Safilios-Rothschild wrote in 1970 "that the concept of the minority group can be applied in the case of the disabled despite minor differences."[52] A decade later a pioneering report on youth with disabilities for the Carnegie Council on Children, which was based exclusively on the minority group model, appeared under the ironic title *The Unexpected Minority*.[53] As a result, the first Harris survey found in 1986 that 45 percent of Americans with disabilities felt that disabled persons are a minority group in the same sense as blacks and Hispanics, and 74 percent reported "a sense of common identity with other disabled people."[54]

There are undoubtedly several reasons for the resistance that the courts have displayed toward the minority group model. First, definitions of disability grounded in the concepts of functional impairment and inability to work are deeply embedded in older and more established government programs. The sociopolitical view, which animates the more recent antidiscrimination laws, is poorly understood by the very lawyers and judges who have for many decades been interpreting and implementing these older programs and who have only recently been charged with the enforcement of disability antidiscrimination laws. In addition, disabled people traditionally have lacked a sense of generational continuity or a shared history that would otherwise have facilitated the dissemination of information about prejudice and oppression. At least until the growth of the disability rights movement, they were commonly burdened by feelings of humiliation and shame that prevented them from drawing upon their own experience to investigate patterns of discrimination.[55]

Part of the responsibility for the reluctance to adopt the minority group model also must be imposed on social scientists. The realization that disabled people constitute a minority group has only been partially acknowledged in medical sociology;[56] it has not yet gained wide acceptance in the academic disciplines or fields that concentrate on the study of social inequality, bigotry, and discrimination. A popular textbook on racial and cultural minorities, for example, specifically excluded the "physically handicapped," even though the authors admitted that such research "can help us to develop a more general theory of discrimination."[57] Attention has been diverted both from the examination of discrimination in the everyday lives of persons with disabilities and from the analysis of the conduct of the nondisabled portion of the population that produces this form of discrimination. As a result, reticence about accepting the minority group model has deprived attorneys and judges of a solid foundation for legal arguments concerning discrimination against citizens with disabilities.[58]

Increased analysis of issues derived from the minority group paradigm could persuade the courts to focus on many dimensions of ADA litigation that might otherwise be neglected or ignored. In fact, the major postulates of the minority group model have been described as follows: *(a)* the basic problems of disabled persons stem from social attitudes; *(b)* all facets of the environment are molded by public policy; and *(c)* policies that have an adverse effect on people with disabilities are a reflection of widespread social attitudes and values. Two important implications can be drawn from these postulates. First, aspects of the environment that have a discriminatory impact on citizens with disabilities cannot be ascribed solely to accident or coincidence. Beneath the level of conscious exploitation, the configurations of the existing milieu reflect the faintly discernible relations of power and privilege that divide disabled and nondisabled segments of society. Social structures were designed to enhance the prestige and authority of the nondisabled,[59] but they were not planned "without any mind to" the needs and interests of people with disabilities. Persons with visible or labeled differences stemming from impairments have existed throughout history, and they have usually been the objects of ridicule or scorn. Instead of assuming that environmental barriers to this group occurred as a result of random influences, it would seem unreasonable to believe that, in constructing human habitats, the dominant nondisabled majority was not affected by the motivation to subordinate and separate itself from such people.[60]

Second, the surroundings created by public policy have almost invariably conferred advantages upon the nondisabled portion of the population and disadvantages on the disabled minority. In a society where nondisabled persons have always had the virtually unchallenged power to determine the shape of the social environment, any other result would seem nearly inconceivable. Yet the task of discovering the advantages bestowed on the nondisabled may be even more difficult than the endeavor to identify the disadvantages faced by Americans with disabilities.[61] Perhaps most significantly, these benefits are such an integral facet of the existing environment that they are "taken for granted," are largely invisible and unnoticed.[62] The advantages granted to nondisabled people by this environment, however, are extremely relevant to the attempt to establish a standard for evaluating equality between the disabled and nondisabled segments of the population.[63] Any effort to assess the issue of equal rights for citizens with disabilities without considering these taken-for-granted privileges would be both incomplete and highly prejudicial.[64]

## Nondisabled Domination of the Discourse

Perhaps the principal reason for the tendency of courts to ignore the basic sources of discrimination against disabled persons in ADA controversies can be traced to the characteristics of the major participants in public discussions about disability. The assessment of this proposition seems especially relevant in a postmodernist age permeated by the philosophical tenets of discursive analysis.[65] In general, words and thoughts bear the imprint of the groups or individuals who express them; hence, they may be expected to shape legal assessments of common features of the lives of adults with disabilities such as unemployment and discrimination.[66] The difficulty, of course, is that nondisabled professionals, such as rehabilitation specialists and other so-called experts, have long dominated the discourse of disability. Disabled people themselves have never had more than a faint voice in debates about their own problems. Even the disability rights movement has had less influence on the interpretation and implementation[67] of the ADA than many of its members expected.

Perhaps the most important determinant of future controversies about the ADA might be the willingness of potential plaintiffs to identify with the disabled minority. In a society where so many taken-for-granted facets of the environment favor their nondisabled peers, most disabled individuals have been socialized to believe that they can only compete on equal terms by relentless striving through overcompensation, or, in the nomenclature of the disability community, by becoming "supercrips." They have not been encouraged to request accommodations, and many have found it difficult to initiate legal action on the basis of a physical trait that they have been taught to "overcome."[68] Yet the effect of court decisions about the ADA may fundamentally depend upon the ability of disabled citizens to achieve a delicate balance between a positive sense of self-esteem and a critical view of society,[69] which seems necessary to sustain a continued struggle for equality and justice.

Many disability professionals still act as though they are more qualified to speak on behalf of citizens with disabilities than disabled people themselves. Yet social workers or service providers appear to have little familiarity with the ADA.[70] Judicial rulings also may be affected by the dearth of lawyers who specialize in ADA litigation. In particular, the development of case law on this subject has been plagued by fragmentation resulting from the tendency of early decisions about disability rights to be shaped by the concerns of individual plaintiffs rather than by a coordinated and cohesive strategy.[71] The outcome of disputes about the ADA could be crucially influenced by the proportions of nondisabled and disabled persons who become involved as litigants, attorneys, and judges. Thus, there appears to be significant support for the proposition that court decisions about statutes prohibiting discrimination on the basis of disability may be shaped as much by differences in the experiences of major groups in the judicial process as by substantive considerations related to the interpretation of specific provisions of the law.[72]

## The Hegemony of Paternalism

Perhaps the most serious and intractable hindrance to the advancement of the rights of people with disabilities is represented by the concept of paternalism, which often appears not only to justify the powerful position of nondisabled persons but also to conceal the comparatively powerless status of the disabled minority. In many respects, paternalistic attitudes may be a natural extension of both nondisabled domination of the discourse about disability, and the persistence of assumptions concerning the alleged biological inferiority of people with disabilities. While research in the social sciences has revealed a deep-seated animosity toward citizens with visible or labeled disabilities,[73] hardly anyone permits their true feelings about these traits to become conspicuous. Nondisabled opposition to the interests of disabled Americans is almost invariably covert instead of open or public. The implicitly patronizing sentiments and the slight tone of condescension that sometimes creep into relationships between the nondisabled and disabled individuals or groups are also revealed by the tendency to interpret disability as a personal tragedy[74] and as an appropriate subject of charity. Perhaps most importantly, the cultural conventions implanted by paternalism constitute an almost indefinite means of perpetuating the social and political oppression of citizens with disabilities.

In many respects, paternalism may be an even more formidable obstacle in the struggle for equality than direct conflict or even hostility. Paternalism often engenders a climate of deceit and hypocrisy that makes it difficult for leaders of the disability rights movement to challenge the opinions of nondisabled professionals who claim to be acting in the best interests of this beleaguered minority.[75] But there does not appear to be any reason to think that issues concerning disability rights are any less likely to involve conflicting political interests than other controversies. Hence, there is little wonder that there is a "backlash" against the ADA; what seems unexpected is that many people are surprised by it. Some critics in the disability rights movement might contend that unfavorable assessments of the ADA simply reflect the animosity toward the disabled minority that many nondisabled persons have harbored in their hearts and minds for years.[76] Some disabled advocates may even welcome this development as an initial break through the veneer of paternalism that has surrounded the analysis of disability rights. The candid acknowledgment of disagreement and opposition would contribute to a healthy debate about the interpretation of the ADA. As an antidote to the deep hostility that may be manifested as backlash, it could be necessary to promote a frank dialogue, which may evoke discord but which might even lead to an increased understanding of the principle of equal rights for Americans with disabilities.

## Judicial Attitudes toward Disability Rights

Perhaps the most crucial manifestation of the sentiments of nondisabled professionals can be found in the unfavorable attitudes toward disability rights displayed by justices of the United States Supreme Court in almost all of the major cases that they have decided about this issue.

The concept of paternalism is especially crucial to an interpretation of the position taken by the Supreme Court on the constitutional status of disabled citizens. Ironically, this question encouraged the justices to investigate whether public opinion about disability is basically positive or negative. The leading case on this issue is, of course, *City of Cleburne v. Cleburne Living Ctr.*[77] At issue in *Cleburne* was the validity of the city's requirement that the Cleburne Living Center obtain a special use permit in order to build and operate a group home for the mentally retarded.[78] The Court concluded that, though the city's actions would be scrutinized only under a rational basis test, the city's requirements were not rational and the requirement violated the Cleburne Living Center's equal protection rights.[79] Writing for the majority, Justice White ignored the judicial convention of avoiding the discussion of issues not essential to the resolution of the case. Instead, he engaged in an extensive assessment of whether or not distinctions in the law based on disability should be constitutionally suspect under the equal protection clause of the Fourteenth Amendment. Although White acknowledged that mentally retarded persons had been subjected to a long history of discrimination and that they lacked the strength to change their subjugation through the political process, he refused to admit that they were powerless.[80] As evidence for this judgment, White referred to numerous state and federal laws, such as the Developmental Disabilities Assistance and Bill of Rights Act and the Education of All Handicapped Children Act, which had been enacted to help retarded citizens.[81] But he also claimed that such persons possessed a "reduced ability to cope with and function in the everyday world."[82] The discrepancy between the assertion about decreased capacities and the conclusion that members of this group are not powerless clearly indicates that the passage of the legislation was achieved primarily by nondisabled leaders acting on behalf of persons who bear the label of retardation rather than by retarded citizens themselves. This need to rely upon others to produce such accomplishments is, of course, one of the defining features of a paternalistic relationship. The approval of government proposals mentioned by White was not due to the endorsement of people in the diagnostic category; rather, the adoption of such policies was based principally on the support of nondisabled experts.

Dependence on this sort of paternalistic alliance does more than prevent members of a disadvantaged group from participating in decisions about their fate. There is also a serious risk that the dominant element in such a coalition might eventually abandon the cause or act contrary to the interest of this group. The danger of such a possibility did not appear to trouble Justice White, who argued that "because both State and Federal Governments have recently committed themselves to assisting the retarded, we will not presume that any legislative action, even one that disadvantages retarded individuals, is rooted in considerations that the Constitution will not tolerate."[83] Disabled or retarded citizens were effectively foreclosed from shaping their own destiny or challenging the decisions made on their behalf by spokespersons from the dominant segment of society. Thus, the concept of paternalism played a pivotal role in the decision by the Supreme Court, which denied the disabled minority heightened scrutiny under the Constitution.

On occasion, the judiciary has even seemed to condone rather than prohibit features of the existing environment that penalize disabled citizens and benefit the nondisabled. Speaking for the Supreme Court in *Garrett*, for example, Chief Justice Rehnquist said, "whereas it would be entirely rational (and therefore constitutional) for a state employer to conserve scarce financial resources by hiring employees who are able to use existing facilities, the ADA requires to 'mak[e] existing facilities used by employees readily accessible to and usable by individuals with disabilities.'"[84] Due to the extraordinarily high rate of unemployment for disabled workers, Rehnquist's plan to limit admission to the workforce by "hiring employees who are able to use existing facilities" may not be entirely inaccurate. But the proposal to restrict employment only to nondisabled employees, however rational it might appear, is totally inconsistent with fundamental American values.

What most courts fail to realize is that legal requirements for workplace and other accommodations are not merely special favors for disabled people; they are predicated on a model of equality that should be fully available to all citizens. In an egalitarian society, disabled workers should not have less right to employment—or any other social and economic advantages—than their nondisabled counterparts. Without a firm commitment to the principle of equality, governments would be compelled to confront the horrific alternative of adopting a eugenics policy to define a physical or mental threshold that every citizen must meet in order to secure legal rights and to deny such rights to anyone who fails to meet such a threshold. The interpretation of the ban on discrimination in the ADA, therefore, is not simply a "distributive" issue involving the allocation of resources; it is, instead, a basic test of whether or not lawyers and courts will honor the principle of equality.

The paternalistic sentiments that permeate public consideration of disability issues have been revealed in numerous ways. The plan for Supplemental Security Income was the only part of Nixon's welfare reforms to be approved by Congress by an overwhelming vote. Other laws such as Section 504 of the Rehabilitation Act of 1973 were adopted without pressure from organized interests,[85] even though the struggle over the formulation of administrative regulations to implement these statutory requirements instigated the birth of the modern disability rights movement.[86] Elected representatives are unwilling to admit that they voted against the interests of disabled people, despite the failure of citizens with disabilities to form powerful voting blocs in their constituencies. As a result, crucial battles over equal rights for Americans with disabilities have shifted from the legislative branch, where they might receive at least a modicum of media attention, to the judiciary and to the subterranean world of the bureaucracy, where the struggle usually focuses on funding and implementation instead of abstract principles.[87] The paternalistic milieu surrounding disability issues, therefore, has impeded public disclosure of the failure of government officials to secure the full enforcement of statutes such as the ADA.

The concept of paternalism has also seemed to produce some slight variations in the Supreme Court's interpretation of public attitudes toward people with visible or labeled disabilities. These inconsistencies appear to parallel the contradictions implicit in *Cleburne,* where Justice White found that mentally retarded Americans were not powerless, even though he admitted that they had endured a history of stigma and discrimination that precluded their altering their subordinate status through the political process.[88] Two years later, in *School Board of Nassau County v. Arline,* Justice Brennan endorsed the statement by Congress acknowledging that "society's accumulated myths and fears about disability and disease are as handicapping as are the physical limitations that flow from actual impairment."[89] Although they were both speaking for a majority of the high court, Justice Brennan's opinion in *Arline* contrasts sharply with the view expressed by White in *Cleburne,* that "the distinctive legislative response, both national and state, to the plight of those who are mentally retarded demonstrates . . . that the lawmakers have been addressing their difficulties in a manner that belies a continuing antipathy or prejudice and a corresponding need for more intrusive oversight by the judiciary."[90]

Perhaps most significantly, in *Alexander v. Choate,*[91] which upheld a "disparate impact" instead of an "intent" test for assessing discrimination against people with disabilities, Justice Marshall contended that such bias was "most often the product, not of invidious animus, but rather of thoughtlessness and indifference—of benign neglect."[92] What appears to be missing from many interpretations of the ADA is a realization that stigmatizing or prejudicial attitudes toward visible or labeled disabilities are often an even greater impediment to disabled citizens than functional impairments, that these attitudes are usually held (but seldom expressed in public) by members of the dominant or nondisabled majority, that such attitudes are frequently permeated by paternalistic feelings, and that bias or animosity is as often the product of a purposefulness (which may barely reach the level of consciousness) as it is of neglect or mindlessness.[93] From this perspective, the legal and cultural meaning of differences that are reflected by visible and labeled disabilities become as relevant to judicial decisions as distinctions based on race or ethnicity, gender, sexual orientation, or age.

The dominant discourse between the nondisabled public and disabled citizens has been shaped by the tendency to confound functional impairments and disability. Yet the Supreme Court has refused to grant disabled Americans even the rights that would flow naturally from a medical understanding. In *Youngberg v. Romeo,*[94] Justice Powell spoke for the Court in holding that a disabled person's constitutional interest in freedom had to be balanced against "the demands of an organized society."[95] He concluded that treatment imposed on the disabled plaintiff was judicially acceptable as long as it reflected the judgment of a qualified expert.[96] In a statement setting a medical standard of care so vague and so low that it could evoke a shudder from many disabled individuals, Powell explained that the "decision, if made by a professional, is presumptively valid; liability may be imposed only when the decision by the professional is such a substantial departure from accepted professional judgment, practice, or standards as to demonstrate that the person responsible actually did not base the decision on such a judgment."[97] Although Powell believed that the plaintiff's request for the training necessary to ensure "safety and freedom from restraints" allowed the justices to avoid the "difficult question" of whether or not a disabled citizen has a constitutional right to any type of habilitation or treatment,[98] he seemed to think that disabled individuals must assume the burden of proving unethical—if not illegal—intent in a confrontation with a nondisabled professional.

Justices Blackmun, Brennan, and O'Connor agreed that the plaintiff should defer to the judgment of professionals, but they believed that he was entitled to the training needed to maintain self-care skills.[99] Chief Justice Burger, in a separate concurring opinion, said that he "would hold flatly that respondent has no constitutional right to training, or 'habilitation' per se."[100] The unanimous judgment of the Supreme Court, therefore, may have been based on a rather dim view of the plaintiff's biological inferiority and his prospects for improvement; but it did not seem to reflect a strong belief either in the legal rights of disabled citizens or in the effectiveness of medical treatment.

In another case involving a resident of the Pennhurst State Hospital in Pennsylvania,[101] Justice Rehnquist employed what some observers might regard as a specious rationale to contend that the Developmental Disabilities Assistance and Bill of Rights Act of 1975 did not extend any rights to disabled Americans after all. In his analysis of legislative intent, Rehnquist alleged that the statute was simply a federal-state spending bill, which conferred no substantive rights to citizens with disabilities. In the dissent, Justice White, joined by Brennan and Marshall, also examined the legislative history of the law and concluded that the enactment had "substantive significance"[102] that extended beyond mere "encouragement."[103] Part of White's analysis was based on the contention that Congress had modeled the 1975 mandate on the Civil Rights Act of 1964. Nonetheless, Justice Rehnquist managed to persuade enough justices to endorse his view to void the carefully enumerated guarantees in the 1975 act. Even though health measures appear to comprise the most popularly and judicially approved method of dealing with the problem of disability, the Supreme Court held that disabled Americans have no legal right to medical treatment.

The Supreme Court decision that most clearly demonstrates the refusal to deviate from the rigid requirements imposed by nondisabled standards of equality is, of course, *Southeastern Community College v. Davis.*[104] Since the plaintiff in the case was already a trained nurse with a hearing impairment who was merely seeking to upgrade her certification, the principal arguments seemed to revolve around the allegation that her acceptance as a student in the nursing program might jeopardize the safety of patients. Justice Powell upheld the college in rejecting her application because her admission allegedly might produce a "fundamental alteration in the nature of [the] program."[105] Beneath the surface of these phrases there seemed to lurk the image of a judicial "horror story" of patients unable to summon attention as they called desperately for help with their dying breath. Yet neither the nursing instructors, the college administrators, the attorneys in the case, nor the Supreme Court justices appeared to possess the imagination to realize that patients might not be able to muster the volume to gasp for help with a dying breath that could be readily heeded by a nurse with perfect hearing, that such a patient might be more likely to have the strength to move a finger slightly to flick a switch to start a system of flashing lights, and that a nurse with a hearing impairment would be more alert to such lights than colleagues attuned to vocal sounds. Hence, in an environment adapted to the needs of people who communicate through visual as well as verbal means, the nurse with a hearing impairment might actually be better able to respond to an emergency than many other professionals. As for the college's argument that it could not provide individual supervision, there would seem to be compelling reasons to indicate that the faculty should include teachers or interpreters who could employ multiple methods of communication through sign language as well as oral speech. The justices seemed to imply that even a slight deviation from a model designed exclusively for a nondisabled person could be construed as a special favor to people with disabilities.

Little attention thus far has been paid by the courts to the vast range of "taken for granted" configurations of the environment that bestow advantages upon the nondisabled and that impose distinct penalties upon citizens with disabilities. The oppression is so ubiquitous that it seems to underscore the fundamental importance of Jacobus tenBroek's simple plea for "the right to live in the world."[106] Discrimination against disabled people is not only more pervasive than other forms of bias in the existing environment, but it also may be especially difficult to prove to the satisfaction of the judiciary. After courts determine that a worker meets the ADA definition of disability, for example, judges must find that the individual is "otherwise qualified"[107] in order to proceed with an investigation of employment discrimination. The phrase was probably inserted into the statute to deflect lawsuits that might, in the present context, seem frivolous or outlandish such as the fear that a blind person might want to become a bus driver.

The conjunction of a restricted functional definition of disability and the clause about qualifications forms a narrow gauntlet through which disabled plaintiffs must pass in order to file lawsuits under the ADA. If employees are qualified, they are not disabled; and if they are disabled, they must not be qualified. The conjunction of these terms obviously produces difficulty in proving that the actions of an employer were prompted by discriminatory attitudes rather than by evaluation of a lack of ability. Nonetheless, these requirements could also be interpreted as an opportunity for judges to assess the legal implications of the inequities resulting from taken-for-granted features of the present environment.

One method of accomplishing this task is indicated by the requirements of employment tests specified by the ADA: "Employers must select and administer employment tests in a manner that will ensure that such tests accurately reflect the skill or aptitude of the applicant or employee, rather than reflecting any impaired sensory, manual or speaking skills."[108] This criterion is designed to provide a setting in which aptitude can be distinguished from functional impairments, but a similar standard could be constructed in an almost experimental context to permit employers to differentiate between true abilities and the stigmatizing effects of visible and labeled bodily differences in the evaluation of disabled and nondisabled workers.[109] The close passageway created by provisions of the ADA concerning qualifications and discrimination seems to make a detailed examination of the concept of equality almost inescapable.

The principal Supreme Court case examining the question of disability and equality directly was the litigation surrounding Amy Rowley, an eight-year-old student with a hearing impairment, whose parents had asked her school to provide a sign-language interpreter.[110] Speaking on behalf of five members of the Court, Justice Rehnquist asserted that the concept of a "free appropriate public education" in the Education of All Handicapped Children Act of 1975[111] simply required "that the education to which access is provided be sufficient to confer some educational benefit upon the handicapped child."[112] In a school of this type where teachers seldom know more than the most rudimentary forms of sign language,[113] Amy Rowley may have had few chances to develop her intellectual skills, even though she managed to receive passing marks and to be advanced from grade to grade. Nonetheless, Rehnquist claimed that the law was designed to offer the disabled student no more than a "basic floor of opportunity."[114] He declared that "the right of access to free public education . . . is significantly different from any notion of absolute equality of opportunity regardless of capacity."[115]

In a concurring opinion, however, Justice Blackmun stated that equality could only be determined by a comparison of disabled and nondisabled students. He thought that "the question is whether Amy's program, *viewed as a whole,* offered her an opportunity to understand and participate in the classroom that was substantially equal to that given her nonhandicapped classmates."[116] Similarly, in a dissent joined by Brennan and Marshall, Justice White endorsed "the conclusion that the Act intends to give handicapped children an educational opportunity commensurate with that given other children."[117]

The notion of parity seems to comprise an appropriate benchmark for interpreting the clause regarding "reasonable accommodations," which is undoubtedly the most important provision in Title I of the ADA. Although some economists and other commentators initially proposed that this provision of the law ought to be characterized as measures that do not impose an "undue hardship" on employers,[118] the meaning of the former phrase has not yet been definitively settled by the Supreme Court. One interpretation of reasonable accommodations is embodied in the principle of equal environmental adaptations, which has been defined as follows:

> To establish a standard of equality that does not require mastery of the present environment, courts can adopt a definition of "reasonable accommodations" based on the concept of Equal Environmental Adaptations. This standard is based on the benefits bequeathed to the non-disabled by conventional features of the present milieu as well as the disadvantages imposed on citizens with disabilities. Any discrepancy between the existing environment, which has been designed to suit the non-disabled, and an environment adapted for people with disabilities is a source of inequality. At a minimum, these features of the environment should be commensurate. Reasonable accommodations is the legal method of reconciling a disparity between these dimensions, and Equality of Environmental Adaptations is the standard for interpreting this statutory requirement.[119]

There are, of course, various legal or philosophical meanings that can be attached to the basic standard of equality.[120] Such conceptualizations range from the notion of equality of opportunity[121] to equality of results,[122] which is frequently designed to ensure that public or private programs or services yield comparable outcomes for different groups, and even equal shares as measured by the extent to which such groups enjoy equivalent social or economic benefits from available services.[123]

Many of the special favors bestowed upon nondisabled individuals are so omnipotent and inconspicuous that lawmakers, attorneys, judges, and members of the public may not even acknowledge them. Analysis of the unique advantages granted to nondisabled people by taken-for-granted facets of the existing environment, however, could also be especially effective means of revealing unequal features of the habitat that impose disadvantages on citizens with disabilities.[124] This type of investigation could promote changes in the legal understanding of many aspects of everyday life including the artificial distinction between home and work. Although courts have generally been reluctant to grant increased transportation costs[125] as part of "reasonable accommodations" in an ADA lawsuit, this expense usually results from the fact that manufacturers design motor vehicles almost exclusively for nondisabled passengers and drivers. The lack of accessible transportation frequently is a major barrier to the employment of adults with disabilities.[126] In an effort to fulfill public policy objectives that would allow disabled persons to join the productive labor force, judges or lawmakers might consider various additional options such as installing technological capacities to permit disabled employees to work at home when necessary and remedies to reimburse the cost of personal assistants who have been paid by the worker with a disability for employment-related duties, especially when the employer had previously refused to grant the worker's request for reasonable accommodations.

Compliance with laws prohibiting discrimination against Americans with disabilities is an important moral and legal obligation that seems to be contradicted by statutory provisions that offer tax incentives or subsidies as a reward for obeying the law.[127] In addition, to prevent the dilution of ADA requirements by lawyers who are sometimes trained to find "reasonableness" almost anywhere,[128] the interpretation of laws prohibiting discrimination against disabled citizens must be guided by the compass embedded in the concept of equality.[129] Emphasis must be placed on the principles of *equality* and *accommodations* instead of *reasonableness* and *individual particularity*.

In addition, there needs to be a change in the status of disabled people as a minority group under the equal protection clause of the Fourteenth Amendment. Although some legal analysts may believe that the question was definitely settled by the opinion of Justice White in *Cleburne*,[130] the controversy could become the focus of additional discussion. As judges begin to recognize that the main problems encountered by the disabled minority consist of stigmatizing and prejudicial attitudes about visible or labeled traits, there is always a possibility that appellate courts might engage in the rare act of changing their minds, although the Supreme Court's recent affirmation of *Cleburne* in *Board of Trustees of the University of Alabama v. Garrett*[131] makes this seem unlikely at best. Some researchers have contended that, since disability is not a suspect classification involving heightened constitutional scrutiny, jurists might be more favorably disposed toward affirmative action programs on behalf of persons with disabilities than other disadvantaged groups.[132]

A possible explanation for the action by the Supreme Court to engage in the classification of disability discrimination under the equal protection clause unnecessarily in the *Cleburne* decision became evident sixteen years later. In *University of Alabama v. Garrett,* the Court held that Section 5 of the Fourteenth Amendment, which gave Congress the right to enforce these prohibitions against discrimination, was not applicable in this case because the test for this kind of discrimination under the equal protection clause was merely "rationality." Instead, the justices chose to employ the Eleventh Amendment to uphold the discrimination against the disabled plaintiffs. Some commentators in the wake of the decision called upon disability rights advocates to fight in Congress, state legislatures, and the courts to "make incremental gains and combat further losses."[133] To other disabled observers, therefore, the decision represented little more than a rationalization to reach a virtually preconceived conclusion adverse to the interests of disabled people. Specifically, in response to the invalid criticism that "Hahn puts his faith in the legal protection of rights, and in particular, the legal protection that antidiscrimination law provides,"[134] this observer sadly concludes that courts and lawyers are not likely to play a supportive role in the quest by disabled people for freedom and equality.[135]

But arguments in favor of equal rights for citizens with disabilities under the Constitution should not be sacrificed for the sake of any other remedial action. The fear that employers might retaliate against workers who disclose health problems or disabilities[136] may interfere with the enforcement of programs that establish timetables or goals, but the concept of individual merit is not apt to be subverted by personnel assessments that encompass environmental as well as personal attributes. More stringent forms of affirmative action such as employment quotas have even been accepted for years in European nations, where experience indicates that their failure to reduce joblessness may be a product of administrative weaknesses. Furthermore, a pilot study conducted in 1978 by the Office of Federal Contract Compliance Programs of contractors covered by Section 503 of the Rehabilitation Act of 1973 found that the 90 percent of the employers were not in compliance with the law and 53 percent did not review job descriptions or other personnel policies that could be discriminatory.[137] Affirmative action and related plans may be helpful in ameliorating discrimination against disabled workers, but they should not supplant the legal remedies potentially offered by the ADA and the Fourteenth Amendment.

## Conclusion

The Americans with Disabilities Act has not fulfilled many of the hopes of its proponents.[138] Major Supreme Court decisions concerning disability rights have been decidedly unfavorable to the interests of this segment of the population. Many of these problems can be traced to confusion surrounding the concepts of impairment and disability, the failure of courts to adopt the sociopolitical definition of disability, which focuses attention on the attitudinal environment as the principal source of discrimination against disabled citizens, and resistance to the minority group model for the assessment of these issues. Additional obstacles have resulted from nondisabled dominance of the discourse about disability and the prevalence of paternalistic sentiments toward disabled persons. To mitigate many of these barriers, the principle of equal environmental adaptations, which seeks to achieve parity between the advantages bestowed on nondisabled people and the disadvantages imposed on disabled citizens in the "taken for granted" environment, is proposed as a means of interpreting the provision regarding "reasonable accommodations" in the ADA.

NOTES

To avoid confusion and misunderstanding, it must be mentioned first that there are major differences in the nature of documentation that both reflect and influence the contrasting perspectives of law and the social sciences. According to conventional assumptions, lawyers should follow a seemingly relentless logic derived from settled precedents and supported by legal authority. By contrast, many social scientists view judicial rulings as simply another form of public policy shaped by social and political values rather than by inexorable rationality. Hence, they are engaged in a continuing search for innovative approaches, creative breakthroughs, and speculative leaps from earlier paradigms; and their citations are designed to demonstrate the limitations as well as the evidence represented by existing information. Moreover, they often believe that proposed solutions to persistent problems are molded by distinct experiences instead of objective reasoning. Thus, the common, though often unspoken, perception that the rights of disabled citizens under the Americans with Disabilities Act (ADA) extend beyond the rights granted other individuals fails to encompass a recognition of "taken for granted" or unacknowledged aspects of the environment that bestow significant advantages upon nondisabled people and corresponding disadvantages upon persons with disabilities. And of course features that contribute to this kind of biased reasoning are never fully documented.

Consistent with the above-stated views, limited legal citations are provided in this article. For those interested in further exposition of my arguments, see HAR-LAN HAHN, EUROPEAN PERCEPTIONS OF EMPLOYMENT POLICY FOR DISABLED PERSONS (1984); Harlan Hahn, *The Appearance of Physical Difference: A New Agenda for Political Research*, 17 J. HEALTH & HUM. RESOURCES ADMIN. 391 (1995); Harlan Hahn, *Disability and the Urban Environment: A Perspective on Los Angeles*, 4 SOC. & SPACE 273 (1986); Harlan Hahn, *Antidiscrimination Laws and Social Research on Disability: The Minority Group Model*, 14 BEH. SCI. & L. 1 (1996); Harlan Hahn, *Equality and the Environment: The Interpretation of "Reasonable Accommodation" in the Americans with Disabilities Act*, 17 J. REHAB. ADMIN. 101, 103 (1993).

1. 42 U.S.C. § 12101 (1994).

2. *See* Saad Z. Nagi, *The Concept and Measurement of Disability, in* DISABILITY POLICIES AND GOVERNMENT PROGRAMS 2–3 (Edward D. Berkowitz ed., 1979).

3. *See* CLAIRE H. LIACHOWITZ, DISABILITY AS A SOCIAL CONSTRUCT 22 (1988).

4. Examples of such diagnostic classifications include polio and Down's syndrome (relating to etiology) or paraplegia and vision impairment (relating to a part of the body).

5. *See* DEBORAH A. STONE, THE DISABLED STATE (1984).

6. Both of these disciplines have developed their own research literatures and their own professional degree programs. The legislative foundation for vocational rehabilitation is the federal Rehabilitation Act of 1920, Pub. L. No. 66–236, *reprinted in* 1973 U.S.C.C.A.N. 2076, 2082–87. The comparable basis for medical rehabilitation can be found in the Barden-LaFollette Act of 1954, Pub. L. No. 83–565, 69 Stat. 652 (*codified as amended at* 29 U.S.C. §§ 31–42) (repealed 1973).

7. *See* CONSTANTINE SAFILIOS-ROTHSCHILD, THE SOCIOLOGICAL AND SOCIAL PSYCHOLOGY OF DISABILITY AND REHABILITATION 230–41 (1970).

8. 29 U.S.C. § 794 (1994).

9. *See, e.g.,* MONROE BERKOWITZ ET AL., PUBLIC POLICY TOWARD DISABILITY 41–63 (1976).

10. For a critique of this orientation, see Paul Abberly, *Disabled People and "Normality," in* DISABLING BARRIERS—ENABLING ENVIRONMENT 107–15 (John Swain et al. eds., 1993).

11. 274 U.S. 200 (1927). One eminent constitutional scholar characterized the final paragraph of this opinion by Justice Oliver Wendell Holmes Jr., by saying,

"Seldom has so much questionable doctrine been compressed into five sentences of a Supreme Court opinion." C. HERMAN PRITCHETT, THE AMERICAN CONSTITU-TION 538 (1977).

12. *See generally* HUGH GREGORY GALLAGHER, BY TRUST BETRAYED: PATIENTS, PHYSICIANS, AND THE LICENSE TO KILL IN THE THIRD REICH (1990).

13. *See* EDWARD H. YELIN, DISABILITY AND THE DISPLACED WORKER 119 (1992).

14. *See* STEPHEN JAY GOULD, THE MISMEASURE OF MAN 30–72 (1981).

15. *See, e.g.,* Bradwell v. Illinois, 83 U.S. 130 (1873) (holding constitutionally valid an Illinois state law prohibiting women from obtaining the requisite license necessary to practice law).

16. *See, e.g.,* JEROME E. BICKENBACH, PHYSICAL DISABILITY AND SOCIAL POL-ICY (1993) (discussing the various models of disablement including the biomedical model, economic model, and the social-political model of disablement).

17. 42 U.S.C. § 12102 (1994).

18. *See* David G. Savage, *Supreme Court to Rule on Disability Act Cases,* L.A. TIMES, Jan. 9, 1999, at A14. *See also* Telephone Interview with Stanley Fleischmen (Jan. 9, 1999) (notes on file with the author).

19. *See* Arlene B. Mayerson, *Restoring Regard for the "Regarded as" Prong: Giving Effect to Congressional Intent,* 42 VILL. L. REV. 587 (1997). Both of these prongs could, of course, be readily interpreted to forbid discrimination on the basis of visible or labeled bodily characteristics. *See infra* text accompanying note 33.

20. School Bd. v. Arline, 480 U.S. 273 (1987).

21. 524 U.S. 624, 637–39 (1998).

22. These issues were placed before the Supreme Court in 1999 in *Sutton v. United Airlines, Inc.,* 527 U.S. 471, 119 S. Ct. 2139 (1999); *Murphy v. United Parcel Serv.,* 527 U.S. 516, 118 S. Ct. 2133 (1999); and *Albertson's Inc. v. Kirkingburg,* 527 U.S. 516, 119 S. Ct. 2162 (1999), respectively.

23. 531 U.S. 356.

24. David G. Strange, *The New Federalism Frontier,* ABA JOURNAL.

25. There is, of course, often a tendency for some lawyers to seize upon new statutes to present novel arguments that have not been successful. Before leaving office, Evan Kemp expressed the opinion that an inordinate number of early ADA lawsuits involved relatively frivolous, trivial matters such as "halitosis and hang-nails." Telephone Interview with Evan J. Kemp Jr., Chairman of the EEOC (Aug. 28, 1991) (notes on file with author).

26. *See, e.g.,* David M. Engel & Frank W. Munger, *Rights, Remembrance, and the Reconciliation of Difference,* 30 L. & SOC'Y REV. 7 (1996).

27. John Anthony White Jr., The Role of Occupation and Adaptation in Ritual Transformation: An Ethnograph Study of Ten People with Mobility Impairments Using Title I of the ADA to Fight Employment Discrimination (1998) (unpublished Ph.D. dissertation, University of Southern California) (on file with author).

28. This issue was accepted for review by the U.S. Supreme Court in 1998 in *Cleveland v. Policy Management Sys.,* 526 U.S. 795 (1999).

29. *See, e.g.,* McNemar v. The Disney Store, 91 F.3d 610 (3d Cir. 1996). *But see* Taylor v. Food World, Inc., 946 F. Supp. 937 (N.D. Ala. 1996), *rev'd.,* 133 F.3d 1419 (11th Cir. 1998).

30. Harlan Hahn, *Toward a Politics of Disability: Definitions, Disciplines, and Policies,* 22 Soc. Sci. J., Oct. 1985, at 87; Harlan Hahn, *Disability Policy and the Problem of Discrimination,* 28 Am. Behav. Sci. 293 (1985).

31. Harlan Hahn, *Reconceptualizing Disability: A Political Science Perspective,* 45 Rehab. Lit. 362, 364 (1989).

32. In many respects, the sociopolitical approach is comparable to the definition of disability formulated years ago in Great Britain by the Union of the Physically Impaired against Segregation:

> In our view, it is society which disables physically impaired people. Disability is something imposed on top of our impairments by the way we are unnecessarily isolated and excluded from full participation in society. . . . Thus we define impairment as lacking part or all of a limb, or having a defective limb, organ or mechanism of the body; and disability as the disadvantage or restriction of activity caused by a contemporary social organisation which takes no or little account of people who have physical impairments and thus excludes them from participation in the mainstream of social activities. Physical disability is therefore a particular form of social oppression.

Michael Oliver, Understanding Disability 22 (1996).

33. This analysis parallels, in some respects, the discussion of "difference" in Martha Minow, Making All the Difference: Inclusion, Exclusion, and American Law (1990). Instead of focusing on a "social relations" approach or "situated knowledge" that reflects the perception of the observed and the observer, however, the emphasis on visibility and labeling as the primary object of discrimination seems to allow distinction to be drawn between the investigator and the subject, and perhaps by extension between impairment and disability, that would permit an empirical study of the bodily variations that elicit prejudice. Moreover, Minow's discussion follows and endorses the comparative approach to the study of political identity and discrimination indicated in her later book, Martha Minow, Not Only for Myself: Identity, Politics, and the Law (1997).

34. *See, e.g.,* Jane R. Mercer, Labeling the Mentally Retarded (1973); Robert A. Scott, The Making of Blind Men (1969).

35. Labeling and visibility could be viewed as an operational measure of "record" and "regarded" in the ADA definition. 42 U.S.C. § 12102 (1994); *cf.* Mayerson, *supra* note 19.

36. At a symposium on disability sponsored by the American Enterprise Institute, the chairman of the EEOC commented on papers presented by four economists for their "failure to recognize the tremendous prejudice against disabled people that exists in our society." Evan J. Kemp Jr., *Disability in Our Society, in* Disability and Work 57 (Carolyn L. Weaver ed., 1991). The implications of such an orientation for the assessment of employment discrimination are indicated by the following statement by two other economists in a book with the same title when they contrasted their approach to the views of most disability rights advocates:

> To them, equal access is a fundamental principle, and its achievement is to be secured as a matter of right, irrespective of cost. An alternative point of view, however, is that the "equal access" goal differs little from other important

objectives in the disability area, such as efficiently sharing the cost of impairments or undertaking efficient investments to reduce the cost of disability. In this perspective, the costs of securing more equal access must be set off against the benefits that a reduction in inequality conveys. And no absolute level of access inequality is to be set as inviolable.

RICHARD V. BURKHAUSER & ROBERT A. HAVEMAN, DISABILITY AND WORK 82 (1982). Many other nondisabled professionals have endorsed the belief that equality for citizens with disabilities is an acceptable goal as long as it does not entail financial costs or impinge on the traditional prerogatives that they have enjoyed. *See, e.g.,* MARK KELMAN & GILLIAN LESTER, JUMPING THE QUEUE (1997).

37.  Harlan Hahn, *Paternalism and Public Policy,* 20 SOCIETY 36, 44 (1983).

38.  *See* Carol K. Sigelman & Louse C. Singleton, *Stigmatization in Childhood, in* THE DILEMMA OF DIFFERENCE 191–92 (Stephen C. Ainlay et al. eds., 1986).

39.  Harlan Hahn, *The Politics of Physical Differences: Disability and Discrimination,* 44 J. SOC. ISSUES 39 (1988).

40.  *See generally* SANDER L. GILMAN, DIFFERENCE AND PATHOLOGY (1985).

41.  *See* Fred Davis, *Deviance Disavowal: The Management of Strained Interaction by the Visibly Handicapped,* 9 SOC. PROB. 120 (1961).

42.  *See, e.g.,* Robert Kleck, *Emotional Arousal in Interactions with Stigmatized Persons,* 19 PSYCHOL. REP. 1226 (1966); Robert Kleck et al., *The Effects of Physical Deviance upon Face-to-Face Interaction,* 19 HUM. REL. 425 (1966).

43.  *See* Norman Goodman et al., *Variant Reactions to Physical Disabilities,* 28 AM. SOCIO. REV. 429 (1963); Stephen A. Richardson, *Age and Sex Differences in Values toward Physical Handicaps,* 11 J. HEALTH & SOC. BEHAV. 207 (1970); Stephen A. Richardson & Jacqueline Royce, *Race and Physical Handicap in Children's Preference for Other Children,* 39 CHILD DEV. 469 (1968).

44.  *See* Kenneth B. Clark & Mamie P. Clark, *Racial Identification and Preference in Negro Children, in* READINGS IN SOCIAL PSYCHOLOGY 551–60 (Guy E. Swanson et al. eds., 1952).

45.  347 U.S. 483, 494 n.11 (1954).

46.  ERVING GOFFMAN, STIGMA: NOTES ON THE MANAGEMENT OF SPOILED IDENTITY 5 (1963).

47.  *See* Lerita M. Coleman, *Stigma: An Enigma Demystified, in* THE DILEMMA OF DIFFERENCE 214 (Stephen C. Ainlay et al. eds., 1986).

48.  *See, e.g.,* EDWARD E. JONES ET AL., SOCIAL STIGMA: THE PSYCHOLOGY OF MARKED RELATIONSHIPS (1984); IRWIN KATZ, STIGMA: A SOCIAL PSYCHOLOGICAL ANALYSIS (1981).

49.  For a more detailed presentation of this analysis, see Harlan Hahn, *Antidiscrimination Laws: The Minority Group Perspective,* 14 BEHAV. SCI. & L. 41 (1996).

50.  *See* Harlan Hahn, *The Minority Group Model of Disability: Implications for Medical Sociology, in* RESEARCH IN THE SOCIOL. OF HEALTH CARE 3–24 (Rose Welt & Jeanne J. Kronenfield eds., 1994).

51.  ROGER G. BARKER ET AL., ADJUSTMENT TO PHYSICAL HANDICAP AND ILLNESS: A SURVEY OF THE SOCIAL PSYCHOLOGY OF PHYSIQUE AND DISABILITY 102 (1953).

52. SAFILIOS-ROTHSCHILD, *supra,* note 7, at 114–15.

53. JOHN GLIEDMAN & WILLIAM ROTH, THE UNEXPECTED MINORITY: HANDICAPPED CHILDREN IN AMERICA (1980).

54. THE ICD SURVEY OF DISABLED AMERICANS 111, 114 (1986) (study on file with author).

55. *See* Harlan Hahn, *An Agenda for Citizens with Disabilities: Pursuing Identity and Empowerment,* 9 J. VOC. REHAB. 31 (1997).

56. ROSE WEITZ, THE SOCIOLOGY OF HEALTH, ILLNESS, AND HEALTH CARE 156–58 (1997).

57. G. E. SIMPSON & J. MILTON YINGER, RACIAL AND CULTURAL MINORITIES: AN ANALYSIS OF PREJUDICE AND DISCRIMINATION 10 (5th ed., 1985).

58. It does not seem inconceivable, for example, that an empirical investigation could be designed to study the degree and extent of avoidance, prejudices, and other forms of discriminatory behavior elicited by variations in the visible or labeled physical characteristics reflected by obvious or hidden disabilities. The difficulty, of course, is that the overwhelming preoccupation with the study of functional impairments has diverted interest and resources from the pursuit of this kind of research.

59. For a discussion of the inordinate emphasis placed on walking in this society from the perspective of a wheelchair user, for example, see OLIVER, *supra* note 32, at 96–109.

60. This analysis parallels, in some respects, the discussion of stigma theory and unconscious racism in Charles R. Lawrence III, *The Id, the Ego, and Equal Protection: Reckoning with Unconscious Racism,* 39 STAN. L. REV. 317 (1987).

61. Perhaps the clearest, though not the most costly, example is chairs, which, for wheelchair users who are considerate enough to bring our own, represent a significant concession to the nondisabled segment of society. Although chairs may comprise a sizable portion of the budget for many facilities, their expense is relatively trivial in comparison with the enormous economic and other rewards bequeathed to the nondisabled by a milieu shaped almost exclusively for their benefit.

62. The question might be asked: What accounts for these environmental inequities, and why are they so widely ignored? The answer to the first portion of the question seems comparatively simple: Nondisabled people throughout history have been relatively powerful, and persons with disabilities have always been numbered among the powerless. The response to the second part also seems rather straightforward: The advantages accruing to the nondisabled are taken for granted. The explanation for this relative neglect can also be partially attributed to the concept of paternalism discussed below in text accompanying *infra* notes 71–74.

63. To a nonlawyer, an appropriate reply to the relentless demand to resolve dilemmas that have puzzled philosophers for centuries by furnishing a simple and precise definition of equality might be summed up by the common-sense formula: equal = equal. More technical and complex efforts to parse the meaning of this word in the manner that seems to appeal to lawyers are discussed below. At a minimum, however, attempts to apply the principle of equality to litigation concerning the status of disabled and nondisabled citizens must be devoid of any assumptions of biological inferiority; and it should fulfill the obligations indicated by the famil-

iar phrase, "a level playing field." Thus, to speak of an "accommodation duty" in the ADA as though it represented an extension beyond the advantages granted to nondisabled persons, or a special favor to disabled citizens, is a serious misinterpretation of the concept of equal rights. In a fundamental sense, the legal responsibility to provide "reasonable accommodations" merely reflects an effort to level the playing field. To querulous critics who may insist on an exact definition of the limits of such accommodations, reference can only be made to the research contemplated in footnote 34. An empirical investigation of the aversion reflected by reactions to visible and labeled bodily differences could be used to define the boundaries of physical characteristics that are especially deserving of the legal protection available in antidiscrimination laws. Beyond this point, the argument becomes tedious and unproductive.

64. One indication of the repertoire of interactions between the human organism and the environment involved in simple routines is provided by an analysis of operational and sensory acts in Anthony F. C. Wallaces, *Driving to Work, in* Urbanman: The Psychology of Urban Survival 23–41 (John Helmer & Neil A. Eddington eds., 1973).

65. *See, e.g.,* Rosemarie Garland Thomson, Extraordinary Bodies: Figuring Physical Disability in American Culture and Literature (1997); Lennard J. Davis, Enforcing Normalcy: Disability, Deafness, and the Body (1995).

66. One political theorist has stated that to understand the meaning of disability "is to describe its location in a field of discursive relations and thereby to locate those persons or groups of persons who control the responsibility prescriptions that attend and constitute the disabled role." Michael J. Shapiro, *Disability and the Politics of Constitutive Rules, in* Cross National Rehabilitation Policies: A Sociological Perspective 87 (Gary L. Albrecht ed., 1981).

67. For a general—and early—appraisal of implementing the ADA, see Implementing the Americans with Disabilities Act (Lawrence O. Goslin & Henry A. Beyer eds., 1993) and Implementing the Americans with Disabilities Act (Jane West, ed., 1996).

68. *See* Jonathan C. Drimmer, *Cripples, Overcomers, and Civil Rights: Tracing the Evolution of Federal Legislation and Social Policy for People with Disabilities*, 40 UCLA L. Rev. 1341 (1993).

69. Renee R. Anspach, *From Stigma to Identity Politics: Political Activism Among the Physically Disabled and Former Mental Patients*, 13 Soc. Sci. & Med. 765 (1979).

70. Richard Beaulaurier, A Study of the Attitudes of Social Workers Toward Disability (1996) (unpublished Ph.D. dissertation, University of Southern California) (on file with author).

71. Susan M. Olson, Clients and Lawyers: Securing the Rights of Disabled Persons (1984).

72. To avoid misinterpretation, it must be emphasized that this statement is purely speculative. It does seem consistent, however, with the theoretical orientation implied by discursive analysis and with the biased or skewed analysis of major issues in the interpretation of ADA created by the nondisabled domination of the discourse of disability. Hence, the failure to consider the advantages or disadvan-

tages produced by "taken for granted" features of the environment and the neglect of the sociopolitical definition of disability can be traced to the differences between the experiences of disabled persons and the dominant participants in this discussion.

73. *See* the research cited in footnotes 41 and 52, *supra*.

74. *See* MICHAEL OLIVER, THE POLITICS OF DISABLEMENT: A SOCIOLOGICAL APPROACH 1–11 (1990).

75. Nondisabled individuals frequently seem to have an almost insatiable desire (or need?) to "help" people with disabilities. This generalization seems to apply with equal effect to judges and legal analysis as well as physicians and bureaucrats.

76. Perhaps it needs to be made clear that this perspective is also speculative. It is not attributed to any specific individual. It simply reflects an opinion that some individuals might form especially after years of struggle in the disability rights movement.

77. *See* City of Cleburne v. Cleburne Living Ctr., 473 U.S. 432 (1985).

78. *Id.* at 435.

79. *Id.*

80. *Id.* at 445.

81. *Id.* at 443–44.

82. *Id.* at 442.

83. *Id.* at 446.

84. *University of Alabama v. Garrett*, 531 U.S. 356, 372.

85. *See* RICHARD K. SCOTCH, FROM GOOD WILL TO CIVIL RIGHTS: TRANSFORMING FEDERAL DISABILITY POLICY 139 (1984).

86. *See* RANDY SHAW, THE ACTIVIST'S HANDBOOK 235–50 (1996).

87. *See* ERWIN L. LEVINE & ELIZABETH M. WEXLER, P.L. 94–102: AN ACT OF CONGRESS (1981).

88. See *supra* notes 75–81 and accompanying text.

89. School Bd. of Nassau County v. Arline, 480 U.S. 273, 284 (1987).

90. *Cleburne*, 473 U.S. at 443.

91. 469 U.S. 287 (1985).

92. *Id.* at 295. Perhaps part of the difficulty with this analysis stems from the belief that "disparate impact" is the only test that can be invoked to prevent injurious inequalities that result from policies enacted through good motives. Little attention has been devoted by the courts to the possibilities that serious harm can be inflicted by laws adopted as a result of paternalistic feelings or noble intentions. *See, e.g.,* Lawrence, *supra* note 60.

93. *See* ELLEN J. LANGER & BENZION CHANOWITZ, *Mindfulness/Mindlessness: A New Perspective for the Study of Disability, in* ATTITUDES TOWARD PERSONS WITH DISABILITIES 68–81 (Harold E. Yuker ed., 1988).

94. 457 U.S. 307 (1982).

95. *Id.* at 320.

96. *See id.* at 322.

97. *Id.* at 323.

98. *Id.* at 318.

99. *Id.* at 328–29.

100. *Id.* at 329.

101. *See* Pennhurst v. Halderman, 451 U.S. 1 (1981).

102. *Id.* at 42 (White, J., dissenting).

103. *Id.* at 36.

104. 442 U.S. 397 (1979).

105. *Id.* at 410.

106. Jacobus tenBroek, *The Right to Live in the World: The Disabled in the Law of Torts,* 54 CAL. L. REV. 841 (1966).

107. The phrase, of course, originally appeared in Section 504 of the Rehabilitation Act of 1973. 29 U.S.C. § 794 (1994). The EEOC regulations defining a similar clause in Title I of the ADA stipulate that a "qualified individual with a disability" is someone "who satisfies the . . . job-related requirements . . . and who, with or without reasonable accommodation, can perform the essential functions of such position." 29 C.F.R. § 1630.2 (m).

108. BONNIE POITRAS TUCKER, FEDERAL DISABILITY LAW IN A NUTSHELL 94 (1998). The need to disentangle these elements is not an easy goal, but perhaps the principal obstacles to the fulfillment of this objective are the constraints on the human imagination imposed by the restrictive contours of the existing environment:

> Clearly, when considering whether some action or situation is an instance of discrimination on the basis of ability, the trick is to distinguish ability to do the relevant things from ability to do irrelevant things. But, given that so many places and activities are structured for people with a narrow range of abilities, telling the two apart is not always easy.

SUSAN WENDALL, THE REJECTED BODY: FEMINIST PHILOSOPHICAL REFLECTIONS ON DISABILITY 54 (1996).

109. Efforts to erect distinctions between abilities and impairments and between abilities and visible or labeled bodily differences in judicial appraisals of employment evaluations may be a difficult, though not impossible, task. It should, however, be supported by basic research. *See supra* notes 56 and 61.

110. *See* Hendrick Hudson Central Dist. Bd. of Educ. v. Rowley, 458 U.S. 176 (1982).

111. Pub. L. 94–142. This law was subsequently renamed the Individuals with Disabilities Education Act, 20 U.S.C. § 1400 (1990) (IDEA).

112. *Rowley,* 458 U.S. at 200.

113. *See generally* HARLEN LANE, THE MASK OF BENEVOLENCE: DISABLING THE DEAF COMMUNITY (1992).

114. *Rowley,* 458 U.S. at 201.

115. *Id.* at 199.

116. *Id.* at 211 (emphasis in original).

117. *Id.* at 214 (White, J., dissenting).

118. *See supra* note 36 for the studies by some four economists published in Weaver, and discussed briefly in that same footnote.

119. Harlan Hahn, *New Trends in Disability Studies: Implications for Educational Policy, in* INCLUSION AND SOCIAL REFORM: TRANSFORMING AMERICA'S CLASSROOM 325 (Dorothy Kezner Lipsky & Alan Gartner eds., 1997).

120. For a discussion of several definitions, see *id.* at 324–27.

121. The difficulty of applying this standard to cases involving disability rights has been described as follows:

> According to this perspective, the basic conditions of equality in "the race of life" are satisfied as long as all of the contestants are lined up evenly at the starting line. In an analogy that is especially compatible with the American economic system, the outcome of this competition is supposedly determined by the principles of meritocracy that have seemingly been reflected in educational policy by a questionable belief in innate intelligence. But this metaphor ignores the context or the environment in which the competition is conducted. If the lane of the race track assigned to disabled contestants is filled with obstacles, for example, the competition can hardly be considered fair. And, for most disabled children and adults, the obstacles presented by architectural inaccessibility, communication barriers, the effects of stigmatizing attitudes, and the demands of a discriminatory environment often appear to be almost insurmountable. The solution, of course, is to "clear the track" by changing the environment instead of the person.

*Id.* at 325.

122. The concept of equality of results for people with disabilities has been explained in the context of educational policy in the following terms:

> Assuming the possibility of defining the skills and knowledge that any person might need to survive or to flourish in a suitable environment . . . education would continue until each student meets the required criteria. . . . This procedure would eliminate the need for tests that attempt to assess aptitude or potential; instead, attention would focus on the creation of standardized evaluations of demonstrated performance and on the identification of necessary or essential requirements for participation in a democratic society. This approach is based on the radical assumption that all human beings have equal dignity and worth.

*Id.* at 326.

123. A natural basis for interpreting "reasonable accommodations" might be derived from educational programs designed to establish parity or commensurate benefits for disabled and nondisabled schoolchildren. The costs of such policies would be difficult to calculate, however, because little systematic attention has been devoted to "taken for granted" advantages conferred on the nondisabled. Future research is likely to uncover many examples of inequality in this form. Ultimately, equal results may be even less expensive than equal opportunities. *Id.* at 327.

124. Again, perhaps chairs serve as the simplest example of an unequal feature of our habitat. *See supra* note 61. Another clear example would be flexible work schedules that might be especially helpful to the vast number of people who have arthritic impairments that entail periods of exacerbation and remission. Many obstacles in the existing environment are a manifestation of the manner in which the nature of the economic system in America inflicts inequalities on citizens with disabilities. For an analysis of the impact of the capitalist system on disabled peo-

ple, see Marta Russell, Beyond Ramps: Disability at the End of the Social Contract (1998).

125. *But see* United States v. Bd. of Trustees for the Univ. of Alabama, 908 F.2d 740 (1990) (holding in part that university's bus system did not make reasonable accommodation for the transportation of handicapped students by providing lift-equipped bus services four hours every day).

126. For an analysis of disability and transportation policy, see Robert A. Katzman, Institutional Disability: The Saga of Transportation Policy for the Disabled (1986).

127. For an analysis of such provisions, see Daniel C. Schaffer, *Tax Incentives, in* The Americans with Disabilities Act 293–312 (Jane West ed., 1991). The objection to such policies is primarily a moral concern that no one should be rewarded for obeying the law. This approach also seems to cheapen the ADA and to impose disrespect on the sociopolitical definition and the minority group model of disability by promoting a belief that a special inducement must be offered to persuade businesses to honor the law. At the same time, of course, there are no tax subsidies for disabled citizens who bear increased costs by living in an inhospitable environment. Disagreements about this matter reflects different political values and must be recognized as such.

128. To those who might think that this statement does not display the proper deference to the legal profession, it must be pointed out that a basic purpose of legal training is to equip a person to construct a rational argument to defend the position of the client in exchange for remuneration. Indeed, elements of this description are at the heart of the advocacy model.

129. Some critics might contend that the principle of equal treatment, which stipulate that likes should be treated alike and unlikes need not be treated alike, must not be applied to disputes concerning disability. Opponents could possibly find a faint trace of assumptions concerning biological inferiority in such criticism. At a minimum, however, it seems possible to state that, with regard to the fundamental rights of citizenship, there are no "unlikes." There are only people created equal. But again, this may reflect only a conflict over political values.

130. 473 U.S. 432 (1985).

131. 531 U.S. 356 (2001).

132. *See* Mark C. Weber, *Beyond the Americans with Disabilities Act: A National Employment Policy for People with Disabilities,* 46 Buffalo L. Rev. 123, 146 (1998).

133. John W. Perry, *Supreme Court Restricts ADA Title I as Applied to the States,* 25 Phys. & Ment.

134. J. E. Bickenbach, S. Chatterji, E. M. Badley, and T. B. Ustun, *Models of Disablement, Universalism, and the International Classification of Impairments, Disabilities, and Handicaps,* 48 Soc. Sci. & Med. (1999) at 1180.

135. Harlan Hahn, *Adjudication or Empowerment: Contrasting Experiences with a Social Model of Disability* in L. Barton, ed., Disability, Politics and the Struggle for Change.

136. An analysis for USA Today by Jury Verdict Research shows that those who file retaliation lawsuits win a higher percentage of cases than victims of age, disability, race, or sex discrimination. *Flood of "Retaliation" Cases Surfacing in U.S. Workplace,* USA Today, Feb. 10, 1999, at 1A.

137.  STEPHEN L. PERCY, DISABILITY, CIVIL RIGHTS, AND PUBLIC POLICY: THE POLITICS OF IMPLEMENTATION 193–220 (1989).

138.  For example, Professor Ruth Colker's research reveals that defendant employers prevailed in "94% of the [Title I] cases from which appeals were taken . . . [and] after the appeal process was completed . . . defendants continued to prevail in 82% of the cases." Ruth Colker, *ADA Title III: A Fragile Compromise,* 21 BERKELEY J. EMP. LAB. L. 376, 399 (2000).

*Matthew Diller*

# Judicial Backlash, the ADA, and the Civil Rights Model of Disability

Sometimes, legislation enacted with little fanfare proves profoundly important. Presumably the converse can be true as well: legislation enacted with great expectations can effectuate little real change.

The Americans with Disabilities Act (ADA) was enacted amid high hopes for the new statute's sweeping impact. Its statement of purpose proclaims the enormous breadth of its scope and goals, to "provide a clear and comprehensive national mandate for the elimination of discrimination against individuals with disabilities."[1] To accomplish this purpose, Congress stated that it was "invok[ing] the sweep of congressional authority . . . in order to address the major areas of discrimination faced day-to-day by people with disabilities."[2] Supporters hailed the ADA as an "emancipation proclamation" for people with disabilities.[3] The bill was signed into law on July 26, 1990, at a White House ceremony attended by two thousand supporters, including many people with disabilities. The event was an emotional watershed marked by tears and jubilation. Many present referred to it as a "second independence day."[4]

More than a decade later, it is clear that the ADA will be no mere footnote in the history of American disability policy. Although difficult to measure, its impact on institutional responses to disability has been profound.

Still, there are reasons to fear that, particularly in the area of employment, the ADA has not yet had the transformative impact its supporters predicted. Indeed, a decade after its enactment, the judicial landscape surrounding claims of employment discrimination under the ADA looks far more bleak than one might expect, given the ambitious hopes placed on the ADA and the celebrations that accompanied its enactment. The law books are littered with court decisions rejecting claims of employment discrimination on every ground imaginable and, in some instances, on grounds that seem inconceivable. A comprehensive study of twelve hundred court decisions by the ABA's Commission on Mental and Physical Disability Law has found that employers have prevailed in 92 percent of final judicial dispositions.[5] Legions of ADA plaintiffs have been thwarted by the many barriers created by judicial interpretations of the statute. Disability advocates have looked on in horror as the ADA case law has unfolded.[6] In 1999, the Supreme Court ratified this trend in significant respects by ruling against plaintiffs in three crucial ADA employment cases concerning the definition of disability.[7] Eighteen months later, in *Board of Trustees of the University of Alabama v. Garrett*,[8] the Court held Title I of the ADA unconstitutional, insofar as it authorized private persons to bring suits for damages against the states in the federal district courts.

This essay seeks to interpret the negative patterns reflected in the federal ADA Title I case law from the mid-1990s into the first years of the twenty-first century. The generally dismal outcomes for plaintiffs can be viewed in a number of ways. First, many ADA claims may fail because they are inherently weak. Under this view, the ADA has generated a wave of meritless cases appropriately rejected by the courts. This interpretation would bear out the opponents of the ADA who predicted that the statute would invite legions of frivolous claims and that in the end, only lawyers would profit from its enactment. As gratifying as it may be to some, this account is unconvincing. As discussed below, many of the court decisions are based on crabbed interpretations of the act that are at odds with its broad purposes. While it is impossible to determine what the success rate for ADA claims should be, it is clear that many plaintiffs who lose have claims that are far from frivolous.

A second explanation for the trend in the case law might be that the ADA is poorly drafted in light of congressional purposes. Under this view, the problem is not that plaintiffs are filing frivolous cases, but that the courts are constrained from enforcing the act in a coherent and effective way by statutory language that fails to reflect the law's broad goals.[9] While the courts certainly have seized on statutory language to create imposing obstacles for plaintiffs, the key phrases in the ADA are, ultimately, vague. Vague language can be interpreted broadly, as well as narrowly. Despite judicial claims that the courts are simply applying the "plain meaning" of the statute, the courts are affirmatively choosing narrow readings over broad ones, even in the face of expansive administrative interpretation and strong evidence that Congress intended the statute to be interpreted expansively. In light of the court decisions, it is easy to criticize the ADA's draftsmanship. But the text itself does not mandate the narrowing approach that the courts have taken.

A third explanation is possible. It may be that the case law merely reflects the confusion that frequently follows the enactment of major legislation.

The ADA introduces a number of concepts that many judges have not dealt with in the past, such as the concepts of "reasonable accommodation," "undue burden," and a new definition of disability. Under this view, the judicial system will eventually right itself, as judges gain experience and expertise in dealing with ADA cases.

This third account may have some validity, as there are a number of areas in which the appellate courts have begun to reject clear misreadings of the statute that they had previously accepted. The Supreme Court's decision in *Bragdon v. Abbott*,[10] holding that HIV infection is a disability under the act, is one example. Similarly, the Court's decision in *Cleveland v. Policy Management Systems Corp*,[11] holding that disability benefit recipients may not be estopped from maintaining ADA cases, should terminate a line of erroneous decisions. The Court's 1999 decisions in *Sutton*,[12] *Murphy*[13] and *Kirkingburg*,[14] however, adopted the kind of narrow approach to the statute that has proven lethal to most plaintiffs' claims. A year and a half later, in *University of Alabama v. Garrett*,[15] the Supreme Court held that provisions of the ADA authorizing individual Title I suits for damages against the states violated the Eleventh Amendment of the Constitution. Although the Court's decision does not directly address the constitutionality of the act's public programs and services, telecommunications, or public accommodations provisions, it leaves open the question of how it might rule on subsequent cases challenging the constitutionality of individual suits for damages against the states under Titles II, III, and IV. These decisions suggest that ADA plaintiffs are not likely to face brighter prospects in the near future.

In any event, the theory that unfamiliarity with the ADA has led to judicial misinterpretation fails to explain why the decisions have so heavily favored employers. If we have simply been in a shakedown period that necessarily precedes consistent and well-reasoned interpretation of the ADA, why have the errors been so persistently one-sided? Why do employers consistently emerge victorious?

A final account of the pattern in ADA decisions is the one suggested by the title of this book: that there is some kind of backlash against the ADA. The term *backlash* suggests an hostility to the statute and toward those who seek to enforce it. The backlash thesis suggests that judges are not simply confused by the ADA; rather, they are resisting it. It suggests that the courts are systematically nullifying rights that Congress conferred on people with disabilities.

Absent a special fondness for conspiracy theories, it is difficult to accept the proposition that federal judges are deliberately sabotaging the ADA.

But the idea of backlash need not be understood as a deliberate or intentional campaign. Resistance to the ADA may result from a failure to comprehend and therefore to accept the conceptual premises underpinning the statute. Such widespread misunderstanding might generate a pattern of erroneous decisions that, on the surface, appear unrelated. If backlash is used in this sense, the case for a judicial backlash against the ADA is strong.

I argue here that the pattern of narrow and begrudging interpretations of the ADA derives from the fact that the courts do not fully grasp, let alone accept, the statute's reliance on a civil rights model for addressing problems that people with disabilities face. In supporting this claim, I first examine several areas of case law in which the courts have taken a restrictive approach to the ADA. In taking this approach, the courts have failed to interpret the ADA as effectuating a coherent civil rights policy. On the contrary, from a civil rights perspective, these decisions often appear perverse.

Next, I examine the implications of the decision to frame legislation intended to make social institutions accessible to people with disabilities as a civil rights measure. The civil rights model identifies discrimination, and a resulting inequality, as the central social issues that people with disabilities face. It establishes a framework of relationships in which employers and public institutions have a responsibility to facilitate the social integration of people with disabilities. Although there are many advantages to framing the issue in terms of civil rights, the civil rights model actually provides a less than an ideal fit with the problems posed by disability.

Judicial resistance to the ADA, I will argue, manifests the more general skepticism that has confronted claims for equality in recent years. With the passage of Amendment 2 in Colorado[16] and Proposition 209 in California[17] it is clear that claims for equality advanced by racial minorities, gays and lesbians, and women are frequently perceived by broad segments of the American public as attempts to gain "special treatment." The ADA relies on notions of equality that have proven especially controversial. The ADA's requirement of "reasonable accommodation" rests on the idea that, in some circumstances, people must be treated differently to be treated equally. This "different treatment" form of equality has long been contested, and in the context of affirmative action, has met with deep resistance from the courts.

Absent a clear understanding that the ADA promotes equality, judges view the act as a kind of subsidy conferred on a class of people singled out by Congress for special treatment. Judges view the ADA as a form of public benefit program for people with disabilities, rather than as a mandate for equality. In deciding whether plaintiffs qualify for these supposed subsidies, courts inevitably focus on the worthiness and need of the plaintiffs. In contrast, under a civil rights framework, the focus of attention is on the question of whether the defendant has responded appropriately to the plaintiff's disability. Judicial decisions in ADA cases, however, seldom reach this issue.

Although reliance on the civil rights model has brought many benefits for people with disabilities, it is not without limitations. People with disabilities have won civil rights protection at a time when such protections are under attack on many levels. The initial wave of judicial decisions interpreting the ADA, which will set the course for judicial enforcement in the future, has crested during a period when cramped readings of civil rights protections represent the norm, rather than the exception.

## Ninety-Nine Ways to Lose a Case

Any discussion of judicial backlash against the ADA must start from the premise that the courts are doing something wrong. For purposes of this discussion it is unnecessary to parse a large number of ADA decisions. Rather, I will outline a few areas in which substantial numbers of courts have relied on restrictive interpretations of the ADA, which unnecessarily and unfairly leave plaintiffs without a remedy. I begin by describing the facts of four cases, which taken together, illustrate the judicial trends I seek to explain.

In the first of these cases, *Ellison v. Software Spectrum, Inc.*,[18] the Fifth Circuit held that an ADA plaintiff with breast cancer who suffered side effects from chemotherapy was not a person with a disability because she managed, despite her impairments, to continue working. As a result of the ruling, not only did Ms. Ellison have no right to reasonable accommodations, she had no legal protection against being fired for having had cancer, regardless of whether she could perform her job. In *Redlich v. Albany Law School*,[19] a district court similarly found that a law professor who had suffered a stroke, resulting in paralysis of the left hand, arm and leg, did not have a disability because he continued to work at his job.

In *McNemar v. Disney Store Inc.*,[20] an employee with AIDS was fired for allegedly failing to replace two dollars that he had taken from the cash register for a pack of cigarettes. The Third Circuit held that he could not maintain an ADA case challenging his dismissal because, after his termination, he had successfully applied for Social Security disability benefits and was therefore estopped from claiming that he was qualified for his past job. The court did not consider the fact that the defendant had never found the plaintiff to be unqualified for the job relevant to the court's analysis.

In *Hileman v. City of Dallas*,[21] the Fifth Circuit found that a plaintiff with a spastic colon aggravated by multiple sclerosis was not entitled to an accommodation that would permit her to arrive at her clerical job twenty minutes late, because her condition did not qualify as a disability. The court angrily chastised the plaintiff for seeking to "misuse" the ADA.

A list of cases like these could go on for pages. These cases make one thing clear: many of the plaintiffs who are losing ADA cases are not raising frivolous claims. Although it is possible to find decisions concerning far-fetched ADA claims, the "garden variety" case involves an employee with a significant medical condition that imposes a variety of work-related restrictions who has been concededly or allegedly terminated because of that condition. In short, many of the unsuccessful cases deal with the core of the ADA's ban on employment discrimination, rather than its periphery.

The fact that so many of these cases fail is troubling in its own right. But the pattern is particularly disturbing because the plaintiffs tend to lose on threshold issues. The problem is not that the courts view all accommodations as "unreasonable" or as imposing "undue burdens" on employers. Courts rarely even get to the point of reaching such issues. Instead, they tend to find plaintiffs simply not covered by the ADA, or, prior to the Court's recent decision in *Cleveland*,[22] they barred plaintiffs from even asserting their claims. In sum, the decisions do not only narrow the scope of the ADA's employment protection, they cut out its heart.

Courts have reached these results through a series of separate but related interpretations of the ADA. Two of the most significant lines of cases are described below. They include decisions constricting the definition of disability and therefore limiting the scope of the law, and decisions barring disability benefit recipients from bringing suit under the ADA.

## No One Has a Disability

The ADA's preamble states that forty-three million Americans have one or more physical or mental disabilities. Despite the enormity of this figure, the court decisions suggest that people who choose to sue under the ADA are seldom among this group. In addition to the cases described above in which courts found individuals with breast cancer, multiple sclerosis and stroke did not have disabilities, courts have also found individuals with lymphoma,[23] brain tumors,[24] heart disease,[25] diabetes,[26] hemophilia,[27] epilepsy,[28] ulcerative colitis,[29] carpal tunnel syndrome,[30] incontinence,[31] depression,[32] bipolar disorder,[33] and paranoia[34] excluded from the definition of disability.[35]

These decisions rest on statutory language defining a disability as an impairment resulting in a "substantial limitation" in the ability to perform a "major life activity." Courts have construed this language narrowly, stressing that the ADA prohibits discrimination based on *disabilities* rather than *medical impairments.* Typically, the ADA defendant argues that the plaintiff's impairments preclude him or her from performing the job at issue, but that the individual is not generally precluded from work, or any other "major life activity." When fully accepted by a court, this line of argument results in a ruling that the plaintiff is not a person with a disability, despite medical impairments that render him or her supposedly unqualified for the job. The import of these cases is that many people are precluded from performing their past jobs because of their employer's reaction to their medical impairments, yet are not viewed as having disabilities within the meaning of the ADA.

The most recent example of this judicial tendency can be found in the U.S. Supreme Court's January 2002 decision in *Toyota Motor Manufacturing v. Williams,* a case brought by a Toyota assembly line worker who had developed a variety of painful musculoskeletal impairments that severely limited her ability to perform manual tasks. In suggesting that Ms. Williams was not a person with a disability within the meaning of the ADA, the Court explicitly stated that the phrases "substantially limited" and "major life activity" must be "interpreted strictly to create a demanding standard for qualifying as disabled."[36]

By now, a number of commentators have pointed out the flaws in this approach to the definition of disability in the ADA.[37] The language of the statute does not compel this result. The legislative history makes clear that Congress did not intend to interpose a stringent functional threshold that would severely restrict the act's reach. Congress included the "substantial limitation" requirement as a means of preventing claims based on *de minimis* impairments, like "an infected finger."[38] Indeed, the legislative history and preamble to the ADA demonstrate that Congress envisioned a comprehensive remedy for discrimination against people with disabilities, not a narrow measure that deals only with a limited piece of the problem. There is simply no evidence that Congress intended to permit discrimination against a broad spectrum of people on the premise that they have "medical conditions" rather than "disabilities." The case law, however, has given employers such license.

Administrative interpretation of the statute also supports a broad construction of the definition of disability. In interpreting the ADA's "substantial limitation" requirement, the EEOC's guidelines suggest that an impairment that inhibits the performance of a job can be deemed "insubstantial" only if the individual cannot perform the job because of some unique requirement.[39] In general, an impairment that prevents performance of one job is likely to prevent performance of at least some other jobs as well.[40]

Courts have used the proposition that inability to perform a single job may be deemed insubstantial to impose onerous burdens of proof on many ADA plaintiffs. These cases require plaintiffs to amass a wealth of demographic and economic data regarding the characteristics of jobs in the geographically relevant labor market, potentially turning individual ADA cases into battles of labor market experts. There is no evidence that Congress desired or contemplated that ADA cases would turn into protracted battles over the ability of plaintiffs to perform jobs not at issue in the case.[41] Given the purposes of the ADA, these decisions make little sense. Indeed, from a policy perspective, it is difficult to discern *any* coherent rationale undergirding these cases, let alone the policies Congress sought to promote in enacting the ADA.

As construed by the courts, the ADA principally prohibits employment discrimination against those individuals who can prove that their ability to perform many jobs is compromised by their impairments. The decisions leave employers free to discriminate when they deal with individuals whose medical impairments do not have such a broad impact. There is no reason why the employer's responsibilities and the employee's rights should depend on the extraneous and ultimately speculative question of how the impairment might affect the individual's ability to perform jobs that he or she does not hold and has not been offered.

The message implicit in this line of cases is that, rather than demanding accommodations, the plaintiffs should simply go out and find jobs where no workplace alteration is necessary. This approach is inimical to the goal of establishing and protecting equal access to the job market. In short, it runs counter to the basic proposition for which ADA Title I stands, that people with disabilities should have access to the fullest possible range of jobs, within the limits of the reasonable accommodation principle. The courts' odd focus on other jobs transmutes the ADA from an equal employment opportunity measure into a means of guaranteeing a low, baseline level of access to at least some segments of the job market. It suggests that accommodation is required only when it is necessary to enable the plaintiff to remain in the workforce, an objective quite different from equal opportunity.

This restrictive interpretation has a number of perverse effects. First, the likelihood that an individual plaintiff will be deemed "disabled" within the meaning of the ADA is directly inverse to the chances that he or she would actually be able to win on the merits. Plaintiffs with more serious medical impairments are less likely to be found qualified for jobs through the provision of reasonable accommodations. Those with less severe impairments would be able to show that they are qualified, but may well be found to have only a medical condition, rather than a disability. In screening out plaintiffs whose impairments are not incapacitating, the restrictive decisions exclude from the act's coverage many of the people most likely to benefit from its protections.

Second, under this restrictive approach, attempts by terminated employees to find other work could be construed as evidence of nondisability.[42] Thus, even though the act is intended to encourage and facilitate the inclusion of people with disabilities in the workforce, courts may view efforts to work as removing an individual from the act's protection. A lawyer counseling a potential ADA plaintiff may well advise him or her *not* to look for another job.[43] This last point underscores how court decisions addressing the definition of disability stand at odds with the fundamental claim underlying the ADA: that disability and work are not mutually exclusive.

## People with Disabilities Are "Not Qualified" for Jobs

In addition to finding that ADA plaintiffs do not have disabilities, courts have been quick to find they are not qualified for the jobs that they seek. Courts have relied on statements made on applications for disability benefits as a basis for granting summary judgment to employers. After being terminated from jobs, many people with disabilities apply for benefits, either under the Social Security Act or long-term disability insurance policies. Many courts have found that assertions of inability to work made on benefit application forms either estop later ADA claims or provide a basis for summary judgment against ADA plaintiffs.[44] The Supreme Court's May 1999 decision in *Cleveland v. Policy Management Systems*[45] should put an end to the widespread practice of barring disability benefit recipients from bringing cases under Title I of the ADA. Nonetheless, pre-

*Cleveland* lower-court decisions remain illustrative of the obstacles courts have placed in ADA plaintiffs' paths.

As the Supreme Court recognized in *Cleveland,* decisions barring benefits recipients from bringing ADA cases frequently overlook critical distinctions between the alternative definitions of disability used in these two different contexts.[46] Specifically, in deciding claims for benefits under the Social Security Act, the Social Security Administration (SSA) does not factor in the possibility of reasonable accommodation. Statements made in connection with Social Security claims must be construed in light of this important difference. An individual may well be "unable" to work, absent provision of reasonable accommodations. General statements on disability benefit applications thus shed no light on the ability of an individual to perform a job, if provided with accommodations mandated by the ADA.

Although many courts have recognized the differences between the ADA's definition of disability and the definition contained in the Social Security Act, they have often failed fully to grasp the implications of these differences. After acknowledging the differences in the statutes, courts have often gone on to treat general statements of inability to work on benefits applications as dispositive of ADA claims.[47] Other courts have viewed the instances of overlap between the ADA and disability benefits programs as only a rare and theoretical possibility.[48] This later view is based on an assumption that the availability of accommodations, the cornerstone of the ADA, will seldom really makes a difference.

The Fifth Circuit's decision in *Cleveland,*[49] which was subsequently overturned by the Supreme Court, exemplified this approach. After suffering a stroke, Ms. Cleveland applied for Social Security Disability Insurance benefits, claiming inability to work. As her condition improved, she returned to her job, despite the fact that her employer denied her request for accommodations. After a number of months, the employer terminated Ms. Cleveland on the ground that she could not perform her job. Following the termination, Ms. Cleveland was awarded disability benefits. Although recognizing the theoretical possibility that a disability benefits recipient could be "qualified" for a job under the ADA because the Social Security Administration does not take the possibility of accommodation into account, the Court nonetheless held Ms. Cleveland estopped from suing under the ADA because her prior assertion of disability was not specifically limited to the Social Security context. In reversing the Fifth Circuit, the Supreme Court correctly noted that "there are too many situations in which a [disability benefit] claim and an ADA claim can comfortably exist side by side"[50] to warrant the assumption that benefit recipients will only rarely be qualified for the jobs they seek.

## Adoption of the Civil Rights Model

The ADA explicitly adopts a civil rights approach to the problems that people with disabilities encounter in the workplace. It characterizes adverse employment decisions based on disability as a form of discrimination, and, going further, identifies the denial of accommodations in the workplace as a form of discrimination as well.[51] The legislative findings that form the act's preamble draw heavily on civil rights discourse. These findings identify people with disabilities as "a discrete and insular minority," historically subjected to isolation, segregation, and "purposeful unequal treatment" that relegates them to a position of "political powerlessness in our society."[52] Further incorporating and reflecting the civil rights paradigm, the ADA draws upon the remedial and administrative scheme of the Civil Rights Act of 1964.[53]

Both the rhetoric and the structure of the ADA are based on an implicit analogy between the problems facing people with disabilities and those facing women and members of ethnic and racial minorities. The analogy rests on the idea that the problems confronting people with disabilities are first and foremost problems of discrimination and structural inequality. The ADA is grounded on the premise that people with disabilities are denied the opportunities accorded to others because of irrational stereotypes and outmoded institutional structures and social arrangements.[54]

The ADA's embrace of the civil rights model represents a break with the tradition of viewing the problems faced by people with disabilities as being principally medical in nature. Under the medical model, the physical or mental effects of a disability on an individual are seen as the paramount problem. The medical model focuses on medical treatment and rehabilitation, attempts to change the individual, rather than society. In contrast, the ADA focuses on the societal response to disability. It seeks to reform social institutions to provide people with disabilities equal access to labor markets, public accommodations, and government programs.

The idea of social reform, however, is not exclusive to the civil rights model. Attempts to restructure society to be more inclusive of people with disabilities can be justified under a medical or public health model as well. First, efforts to increase employment for people with disabilities can be viewed as a means of improving their quality of life. Greater access to the job market can be seen as a means both of increasing the income of people with disabilities and of enabling them to have richly rewarding life experiences. This claim can be seen either as an unadorned appeal to altruism or as part of a social vision in which society as a whole is seen as having an obligation to facilitate the self-actualization of its members. Arguments of this nature underpinned the growth of the welfare state during the twentieth century.

An economic argument can also be made, asserting that expenditures that enable people with disabilities to work will reduce sums spent on income maintenance and will add needed skills and talents to the job market. The idea of promoting the employment of people with disabilities as an investment has often been advanced to support funding for physical and vocational rehabilitation. The power of this idea can be discerned from the fact that federal funding for vocational rehabilitation was established in 1920, before the New Deal. In sum, the civil rights model is not the only conceptual tool available for promoting the use of governmental power as a means of increasing employment and related opportunities for people with disabilities.

Although these arguments can be used to advance goals shared by a civil rights approach, they suggest very different methods of government intervention. Because they focus on overall societal objectives, they lend themselves to the creation of government programs that fund, through direct spending or tax subsidies, the desired changes in the workplace. In contrast, the civil rights approach places the responsibility for the necessary changes on individual employers. The premise of civil rights law is that the provision of equal opportunity and equal access is a basic responsibility of every employer, government program, and public accommodation. The idea of socializing the cost through public funding of compliance by private entities cuts against the grain by suggesting that the responsibility for effectuating equality is collective rather than individual.[55]

This discussion highlights the fact that advocates for and among people with disabilities have made a strategic decision to cast the claim for government protection as an issue of civil rights, rather than simply as an appeal for a new social welfare program, or an investment in the labor force. This strategic decision was not made at any specific point in time or by any select group of individuals. Rather, the momentum for a civil rights–based strategy grew over a twenty-year period, during which it gathered increasing support both among people with disabilities and among political leaders,[56] and culminated in the passage of the ADA. The decision to adopt a civil rights framework to address the problems of people with disabilities has had enormous consequences, a number of which can help us understand the trend now emerging in court decisions construing the ADA.

## Advantages of the Civil Rights Model

The struggle of African Americans for equality represents the prototype of a successful movement combining political mobilization, activism, litigation, and legislation to bring about major social change. Although African Americans' quest for racial justice is certainly incomplete, and in recent years has suffered a number of political and legal setbacks, during the 1970s, when the civil rights approach to disability was developing and growing in strength, the cause of racial equality appeared to move from success to success. It is not surprising that other groups sought to adopt the civil rights model of advocacy, legislation, and litigation in their own struggles for equality. Advocates for women's rights have perhaps been most successful in this effort, while advocates for the rights of poor people have been largely unsuccessful.

The use of sociopolitical concepts and regulatory frameworks provided by the civil rights movement to address the problems confronting people with disabilities has brought enormous benefits. Principally, it has furnished a vocabulary and a conceptual frame of reference through which people with disabilities can articulate, and others understand, the difficulties they face in seeking to participate fully in society. The benefits of reliance on the civil rights model can be seen on many levels. It helped mobilize people with disabilities and forge them into a distinct and vocal political constituency. It provided a framework through which the larger public can gain greater understanding of the problems facing people with disabilities. It supplied a conceptual structure for legislation intended to benefit people with disabilities and helped build alliances with other interest groups. Finally, it has enabled arguments on behalf of people with disabilities to be cast as claims of right in a way that reinforces rather than threatens fundamental values of our society.

Civil rights discourse provides a means through which people with disabilities can understand their experience and communicate that understanding to others. Its focus on lack of equal opportunity and negative treatment stemming from denigrating stereotypes, irrational fear, and hostility resonates deeply with many people with disabilities and reflects the reality they have experienced. It also enables people with disabilities to communicate this reality in a way that is familiar and understandable to the nondisabled majority. The civil rights framework thus gives the nondisabled majority a means of comprehending many of the problems faced by people with disabilities.

Further, the civil rights framework establishes a set of legal relationships between those who act on biases and those who are treated adversely as a result. The key concept is the idea of discrimination—the principle that it is improper for government agents, employers, or public accommodations to act on biases, hostility, or stereotypes relating to the group in question. Under the civil rights rubric, the discriminator is a wrongdoer who has violated legal and social norms, while the person discriminated against is a victim entitled to redress. Thus, the civil rights paradigm posits the legal prohibition of discrimination as the principal solution to the problem of inequality.

The civil rights framework also provides a means of achieving this goal—the use of the state's coercive power to compel compliance and remedy violations of the nondiscrimination principle. Indeed, the civil rights model incorporates a distinctively judicial strategy for dealing with social problems. The courts are expected to take an active role in enforcing newly established norms. During the civil rights struggles of the 1950s and 1960s, the federal judiciary played a critical role in articulating new norms and delegitimating old ones.

The legal framework provided by the civil rights model casts the claims of people with disabilities as assertions of the fundamental right to be free from invidious discrimination. In this way, the claims raised by people with disabilities can be presented as imperatives rather than mere policy preferences.[57] Moreover, the civil rights approach potentially enables advocates to frame the issue as one of equal opportunity rather than economic redistribution. Over the long run, arguments framed as appeals for equal opportunity have proven far more resilient, both in the political process and in the courts, than attempts to secure resource redistribution.[58] Indeed, advocates for the poor and other marginalized groups have long sought to avoid unadorned claims for the redistribution of resources by clothing their arguments in the garb of traditional rights and entitlements.[59] Instead of seeking redistribution and subsidization, the use of a civil rights model enables advocates for people with disabilities to present their claims as congruent with traditional and broadly accepted values, such as equality, fair play, and meritocracy. Because it was anticipated that civil rights protection would enable people to leave the disability benefits rolls, the ADA was even promoted as a means of curtailing redistributive social welfare programs.[60]

Further, by framing the issue as one of civil rights, advocates could argue that legal protections for people with disabilities would not be overly disruptive. The Civil Rights Act of 1964 had already established the basic principles and statutory protections that were sought; all that needed to be done was to add discrimination on the basis of disability to the list of prohibited conduct. The Rehabilitation Act of 1973 established this core principle with respect to federal agencies and entities that receive federal funding.[61] By the late 1980s, ADA advocates could point to experience with the Rehabilitation Act as evidence that protection of people with disabilities was feasible, and could cite the regulations and case law based on the Rehabilitation Act as a workable blueprint for extending the protection more generally. Lastly, civil rights protection would place the economic costs of social change on employers, public accommodations, and state and local governments, rather than on the federal government—a vital point during a period when federal budget deficits constituted a major political issue.

For all of these reasons, the civil rights focus of the ADA was critically important to establishing a strong federal commitment to the goals of employing people with disabilities and providing them with vastly expanded access to public programs, services, and accommodations. Although a number of amendments were introduced in attempts to water down the legislation,[62] by the time it was enacted, the ADA garnered broad bipartisan support.[63] A vote for the ADA was a vote for traditional American values, such as fairness, tolerance, self-sufficiency, and the work ethic.

## Limitations of the Civil Rights Model

Although reliance on the civil rights model made it possible to enact the ADA during a conservative period in which a Republican administration held power in Washington, that model has contributed to the problems plaintiffs have faced in enforcing the statute in at least two ways. First, in some respects, the barriers faced by people with disabilities differ from those experienced by other groups protected by civil rights laws. Applying the civil rights model to the problem of disability raises many difficult issues and questions. Second, public attitudes toward the civil rights model have themselves shifted. Apart from some core principles, the civil rights model has become highly controversial, and judges have become much less sympathetic to civil rights claims in any context. Putting these two problems together, one finds a judiciary ill disposed toward civil right principles answering the many difficult questions raised by the ADA. Not surprisingly, courts are responding in ways that narrow the coverage and limit the efficacy of the statute. Ironically, people with disabilities have gained civil rights protection at a point when civil rights are under attack.

## Defining Protected Classes

The civil rights model has traditionally been applied in situations in which the protected group is relatively easy to define. Unlike race and gender, however, there is no social consensus surrounding the definition of disability. Thus, the question of whom Congress sought to protect in enacting the ADA is a legitimate point of contention. However, in addressing these questions, the courts have tended to draw on stereotyped images of what it means to be "disabled." Although the person who uses a wheelchair would clearly seem to fit the conceptual mold, its application to an individual with a lifting, bending, or manipulative restriction is much less clear. Indeed, according to prevailing stereotypes, most people with disabilities cannot work. Thus, an individual who can work is apt to be seen as "not disabled." The stereotype therefore suggests exclusion of those most able to work from the class protected by the statute. There is more than a bit of irony in the fact that the interpretation of a statute whose purpose is to break down stereotypes has become ensnared by their application.

Aspects of the civil rights model reinforce this inclination toward a restrictive definition of disability. The civil rights model rests on the premise that a powerless minority group is systematically subordinated by the majority. Drawing on this model, the preamble to the ADA defines people with disabilities as a "discrete and insular minority,"[64] a phrase imbued with great significance in civil rights law.[65] The idea of the discrete and insular minority suggests that a civil rights statute will provide protection for a narrow and clearly defined group, which has been subjected to a particular history of discrimination. It encourages people to think about the disabled as a group distinct and separate from the nondisabled. In sum, it invites judges to view the problem of disability narrowly, rather than broadly. As earlier noted, in *Toyota Motor Manufacturing v. Williams,* Justice O'Connor, writing for a unanimous Supreme Court, explicitly stated that the ADA's definition of disability must be "interpreted strictly to create a demanding standard for qualifying as disabled," so as to effectuate Congressional intent as expressed in the ADA's preamble. In like fashion, in her concurrence in *Sutton,* Justice Ginsburg relied on the ADA preamble's reference to a "discrete and insular minority" to support a narrow reading of the statute.[66] In reality, the problems addressed by the ADA are experienced by a wide-ranging and amorphous spectrum of people. In this sense, the minority group model provides an uneasy fit with the problem of human variation and access to the workplace addressed by the ADA.

### Contested Visions of Equality: The ADA and the Landscape of Civil Rights Law

That disability does not easily fit into the "discrete and insular" minority group model need not present an insuperable obstacle. The civil rights model has been successfully adapted to address sex discrimination and age discrimination, even though neither women nor the elderly can be characterized as constituting a discrete and insular minority. The problems that emerge in adapting the civil rights model to the disability context have developed into serious impediments because of the larger judicial landscape in which the ADA is being interpreted. Courts are resolving critical issues concerning the ADA's scope at a time when they are decidedly inhospitable to expansive interpretations of civil rights protections more generally. In contrast, the initial decisions construing the Civil Rights Act of 1964 were issued during a period when the federal judiciary was substantially more willing to play an active role in the articulation and enforcement of civil rights statutes. In short, the civil rights model's reliance on judicial enforcement has proven to be a major obstacle to effective enforcement of the ADA.

Many of the problems emerging from judicial decisions concerning the ADA stem from the statute's reliance on a conception of equality that is particularly controversial: the principle that deferential treatment, rather than same treatment, is sometimes necessary to effectuate equality. Although the proposition that members of minority groups should be treated the same as others enjoys broad consensus,[67] notions of equality that call for protected groups to be treated differently as a means of establishing equal opportunity in the labor market or providing equal access to programs and institutions are hotly disputed. The justifications for requiring reasonable accommodation as a means of promoting equality are similar to the arguments presented in support of affirmative action programs. Courts have been increasingly unreceptive to these arguments in the context of affirmative action, and it should not be surprising that they are proving resistant to the same arguments in the ADA context.

The ADA relies on a different treatment vision of equality to address the reality that, given the structure of our social institutions, disabilities frequently *do* have an impact on an individual's ability to perform a job. Thus, unlike race, disability is often a legitimate consideration in employment decisions. For this reason, the ADA relies on the reasonable accommodation principle, which requires employers to alter job requirements in response to an individual's disability.[68]

Under the reasonable accommodation principle, an employer is not simply required to treat a person with a disability like a nondisabled person. Rather, the statute requires the employer to take the disability into consideration and change its workplace accordingly. Moreover, because every disability is unique, the ADA relies on a highly individualized and contextualized vision of equality. The reasonable accommodation requirement does not simply mandate that a group be treated differently; it requires that each person within a group be treated differently. The reasonable accommodation requirement therefore is based on a more complex and richer conception of equality than a simple requirement that the disabled and nondisabled be treated the same.[69]

The case for reasonable accommodation as a means of establishing equality can be made in a number of different ways. First, the reasonable accommodation mandate can be seen as a means of enforcing the more traditional civil rights requirement that employers refrain from acting based on stereotype or bias. Since employers are often not consciously aware of their own biases with respect to disability, an edict simply prohibiting discrimination would likely have little effect on their conduct. As the Supreme Court stated in *Alexander v. Choat*, the reasonable accommodation requirement can be understood as a way of addressing the problem of subliminal discrimination against the handicapped.[70] It forces an employer to focus on whether an applicant or employee with a disability can indeed perform the essential elements of a job. The process of considering whether an individual can be accommodated may well lead the employer to realize that the person would in fact be able to perform the job, after certain adjustments are made. If, however, an employer is unwilling to make reasonable adjustments to accommodate a disability, then there is a good chance the employer is indeed biased against the disabled plaintiff.

Second, and more importantly, the reasonable accommodation requirement can be viewed as a response to the fact that social institutions are not structured neutrally—they are shaped by and for a nondisabled majority. Social institutions that do not provide accommodation to the needs of people with disabilities give a competitive edge to individuals who do not have disabilities and subordinate those who do. Thus, the establishment of equal opportunity requires alterations in existing norms and institutionalized practices. Seen in this light, the reasonable accommodation requirement is not a means of giving people with disabilities a special benefit or advantage. Rather, it protects people with disabilities from disadvantage resulting from the tendency of those who design the workplace and organize the means of production to ignore their needs.

The limitation permitting employers to withhold accommodations if they would impose an "undue burden" cabins the accommodation duty. The statute's requirement of a level playing field is thus not absolute. The fact is that with respect to disability, effectuating equality imposes costs.

In the area of racial justice, and especially in the debate over affirmative action, conceptions of equality that require differential treatment have been hotly contested. Supporters of affirmative action maintain that American society continues to suffer from pervasive and often unconscious racism that cannot be eliminated by a simple statutory requirement of color-blind treatment.[71] The problem is too ingrained in American society to be rooted out by a simple statutory prohibition against biased conduct. As Christopher Edley has argued, "within a broader conception of discrimination, our attention to racial progress must not be diverted by scattered investigations of isolated cases of provable bigotry. We care, too, about the big picture, the larger forces sustaining racial inequality."[72] The achievement of equality requires "active efforts attacking and preventing discrimination, not merely opposing it whenever one happens on it."[73]

Affirmative measures to promote the employment of racial minorities are generally justified by reference to a past history of discrimination that has a continuing impact. Because social and economic institutions have been shaped by explicitly or implicitly biased practices, a requirement that blacks and whites be treated identically does not effectuate equality. The history and lingering effects of racism create structural conditions that disadvantage racial and ethnic minorities. Under this argument, equal opportunity requires affirmative efforts to overcome these disadvantages. As Charles Lawrence and Mari Matsuda have recently explained: "Social systems three centuries in the making can be dismantled only through affirmative action; it requires affirmative efforts to tear down the walls that white supremacy took centuries to build."[74]

There has been some confusion about whether the reasonable accommodation requirement of the ADA should be viewed as an "affirmative action" provision. In *Southeastern Community College v. Davis,*[75] the Supreme Court referred to the modification of basic program requirements to accommodate a person with a disability as a form of "affirmative action."[76] In *Alexander v. Choate,*[77] however, Justice Marshall responded to criticism of this proposition by explaining that substantial or fundamental alterations of a program could be considered "affirmative action," but that the Court had not intended to classify reasonable accommodation as affirmative action.[78] Commentators have also offered differing views on the issue.[79]

Although there exist significant differences between policies that provide for racial preferences as a means of countering historic discrimination and the ADA's mandate of reasonable accommodation, both concepts rely on visions of equality calling for differential treatment of the subordinated individual or group. Moreover, one can identify obvious parallels between the normative and empirical claims supporting the two policies.

The concept that equality requires differential treatment has long been contested in American society, and many have argued that such differential treatment is inherently discriminatory.[80] Since its inception in the late 1960s, affirmative action has proven controversial at every turn. Thus, the strategy of linking the goals of people with disabilities to a civil rights model does not place questions concerning the treatment of people with disabilities into an area of broad social consensus. Instead, it situates the issue of disability access at the center of a hotly contested and long-running legal and sociopolitical battle. In short, with the passage of the ADA and the adoption of the civil rights model, people with disabilities find themselves on the front lines of a sociolegal culture war.

In recent years, this war has not been going well for those asserting that equality sometimes requires differential treatment of socially subordinated groups. The passage of Proposition 209 in California banning the use of racial preferences in higher education illustrates a renewed hostility to this proposition. More importantly, the federal courts, led by the Supreme Court, have grown increasingly wary of policies based on this richer notion of equality. In the *Bakke* case, decided in 1978, the Court splintered so thoroughly on the use of affirmative action by the University of California that it could not produce a majority opinion.[81] In *Richmond v. J. A. Croson Co.*,[82] the Court struck down a municipal contracting minority set-aside program, holding that all racial classifications are subject to strict scrutiny. The Court rejected the argument that classifications benefiting historically subordinated groups should be evaluated under a different standard than classifications disfavoring such groups. Although the Court initially held in *Metro Broadcasting Inc. v. FCC*[83] that racial classifications used by the federal government to benefit minority groups were subject only to intermediate scrutiny, the Court reversed itself in *Adarand Constructors, Inc. v. Pena*[84] and held strict scrutiny applicable to congressional action as well.

Moreover, the Court has explained that strict scrutiny in this context can only be satisfied by a strong showing that there has been specific discrimination in the past and that the remedial plan is narrowly tailored to redress this history of discrimination.[85] Absent such a showing, the Court has concluded, affirmative action may "in fact promote notions of racial inferiority and lead to a politics of racial hostility."[86] Although the Court has applied a less restrictive standard in reviewing affirmative action programs by private actors,[87] the distinction may merely result from the fact that the Supreme Court has not heard a case involving a Title VII challenge to an affirmative action program in fifteen years.[88]

In another line of cases, the Court has rejected the use of race as a criterion in establishing voting districts, rejecting the argument that the use of race is appropriate to ensure that African Americans can participate effectively in the political process. In *Shaw v. Reno*,[89] the Court announced that it would apply strict scrutiny to congressional districting decisions made on racial lines. In a series of cases, the Court has rejected various arguments that particular districting schemes can be justified as narrowly tailored to serve a compelling government interest.[90]

Court decisions regarding affirmative action reveal mounting judicial skepticism toward the proposition that differential treatment of minority groups may be necessary to establish equal opportunity and equal access. This skepticism is reflected in judicial ratcheting up of the showing needed to support affirmative action programs. The courts have firmly rejected claims that some kind of generalized, societal mistreatment of minority groups in the past will justify differential treatment by government entities today.

This same skepticism toward claims that equal opportunity requires that protected groups be treated differently underpins many of the negative trends in the ADA case law. Of course, the legal context of these cases is far different from those dealing with affirmative action. Courts deciding ADA cases are called upon to enforce a statutory mandate requiring differential treatment, rather than to pass judgment on the legality of voluntarily undertaken policies of differential treatment. Nonetheless, the underlying equality issues are similar in ADA and affirmative action cases. Simply put, many judges do not buy the idea that basic civil rights are at stake in ADA cases. Many do not accept or even understand that the employer who refuses to provide an accommodation has violated someone's basic civil rights. Thus, the civil rights model has, to date, met with only limited success—judges are reluctant to label employers who fail to provide accommodations as civil rights violators for simply carrying on with business as usual.

In addition, the ADA impinges on the long-held doctrine of at-will employment, under which employers are free to make arbitrary, absurd, or seemingly ridiculous demands on their employees.[91] Although at one level, the requirement of "reasonable" accommodation appears difficult to dispute—who can object to a requirement that people act reasonably?—on another level, American employers have long been free to act unreasonably and have zealously guarded this prerogative. If one proceeds from the premise that employers are at liberty to act unreasonably, then the refusal to provide an accommodation, however reasonable, may not be viewed as a heinous act. Indeed, for this reason, even requirements that people be treated the same may be labeled "special" rights. In a context in which employers have complete control, the protection from discharge due to race, gender, disability, or sexual orientation can be seen as exceptional. Hence, even civil rights protections without affirmative requirements have provoked ire.[92]

Finally, the conception of equality reflected in the reasonable accommodation requirement of the ADA is not only controversial, it is threatening. Acceptance of the ADA's vision of equality can have consequences beyond the disability context. If differential and individualized treatment is necessary for the establishment of equal opportunity for people with disabilities, it may also be necessary for other groups, including women and minorities. In fact, several commentators have made just this point, arguing that the ADA's insights concerning equality should be made applicable in other areas.[93] Thus, the ADA introduces concepts that, once accepted, are difficult to contain.

The reluctance of courts to view the ADA as a civil rights measure culminated in the Supreme Court's 2001 decision in *Board of Trustees of the University of Alabama v. Garrett,* in which a narrow majority of the justices found that the ADA is not a valid exercise of Congress's power to enforce the Fourteenth Amendment to the United States Constitution.[94] *Garrett* holds that the reasonable accommodation requirement is not a permissible means of enforcing the Fourteenth Amendment's mandate that states accord people with disabilities equal protection of the laws. The practical effect of *Garrett* is to render Title I of the ADA unenforceable against state employers, but it does not disturb the ADA's applicability to local government entities or to the private sector.[95]

The Court reached its conclusion in two steps. First, it concluded that state action with respect to people with disabilities is subject only to rational basis review, the weakest level of scrutiny under the equal protection clause.[96] Second, the justices held that because it would be rational for an employer to withhold accommodations in order to save money, "the accommodation duty [of the ADA] far exceeds what is constitutionally required." In essence, *Garrett* holds that the ADA may be a legitimate form of social legislation enacted under the commerce clause, but that it is not, for constitutional purposes, a civil rights law. At least with respect to disability, *Garrett* rejects the idea that "equal protection" under the Constitution requires that people with disabilities be treated differently than others to provide equal access or equal opportunity.

## Construing the ADA as a Public Benefits Law

The failure of many judges to embrace the model of equality reflected in the ADA has led courts to construe the statute in ways that make no sense from the perspective of civil rights policy. If judges do not view the ADA as a civil rights statute, how do they view it? Is there any coherent set of principles that guides their interpretation of the ADA? The answer is that in the absence of any principles grounded in equality, the ADA can only be read as a means of dispensing subsidies to a targeted group of people. Seen from this vantage point, the case law has a certain coherence, though not that intended by the ADA's framers.

Viewed from the perspective of public benefits law, judges do not view ADA plaintiffs as potential victims of civil rights violations. Rather, these plaintiffs are viewed as supplicants. In dispensing benefits, the moral worth and need of the applicant are traditionally viewed as paramount. ADA decisions tend to focus on threshold issues because judges are concerned with the character of the plaintiff, rather than the conduct of the defendant. Thus, the animating force behind the judicial estoppel cases is, in part, a belief that disability benefits recipients are already being "taken care of" by the social welfare system. The attempt to maintain an ADA case is seen as a form of double dipping. Similarly, the cases imposing strict definitions of disability can be seen as evaluating the extent to which the plaintiff needs the job in question. If the plaintiff is able to perform many other jobs, then the "benefit" of accommodation may appear unnecessary because the plaintiff can simply work somewhere else.

Reflecting this view, both the Fifth and Tenth Circuits have reproached plaintiffs who failed to show that their impairments had a broad negative effect on employability: "We refuse to construe the . . . Act as a handout to those who are in fact capable of working in substantially similar jobs."[97] Presumably, the "handout" to which the courts refer is the accommodation the plaintiff requested. The courts' anger stems from the belief that the plaintiff is making demands on his or her employer when he could simply be looking for another job. Clearly, it is the courts that are construing the ADA as a handout, not the plaintiffs in these cases. The emphasis that courts have placed on the definition of disability is much more apropos of determinations concerning categorical eligibility for benefits programs than it is to the adjudication of a civil rights claim.

Courts adjudicating the enforceability of the ADA against the states have similarly viewed the ADA as a social welfare statute, rather than as a piece of civil rights legislation. Thus, in *Garrett,* the Court noted that a state employer that denies a reasonable accommodation may be acting "hard-heartedly," but not unconstitutionally, suggesting that the ADA embodies an appeal to charitable impulses, rather than a guarantee of basic civil rights.[98] In like fashion, a Fourth Circuit decision concluded that, in prohibiting states from charging fees for the provision of handicapped parking stickers, the ADA simply creates "a positive entitlement to a free handicapped parking space," rather than a guarantee of equal access.[99] Similarly, Judge Cox of the Eleventh Circuit perused the legislative history of the ADA and concluded that despite Congress's protestations, the true basis of the statute is simply to help people with disabilities and to get them off the public benefit rolls: "Altruistic and economic concerns motivated this Act," not defense of the Constitution.[100]

When viewed from a civil rights perspective, however, it becomes clear that the definition of disability under the ADA should not be drawn so narrowly. After all, a finding that a person is protected by the ADA only leads to the central question of whether the employer has improperly discriminated against the individual. In other words, it leads to an individualized inquiry into whether the particular employer has treated a particular individual in ways that reflect the biases the ADA was enacted to address. Moreover, the goal of providing equal access to the job market suggests that, to the extent possible under the reasonable accommodation principle, the individual should have access to the entire range of jobs available in the relevant labor market, not simply a means of obtaining some minimal foothold in the world of paid labor. From a civil rights perspective, if an individual needs accommodation to perform a class of jobs, it should not matter whether there are other jobs that he or she could do.

Courts have seized upon the statutory definition of disability to erect a formidable categorical barrier, which often operates to shield a biased employer's conduct from ADA scrutiny. In the view of many courts, if the plaintiffs' impairments do not appear serious enough, then there is no basis for distinguishing them from the general mass of workers who are subject to the vicissitudes of at-will employment and no reason to grant them the "benefit" of accommodation and protection from arbitrary discharge.

When plaintiffs are not seen as members of a narrowly drawn category deemed worthy of "special benefits" conferred by the ADA, they appear to judges merely as a bunch of whiners making excuses for poor performance. A request for accommodation is likewise seen as a crass attempt to capitalize on a medical condition.[101] This perception is ironic, in view of the fact that on another level, ADA plaintiffs can be seen as individuals who are struggling to do exactly what in other contexts society demands—they seek to work, rather than to rely on public benefits. Moreover, absent a clear understanding that principles of equality are at stake, ADA cases appear as a tangle of petty disputes that clutter up the dockets of federal courts.[102]

Federal judges are generally imbued with a strong sense that their role is to resolve "important" cases, rather than run-of-the-mill disputes that are more appropriately heard in state courts.[103] In recent years, federal judges have complained openly about statutes that create new federal causes of action without, in their view, sufficient justification.[104] Although specific statutes are rarely identified, I suspect that many federal judges would count the ADA as among the most guilty culprits. In sum, rather than viewing ADA cases as disputes about fundamental civil rights, many judges treat them as requests for special benefits made by undeserving employees who are performing poorly. They are both unsympathetic to these requests and, at some level, annoyed that Congress has compelled the federal judiciary to hear them. The result has been disastrous for ADA plaintiffs.

## Conclusion

The enactment of the ADA illustrates the discursive power of analogy. By analogizing the problems facing people with disabilities to those confronted by racial minorities, ADA advocates were able to harness some portion of the rhetorical power of the civil rights struggle. The analogy provided a powerful new way of thinking and talking about the problems facing people with disabilities and suggested a series of concrete and achievable legislative solutions to those problems.

The case law interpreting the ADA, however, reveals that the analogy has limitations as well as discursive power. The risk involved in a strategy that calls for convincing mainstream America that people with disabilities are comparable to racial minorities seems obvious: White America has only sporadically and superficially been willing to redress racial inequalities in society. Putting people with disabilities on the same footing as racial minorities places them in a somewhat unenviable situation.

This problem may have been obscured at the time the civil rights strategy for people with disabilities was formulated. The struggle for racial equality seemed a clear model of success. The real story, however, was far more complex.[105] Sweeping Supreme Court language in civil rights decisions often failed to presage comparable transformations in social and economic conditions.[106] Moreover, a sort of civil rights backlash has set in over time, and the series of broad victories in the courts have given way to a wave of losses. In actuality, as civil rights leaders have long known, the achievement of racial equality is a long-term goal toward which society moves only tentatively, confronting many barriers along the way.

The same is true with respect to civil rights for people with disabilities. The case law illustrates something that should have been apparent when the statute was enacted; the signing of the act was not the end of the struggle for civil rights for people with disabilities. Rather, it was an interim victory, which shifted and redefined the fields of the battle. The ADA's drafters were aware of this reality. They recognized the critical importance of judicial interpretation and the inhospitable orientation of the Supreme Court.[107] To guard against crabbed judicial interpretations, they drafted the ADA and the accompanying committee reports with painstaking care and attention to detail.[108]

In the end, however, laws are necessarily subject to interpretation. Judges construing and applying statutes are inevitably affected by the broader social and political environment, even as they disclaim any such influence. Only broad-based social understanding of and support for the principles undergirding the ADA will make the statute's promise a reality. Although enactment of the law and efforts to enforce it can play an important role in helping to create such understanding and support, neither ringing statutory language, nor seemingly tough provisions for judicial enforcement are sufficient to carry the day. Whether the ADA has the transformative effect that its supporters predicted will ultimately not be resolved in the courtroom.

We should not forget that the ADA and the civil rights model are strategic tools for achieving change; they are not ends in themselves. The search for new tools and analogies should continue. For example, the goal of protecting people with disabilities from discrimination in the workplace may be more closely connected to a broader struggle for workers' rights. Strategies that emphasize the universal nature of the problems faced by people with disabilities, rather than their uniqueness, may help build public support the ADA.[109] In sum, there is plenty of work to be done, both to make the vision of the ADA a reality and to devise new strategies to accord people with disabilities the fullest possible range of access and opportunity.

NOTES

1. 42 U.S.C. § 12101(b)(1) (1994).

2. 42 U.S.C. § 12101(b)(4) (1994).

3. 136 Cong. Rec. S9689 (July 13, 1990) (statement of Sen. Harkin).

4. *See* Terry Wilson, *For the Disabled, It's "Independence Day,"* Chi. Trib., July 27, 1990, at 1.

5. *See Study Finds Employers Win Most ADA Title I Judicial and Administrative Complaints,* 22 Mental & Physical Disability L. Rep. 403 (1998) at 403. The authors found that these results were due largely to "the gap between what Congress claimed it was doing in enacting the ADA and what interpretation of the actual language of the Act allows." *Id.* at 405. A follow-up study found that in 1998, employers actually increased their win rate to 94 percent. John W. Parry, *Employment Decisions Under ADA Title I B Survey Update,* 23 Mental & Physical Disability L. Rep. 290, 294 (1999). *See also* Ruth Colker, *The Americans with Disabilities Act: A Windfall for Defendants,* 34 Harv. C.R.-C.L. L. Rev. 99, 160 (1999) (describing empirical study of appellate employment discrimination decisions under the ADA and concluding that "defendants prevail at an astonishingly high rate on appeal" in ADA cases).

6. Robert L. Burgdorf Jr., one of the drafters of the ADA, has written the most comprehensive analysis of the early ADA Title I decisions. *See* Robert L. Burgdorf Jr., *"Substantially Limited" Protection from Disability Discrimination: The Special Treatment Model and Misconstructions of the Definition of Disability,* 42 Vill. L. Rev. 409 (1997) [hereinafter Burgdorf, *The Special Treatment Model*]. Professor Burgdorf concludes that "legal analysis under [the ADA] has proceeded quite a long way down the wrong road. . . ." *Id. See also* Arlene B. Mayerson, *Restoring Regard for the "Regarded as" Prong: Giving Effect to Congressional Intent,* 42 Vill. L. Rev. 587, 612 (1997) (referring to the "disturbing trend" in the case law and criticizing the "hypertechnical, often illogical, interpretations of the ADA" in recent decisions).

7. Sutton v. United Airlines, Inc., 527 U.S. 471, 119 S. Ct. 2139 (1999); Murphy v. United Parcel Serv., 527 U.S. 516, 119 S. Ct. 2133 (1999); Albertson's, Inc. v. Kirkingburg, 527 U.S. 555, 119 S. Ct. 2162 (1999). *But see* Cleveland v. Policy Management Sys. Corp., 526 U.S. 795, 119 S. Ct. 1597 (1999) (ruling in favor of the plaintiff).

8. 531 U.S. 356, 121 S. Ct. 955 (2001).

9. For an example of this view, see Lisa Eichhorn, *Major Litigation Activities Regarding Major Life Activities: The Failure of the "Disability" Definition in the Americans with Disabilities Act of 1990,* 77 N.C. L. Rev. 1405, 1423 (1999) (the ADA's "compromising, unworkable definition [of disability] too often has prevented legitimate lawsuits from going forward").

10. 524 U.S. 624 (1998).

11. 526 U.S. 795, 119 S. Ct. 1597 (1999).

12. 527 U.S. 471, 119 S. Ct. 2139 (1999) (considering corrective measures in determining whether an impairment constitutes a disability).

13. 527 U.S. 516, 119 S. Ct. 2133 (1999) (holding that employee with controlled high blood pressure does not satisfy the ADA's definition of having, or being regarded as having, a disability).

14. 527 U.S. 555, 119 S. Ct. 2162 (1999) (finding that employer may use federal safety standard as justification for job requirement regardless of possibility of obtaining a waiver of the standard as part of an experimental program).

15. 531 U.S. 356, 121 S. Ct. 955 (2001).

16. Amendment 2 prohibited localities from enacting ordinances outlawing discrimination based on sexual orientation. *See* Romer v. Evans, 517 U.S. 620 (1996).

17. Proposition 209 forbids state programs from using race as a factor in hiring/admission decisions. *See* Coalition for Economic Equity v. Wilson, 122 F.3d 692 (1997), *cert. denied*, 522 U.S. 963 (1997).

18. 85 F.3d 187 (5th Cir. 1996); *see also* Gordon v. E.L. Hamm & Assocs., Inc., 100 F.3d 907 (11th Cir. 1996) (finding that cancer with side effects from chemotherapy is not a disability); Schwertfager v. City of Boynton Beach, 42 F. Supp. 2d 1347 (S.D. Fla. 1999) (same); Madjlessi v. Macy's West, Inc., 993 F. Supp. 736 (N.D. Cal. 1997) (same).

19. 899 F. Supp. 100 (N.D.N.Y. 1995).

20. 91 F.3d 610 (3d Cir. 1996), *cert. denied*, 117 S. Ct. 958 (1997).

21. 115 F.3d 352 (5th Cir. 1997); *see also* Sorensen v. University of Utah Hosp., 1 F. Supp. 2d 1306 (D. Utah 1998) (finding that plaintiff with multiple sclerosis did not have a disability).

22. 526 U.S. 795, 119 S. Ct. 1597 (1999).

23. *See* Heyman v. Queens Village Committee for Mental Health, 97 CV 3063, E.D.N.Y. 1999 Westlaw 118783; Hirsch v. National Mall & Serv., 989 F. Supp. 977 (N.D. Ill. 1997); *see also* Olmeda v. New York State Dep't of Civil Service, 96 CV 7557, S.D.N.Y. 1998 Westlaw 17729 (S.D.N.Y. Jan. 16, 1998) (leukemia).

24. *See* Cook v. Waters, 980 F. Supp. 1463 (M.D. Fla. 1997).

25. *See* Korzeniowski v. ABF Freight Sys., 38 F. Supp. 2d 688 (N.D. Ill. 1999); Muthler v. Ann Arbor Mach., Inc., 18 F. Supp. 2d 722 (E.D. Mich. 1998); Hilburn v. Murata Elecs. of North America, 17 F. Supp. 2d 1377 (N.D. Ga. 1998).

26. *See* Berg v. Norand Corp., 169 F.3d 1140 (8th Cir. 1999); Cupola v. Central Can Co., 97-C-3819, N.D. Ill. 1999 Westlaw 199621; Moore v. Time Warner GRC 9, 18 F. Supp. 2d 257 (W.D.N.Y. 1998).

27. *See* Bridges v. City of Bossier, 92 F.3d 329 (5th Cir. 1996).

28. *See* Deas v. River West L.P., 152 F.3d 471 (5th Cir. 1998).

29. *See* Ryan v. Grae & Rybicki, 135 F.3d 867 (2d Cir. 1998).

30. *See* Toyota Motor Manufacturing v. Williams, 122 S. Ct. 681 (2002); Gutridge v. Clure, 153 F.3d 898 (8th Cir. 1998); McCay v. Toyota Motor Mfg., 110 F.3d 369 (6th Cir. 1997).

31. *See* Swain v. Hillsborough County School Bd., 146 F.3d 855 (11th Cir. 1998).

32. *See* Miller v. City of Springfield, 146 F.3d 612 (8th Cir. 1998); Olson v.

Dubuque Community School Dist., 137 F.3d 609 (8th Cir. 1998); Cody v. Cigna Healthcare of St. Louis, 139 F.3d 595 (8th Cir. 1998); Polderman v. Northwest Airlines, 40 F. Supp. 2d 456 (N.D. Ohio 1999); Powell v. Morris, 37 F. Supp. 2d 1011 (S.D. Ohio 1998).

33. *See* Hoeller v. Eaton Corp., 149 F.3d 621 (7th Cir. 1998); Dupre v. Harris County Hosp. Dist., 8 F. Supp. 2d 908 (S.D. Tex. 1998).

34. *See* Patterson v. Chicago Ass'n for Retarded Children, 150 F.3d 719 (7th Cir. 1998).

35. *See* Burgdorf, *The Special Treatment Model, supra* note 6, at 539–41 & nn.643–60 (listing conditions that courts have found not to constitute disabilities).

36. Toyota Motor Mfg. v. Williams, 122.S.Ct. at 691. For a less recent, but in some ways more disturbing example, see Christian v. St. Anthony Med. Ctr., Inc., 117 F.3d 1051, 1053 (7th Cir. 1997) (offering a hypothetical scenario used to "illustrate" the claim that, if an ADA plaintiff is terminated because of an unsightly skin disease that the employer found "revolting" but did not interfere with the plaintiff's ability to do the job, the ADA would not accord protection because the plaintiff is not limited in a major life activity, and because the employer did not perceive the individual to have a disability).

37. *See* Burgdorf, *The Special Treatment Model, supra* note 6, at 539–46; Locke, *supra* note 31 at 107; Mayerson, *supra* note 6, at 591–609.

38. *See* S. Rep. No. 101–116, at 23 (1989). Congress also relied on the Supreme Court's broad reading of the definition of disability in the Rehabilitation Act set forth in *School Board of Nassau County v. Arline,* 480 U.S. 273 (1987). *See* H.R. Rep. No. 101–485, pt. 3 (1990). The *Arline* decision created an expectation that the courts would interpret the vague language drawn from the Rehabilitation Act broadly.

39. 29 C.F.R. § 1630.2(j) (app.) (1991) (interpretative guidance). For example, a baseball pitcher with a sore arm would be considered to have an insubstantial limitation because the requirement of throwing a ball ninety miles an hour is truly unique to that job and the player's ability to use his arm is reduced only from extraordinary to merely average.

40. The proposition that an impairment is not a disability if it precludes performance of only a single job derives from *E.E. Black v. Marshall,* 497 F. Supp. 1088 (D. Haw. 1980), a Rehabilitation Act case. In *E.E. Black,* the court concluded that labor market and vocational factors such as the number and types of jobs from which an individual is disqualified, the individual's training and skills, and the geographic area are relevant to the determination of whether an impairment is a disability. The *E.E. Black* court, however, stressed that in making this determination the inquiry must focus on whether the individual would be precluded from a class of jobs if all employers viewed the impairment the way that the employer in question did. *Id.* at 1100. In other words, if all employers acted like the defendant, would the individual's ability to work be substantially impaired? Moreover, the *E.E. Black* court implicitly recognized that if this analysis is applied, then in most cases disqualification from one job would signal likely disqualification from many jobs. *Id.* at 1102. Accordingly, the court placed the burden on the employer to demonstrate that the task at issue is unique to the job in question. *Id; see also* Arlene Mayerson, *Title I—Employment Provisions of the Americans with Disabilities Act,* 64 Temple L. Rev. 499, 505–7 (1991).

41. The ADA's legislative history suggests that Congress viewed even the *E. E. Black* approach as too restrictive. *See* S. REP. NO. 101–116, at 23 (1989) ("if the person is severely restricted in the performance of the particular job, then coverage is triggered"); H. REP. NO. 101–485, pt. 3, at 29 (1990) ("A person with an impairment who is discriminated against in employment is also limited in the major life activity of working. However, a person who is limited in his or ability to perform only a particular job *because of circumstances unique to that job site* or the materials used, may not be limited in the major life activity of working") (emphasis added); *see also* 136 CONG. REC. H4626 (1990) (statement of Rep. Waxman that the ADA relies on a "broad, flexible definition of disability").

42. *See, e.g.,* Szalay v. Yellow Freight Sys., 127 F.3d 1103 (6th Cir. 1997); Adair v. W. H. Braum's, Inc., 1999 Westlaw 242696, 6 (N.D. Tex. 1999) ("The fact that [plaintiff] is presently employed is dispositive of her alleged substantial limitation on working").

43. Of course, not looking for work may be construed as a failure to mitigate damages. *See* Greenway v. Buffalo Hilton Hotel, 143 F.3d 47, 53 (2d Cir. 1998).

44. *See* Pena v. Houston Lighting & Power Co., 154 F.3d 267 (5th Cir. 1998); McConathy v. Dr. Pepper/Seven Up Corp., 131 F.3d 558, 562–63 (5th Cir. 1998); Downs v. Hawkeye Health Serv., Inc., 148 F.3d 948 (8th Cir. 1998); Moore v. Payless Shoe Source, Inc., 139 F.3d 1210 (8th Cir. 1998); Budd v. ADT Sec. Sys., 103 F.3d 699 (8th Cir. 1996); McNemar v. Disney Stores, Inc., 91 F.3d 610 (3d Cir. 1996), *cert. denied,* 117 S. Ct. 958 (1997); Lemons v. U.S. Air Group, 43 F. Supp. 2d 571 (M.D.N.C. 1999), *vacated,* 1999 U.S. App. LEXIS 22472 (4th Cir. 1999); Graf v. Wal-Mart Stores, 4 F. Supp. 2d 680 (S.D. Tex. 1998); Lowe v. Angelo's Italian Foods, Inc., 966 F. Supp. 1036 (D.Kan. 1997); Violette v. International Business Mach. Corp. 962 F. Supp. 446 (D.Vt. 1996), *aff'd,* 116 F.3d 466 (2d Cir. 1997); Johnson v. Georgia Dep't of Human Resources, 983 F. Supp. 1464 (N.D. Ga. 1996); Mitchell v. Washingtonville Cent. School Dist., 992 F. Supp 395 (S.D.N.Y. 1998), *aff'd,* 190 F.3d 1 (2d Cir. 1999); *see also* Matthew Diller, *Dissonant Disability Policies: The Tensions Between the Americans with Disabilities Act and Federal Disability Benefit Programs,* 76 TEXAS L. REV. 1003, 1033 n.141 (1998) (listing additional cases).

45. 526 U.S. 795, 119 S. Ct. 1597 (1999).

46. 119 S. Ct. at 1602–3.

47. *See* Kennedy v. Applause, Inc., 90 F.3d 1477, 1481–82 (9th Cir. 1996) (granting summary judgment to employer based on plaintiffs' statements on benefits application).

48. *See, e.g.,* Pena v. Houston Lighting & Power Co., 154 F.3d 267 (5th Cir. 1998) (applying rebuttable presumption of estoppel); McConathy v. Dr. Pepper/Seven Up Corp., 131 F.3d 558, 562–63 (5th Cir. 1998) (same); Downs v. Hawkeye Health Serv., Inc., 148 F.3d 948 (8th Cir. 1998) (requiring disability benefit recipient to meet a heightened burden in ADA case); Moore v. Payless Shoe Source, Inc., 139 F.3d 1210 (8th Cir. 1998) (same); Dush v. Appleton Elec., 124 F.3d 957 (8th Cir. 1997) (same).

49. 120 F.3d 513 (5th Cir. 1997), *rev'd,* 119 S. Ct. 1597 (1999).

50. *Cleveland,* 119 S. Ct. at 1602.

51. 42 U.S.C. § 12112 (1994).

52. 42 U.S.C. § 12101(a)(1) & (7) (1994).

53. 42 U.S.C. § 12117 (1994).

54. 42 U.S.C. § 12101(a) (1994) (congressional findings detailing history of discrimination).

55. Many ADA critics oppose the statute's focus on individual rights and responsibilities and argue in favor of socializing the costs of providing people with disabilities access to the societal mainstream. *See* RICHARD EPSTEIN, FORBIDDEN GROUNDS: THE CASE AGAINST EMPLOYMENT DISCRIMINATION LAWS 480–94 (1992) (arguing for federal grant program, rather than civil rights protection); Carolyn Weaver, *Incentives Versus Controls in Federal Disability Policy, in* DISABILITY AND WORK: INCENTIVES, RIGHTS, AND OPPORTUNITIES 3–17 (Carolyn Weaver ed., 1991) (arguing for incentives rather than rights-based policies toward disability); Christopher Willis, Comment, *Title I of the Americans with Disabilities Act: Disabling the Disabled,* 25 CUMB. L. REV. 715, 752 (1994) (supporting a program that would award federal grants routed through charities to employers who voluntarily hire disabled workers).

56. For a thorough discussion of the development of the civil rights strategy, see RICHARD SCOTCH, FROM GOOD WILL TO CIVIL RIGHTS: TRANSFORMING FEDERAL DISABILITY POLICY (1984). A key event was the passage of Sections 503 and 504 of the Rehabilitation Act of 1973, which prohibited discrimination on the basis of disability by entities that receive federal funds. As the title suggests, the Rehabilitation Act was originally drafted as a measure to reauthorize funding for vocational rehabilitation. The antidiscrimination provisions were added by Senate committee staff members at a late stage in the legislative process. Scotch argues that the assignment of the task of drafting implementing regulations to HEW's Office of Civil Rights, rather than to the Rehabilitation Services Agency, was critical to the issuance of regulations that reflected a strong civil rights orientation. *Id.* at 60–64.

57. Many scholars have noted the importance of claims of "right" to the achievement of political aspirations. *See, e.g.,* PATRICIA WILLIAMS, THE ALCHEMY OF RACE AND RIGHTS 159–65 (1991); Ed Sparer, *Fundamental Human Rights, Legal Entitlements, and the Social Struggle: A Friendly Critique of the Critical Legal Studies Movement,* 36 STAN. L. REV. 509 (1984); *cf.* MARY ANN GLENDON, RIGHTS TALK: THE IMPOVERISHMENT OF POLITICAL DISCOURSE (1991); Mark Tushnet, *An Essay on Rights,* 62 TEX. L. REV. 1363 (1984).

58. *See* Dennis Hirsch, *The Right to Economic Opportunity: Making Sense of the Supreme Court's Welfare Rights Decisions,* 58 U. PITT. L. REV. 109 (1996) (arguing that welfare rights advocates would be wise to recast their claims in terms of economic opportunity).

59. *See* William Simon, *Rights and Redistribution in the Welfare System,* 38 STAN. L. REV. 1431 (1986).

60. For example, in supporting enactment of the ADA, Representative Hammerschmidt stated, "The disabled do not want charity or a government handout; they want to work." 136 CONG. REC. H4627 (1990).

61. Rehabilitation Act of 1973, Pub. L. No. 93–112, 87 Stat. 355 (1973). The drafters of the Rehabilitation Act adapted language directly from Title VI of the Civil Rights Act.

62. *See* 136 CONG. REC. H4629 (1990) (motion to recommit bill to committee for consideration of amendment concerning food-handling jobs); Robert L.

Burgdorf Jr., *The Americans with Disabilities Act: Analysis and Implications of a Second Generation Civil Rights Statute,* 26 Harv. C.R.-C.L. L. Rev 413, 451–52 (1991) (describing unsuccessful attempts to amend the ADA).

63. The vote in the House of Representatives was 377 to 28. 136 Cong. Rec. H4629 (1990). In the Senate, the vote was 91 to 6. *Id.* at S9695.

64. 42 U.S.C. § 12101(a)(7) (1994).

65. The phrase comes from Justice Stone's famous footnote in *United States v. Carolene Products Co.,* 304 U.S. 144 n.4 (1938) (defining the bases for heightened judicial scrutiny of legislative enactments). *See generally* Bruce Ackerman, *Beyond Carolene Products,* 98 Harv. L. Rev. 713 (1985) (questioning the assumption that discreteness and insularity can be equated with political powerlessness).

66. In her concurrence in *Sutton,* Justice Ginsburg relied on the references in the ADA to a discrete and insular minority to support a narrow reading of the statute. Sutton v. United Airlines, Inc., 119 S. Ct. at 2152 (Ginsburg, J., concurring).

67. Opposition to civil rights protections based on sexual orientation is a notable exception to this acceptance. *See* Romer v. Evans, 116 S. Ct. 1620 (1996).

68. *See* 42 U.S.C. § 12112(b)(5)(A) (1994) (defining discrimination to include the failure to make reasonable accommodations).

69. *See* Pamela S. Karlen & George Rutherglen, *Disabilities, Discrimination, and Reasonable Accommodation,* 46 Duke L.J. 1, 10–11 (1996) (discussing how the "difference model" of discrimination differs from the "sameness model" in that it requires employers to treat some disabled persons differently than other individuals).

70. 469 U.S. 287, 295 (1985) (observing that discrimination against the handicapped is "most often the product, not of invidious animus, but rather thoughtlessness and indifference.").

71. *See* Charles Lawrence & Mari Matsuda, We Won't Go Back: Making the Case for Affirmative Action 67–81 (1997); Charles Lawrence, *The Id, the Ego, and Equal Protection: Reckoning with Unconscious Racism,* 39 Stan. L. Rev. 317 (1987) (arguing that judicial exploration of the cultural meaning of governmental actions with racially discriminatory impact is the best way to discover the unconscious racism of governmental actors); David Oppenheimer, *Understanding Affirmative Action,* 23 Hastings Const. L.Q. 921 (1996).

72. Christopher Edley, Not All Black and White: Affirmative Action, Race, and American Values 112 (1996).

73. *Id.* at 113 ("By engaging in appropriate affirmative action an employer, for example, can help dismantle subtle forms of discrimination that occur in ill-conceived recruitment, hiring, and promotion practice—discrimination that might otherwise go undetected or be detected but left unchallenged because of the transaction costs and imperfections in the enforcement system"). *See also* Linda Hamilton Krieger, *Civil Rights Perestroika: Intergroup Relations after Affirmative Action,* 86 Cal. L. Rev. 1251, 1258 (1998) ("antidiscrimination policy grounded in an individualized search for discriminatory intent cannot be expected to succeed either in identifying and preventing intergroup bias or in managing social tendencies toward intergroup conflict").

74. Lawrence & Matsuda, *supra* note 71, at 26. Lawrence and Matsuda elaborate:

[T]he only remedy for racial subordination based on systematic establishment of structures, institutions, and ideologies is the systemic disestablish-
ment of those structures, institutions, and ideologies. Radical affirmative
action goes beyond the remedy of simply declaring that discrimination is
illegal and pretending that our culture is color blind. It is not enough for the
discriminator to remove his boot from the victim's throat and call it equal
opportunity.

*Id.* at 27. *See also* MARTHA MINOW, NOT ONLY FOR MYSELF 153–54 (1997) ("in a
society that has made race matter so pervasively, colorblindness simply leaves in
place racialized thinking that benefits whites"); Susan Sturm & Lani Guinier, *The
Future of Affirmative Action: Reclaiming the Innovative Ideal,* 84 CAL. L. REV. 953
(1996) (arguing that affirmative action is necessary because so-called meritocratic
systems are in fact arbitrary and exclusionary).

75.  442 U.S. 397 (1979) (finding that, under some circumstances, a refusal to
modify an existing program might become unreasonable and discriminatory).

76.  *Id.* at 411.

77.  469 U.S. 287 (1985).

78.  *Id.* at 300 n.20; *see also* Dopico v. Goldschmidt, 687 F.2d 644, 652 (2d Cir.
1982) ("Use of the phrase 'affirmative action' in this context is unfortunate, making
it difficult to talk about any kind of affirmative efforts without importing the special legal and social connotations of that term"). Under the Rehabilitation Act the
distinction is of some importance, as federal contractors are required to engage in
affirmative action, while recipients of federal funds are not. *See* 41 C.F.R. §
60–741.21 (1978) (contractors); 45 C.F.R. § 84.12 (1977) (grantees). *Compare* 29
U.S.C. § 793 (1973) *with* 29 U.S.C. § 794 (1973). Applicable regulations, however,
make both groups subject to the obligation to provide reasonable accommodations.

79.  *See, e.g.,* Mark Martin, *Accommodating the Handicapped: The Meaning of
Discrimination Under Section 504 of the Rehabilitation Act,* 55 N.Y.U. L. REV. 881, 885
(1980) (arguing that it is essential to keep the two concepts of accommodation and
affirmative action separate); *Toward Reasonable Equality: Accommodating Learning
Disabilities Under the Americans with Disabilities Act,* 111 HARV. L. REV. 1560, 1574
(1998) (arguing that the analogy between reasonable accommodation and affirmative action is misplaced). *Compare* Karlen & Rutherglen, *supra* note 69, at 12 ("Reasonable accommodation is affirmative action in the sense that it requires an
employer to take account of an individual's disabilities and to provide special treatment for that reason") *with* Mark C. Weber, *Beyond the Americans with Disabilities
Act: A National Employment Policy for People with Disabilities,* 46 BUFF. L. REV. 123,
147–50 (1998) (distinguishing reasonable accommodation and affirmative action as
different in "degree and character").

80.  This argument is commonplace with respect to race. *See, e.g.,* William
Bradford Reynolds, *An Experiment Gone Awry, in* THE AFFIRMATIVE ACTION
DEBATE 130 (George Curry ed., 1996); Charles Canady, *The Meaning of American
Equality. Id.* at 277. In the area of disability, Sherwin Rosen has articulated a variant
of the argument:

> Fundamentally the ADA is not an antidiscrimination law. By forcing employers to pay for work site and other job accommodations that might allow workers with impairing conditions . . . to compete on equal terms, it would require firms to treat unequal people equally, thus discriminating in favor of the disabled.

Sherwin Rosen, *Disability Accommodation and the Labor Market, in* DISABILITY AND WORK, *supra* note 90, at 18, 29. *Cf.* Amy Wax, *Discrimination as Accident,* 74 IND. L. J. 1130, 1184–91, 1226–29 (1999) (rejecting differential treatment of protected groups as a remedy for unconscious discrimination).

    81. Regents of University of California v. Bakke, 438 U.S. 265 (1978).

    82. 488 U.S. 469 (1989).

    83. 497 U.S. 547 (1990).

    84. 515 U.S. 200 (1995).

    85. Richmond v. Croson, 488 U.S. at 500–506 (1989). After *Croson,* lower courts have split over whether the specific entity engaging in affirmative action must have discriminated in the past or whether government entities can use affirmative action to remedy discrimination by private actors. *See* Ian Ayres & Frederick Vars, *When Does Private Discrimination Justify Public Affirmative Action?* 98 COLUM. L. REV. 1577 (1998).

    86. *Croson,* 488 U.S. at 493.

    87. *See* Johnson v. Transportation Agency, Santa Clara County, Cal., 480 U.S. 616 (1987) (rejecting Title VII challenge to use of affirmative action to eliminate pattern of segregation in an industry); Steelworkers v. Weber, 443 U.S. 193 (1979) (same).

    88. In fact, civil rights advocates have taken steps to avoid such cases being heard by the court. One such case was settled at the Supreme Court level at the urging of civil rights advocates in order to keep the matter off the court's docket. Piscataway Township Board of Educ. v. Taxman, 118 S. Ct. 595 (1997) (dismissing writ of certiorari). In the *Piscataway* case, the Third Circuit held that an affirmative action plan violates Title VII if its purpose is to promote diversity, rather than remedy past discrimination. Taxman v. Board of Educ. of Township of Piscataway, 91 F.3d 1547 (3d Cir. 1996) (en banc), *cert. granted,* 117 S. Ct. 2506 (1997). *See* Joan Biskupic, *On Race, a Court Transformed; Affirmative Action Defenders Now Avoid Justices,* WASH. POST, Dec. 15, 1997, at A1 (discussing efforts of civil rights advocates to avoid the Supreme Court). Recently, advocates persuaded another defendant not to seek certiorari following a decision striking down an affirmative action plan. *See* Tony Mauro, *Civil Rights Groups Avoiding High Court,* USA TODAY, Feb. 8, 1999, at 2.

    89. 509 U.S. 630 (1993).

    90. Shaw v. Hunt, 517 U.S. 899 (1996); Bush v. Vera, 517 U.S. 952 (1996); Miller v. Johnson, 515 U.S. 900 (1995).

    91. The doctrine of "at will" employment has long been debated in the literature. *Compare* Cynthia Estlund, *Wrongful Discharge Protections in an At-Will World,* 74 TEX. L. REV. 1655 (1996) (arguing for greater protections of employees from wrongful discharge) *with* Richard Epstein, *In Defense of the Contract at Will,*

51 U. Chi. L. Rev. 947 (1984) (opposing protections against wrongful discharge) and Andrew Morris, *Bad Data, Bad Economics, and Bad Policy: Time to Fire Wrongful Discharge Law*, 74 Tex. L. Rev. 1901 (1996) (opposing protections against wrongful discharge).

92. *See* Peter Rubin, *Equal Rights, Special Rights, and the Nature of Antidiscrimination Law*, 97 Mich. L. Rev. 564 (1998) (discussing how requirements that people be treated the "same" can be viewed as "special" treatment).

93. For example, Pamela Karlen and George Rutherglen have observed that the insights gained from fleshing out the meaning of reasonable accommodation in disability cases present an opportunity to rethink antidiscrimination in employment law more generally. *See generally,* Karlen & Rutherglen, *supra* note 69, at 39–40.

94. 531 U.S. 356 (2001). Title I of the ADA was enacted as an exercise of Congress's power under both the Fourteenth Amendment and the commerce clause.

95. This result flows from the Supreme Court's decision in *Seminole Tribe of Florida v. Florida,* 517 U.S. 44 (1996), which held that Congress can abrogate state sovereign immunity when it acts through its powers under the Fourteenth Amendment, but not when it relies on its powers under the commerce clause. Because the Court concluded that the ADA cannot be sustained under the Fourteenth Amendment, its only remaining source of authority is the commerce clause.

96. In earlier cases, the Court had also used the rational basis standard, but had done so in a way that suggested the Court's inquiry would be more searching when it considers discrimination based on disability than in other contexts where it uses rational basis scrutiny. See, e.g., Cleburne v. Cleburne Living Center, Inc., 473 U.S. 432 (1985) (striking down city ordinance requiring special permit for operation of group home for the mentally retarded).

97. Sutton v. United Airlines, 130 F.3d 893 (10th Cir. 1997), *aff'd,* 527 U.S. 471, 119 S. Ct. 2139 (1999); Hileman v. City of Dallas, 115 F.3d 352 (5th Cir. 1997).

98. 121 S. Ct. at 964.

99. Brown v. North Carolina Div. of Motor Vehicles, 166 F.3d 698 (4th Cir. 1999).

100. Kimel v. Florida Board of Regents, 139 F.3d 1426, 1449 (11th Cir. 1998) (Cox, J., concurring in part and dissenting in part), *aff'd,* 528 U.S. 62, 120 S. Ct. 631 (2000).

101. The judicial estoppel cases most clearly reflect the view that ADA plaintiffs are unscrupulous people seeking to manipulate the system to their own advantage. *See, e.g.,* McNemar v. The Disney Stores, 91 F.3d 610, 617–18 (3d Cir. 1996), *cert. denied,* 117 S. Ct. 958 (1997) (accusing plaintiff of "playing fast and loose with the courts"); Hindman v. Greenville Hosp. Sys., 947 F. Supp. 215, 223 (D.S.C. 1996), *aff'd,* F.3d (4th Cir. 1997) ("This court . . . will not allow [the plaintiff] to treat her disability as a garment that she can don and remove as the mood strikes her").

102. Civil rights filings in federal court rose 63 percent between 1993 and 1997. *See* Administrative Office of the United States Courts, Federal Judicial Caseload: A Five Year Retrospective 5 (1998).

103. *See* Stephen Reinhardt, *Whose Federal Judiciary Is It Anyway?* 27 Loy. L.A. L. Rev. 1, 3 (1993) (describing and critiquing the view that "federal judges are too important for routine matters that only affect ordinary persons").

104. The Judicial Conference has recommended that "Congress should be

encouraged to exercise restraint in the enactment of new statutes that assign civil jurisdiction to the federal courts and should do so only to further clearly defined and justified federal interests." UNITED STATES JUDICIAL CONFERENCE, LONG RANGE PLAN FOR THE FEDERAL COURTS 28 (1995) (recommendation 6). Although the commentary to the recommendation cites the vital role "of the federal courts in promoting civil rights," and notes that this role should continue, it also urges that Congress should rely on state courts to a greater extent than it has to enforce federal rights. *Id.*

105. For discussions questioning whether the integration strategy of the civil rights movement has promoted equality, see Derrick Bell, *Serving Two Masters: Integration Ideals and Client Interests in School Desegregation Litigation,* 85 YALE L.J. 470 (1976); Alan David Freeman, *Legitimizing Racial Discrimination Through Antidiscrimination Law: A Critical Review of Supreme Court Doctrine,* 62 MINN. L. REV. 1049 (1978); *see also* Cheryl Harris, *Whiteness as Property,* 106 HARV. L. REV. 1707, 1757 (1993) (describing *Brown*'s legacy as "mixed" because it did not address government's responsibility to eradicate inequalities in resource allocation that support white domination); Kimberle Crenshaw, *Race, Reform, and Retrenchment: Transformation and Legitimization in Antidiscrimination Law,* 101 HARV. L. REV. 1331, 1377–79 (1988) (arguing that the civil rights movement removed most of the formal barriers and symbolic manifestations of racial subordination, but left much of the reality of white domination intact).

106. *See* DERRICK BELL, AND WE ARE NOT SAVED: THE ELUSIVE QUEST FOR RACIAL JUSTICE 59–74 (1987) (discussing disappointment of civil rights activists with reliance on the judiciary).

107. At the time that Congress enacted the ADA, the Supreme Court had already revealed its tendency toward narrow interpretation of civil rights laws. *See, e.g.,* Wards Cove Packing Co. v. Atonio, 490 U.S. 642 (1989). In fact, at the same time that Congress enacted the ADA, it was also considering the bill that ultimately became the Civil Rights Restoration Act of 1991, a measure designed to overturn narrow interpretations of Title VII. *See* Pub. L. No. 102–166, 105 Stat. 1071 (codified in scattered sections of 42 U.S.C.).

108. *See* Burgdorf, *The Americans with Disabilities Act, supra* note 62 (contrasting the detail of the ADA with the broad language of other civil rights statutes).

109. For example, the Family and Medical Leave Act, 29 U.S.C. §2601, is built on the idea that all workers, instead of a narrowly defined group, should be permitted to take leave when various exigencies arise; *see also* Estlund, *supra* note 91, at 1678–82 (arguing for protections for all employees against wrongful discharge, in part to alleviate resentments caused by targeted antidiscrimination laws).

*Lennard J. Davis*

# Bending Over Backwards
## Disability, Narcissism, and the Law

I am not a lawyer. But when I was a child growing up in the Bronx, my Deaf mother highly recommended that I become one because I was so good at arguing for my position against my parents' accusations. Instead, I became an English professor and now spend much of my time arguing for my interpretations against those of others. So perhaps things are not so different.

I began this presentation with a brief story about myself. In the previous statement, I allowed a snippet of biographical detail that would permit readers to make certain judgments about me. As a result of those few words, those readers who are lawyers probably feel they can let me off the professional hook. Such readers are probably now settling back, putting their pens down, and expecting a literary jaunt, a kind of breezy, erudite entertainment rarely found in legal books or journals. In making such judgments, readers are relying on stereotypes about English professors arrived at by interpreting my tone and my style of writing, and they are indexing their expectations from previous life-events that were similar. In other words, such readers are interpreting me as they might any text or person, and my meager narrative has provided some grist for their mill.

I too am interpreting texts—in this instance, some legal cases concerning people who have brought suits under the Americans with Disabilities Act. Before I do that, I need to justify the value of having an English professor read through some of these cases. It has been established by many in the relatively new endeavor of critical legal studies that cases are forms of narrative that can therefore be subject to the same kind of analyses that we tend to employ on novels or poetry.[1]

A second point involves the understanding that such cases are far from objective. Although cases are written in a style that suggests objectivity, impartiality, and authority, they are, after all, simply the written words of people. That style of writing, described by one scholar as comprising a "profoundly alien linguistic practice, . . . an archaic, obscure, professionalised and impenetrable language," which judges use to decide cases,[2] is simply a literary style like any other. Because words are part of language and language is a communal practice, there can be no use of language that transcends the sociability and biases of any linguistic community. It might therefore make sense for a literary critic to analyze the way legal language is used to create the illusion of objectivity, impartiality, and so on. In this sense, the role of the critic is an unmasking one, an attempt to show how many factors come into the writing of a case, just as many strands of culture come into the making of a novel or an opera.

A third and related point is that, because cases are both analyzable and instantiations of a larger culture, they are therefore ideological by definition. By ideological, I don't mean that cases are polemical, but rather that they contain the predilections, politics, nuances, and biases of their authors' particular culture or class within that culture. It is the job of a critic to tease out those predilections and nuances.

Having justified, however sketchily, the claim that legal cases are narratives and in need of interpretation by literary critics, among others, I need to make another assertion. Cases involving disability, because they are often not so much about fact as they are about personal and social attitudes, tend to involve the states of mind of the various players in the story. We are asked, for example, to imagine the state of mind of a potential employer who faces an obese job applicant and tries to decide whether or not to hire her,[3] or the state of mind of a supervisor who fires an employee who happens to have nonsymptomatic AIDS.[4] When judges and juries rule on such cases, they have to perform a complex and creative act of identification. Since the Supreme Court advises us to consider trial participants not as "members of a faceless, undifferentiated mass" but as "uniquely individual human beings,"[5] we then have an obligation to imagine and bring to life these individual states of mind through an act of what Martha Nussbaum calls "the literary imagination."[6] When we follow the narrative of the alleged crime, we must be readers, and as readers, we must place ourselves in a position to enter the state of mind of the players involved.

Two kinds of people do this for a living. One group is composed of dramaturges, directors, actors, and literary critics. The other group is composed of psychologists, psychoanalysts, or therapists. Therefore, along with saying that we need to know something about narrative to analyze these cases, we also need to know a lot about psychology. Indeed, a judge in writing such cases is acting as a kind of analyst, both literary and psychological, who attempts to resolve the questions of the case. A judge will have the same problems psychotherapists have—problems of interpretation, transference, and so on. However, judges do not seem to be very good at reflecting on these problems, so it will be the job of someone like me to do that for them.

We might begin with the first judge of psychoanalysis, Sigmund Freud. In his analysis of Shakespeare's *Richard III*, Freud identifies the deformed person or the disabled person as a characteristic personality type met in psychoanalysis.[7] Freud begins by reading Richard's well-known opening soliloquy in which the would-be king explains his character by saying:

> I, that am not shaped for sportive tricks,
> Nor made to court an amorous looking-glass;
> I, that am rudely stamp'd, and want love's majesty
> To strut before a wanton ambling nymph;
> I, that am curtail'd of this fair proportion,
> Cheated of feature by dissembling Nature,
> Deform'd, unfinish'd, sent before my time
> Into this breathing world, scarce half made up,
> And that so lamely and unfashionable,
> That dogs bark at me as I halt by them;
>
> .  .  .  .  .  .  .  .  .  .  .  .
>
> . . . since I cannot prove a lover,
> To entertain these fair well-spoken days,
> I am determined to prove a villain,
> And hate the idle pleasures of these days.[8]

According to Freud, Richard's soliloquy would serve to alienate the audience if Richard were merely saying: "I find this idle way of life tedious, and I want to enjoy myself. As I cannot play the lover on account of my deformity, I will play the villain."[9] This is the case, according to Freud, because "[s]o wanton a cause of action could not but stifle any stirring of sympathy in the audience, if it were not a screen for something much more serious."[10] Freud's point is that audiences generally tend to identify with a sympathetic rather than a villainous character, as the most elementary screenplay manual will inform the neophyte writer. If we remove the "screen" and reveal the "something much more serious," Freud tells us what we find is that the "wantonness vanishes" and what remains is the "bitterness and minuteness with which Richard has depicted his deformity."[11]

Here Freud begins to act like the judge in a disability case. He is pene-
trating beneath the words of the plaintiff's complaint to the intent behind
it. Freud explains Richard's real motive by reanalyzing the soliloquy, pointing to Richard's true message:

> Nature has done me a grievous wrong in denying me that beauty of
> form which wins human love. Life owes me reparation for this, and I
> will see that I get it. I have a right to be an exception, to overstep those
> bounds by which others let themselves be circumscribed. I may do
> wrong myself, since wrong has been done me.[12]

In this explanation, we begin to see how the analyst—and we might add
the judge and even the jury—begins to perceive people with disabilities.
Such disabled people claim that Nature has done them a wrong, and for
this wrong they seek reparation. This reparation is really an attempt to
claim themselves as an exception to the rules of society, which allows them
to overstep the bounds assigned to normal people. Thus, they see themselves as entitled to do a wrong to correct a wrong—thereby violating both
universal imperatives taught by parents to their children: "Two wrongs
don't make a right" and "If I make an exception for you, I have to make an
exception for everyone else." But, as children remain unconvinced by such
parental logic, so it is with audiences. As Freud writes:

> Richard is an enormously magnified representation of something we
> can all discover in ourselves. We all think we have reason to reproach
> nature and our destiny for congenital and infantile disadvantages: we
> all demand reparation for early wounds to our narcissism, our self-
> love. Why did not nature give us the golden curls of Balder or the
> strength of Siegfried or the lofty brow of genius or the noble profile of
> aristocracy? Why were we born in a middle-class dwelling instead of
> a royal palace?[13]

Freud tells us that as audience members we can put ourselves in the
position of Richard and identify with his sense of injustice, since we all are
deprived of something physical, mental, or economic that we might wish to
have redressed. Freud further tells us that the core of these feelings of deprivation is "early wounds to our narcissism, our self-love."[14]

An application of Freud's theory thus characterizes people with disabilities as narcissists, particularly when evaluated in psychoanalysis, as Tobin
Siebers has recently pointed out.[15] People with disabilities are regarded by

psychoanalytic theory as inherently viewing themselves as "exceptions" to the rule. Freud says as much when he talks about a woman with "organic pain" and a man who was accidentally infected by his wet nurse.[16] He describes these patients' personalities as "deformities of character resulting from protracted sickliness in childhood."[17] In his work *On Narcissism*, Freud again refers to the "familiar egoism of the sick person."[18] Siebers points out that current psychoanalytic theory continues this tradition, citing William G. Niederland's assertion that "minor physical anomalies or imperfections" are associated with "compensatory narcissistic self-inflation."[19]

An analyst, or in our case a judge or jury, may find that the narcissism of the person with disabilities spills over to the observer. For example, Siebers cites analyst Kenneth R. Thomas, who states that, in treating a patient with a disability, "therapists may experience a variety of reactions including 'imaginary' pangs of pain in the genital area, headaches, dizziness, or other physical symptoms."[20] This psychoanalytic theory further argues that such reactions are a sign that the therapist "has identified with the patient" and is "mirroring what the patient is feeling."[21] In other words, the narcissistic attitude of the person with disabilities is catching, and the observer can mimic or acquire the symptoms like a kind of non-birth-related couvade.

Such insights or prejudices carry over into the judicial realm. For example, in the quest to identify with the state of mind of the plaintiff with disabilities, the judge may find him- or herself reacting much in the same way that Freud and others suggest the culture demands "normal" people react to people with disabilities. This reaction causes the judge to see the disabled plaintiff as first and foremost narcissistic and egoistic. By definition, a concern for one's disability is seen as a self-concern rather than a societal concern. One of the major struggles of the disability rights movement has been to create public awareness that the problem of disability is not solely located in the individual using a wheelchair or in the Deaf person, but rather that the problem resides in the society that does not mandate curb cuts or allow American Sign Language to satisfy foreign language requirements in high schools and colleges.[22]

Many people with disabilities can testify to this general reaction in areas of accommodation and employment. When "special needs" (and let us notice the valence of that term) are required, too often the requester is seen as overly self-concerned, overly demanding. Indeed, this attitude is evident in the case of *DeSario v. Thomas*,[23] recently vacated by the Supreme Court in *Slekis v. Thomas*,[24] in which the Second Circuit Court of Appeals had ruled that states could refuse to provide equipment that met the medical needs of a small number of people as long as the state's plan for "home health services" provided adequately for "the needs of the Medicaid population as a whole."[25] In vacating that lower-court ruling, the Supreme Court countermanded the notion expressed by the lower court that people with unusual needs "will have to look for other sources of assistance."[26] This lower-court ruling saw people with even more specialized needs as overly demanding beyond the regular needs of people with disabilities. Because they are regarded as narcissists, people with disabilities are seen as demanding exceptions for themselves that overstep what employers can or should provide.

This theory of narcissism is further elaborated when we consider the very particular nature of many cases brought under the ADA. The act defines a disability as a physical or mental impairment that substantially limits one or more of the major life activities, a record of such an impairment, or being regarded as having such an impairment.[27] The ADA also bars discrimination against a person with a disability who can perform a job with reasonable accommodation.[28] But the act has not specified the range of definitions. For example, the Supreme Court recently decided that a correctable disability is not a disability under the ADA in three cases that involve correctable vision in airline pilots and truck drivers and high blood pressure in a mechanic.[29] A second area of ambiguity is the nature of reasonable accommodation, and a third is the very gray area that asks whether the impairment is such that it interferes with the employee's ability to perform the job. This last issue is almost the litmus test for many of these cases because, if a person claims to have been discriminated against on the basis of disability, the accuser must establish that, although she is disabled, she is not *so* disabled as to warrant that the employer was correct in not hiring or in dismissing her.

In all of these instances, the claimant must rely on very fine distinctions. In other words, these are not cases in which the matters of fact are clear. Of course, many cases revolve around such ambiguities, but it is fair to say that in disability cases these ambiguities abound. To argue that one was discriminated against because, for example, a potential employer thought the claimant was obese is to make a strident claim about a subtle thing. To claim that an employer did not provide reasonable accommodation because it installed ramps and provided many other structural changes, but did not lower a sink, is to make a strident claim about a subtle thing. Indeed, it almost seems that, in some cases, the claimant is biting the hand that feeds her, is unappreciative of what has been done for her, or is acting in a paranoid manner. In other words, the claimant is being self-centered and narcissistic.

Let us give the attempt to accommodate this narcissistic demand for exceptions a phrase, one that occurs in the language of legal cases: "bending over backwards." Take, for example, *Vande Zande v. State of Wisconsin Department of Administration,* a case I will analyze in greater depth later in this article, wherein the court describes the employer as one who "bends over backwards to accommodate a disabled worker."[30] The metaphor of "bending over backwards" to accommodate a disabled worker is one worth considering. The *Dictionary of English Colloquial Idioms* defines the phrase as to "go to extreme limits to try and satisfy someone."[31] The implication is that to redress a problem, the redresser must engage in a painful, extreme action. Indeed, the image is somewhat contradictory, since by bending over backwards in an awkward position, how can one help anybody? The meaning, perhaps, is that the contortion is out of the ordinary, since normally we bend forward. Bending backwards is distinctly uncomfortable for most people, except perhaps those in circuses or on videos that feature "abs of steel." The implication in this legal usage can be construed as saying that the pain felt by the person with a disability, as a result of either being disabled or being discriminated against on account of the disability, is now felt by the employer seeking to provide reasonable accommodation.[32] This sense of parity in the feelings of both employer and discriminated-against-employee creates a sense that justice has been served.

The concept of parity or equivalence in the law is expressed by Friedrich Nietzsche in *The Genealogy of Morals* when he describes "the notion that for every damage there could somehow be found an equivalent, by which that damage might be compensated—if necessary in the pain of the doer."[33] Nietzsche goes on to speak of "that ancient, deep-rooted, still firmly established notion of an equivalency between damage and pain."[34] In essence, the judge in this case is telling us that the pain felt by the employee is weighed against the compensatory pain felt by the employer. In this equation one pain is equivalent to the other, and the scales of justice are balanced by this awkward bending. But further, the compensatory pain is like a referred pain in that the judge feels the pain much as does the therapist who experiences in transference the pain of the narcissistic, disabled person. In fact, the judge and the employer, as observers, have to take "pains" to accommodate a narcissistic plaintiff.

An episode of *Ally McBeal* serves to illustrate this point as it exists in popular culture and consciousness. A man who claimed to be a sex addict argued that his marital contract was invalid because he married his wife in a state of lust that was close to insanity. In other words, he argued that his sexual addiction constituted a disability that should get him out of his marriage vows. Although this case is clearly invented, the television audience was meant to see that his claim for disabled status was the ultimate claim of a narcissistic personality. Although marriage vows are considered universally binding, the plaintiff wanted to make an exception for himself based on his disability and receive legal and financial rewards for behavior for which even the president of the United States could not expect recompense.

Returning to Shakespeare for a moment, let us consider his other outcast villain, Shylock. While he is not a person with disabilities, there are certainly parallels between Shylock and Richard III. There is much historical and sociological work to indicate that Jews were considered by European gentile society to be disabled or physically inferior.[35] As a Jew and an "alien,"[36] Shylock inhabits a body that is scorned by the general Christian populace, and he specifies this perceived physical inferiority in the now-famous "Doth not a Jew have eyes?" speech. Shylock turns hateful and demands his pound of flesh in court specifically because of his treatment as an outcast, much as Richard seeks his revenge for his treatment by others. Moreover, Shylock is perceived by the characters in the play as not being "touched with human gentleness and love"[37] when he insists on "the due and forfeit of my bond."[38] Shylock, like the claimants in a disability case, must counter, "I stand here for law."[39] But Portia's responsive speech on the "quality of mercy" asks Shylock to "mitigate the justice of thy plea."[40] Shylock is thus made to seem the self-centered, irrational, vengeful claimant who is redressing past wrongs through his legal suit. He demands his pound of flesh for no reason other than that "it is my humor."[41] In this sense, he provides yet another instance of a narcissistic person with wounds demanding his right to receive redress.

Let us now take a case not from the court of television or the stage but rather from the annals of the law: *Vande Zande v. State of Wisconsin Department of Administration*,[42] where the judge[43] felt that the employer had "bent over backwards." Lori Vande Zande was a thirty-five-year-old paraplegic woman who used a wheelchair. She developed pressure ulcers from time to time that made it difficult for her to work in the office. Ms. Vande Zande worked for the housing division of the State of Wisconsin for three years as a program assistant, which involved her preparing information, attending meetings, typing, mailing, filing, and copying. The state made modifications at her request including improving bathroom access, providing adjustable furniture, paying one-half the cost of a cot, and changing plans for a locker room in a not-yet-constructed building. Ms. Vande Zande complained that the state did not accommodate her requests to work full time at home during an eight-week bout of pressure ulcers and to provide a laptop computer during that period. Instead, she was told she would have to make up the difference between a reduced schedule and a full work week by subtracting days from her accumulated sick leave.

Ms. Vande Zande had also requested that a sink in the office kitchenette be lowered to accommodate her wheelchair. If the building had been constructed after the passage of the ADA, accessible facilities would have been required; however, since the planning had occurred prior to 1990, no such requirement existed. The plaintiff did not argue that the failure to include thirty-four-inch high sinks violated the act, but she did argue that once she brought the complaint to the attention of her supervisors, they should have made the alteration as a reasonable accommodation. Her employer claimed that it agreed to lower a counter in the kitchenette but could not lower the sink because the plumbing was already in place. However, that repair would have cost only $150, or $2,000 if the employer lowered similar sinks on every floor of the building. The employer argued that Ms. Vande Zande could use the sink in a nearby accessible bathroom. Ms. Vande Zande claimed that being forced to use the bathroom sink "stigmatized her as different and inferior."[44]

By nature, these cases tend to be about rather small matters. A series of small matters may add up to a large matter, but each individual request—cot, ramp, sink, shelf, and so on—seems rather insignificant and petty. Indeed, the plaintiff in this case appeared to violate a series of agreed-upon behaviors for team players, stoical American individualists, and generally agreeable people. Rather than take the self-abnegating road and wash her coffee cup out in the bathroom sink, Ms. Vande Zande protested the indignity of having to use a bathroom to fill a drinking cup. Also, rather than just accept the donation of her time, and therefore money, from accumulated sick leave, she contested such a quid pro quo. Plaintiffs making these types of claims will, by definition, seem to be bad sports, whiners, and, most of all, self-centered.

Ms. Vande Zande ultimately violates the understanding that people should be self-sufficient, and, in a culture based on independence rather than interdependence, she appears to be asking for too much. Indeed, the Seventh Circuit Court of Appeals notes as much when it critiques her demand to have a laptop at home: "Most jobs in organizations . . . involve team work . . . rather than solitary unsupervised work."[45] Thus, the court's attitude is dismissive, because it envisions the plaintiff to be asking for an even more narcissistic accommodation—to work at home as a solitary player, rather than as part of a team. Next, the court implies, she'll be asking for massages and cappuccinos. The court further states, "It is plain enough what 'accommodation' means."[46] This appeal to common sense is then belied by the court's next sentence, "The difficult term is 'reasonable.'"[47] Signaling a profound lack of knowledge about current nonableist terminology, the court notes that the plaintiff "is confined to a wheelchair."[48] So the analysis begins immediately with a central paradox. Accommodation is seen as a limpid category, while reasonableness in accommodation is not clear. Meanwhile, the court's ableist phraseology indicates that issues around disability are not, in fact, "plain enough" to those unfamiliar with these issues.

The court refers to the fact that even if the employer is large or wealthy (or a state bureaucracy, as in this case) and cannot plead undue hardship, "it would not be required to expend enormous sums in order to bring about a trivial improvement in the life of a disabled employee."[49] The point here is that, although the court does not know what "reasonable" accommodation may be, it feels comfortable judging whether a particular accommodation is "trivial" or not. Therefore, as I have suggested, most of the kinds of complaints made in these types of cases are going to be seen by people without a disability consciousness as "trivial." At this point, an analogy to earlier civil rights struggles might be instructive. For example, one can easily envision a southern judge in a 1960s civil rights case concluding that lack of access to a drinking fountain when another by its side was made available would be trivial, or that being seated in one seat versus another on a bus would be trivial. In cases of discrimination and civil rights, however, attention to the trivial is precisely the way to stop discrimination, because discrimination often operates on a trivial level or on many trivial levels, all of which add up to a substantial level of discrimination in the aggregate.

The court then fashions a reductio ad absurdum argument, saying that "if the nation's employers have potentially unlimited financial obligations to 43 million disabled persons, the Americans with Disabilities Act will have imposed an indirect tax potentially greater than the national debt."[50] Considering that the national debt is in the trillions of dollars, this assertion is clearly an overstatement. The court balances on one side of the scales trivial improvements and on the other side imposition of crushing taxes equaling the national debt. In an employer-centered, pro-tax-cut world, the decision is suddenly made easy: tax the engine of prosperity or indulge the narcissistic whiners.

The court adds another color to its discussion by noting, "We do not find an intention to bring about such a radical result in either the language of the Act or its history."[51] The new color is clearly "red"—that is, the desire to avoid going into the red because of "radical" reinterpretations of the

ADA. The court's statement further suggests another kind of "red" threat, because it contains an implication that leftist radicals may be trying to use the ADA to attack the very nature of capitalism itself. It is important for the court that the history of activism that led to the passage of the ADA not be seen as radical in nature, nor the effect become radical in intent or action. Thus, the court cites the preamble of the ADA as something that "'markets' the Act as a cost saver, pointing to 'billions of dollars in unnecessary expenses resulting from dependency and nonproductivity.'"[52] This move is important because it casts the ADA as a putatively pragmatic, but fundamentally conservative, statute that appears to espouse cost-saving as its main goal. Seizing that Occam's razor, the court slices through the complex issue of civil rights, proclaiming: "The savings will be illusory if employers are required to expend many more billions in accommodations than will be saved by enabling disabled people to work."[53] So, on a simple cost basis, employing a reductionist double-entry bookkeeping model, accommodation on a "trivial" level is a tax on businesses and does not live up to the cost-saving goal of the drafters of the ADA.

It is important to note the court's premise that the accommodation of removing barriers would be, on a national scale, too costly to enforce. So costly, in fact, that it would—and here I chose my words carefully—cripple the national economy. Again, we see the transference inherent in the analytic relation between the disabled person and the nondisabled observer— the observer feels the pain. If one weighs the discomfort of the trivializing narcissist against the crushing anguish of the crippled national economy, the former inevitably loses to the latter. Yet the government's own statistics show that the costs of removing barriers are relatively low. In fact, tax credits give employers back at least 50 percent of barrier removal expenses: the IRS figures for 1993 indicate that small businesses (defined as making less than $1 million in gross receipts and employing thirty or fewer employees) taking advantage of the Disabled Access Tax Credit spent on the average $3,327 for such accommodations, half of which was reimbursed for expenditures up to $10,250.[54] For individually owned businesses the average expenditure for accommodations was lower, about $2,500 per employer.[55] Clearly, the national economy can handle and will more than benefit from these improvements, but the Seventh Circuit Court of Appeals has unfortunately not taken even the basic steps to ascertain the nature of the expenditure on which it predicates the fall of America.

To put the final touch on this argument, and completely eviscerate any notion of civil rights inherent in the ADA, the Seventh Circuit in *Vande Zande* states that the district judge had granted summary judgment to the defendants because they "had gone as far to accommodate the plaintiff's demands as reasonableness, in a sense distinct from either aptness or hardship—a sense based, rather, on considerations of cost and proportionality—required."[56] Although the Seventh Circuit critiques the district court's analysis, it ultimately accepts the lower court's conception of what makes an accommodation "reasonable." The Seventh Circuit states:

> The employee must show that the accommodation is reasonable in the sense of both efficacious and of proportional to cost. Even if this prima facie showing is made, the employer has an opportunity to prove that upon more careful consideration the costs are excessive in relation either to the benefits of accommodation or to the employer's financial survival or health.[57]

In accepting the lower court's reasoning, the court of appeals has reinstated the "bending over backwards" test in what appears to be a supreme act of logic. Although the court allows that *reasonable* is a loaded word, it decides that reasonableness is based on common sense. And what constitutes that common sense? Cost and proportionality. Cost is put into a proportional equation with accommodation, while rights are magically left out of the equation.

Thus, the court concludes in effect that almost no accommodation except one that is deemed not trivial could be considered reasonable. Employers who grant any accommodations whatsoever, then, are seen as the ones who "bend over backwards."[58] That is, this defendant employer "goes further than the law requires—by allowing the worker to work at home."[59] How exactly compliance in regard to the ADA is seen as "going further" than the law requires is an interesting turn of phrase. If the law requires reasonable accommodation, and reasonable accommodation might require allowing the employee to work at home, then how is this "going further?" The court implies that workers with disabilities are approaching asymptotically that classic stereotype of the worker who fakes a disability to shirk work. It notes, "An employer is not required to allow disabled workers to work at home, where their productivity inevitably would be greatly reduced."[60] In this deteriorating chain of pseudologic, the court now sees the disabled employee as seeking institutionally sanctioned absenteeism as a way of life. Such absenteeism is automatically assumed to be linked to reduced productivity, which the court sees as an inevitable consequence of working at home (where, by the way, I am currently unproductively writing this essay). Thus, the largesse of the accommodating employer is placed in stark contrast with the trivializing, unproductive shirker using the ADA as convenient shield to cover basic laziness.

Notice how this way of putting things leads to the court's next conclusion. The employer "must not be punished for its generosity by being deemed to have conceded the reasonableness of so far-reaching an accommodation."[61] Compliance is now seen as an act of "generosity" with all its resonance of charity, almsgiving, philanthropy, and altruism—that general attitude which disability activism and laws have sought to change into a discussion of rights, fairness, and equity. In the court's scenario, though, the employer is generous to a fault, while the disgruntled, disabled employee is faulted for lacking the same generosity and team spirit. In a complete reversal of intention and logic, the court concludes that to punish such a generous employer "would hurt rather than help disabled workers."[62] Now, the notion of enforcing compliance with the ADA is seen as something that would paradoxically injure disabled employees. This argument brings to mind the old slogan "What's good for General Motors is good for America!" and implies that, if we impede the function of industry by insisting that it comply with the provisions of reasonable accommodations, we will reduce cash flow and thus limit industry's ability to pay for the costly barrier removal insisted on by the law.

This logic is so apparently clear to the court that it comments, "[W]e therefore do not understand what she [Vande Zande] is complaining about."[63] It is no wonder that the court is in such a state of incomprehension; it has so mangled the intent of the ADA that the transformed act now seems merely to amount to a governmental injunction for business to cut unnecessary costs. Under that set of misapprehensions, we should not be surprised that the Seventh Circuit cannot understand the discrimination about which Vande Zande is complaining. Neither could slave owners understand why slaves were carrying on about freedom so insistently.

The court's lack of comprehension becomes obvious in its analysis of the issue of the sink in the kitchenette. The court notes that Vande Zande complains about having to use the bathroom sink to wash out her coffee cup or fill a glass with water. She claims that this situation "stigmatized her as different or inferior."[64] The court notes that "she seeks an award of compensatory damages for the resulting emotional distress."[65] Here we have the crux of the Richard III or the Shylock problem. The aggrieved disabled party is injured by the way people treat him or her; the person with disabilities is therefore distressed and embittered, seeks revenge or compensation, and will not be deterred. Vande Zande wants her pound of flesh, only she'll take cash to sooth her emotional distress. Its perception of how trivial and narcissistic this claim is causes the court to respond in measured, objective cadences completely devoid of understanding. The specific ways in which disability operates within the culture and throughout the economy are a mystery to the court.

Of Vande Zande's claim that she is "stigmatized," the court responds, "That is merely an epithet."[66] This parsing of the word is particularly strange. The court's statement that being stigmatized is merely an "epithet," which the dictionary defines as "a disparaging or abusive word or phrase,"[67] without further examination of the concept of stigmatization is itself no more than an epithet. In fact, the *Vande Zande* court pays only lip service to the concept of stigmatization. For example, while the court is willing to assume that "emotional as well as physical barriers . . . are relevant in determining the reasonableness of an accommodation,"[68] the very next sentence of its opinion discounts the emotional barrier by retreating to the earlier cost-saving argument: "But we do not think an employer has a duty to expend even modest amounts of money to bring about an absolute identity in working conditions between disabled and nondisabled workers."[69]

Here, the court seeks to attack the claim of being stigmatized by presenting it in turns as merely emotional and at the same time as impossible to fix by economic means. But it must be pointed out that, although the stigmatization at issue may have caused emotional distress, the basic act of stigmatization is not so much an emotional issue as it is a sociological one. The term was virtually recoined for use in relation to disability by Erving Goffman in his classic book *Stigma,* which focuses not on emotional distress but on a pattern of behavior inherent in ableist society.[70] To link emotion with stigma is to denigrate the rationality inherent in the study of stigma and to negatively feminize it, as it were, since women are perceived in patriarchal society to be "emotional" rather than "rational." Further, taking the complex concept of stigma and reducing it to a simple and absurd claim that any attempt to remove or lessen a stigma requires creating an "absolute identity in working conditions between disabled and nondisabled workers,"[71] eviscerates any notion that stigma can ever be lessened or neutralized because employers would be forced to such lengths of bending over backwards that they would end up virtually upside down. Under these circumstances it is no wonder the *Vande Zande* court thinks that stigmatizing is "merely an epithet."[72]

Under this logic, the court can likewise conclude that Vande Zande could not have experienced a "pattern of insensitivity or discrimination,"[73] as she had claimed. First, all the events in question are "minor incidents,"[74] too trivial to rise to the level of a pattern of discrimination. Second, the experiences of stigma and emotional distress are not possible since these words are merely epithets. Third, this stigma can never be removed since removal requires "an absolute identity in working conditions."[75] Finally, all accommodations done by an employer are reasonable, and reasonableness is a cost-related concept determined by the employer's and the nation's economic ability to pay. Even if an employer can afford an accommodation, the national economy cannot afford such remedies because it will be devastated by the exponential expenditures of millions of employers. Thus, there can never really be a pattern of insensitivity or discrimination sufficient for redress. The logic of the court becomes consistent and impeccable, with only the minor failing of being completely wrong.

If my reading of the case is at all accurate, then it is necessary to try and specify how we can fix the court system, if possible, to decrease the likelihood that decisions like this one will continue to appear throughout cases related to the ADA. Certainly, it would be grandiose, to say the least, for me to claim that I had the broom that could clean out these Augean stables, or that this paper could even begin to provide the impetus for that housecleaning. Nonetheless, and because my mother was probably right about my argumentative nature, I will make the first attempts at housecleaning measures.

The first point that needs to be acknowledged is that the general public, including those members of it in the judiciary and on juries, is by and large ableist. I don't mean to use this brush to tar the good people of America. I am sure that each and every person, when asked, "Are you biased against people with disabilities?" will proclaim, one more loudly than the other, that they are as likely to be biased in that regard as they would be biased against mothers or national heroes. Yet my experience, and I am sure the experience of most people who work in disability studies, sheds a different light.

The point is not that rampant, overt prejudice abides in the hearts of citizens. Rather, the discrimination I am speaking about appears to be, to choose *le mot just*, trivial. The ordinary encounter, the glancing gaze, the innocent observation are the stock in trade of this kind of discrimination. We are not speaking of people with tattoos that say, "I hate cripples" or "Death to Deaf!" What we are speaking of is well-meaning people who simply do not have progressive information and education, in part because we do not teach disability in the public schools and colleges as we now teach race and gender. Few educated people nowadays would dare say that African Americans are not good long distance runners but are good basketball players and dancers; yet such observations were commonplace twenty years ago and were thought to be simple observations of fact. A friend of mine who trained as a lifeguard in the 1950s was told in a matter-of-fact way by his instructor not to save African Americans if they were drowning because "they're sinkers." This wasn't deemed to be a racist comment, but rather a simple bit of fact passed on by one lifeguard to another to avoid being pulled down to one's death. But, thanks to an educational policy that recognized the injustices being done to minorities by well-meaning folks, racism—while hardly eliminated—has been highlighted and discouraged. Sexism is also dying a slow and protracted death.

Ableism, on the other hand, is alive, well, and playing in your local theater, if you judge by the never-ending roster of movies filled with stereotypical disabled people triumphing over their afflictions. During the period in which this essay has been written, I have also been trying to place an op-ed piece in the *New York Times* and *The Nation,* both rather progressive newspapers. My piece is about the dragging death of James Byrd Jr. in Jasper, Texas, a subject much covered in the news. I point out that Byrd, in addition to being an African American, was also a person with disabilities, and I question why that fact was essentially suppressed in the news. I also discuss the long history of people with disabilities who have been abused and murdered. In trying to place this essay, I spoke with an editor at *The Nation* who immediately said, "But there's a long history of blacks being murdered and abused." When I said that there was also a history of such abuse toward people with disabilities, she was surprised. Having absolutely no knowledge of that history, she nonetheless presumed to tell me there was no such history. Likewise, when I spoke to a member of the editorial board of the *New York Times,* he protested that although the issues about which I spoke were valid, it was wrong perhaps to link them to the Byrd story. "People will see you as an opportunist trying to promote a cause that's unrelated to the story." I replied, "Oh, yes, because people are 'ableist,'" and he immediately shot back. "Not at all. It just seems like one thing has nothing really to do with the other." *The Nation* had agreed to publish the piece, but several months later has not yet done so because of the more "pressing" nature of other issues.

I give these examples not to grind personal axes, but rather to show how intelligent progressives simply do not see a connection between racism and ableism. Further, and this is a telling point, many people don't realize that there is a history or a politics to disability. There is nothing to be learned that an ordinary, sensitive person (and aren't we all?) can't simply intuit in the "I feel your pain" scenario I laid out earlier. Just as anyone can go to the cinema and be moved by a story about a mentally retarded woman or a blind man, so too anyone, judge or jurist, can sympathize with the plight of a person with disabilities. Empathy is cheap and there's plenty to go around. But, as many of us know, there is more to disability than meets the eye (if yours happen to be able to see). Indeed, the aim of disability studies and disability activism has been to fight exactly these common-sense notions of disability. Much of this knowledge is counterintuitive and for this reason especially needs to be taught in organized curricula and through the media in special series on radio and television parallel to those multi-part extravaganzas on the oppression of other groups. To counter the notion that disability is a personal tragedy, we propose the conception that disability is a social and political problem. To counter the stereotype that people with disabilities are either bitter, lustful, and resentful, or else inno-cent, asexual, and resigned, we propose very different ways of thinking. To the idea that language is neutral, we expose the lexicon that contains mor-alized and demoralizing words associated with impairment. And so on. The answer is a radical project of education on a national level. How we could achieve this cannot be the topic of this paper, but it is clear to me that the backlash against the ADA will not be halted by legal measures alone. The people that make up the court system need more knowledge.

Thus, it should come as no surprise that legal cases are filled with such a lack of knowledge and understanding. Let me take a few concrete examples. In the case of *Runnebaum v. Nationsbank*,[76] there are a host of uneducated assumptions concerning homosexuality and disability. The court notes as an example of Runnebaum's "inappropriate" behavior that "[h]e brought his gay lover to the reception and introduced him . . . as his 'boyfriend.'"[77] This example, among others, is seen as "failing to present a professional image."[78] I won't go into more detail about this issue, except to say that the court never questions its own attitudes toward homosexuality.

The same is true of the court's attitudes toward disability. In order to determine whether Runnebaum's asymptomatic HIV is an "impairment" and, thus, a disability covered under the ADA, the court's first recourse is to look up the words *impair* and *impairment* in *Webster's New Collegiate Dictionary*. What it finds is that *impair* means to "make worse by or as if by diminishing in some material respect" and that *impairment* means a "decrease in strength, value, amount, or quality."[79] While I understand that this refreshing approach to language is characteristic of such progressive judges as Richard Posner, who would prefer to use plain or common mean-ing of words, it is a uniquely inappropriate strategy for dealing with words like *disability* or *impairment*, which are in the process of being defined and redefined in complex ways to combat the kind of ableism one might indeed find in a dictionary.

In this case, the judge acts like a mediocre student attempting to write a freshman essay without doing much research. He simply reaches over to the shelf and selects a dictionary, and one indeed that was published in 1986, four years before the ADA was passed and eleven years before the case was heard. To beef up the serious scholarship inherent in this cantilevered swivel from desk to shelf, the court also cites two other Webster's dictionaries of the same era and concludes that "under these definitions, asymptomatic HIV infection is simply not an impairment."[80] The court cites an earlier case, *de la Torres v. Bolger,*[81] which states that "the term 'impairment,' as it is used in the Act, cannot be divorced from its dictionary and common sense connotation of a diminution in quality, value, excellence or strength."[82] Yet, the act referred to in this citation obviously cannot be the ADA because *de la Torres* was written four years before the passage of the ADA.

The point here is that the *Runnebaum* court, precisely because it has no knowledge of disability history or terminology and doesn't care to find out, deems that the only recourse is to a dictionary. Dictionaries, however, frequently contain antiquated and inappropriate definitions, particularly with regard to terms relating to race and disability. For example, had the court looked up the word *nigger* in a Merriam-Webster *Collegiate Dictionary,* it might have found the definition "a black person," one that has recently been protested and will be removed in subsequent editions.[83] Likewise, *blind* would have yielded among its definitions "defective" and "unable or unwilling to discern or judge."[84] By that usage, the statement "justice is blind" would come out "justice is defective, unable or unwilling to discern or judge." Actually, not a bad definition given these cases. Furthermore, the word *deaf* would produce "unwilling to hear or listen,"[85] and the word *lame* hobbles in as "weak."[86] What all this proves is that you don't go to the dictionary to find out about constructions within society that undergird prejudice because the language itself will necessarily contain or reflect that prejudice.

But the bigger misapprehension in *Runnebaum,* found both in the majority and minority opinions, is that the term *impairment* is a specific term, like *stigma,*[87] that relates to the history and conceptualization of disability as it developed within disability activism and scholarship over the past twenty years. I am speaking of the distinction, widely known and no doubt used by the drafters of the ADA, between *impairment* and *disability.* The previously used term *handicapped* did not allow a distinction between the physical condition and the barriers that cause that condition to become a problem. As a result, disability activists came to define *impairment* as the physical limitation of a particular illness or a chronic physical limitation, while defining *disability* as the social and political conditions that place barriers in the way of that impairment, thereby creating a disabling condition.[88]

Thus, an impairment might be anything from HIV to paraplegia, and the disability anything from targeted discrimination to the absence of curb cuts or ramps. Since the peculiar history of the passage of the ADA included the input of many disability activists in the actual wording of legislation, particularly in the sense of encouraging civil rights–associated wording in the act, the folly of looking up the meaning of the word *impairment* in Webster's is obvious. The equivalent would be to look up the meaning of *atom* and *bomb* in the dictionary in an attempt to understand how to build a tactical nuclear weapon. Instead, the judge should have looked up works about the drafting of the ADA and about the history of disability rights in the United States, works such as those by Paul Longmore, David Pfeifer, Irv Zola, and many others.[89] But that would require what we might call "disability literacy," something that the courts don't seem to demand for the citizens who occupy the bench.

Indeed, one case shows us by its metaphors how foreign a country disability is for many judges. In *Cook v. State of Rhode Island, Dept. of Mental Health, Retardation, and Hospitals*,[90] the judge describes the case as one that "calls upon us to explore new frontiers."[91] He therefore embarks on "our journey into the *terra incognita* of perceived disabilities [which] requires us to explore"[92] the subject. The metaphor is of the pith-helmeted adventurer going into the heart of darkness to bring light. At another moment, the court describes a consideration of evidence as "[t]he next stop on our odyssey."[93] The pith helmet is now replaced by battle helmet and shield as the judge continues as an epic hero wandering through the Scylla and Charybdis of disability. And a final determination is referred to as "[o]ur last port of call."[94] Now the errant nautical type, like Odysseus, and even a bit like Lord Jim or Marlowe, travels from one insecure port to another across ever more treacherous seas. At the conclusion of the decision, the judge announces, "We need go no further."[95] The journey of exploration need go on no more as the judge brings light and security to the chaotic world of disability claims.

The plaintiff, on the other hand, is described as one who "did not go quietly into this dark night" of discrimination.[96] But the plaintiff, to make her case, must "prove each element of her chain," and the court must "turn, then, to the remaining links that forge the chain."[97] So, while the court is the active explorer, out in the dangerous world of disability, the plaintiff is much more stationary. She doesn't go into "this dark night" but stays at home forging chains like a blacksmith to make her own case.

While the plaintiff in *Cook* ultimately prevailed amid this orgy of purple prose and the journey of the court led to an enlightened land, the metaphors used still tell us that the court is out there in the dark. Despite the heroic efforts of this decision and the self-referential congratulations for this exploration and bringing of light to the darkness, which perhaps comprehendeth it not, the basic problem remains. For intelligent and just decisions to be made, decisions based on knowledge and rationality rather than impulsive tropisms, bad faith, common sense, stereotyping, and a patronizing condescension to the issues, the judiciary will have to learn a lot more. Law schools should certainly teach courses on disability, and K–12 as well as college courses need to be developed. All of us will have to do much more to educate America.

Here are some suggestions:

1. Write op-ed pieces and articles for local and national magazines and newspapers.
2. Create a demand for radio and television documentaries and help to develop these.
3. Set up a public relations bureau that will make information available to the entertainment industry. Such entities already exist for other identity groups and foreign nationals.
4. Actively protest targeted legal cases, as for example ADAPT did on May 12, 1999, before the *Olmstead* case was decided by the Supreme Court,[98] and coordinate such demonstrations with educational outreach programs.

These are only a few suggestions among many. But we will never see a reversal in the backlash against the ADA until the majority of Americans, or at least what pollsters call "the opinion makers," are educated on this subject, or until enough of these opinion makers are themselves people with disabilities. The new millennium may see the number of people with disabilities rise to 20 or 25 percent of the population as the baby boomers age and if the trend of increasing disabilities among the young continues. But short of sheer numbers, we need to let the world know that people with disabilities who become whistle-blowers aren't trivializing narcissists who are just whistling "Dixie." In fact, they are really whistling "The Star-Spangled Banner."

NOTES

1. *See, e.g.,* Wai Chee Dimock, Residues of Justice: Literature, Law, Philosophy (1996); Stanley Fish, Doing What Comes Naturally: Change, Rhetoric, and the Practice of Theory in Literary and Legal Studies (1989); Patricia Williams, The Alchemy of Race and Rights (1991).

2. Peter Goodrich, Legal Discourse: Studies in Linguistics, Rhetoric, and Legal Analysis 1 (1987).

3. *See* Cassista v. Community Foods, 5 Cal. 4th 1050 (1993).

4. Runnebaum v. Nationsbank of Maryland, N.A., 123 F.3d 156 (4th Cir. 1997).

5. Woodson v. North Carolina, 428 U.S. 280, 304 (1976).

6. Martha C. Nussbaum, Poetic Justice: The Literary Imagination and Public Life 1–4 (1995).

7. *See* Sigmund Freud, Character and Culture 158–62 (Philip Rieff ed., 1963).

8. *Id.* at 160–61 (quoting William Shakespeare, Richard the Third, act 1, sc. 1).

9. *Id.* at 161.

10. *Id.*

11. *Id.*

12. *Id.*

13. *Id.*

14. *Id.*

15. Tobin Siebers, *Tender Organs, Narcissism, and Identity Politics, in* Disturbing Discourses: A Disability Studies Sourcebook (Brenda Jo Brueggemann et al. eds., forthcoming).

16. Freud, *supra* note 7, at 159–60.

17. *Id.* at 160.

18. Sigmund Freud, *On Narcissism, in* 14 The Standard Edition of the Complete Psychological Works of Sigmund Freud 82 (James Strachey ed. & trans., 1974).

19. Siebers, *supra* note 15.

20. *Id.*

21. *Id.*

22. Lennard J. Davis, *The Linguistic Turf Battles over American Sign Language,* Chron. Higher Educ., June 5, 1998, at A60.

23. 139 F.3d 80 (2d Cir. 1998).

24. 119 S. Ct. 864 (1999).

25. Linda Greenhouse, *"Three Strikes" Challenge Fails, but Others Are Invited,* N.Y. Times, Jan. 20, 1999, at A12.

26. *Id.*

27. The Americans with Disabilities Act of 1990, 42 U.S.C.A. § 12102(2) (1994).

28. *Id.* at §§ 12112(a), 12112(b)(5)(A).

29. Murphy v. United Parcel Serv., Inc., 527 U.S. 516, 119 S. Ct. 2133 (1999) (high blood pressure controllable by medication does not constitute a disability under the ADA); Sutton v. United Airlines, Inc., 527 U.S. 471, 119 S. Ct. 2139 (1999) (correctable myopia does not constitute a disability under the ADA); and Albertson's,

Inc. v. Kirkingburg, 527 U.S. 516, 119 S. Ct. 2162 (1999) (individuals with monocular vision are not per se "disabled" within the meaning of the ADA, but must prove on a case-by-case basis that their conditions substantially limit a major life activity).

30. 44 F.3d 538, 545 (7th Cir. 1995).

31. FREDERICK T. WOOD, DICTIONARY OF ENGLISH COLLOQUIAL IDIOMS 30, 191 (1979).

32. The original meaning of *bend* is actually "to bind," related to the use of the noun *band,* as in "fetters." OXFORD ENGLISH DICTIONARY 104 (2d ed., 1989). Thus the original meaning of the word implied coercion and imprisonment, and *bend* derived from the sense of binding something by twisting it into an unnatural position, similar to forming a knot. *Id.* Therefore, it is possible that our phrase "to bend over backward" was originally to "to bind over backward," indicating an even greater degree of suffering, pain, and deformation. However, the phrase is also found in the form of "lean over backwards." In any case, that notion of pain is now retained in the current expression.

33. Friedrich Nietzsche, *The Genealogy of Morals, in* THE BIRTH OF TRAGEDY AND THE GENEALOGY OF MORALS 195 (Francis Golffing trans., 1956).

34. *Id.*

35. *See, e.g.,* Sander Gilman, THE JEW'S BODY (1991).

36. William Shakespeare, *The Merchant of Venice, in* WILLIAM SHAKESPEARE: THE COMPLETE WORKS 238 (Alfred Harbage ed., 1969).

37. *Id.* at 234.

38. *Id.*

39. *Id.* at 235.

40. *Id.* at 236.

41. *Id.* at 234.

42. 44 F.3d 538 (7th Cir. 1995).

43. Fans of legal theory might be interested to note that Judge Posner was the judge who ruled in this case.

44. 44 F.3d at 546.

45. *Id.* at 544.

46. *Id.* at 542.

47. *Id.*

48. *Id.* The preferred phrase among people with disabilities is "uses a wheelchair," rather than "confined to a wheelchair."

49. *Id.* at 542–43.

50. *Id.* at 543.

51. *Id.*

52. *Id.*

53. *Id.*

54. *See* H. STEPHEN KAYE, DISABILITY RIGHTS' ADVOCATES, DISABILITY WATCH: THE STATUS OF PEOPLE WITH DISABILITIES IN THE UNITED STATES 54 (1997).

55. *Id.*

56. *Vande Zande,* 44 F.3d at 543.

57. *Id.*

58. *Id.* at 545.

59. *Id.*

60. *Id.*

61. *Id.*

62. *Id.*

63. *Id.*

64. *Id.* at 546.

65. *Id.*

66. *Id.*

67. Webster's Ninth New Collegiate Dictionary 419 (1983).

68. *Vande Zande,* 44 F.3d at 546.

69. *Id.*

70. Erving Goffman, Stigma: Notes on the Management of Spoiled Identity (1963).

71. *Vande Zande,* 44 F.3d at 546.

72. *Id.*

73. *Id.*

74. *Id.*

75. *Id.*

76. Runnebaum v. Nationsbank of Maryland, N.A., 123 F.3d 156 (4th Cir. 1997).

77. *Id.* at 162.

78. *Id.* at 163.

79. *Id.* at 168.

80. *Id.*

81. 781 F.2d 1134 (5th Cir. 1986).

82. *Runnebaum,* 123 F.3d at 168.

83. *Dictionary Will Revise Definitions of 200 Slurs,* N.Y. Times, May 3, 1998, at 34.

84. Webster's Ninth New Collegiate Dictionary 159 (1983).

85. *Id.* at 327.

86. *Id.* at 671.

87. And one wouldn't want to look up *stigma* in Webster's Ninth New Collegiate Dictionary because the definitions provided do not adequately describe the sociological term. Out of seven definitions, all but one are about marks, scars, or spots on the skin; only "a mark of shame or discredit: stain" comes close to the currently accepted sociological meaning. *Id.* at 1158.

88. *See* Tom Shakespeare, *What Is a Disabled Person? in* Disability, Divers-Ability, and Legal Change 25–34 (Melinda Jones & Lee Ann Basser Marks eds., 1999).

89. There are cases that trace disability history such as *Cassista v. Community Foods,* 5 Cal. 4th 1050 (1993), although that case ends up using a kind of spurious continuity between older and newer legislation insofar as the distinction between disability and impairment is concerned.

90. 10 F.3d 17 (1st Cir. 1993).

91. *Id.* at 22.

92. *Id.* at 25.

93. *Id.* at 26.

94. *Id.* at 28.

95. *Id.*

96. *Id.* at 21.

97. *Id.* at 22.

98. *ADAPT Anticipates Affirmation of Housing Rights of the Disabled,* U.S. NEWSWIRE, May 12, 1999, available in LEXIS, News Group File, at A11. The case at issue, *Olmstead v. L.C. ex rel. Zimring,* was ultimately decided at 527 U.S. 581, 119 S. Ct. 2176 (1999).

*Wendy E. Parmet*

# Plain Meaning and Mitigating Measures
## Judicial Construction of the Meaning of Disability

When I use a word, it means just what I choose it to mean,
neither more nor less.

—Lewis Carroll

When the Americans with Disabilities Act[1] was enacted in 1990, supporters heralded it as broad and transformative legislation. Senator Tom Harkin, one of the act's chief sponsors, asserted that the ADA was "the most important legislation Congress will ever enact for persons with disabilities."[2] No less enthusiastic, President George Bush signed the bill into law stating that "with today's signing of the landmark Americans for [*sic*] Disabilities Act, every man, woman and child with a disability can now pass through once closed doors into a bright new era of equality, independence and freedom."[3]

Central to their enthusiasm was a belief that the new act would promote the independence and economic self-sufficiency of millions of people with disabilities. As Jane West has noted, to achieve these lofty goals, the ADA "require[d] us to change our thinking about people with disabilities. The ADA demands that we focus on *people,* not on *disabilities;* that we focus on what they *can* do, not on what they *cannot* do."[4]

Unfortunately, the impact of the ADA has been less dramatic than predicted. An overwhelming number of plaintiffs have lost their claims.[5] In part, this is because much of the focus in ADA litigation has been on what people *cannot* do, rather than what they *can* do.[6] Frequently, courts have assumed that under the ADA, protection from discrimination is only available when the plaintiff demonstrates substantial inabilities. Thus as the Supreme Court made clear in *Toyota Motor Manufacturing, Kentucky, Inc. v. Williams,* a plaintiff who can lead an independent life, undertaking most activities of daily life, will have trouble establishing his or her disability.[7] In a sense, a plaintiff who can *do* is not viewed as *truly disabled.*

This reluctance to apply the ADA when individuals are able to overcome the effect of their impairments was dramatically evident in three cases decided by the Supreme Court in 1999. In *Sutton v. United Airlines*,[8] *Murphy v. United Parcel Service, Inc.*[9] and *Albertson's, Inc. v. Kirkingburg*,[10] the Supreme Court held that the beneficial impact of medication and other mitigating measures should be considered in determining whether an individual has a disability within the meaning of the ADA. According to the Court, if an individual is not substantially limited in a major life activity when the impairment is mitigated, that individual does not have a disability and is not entitled to protection from discrimination under the ADA. In so holding, the Court followed a path set by many lower courts in reading the ADA's definition of disability narrowly to apply only to individuals with irremediable impairments.

What is striking about the Supreme Court's decisions, as well as the lower-court cases that preceded them, is the Court's refusal to follow both the act's legislative history and regulatory guidance provided by the enforcing administrative agencies. Indeed, only by starkly dismissing an extraordinarily rich legislative history, along with a voluminous set of administrative materials, could a court have concluded that individuals with mitigated impairments do not have disabilities.

This paper discusses the mitigating measures issue and the role that different methods of statutory interpretation have played in the courts' analysis of it. The courts' treatment of the mitigating measures problem, I argue, results in large part from many courts' refusal to defer to either the ADA's legislative history or the administrative interpretations that have been drafted to guide the statute's implementation. That refusal, in turn, reflects the increasing preference among federal judges for textualism as a method of statutory interpretation. Textualism, I suggest, relies heavily upon "plain meanings" of terms that bring the interpreter back to the colloquial and stereotypical meanings that the statute was designed to transform. Thus, the rise of textualism presents a formidable obstacle to the realization of the broad goals shared by those who fought to enact the ADA.

To explore the relationship between the ADA and textualism, I begin by briefly reviewing the history of the ADA and the vision of social discrimination that informed it. Next, I consider more specifically the problem of mitigating measures, reviewing both the legislative history pertaining to the issue and the administrative guidance on the subject. I also discuss the current debates over methods of statutory construction and the rise of the so-called new textualism. I then relate this debate to the courts' analysis of the mitigating measures issue to demonstrate the close affinity between textualism and an insistence that the determination of disability be made with regard to the impact of mitigating measures. In so doing, I look not only to the Supreme Court's recent cases, but to earlier lower-court opinions on the subject. Even though many of these cases have been superseded by the Supreme Court's analysis, they provide a larger sample for analyzing the relationship between textualism and alternative resolutions of the mitigating measures issue. Finally, I explore why textualism has led courts to conclude that only individuals with irremediable impairments have disabilities. The answer, I suggest, lies in the common or colloquial understanding of disability upon which the textualist relies. By using preexisting meanings of social categories, textualism makes it difficult to implement truly transformative legislation without first transforming wider understandings. With textualism ascendant, advocates for disability rights will need to look beyond the legislature and federal bureaucracy in order to achieve the goals that inspired the ADA.

## A Brief History of the ADA's Definition of Disability

### A New Conception of Disability

What it means to have a disability—or to be a person with a disability—is critical to the implementation of the ADA. Unlike other civil rights statutes, the ADA generally protects only those who fall within its protected class. In contrast to Title VII of the Civil Rights Act of 1964,[11] the ADA does not so much prohibit discrimination *on the basis of disability* as it does discrimination against *individuals with a disability* on that basis.[12] Hence cases brought under the statute must face the initial, gatekeeping question, what does it mean to be a person with a disability?

For much of Western history, religious views shaped the answer to that question. Disability was associated with moral failing. Those who had disabilities were often assumed to have committed some sin that brought on their affliction.[13] Early in the more secular twentieth century, perspectives changed, and disability was conceptualized in medical terms.[14] Individuals with disabilities were now seen as having medical "problems" that could be diagnosed, treated, and sometimes, but not always, "cured" by medical practitioners. From this perspective, treatment, care, and pity were the typical social responses.

Slowly, in the wake of World War II and the concomitant reaction against Nazi eugenicist policies, and the rise of the civil rights movement, a new disability rights movement emerged. This movement decried both discrimination and paternalism. Instead, it promoted independent living and the full recognition of the capacities of all individuals with disabilities.[15] Building upon understandings developed and popularized by the civil rights and feminist movements, disability rights activists suggested that the difficulties faced by individuals with disabilities are caused not so much by the physical attributes of affected individuals, nor by anything they had done, but rather by the social treatment they encountered.[16] This perspective was elegantly articulated in 1969 by Leonard Kriegel in *Uncle Tom and Tiny Tim: Some Reflections on the Cripple as Negro.*[17] In that seminal work, Kriegel compared the individual with a disability to the "Negro." In both cases, the individual's experience and identity were formed as much (if not more) by social conditions and his or her status as an outsider, rather than by the actual physical attributes (paralysis of the limbs or skin color) that were used to identify the condition. From this perspective, disability was not so much a biological as a social phenomenon.

Remarkably, this vision of disability found its way into some of our earliest disability rights laws. Consider, for example, the 1968 Architectural Barriers Act,[18] which required that all new facilities built with federal money be made accessible to people with disabilities. This act sought to achieve accessibility not merely by prohibiting the exclusion of a discrete class of individuals, but by modifying future building designs to ensure universal accessibility. Thus, rather than focusing on the particular attributes or character of those to be protected, the act recognized the problem of disability as one of building designs that (inadvertently) created barriers. Disability, therefore, was not so much within the individual as within the built environment.[19]

The importance of this social vision of disability became more apparent with the enactment of Section 504 of the Rehabilitation Act of 1973.[20] Originally, the Rehabilitation Act provided financial support for vocational programs for individuals with disabilities. As such, the program assumed that disability was an individual characteristic that interfered with an individual's ability to hold a job. The training provided, therefore, would help a person compensate for his or her own incapacities.

In 1973 the Rehabilitation Act was substantially amended. With virtually no debate, Congress included a new provision that prohibited all recipients of federal financial assistance from discriminating against "otherwise qualified" individuals with a handicap "solely by reason of . . . handicap."[21] Exactly what that would mean was left, in large part, to the Department of Health, Education, and Welfare to decide through the regulatory process.

Although fundamentally a civil rights statute, Section 504 originally relied upon the narrow definition of disability associated with the broader statute's emphasis on vocational programs. This definition, which focused on an individual's inherent inability to work, made little sense in conjunction with a civil rights statute that prohibited discrimination. Recognizing this incongruity, in 1974, Congress amended that act to include a new definition of disability that would apply solely to the act's nondiscrimination provisions. The new definition characterized an individual with a disability as "Any individual who (i) has a physical or mental impairment which substantially limits one or more of such person's major life activities, (ii) has a record of such an impairment, or (iii) is regarded as having such an impairment." By adding this amendment, Congress opened the door to Section 504's application to individuals whose disability does not necessarily affect their ability to work, but rather their ability to engage in some other important life endeavor, such as being educated. At the same time, by inserting the second and third prongs to the definition, Congress recognized that discrimination on the basis of disability could extend not only to those who actually have a current disability, but also to those who either previously had a disability, or were erroneously assumed to have one.[22] In effect, Congress had adopted a social conception of disability.

## The ADA's Definition

By the mid-1980s, the federal government had made a significant, albeit partial, commitment to guaranteeing the rights of individuals with disabilities. Discrimination, however, remained rampant.[23] Individuals with disabilities remained disproportionately poor, unemployed, and undereducated.[24] Legal protections remained scattered. Most glaring was the absence of any federal law pertaining to private-sector employers who did not receive government contracts. To remedy this defect, several attempts were made during the 1970s and 1980s to amend the Civil Rights Act of 1964 to provide just such protection. Initially these efforts were opposed by many civil rights advocates who feared that reopening the 1964 act could lead to its general weakening. Yet, slowly, a coalition of previously disparate groups united to endorse comprehensive, federal legislation.[25]

The original supporters of the ADA saw disability as a broad and malleable concept, with deep social roots. The act's initial blueprint appeared in a 1984 article by Robert Burgdorf Jr., an attorney for the United States Commission on Civil Rights, and Christopher Bell, an attorney for the Equal Employment Opportunity Commission.[26] Their article began by surveying the diversity that exists among individuals with disabilities. Rather than treating disability as a discrete and inherent characteristic, the law, they argued, "must . . . acknowledge the existence of functional impairments, but it must also focus on ways society can reasonably adapt to a wider range of mental and physical differences than the handicapped-or-normal dichotomy has permitted."[27]

As support for the ADA developed in the 1980s, the idea of disability as a social condition merged with a call for "independence" that was quite consonant with the individualism of the Reagan eighties.[28] From this perspective, social discrimination against individuals with disabilities impeded their ability to function independently and be economically self-sufficient. What people with disabilities needed, therefore, was not government benefits, but freedom from the discrimination that turned their physical or mental attributes into disabilities.[29] The focus, therefore, was not on physical incapacities affecting individuals, but on the social dimensions of disability.[30]

This perspective is reflected in the ADA's legislative history. Robert Burgdorf's original draft of the ADA did not create a class of individuals with disabilities; rather it prohibited discrimination on the *basis* of disability.[31] The draft that was ultimately adopted, however, used a definition that mirrored, almost exactly, the definition employed by the Rehabilitation Act. This approach, it was felt, had the advantage of incorporating all of the case law and precedent developed under the Rehabilitation Act. That this was the intent was made explicit by the enactment in Title V of a specific provision directing that the act be interpreted not to provide lesser protections than were previously available under the Rehabilitation Act and its regulations.[32]

As of 1990, both the case law construing that definition and the model regulations issued by various administrative agencies pointed toward a broad understanding of disability. Indeed, in reviewing Rehabilitation Act case law of the 1970s and 1980s, one is struck by how seldom the question of disability was litigated. For the most part, courts simply assumed that the plaintiff had a disability.[33] Moreover, in the only Supreme Court case on the issue, *School Board of Nassau County v. Arline*,[34] the Court, in an opinion written by Justice Brennan, provided a broad interpretation of disability, finding that the Rehabilitation Act's definition could apply to a nontraditional disability such as a contagious disease. Justice Brennan went further, suggesting that under the third, "regarded as" prong of the definition, an individual could have a disability if the individual was hindered due to fear of her condition.[35] Thus Justice Brennan signaled approval of a social understanding of disability.

This was the backdrop against which Congress decided to adopt the Rehabilitation Act's definition in the ADA. Indeed, the evidence that the ADA's drafters and supporters understood the definition's potential breadth is overwhelming. Perhaps most apparent is the statute's own preamble, with its estimate that there are forty-three million Americans with disabilities.[36] Moreover, in apparent recognition of the statute's wide scope, Congress took care to explicitly exclude some disfavored conditions from the definition.[37] That the definition was to be expansive, moreover, was evident from a series of committee reports discussing the construction of the term.[38] True, the application of the definition to certain specific conditions was not fully delineated. However, that uncertainty was inevitable, given an understanding of disability as a socially constructed phenomenon.[39] If we accept that disability is as much a creation of the way society treats an individual as of concrete biological conditions, a list of disabilities cannot be provided. Nor, from the perspective of the ADA, would there be any need to provide an all-inclusive list. The goal of the statute, after all, was the promotion of economic independence rather than the provision of scarce government benefits.[40] Thus, seeing disability broadly,[41] the statute's drafters were content to provide a general definition of disability, comfortable with the thought that it would help promote the self-sufficiency of some unspecified group of over forty million Americans.[42]

## The Problem of Mitigating Measures

### What Is at Stake?

Central to understanding the nature of disability and the purpose of disability law is the question the Supreme Court reviewed in the summer of 1999:[43] whether individuals whose impairments are mitigated by medication, assistive devices, or other creations of human ingenuity still have a disability.[44] The answer to this question relates to how we conceive of disability. If we think of disability as a narrow category, as an exception to a norm of independence and self-sufficiency,[45] then the term should apply infrequently, only to those individuals who by virtue of their condition are incapable of living an independent, economically productive life.[46] From such a perspective, an individual whose condition is mitigated or controlled by medication, surgery, or an assistive device is, in a sense, no longer disabled. Because of the mitigating measure, that individual has "overcome" his or her physical incapacity and is now able to be self-sufficient. Such an individual, it may be argued, no longer requires reasonable accommodations and is no longer in need of the protections of disability law.[47]

If, on the other hand, we conceptualize disability more liberally, applying the term to individuals who encounter unnecessary hindrances in their quest for self-sufficiency[48] because the interaction of their biological selves and the social world around them, the existence of mitigating measures should not preclude a finding of disability. Indeed, from this perspective, individuals with disabilities are rarely physically incapable of self-sufficiency; rather it is the social reaction to their conditions that is both the problem to be solved by and the proper focus of the law. The fact that an individual's condition can be mitigated does not mean that the person no longer has a disability. Rather, the assumption is that all, or almost all, disabilities may be mitigated if society responds differently to human difference. From this view, a person with a disability is not necessarily, indeed is rarely, one who is incapable of independence. To insist that mitigation denies disability, then, is to treat disability as total incapacity, and to deny both the abilities of individuals with disabilities as well as the way in which social responses to biological differences have created the problem in the first place.

It is, of course, possible to contend that even if mitigated impairments are not "real disabilities" falling within the parameters of the first prong of the definition of disability, they can nevertheless "be regarded" as "such impairments" and therefore would qualify as a disability under the third prong of the statutory definition.[49] After all, the insertion of the third prong of statutory definition was made in the recognition that disability is, in part, a social condition, and that discrimination may occur even when an impairment does not in and of itself substantially limit a major life activity.

In practice, however, the narrow understanding of disability that excludes mitigated conditions under the first prong will often also exclude them under the third prong.[50] If the impact of an impairment can be mitigated, then the fact that an individual "is regarded as having such impairment" will usually not fall within the definition of disability, because "such impairment" can be mitigated. Only when a defendant subjectively misunderstands the impact of mitigation, as for example, when an employer fails to understand that insulin may control diabetes and enable someone with diabetes to continue working, will the third prong apply. But if the employer understands the impact of insulin, but still feels uncomfortable, perhaps for irrational reasons, with hiring an individual with diabetes, the narrow conception of disability that precludes inclusion of controlled diabetes under the first prong of the definition will generally prevent inclusion under the third prong.[51]

Thus if mitigating impacts are considered, few, if any, of the millions of individuals who depend upon medication, prosthetic devices, or other means to function independently and successfully despite their impairments will be entitled to the benefits of the ADA. A statute that was conceived broadly will be applied only to those with impairments that neither medical science nor human ingenuity can overcome.

## The Legislative and Administrative Record

The drafters of the ADA were remarkably cognizant of the mitigating measures issue. The matter was explicitly addressed in several committee reports. For example, the report of the Senate Committee on Labor and Human Resources stated that "whether a person has a disability should be assessed without regard to the availability of mitigating measures, such as reasonable accommodations or auxiliary aids."[52] Identical language appeared in the report of the House Committee on Education and Labor.[53]

> For example, a person who is hard of hearing is substantially limited in the major life activity of hearing, even though the loss may be corrected through the use of a hearing aid. Likewise, persons with impairments, such as epilepsy or diabetes, which substantially limit a major life activity, are covered under the first prong of the definition of disability, even if the effects of the impairment are controlled by medication.[54]

The House Committee on the Judiciary made similar observations.[55]

This is not to say that there is no ambiguity in the legislative history. For example, the drafters were clear that the ADA should be generally read in accordance with the Rehabilitation Act precedent.[56] Yet, while most cases decided under that act either interpreted the definition of disability broadly,[57] or simply assumed the existence of a disability,[58] by the late 1980s a few courts had begun to parse the statute's definition of disability, questioning its application to certain "nontraditional" disabilities.[59] None of these courts, however, appears to have relied explicitly upon the existence of mitigating measures as a rationale for rejecting a finding of disability.[60]

Still the ADA's drafters did not intend that *every* conceivable condition would constitute a disability. As both Justice O'Connor and Justice Ginsburg discussed in their opinions in the *Sutton* case,[61] the ADA's drafters clearly did not assume that every individual, or even a majority of individuals, had a disability, at least under the first prong of the statutory definition.[62] The House Judiciary Committee's report stated that "[p]hysical or mental impairment does not include simple physical characteristics, such as blue eyes or black hair. Nor does it include environmental, cultural or economic disadvantages, such as having a prison record, or being poor. Age is not a disability."[63] Moreover, the legislators did not believe that their definition would cover "minor, trivial impairments, such as a simple infected finger."[64] They insisted that in order for a condition to constitute a disability under the first prong of the statutory definition, it must be an *impairment* (not a social condition) that restricts an individual's major life activities "as to the conditions, manner, or duration under which they can be performed in comparison to most people."[65] Hence, the drafters seemed to have assumed that in order to find a disability under the first prong, at least, a condition must be a "real" impairment, which can restrict an individual substantially in a major life activity. Still, the legislators assumed that the definition would encompass many millions of individuals,[66] including those who relied upon mitigating measures. After all, the statute was enacted to require some mitigating measures—those that constitute reasonable accommodations.

The federal agencies authorized to enforce the statute quickly reached a similar conclusion. The EEOC, which has authority under Title I of the act,[67] adopted regulations defining the term *disability*. For the most part, these regulations followed the model set forth by the Department of Health and Education in its earlier model regulations for the Rehabilitation Act.[68] The EEOC regulations do not explicitly address the issue of mitigation. However, the appendix to the regulations, known as the Interpretative Guidance, stated that "[t]he determination of whether an individual is substantially limited in a major life activity must be made on a case by case basis, without regard to mitigating measures, such as medicines, or assertive or prosthetic devices."[69] The *Technical Assistance Manual* published by the EEOC to assist employers was even more emphatic. It stated that a "person's impairment is determined without regard to any medication or assistive device that s/he may use."[70] The manual went on to give the following example: "A person who has epilepsy and uses medication to control seizures, or a person who walks with an artificial leg would be considered to have an impairment, even if the medicine or prosthesis reduces the impact of that impairment."[71]

The Department of Justice, which has administrative jurisdiction over Titles II and III of the act,[72] took a similar view.

> Whether a person has a disability is assessed without regard to the availability of mitigating measures, such as reasonable modifications, auxiliary aids and services, services and devices of a personal nature, or medication. For example, a person with severe hearing loss is substantially limited in the major life activity of hearing, even though the loss may be improved through the use of a hearing aid. Likewise, persons with impairments, such as epilepsy or diabetes, that, if untreated, would substantially limit a major life activity, are still individuals with disabilities under the ADA, even if the debilitating consequences of the impairment are controlled by medication.[73]

Of course, this guidance was not meant to imply that every controlled condition constituted a disability. Although the departments were insisting that the effect of an impairment should be determined without regard to mitigating measures, they still presumed that in order for there to be a disability under the first prong of the definition, there had to be a "real impairment," and that impairment in the absence of mitigating measures would substantially limit an individual in a major life activity.[74] Thus, gray hair would not be a disability not because it can be mitigated through dying, but because it is not generally, even in the absence of hair coloring, an impairment that substantially limits one or more major life activities. Minor vision problems that are no worse than those experienced by the average person in the population might well be analyzed similarly. Still, according to the departments, the fact that an impairment's impact can be ameliorated, due either to the mandates of the statute or the wonders of medicine, did not in itself negate a finding of disability and concomitant protection under the law. An individual in a wheelchair does not cease to have a disability merely because he or she can be mobile in the chair.

## Statutory Construction and Judicial Interpretation of the Role of Mitigating Measures

### The Interpretative Debate: Intentionalism versus Textualism

In the last two decades, federal judges and commentators have waged a lively debate over how courts should go about interpreting ambiguous terms or phrases appearing in statutes.[75] Although courts have traditionally begun the task of construing a statute by looking at its text, for much of this century, their reliance on text was limited at best.[76] Seeing statutory construction as an attempt to discern and fulfill the intent of Congress,[77] courts would quickly and readily turn to a wide variety of nontextual sources.[78] Chief among these were legislative history, conceived broadly,[79] as well as the interpretations and opinions of administrative agencies.[80]

This mixed method of statutory construction, which may be termed *intentionalism*,[81] was well exemplified by Justice Brennan's opinion in *School Board v. Arline*.[82] The chief question in *Arline* was whether a teacher with tuberculosis has a "handicap" within the meaning of the Rehabilitation Act. Writing for the Court, Justice Brennan began his analysis not with the textual definition of *handicap*, but with statements by Senator Humphrey in the *Congressional Record* describing the statute's goal as sharing "with handicapped Americans the opportunities for an education, transportation, housing, health care, and jobs that other Americans take for granted."[83] Only after framing the issue in that light did Justice Brennan turn to the actual statutory definition of *handicap*,[84] which he quickly noted was enacted in 1974 to "reflect Congress's concern with protecting the handicapped against discrimination stemming not only from simple prejudice, but also from archaic 'attitudes and laws'" and from the "fact that the American people are simply unfamiliar with and insensitive to the difficulties confront[ing] individuals with handicaps."[85]

After setting forth the statute's text and legislative history, Justice Brennan turned to the regulations promulgated by the Department of Health and Human Services, finding them of "significant assistance" in helping to determine whether an individual has a handicap within the meaning of the statute.[86] Having thus laid the foundation for the proposition that the Rehabilitation Act's definition should be construed broadly to support the statute's goals, Justice Brennan spent little time demonstrating that the actual words of the text supported his conclusion that tuberculosis was a handicap. Indeed, what is striking about the opinion is its ambiguity as to which prong of the definition of handicap provided the basis for the decision. For while Justice Brennan briefly noted that Arline's previous hospitalization "suffices" to establish a "record of . . . impairment," suggesting that he was relying upon either the first or second prong of the definition, he also spent considerable time discussing the third, "regarded as" prong, explaining how it reflected Congress's concern "about the effect of an impairment on others."[87] From a contemporary perspective, Justice Brennan's discussion was remarkably conclusory. All he told us was that Arline had a respiratory infection that once required hospitalization. To Brennan, that was sufficient to demonstrate either the present or past substantial limitation of a major life activity.

Even in 1987, however, Justice Brennan's approach was not without its detractors. Throughout the 1980s, intentionalism, with its great reliance on legislative history, came under sharp attack from a variety of critics.[88] Public choice theorists, historicists, and formalists all questioned the idea that a court could look to legislative history to determine Congress's intent (and even that there is such a thing as congressional intent).[89]

Leading the attack within the judiciary was Supreme Court Justice Antonin Scalia. To Scalia and other so-called textualists, statutory interpretation must depend primarily upon the "plain meaning" of the statute in question.[90] When the particular words at issue are not completely clear, their meaning may be discerned by analysis of the statute's text as a whole, dictionaries,[91] grammar books, and the traditional common-law canons of statutory construction.[92] Legislative history is to be used sparingly, if at all,[93] and reliance upon such lofty notions as "statutory goals" is condemned as an illegitimate imposition of a judge's own values and policy preferences into the supposedly "neutral" task of applying the law as written by the legislature.[94]

Justice Scalia's attitude toward administrative interpretation is somewhat more complex. Because he questions the legitimacy of judges citing statutory goals,[95] he has at times been a strong advocate of judges deferring to administrative agencies, thereby eschewing their own policy choices.[96] On the other hand, the textualists' insistence on textual supremacy and their critique of extratextual considerations may result in reluctance to defer to administrative interpretations in the face of what the textualist believes to be a clear statutory meaning,[97] particularly when the statutory source for such deference is not absolutely explicit.[98] Thus the textualist judge may often appear to disregard the so-called *Chevron* doctrine, under which courts are obligated to defer to an administrative agency's interpretation of the statute it is charged with enforcing.[99] This refusal to defer to administrative interpretations has been most apparent with respect to the EEOC,[100] the agency charged with enforcing Title I of the ADA.

Although textualism is by no means fully triumphant in the courts,[101] its influence is substantial.[102] According to Professor Eskridge, textualism has become "agenda-setting."[103] At the Supreme Court, the method's influence may often be discerned, even when it is not fully embraced.[104] This was evident in the Court's opinion in *Bragdon v. Abbott*.[105] In writing the Supreme Court's first case construing the definition of disability under the ADA, Justice Kennedy took an approach strikingly different from that employed in *Arline*. Although Justice Kennedy found that the definition of disability could apply to HIV infection, he did so without referring at all to the goals or policies underlying the ADA. Indeed, his discussion of the definitional problem lacks any mention of statute's remedial goals.[106] And while he relied heavily upon administrative interpretations, he did so only after establishing clear textual support for such reliance. Citing 42 U.S.C. sec. 12201, Justice Kennedy noted that Congress explicitly stated that the ADA should be construed in light of the Rehabilitation Act and its regulations.[107] Therefore the administrative precedent Justice Kennedy relied upon was, in his mind, effectively codified into the text of the ADA. Moreover, while he did cite legislative history, he did so narrowly, avoiding consideration of broad congressional goals, and focusing instead upon explicit references in the legislative history to the specific issue before the Court.[108] Moreover, in contrast to Justice Brennan, Justice Kennedy turned to this history only after he established his text-based conclusion. To Justice Kennedy, legislative history served to confirm textual interpretation, not to guide it.

Many lower federal courts have proven even more dependent on textualist methodology. For the plaintiff who used mitigating measures to limit the impact of an impairment, this preference for text over extratextual material was devastating.

## The Sutton Case

The question of whether mitigating measures should be considered in determining disability and, more particularly, whether an impairment the effects of which are mitigated may still be substantially limiting within the meaning of the ADA was before the Supreme Court in three cases decided in the summer of 1999. The plaintiffs in the lead case, *Sutton v. United Airlines, Inc.*,[109] were twins with severe myopia who wished to be commercial airline pilots.[110] The district court had dismissed the twins' complaint, finding that they did not have a disability within the meaning of the act because their visual impairments were not substantially limiting when they wore corrective lenses. The district court also found that the plaintiffs did not qualify as having a disability under the third prong of the ADA's definition of disability because the defendant did not "regard" the plaintiffs as substantially limited in performing a class of jobs, but rather merely as being unable to do the single job of being a commercial airline pilot.[111] The Court of Appeals for the Tenth Circuit affirmed, accepting the lower court's analysis and finding that the determination of disability under the first prong should be made with regard to the beneficial impact of the twins' corrective lenses.[112]

In considering the impact of the plaintiffs' corrective lenses on the determination of disability, the Tenth Circuit parted company with the majority of appellate courts that had considered the issue.[113] The court of appeals' decision, however, was affirmed by the Supreme Court, in an opinion written by Justice O'Connor and joined by six of her colleagues. Justices Stevens and Breyer dissented.

Although Justice O'Connor never used the word, her opinion vividly demonstrated textualism's influence. Like any good textualist, she began with the statute's text, and relied heavily upon rules of grammar. She pointed out that the statute's definition of disability used the term "substantially limits" in the "present indicative verb form," and hence could not apply when an impairment "'might,' 'could' or 'would' be substantially limiting if mitigating measures were not taken."[114] She also noted that the statute's preamble claimed that forty-three million Americans had disabilities, thereby making the inclusion of the many more millions of individuals with hypertension, diabetes, and other controlled chronic impairments incompatible with the statute's text.

Equally revealing were the sources of interpretation that Justice O'Connor rejected. She refused to accept the administrative guidance on the subject, as well as the legislative history specifically on point. Nor did she worry much about the impact her decision would have on the statute's ability to realize its fundamental goals. In short, she rejected firmly, although not explicitly, the basic tools of intentionalist interpretation.

In contrast, Justice Stevens's dissent provides a striking illustration of intentionalist methodology. He relied heavily on congressional "purpose,"[115] as well as the relevant legislative history on the subject. He also looked to the guidance of the enforcing administrative agencies. In essence, he used an approach far more similar to the one Justice Brennan used in *Arline* than to that used by Justice O'Connor for the majority.

The disparity between the methods of statutory interpretation used by the majority and dissent in *Sutton* echoes the division found in the lower courts. Indeed, before *Sutton* the lower courts' conclusions about the mitigating measures issue were correlated closely with their views about administrative guidance, legislative history, the importance of searching for congressional purpose, and the weight to be given to the "plain meaning" of a text. In the discussion that follows, I consider the weight given by the courts to each of these sources of interpretation by looking more closely at the opinions in *Sutton* and at earlier lower-court decisions on the mitigating measures problem.

## The Role of Administrative Interpretations

Given that the text of the ADA is silent on the issue of mitigating measures, but that the administrative agencies that enforce the statute had addressed the matter explicitly, it should not be surprising that the amount of deference that courts were willing to give to agency interpretations was often critical to determining the outcome of the mitigating measures issue.[116] Indeed, the correlation is striking. Almost every court that decided to exclude the impact of mitigating measures in the determination of disability did so by relying heavily upon the interpretative guidelines issued by the EEOC and Department of Justice.[117] As noted above, these guidelines were quite explicit and appeared to provide a strong basis for excluding the impact of mitigating measures.

Deference to administrative guidance was clearly evident in the two *Sutton* dissents. In the lead dissent, Justice Stevens noted,

> Each of the three Executive agencies charged with implementing the Act has consistently interpreted the Act as mandating that the presence of disability turns on an individual's uncorrected state. We have traditionally accorded respect to such views when, as here, the agencies "played a pivotal role in setting [the statutory] machinery in motion."[118]

Justice Breyer's dissent gave even greater weight to the enforcing agencies. Justice Breyer noted that the EEOC had regulatory authority with respect to the definition of disability,[119] and that the agency could, if it wanted to, "draw finer definitional lines."[120] In other words, for Justice Breyer, the question of whether mitigating measures should be considered was one best left to the administrative agencies. Because the relevant agencies had concluded that mitigating measures should not be considered, the courts should follow suit.

The views of the administrative agencies were also critical to those lower courts that, prior to *Sutton,* had determined that mitigating measures should not be considered. For example, in *Roth v. Lutheran General Hospital,*[121] the Seventh Circuit simply accepted the EEOC's interpretation of the matter, without providing substantial discussion of either the amount of deference properly given to the agency nor the textual validity of the agency's interpretation.[122] Other courts provided a fuller explanation of why they should accept the EEOC's position.[123] For example, in one of the earliest court of appeals decisions on point, the Eleventh Circuit began its discussion of the issue stating, "At first glance, it is difficult to perceive how a condition that is completely controlled by medication can substantially limit a major life activity."[124] The answer to that paradox, according to the court, lay in the fact that under the Supreme Court's *Chevron* doctrine, courts are to give "considerable weight" to an administrative agency's interpretation of the statute it is entrusted to enforce.[125] Thus, because the EEOC had taken a clear position on the matter, the agency's view should be followed as long as it was not in "direct conflict" with the language of the statute.[126] Looking then at the language of the statute and its legislative history, the court concluded that the EEOC's position could not be "disregarded," as it was based on a "permissible construction of the statute" and was supported by the statute's legislative history."[127]

For some courts, the fact that the EEOC's construction appeared in interpretative guidelines, rather than actual regulations, proved troubling.[128] The weight to be given to such "nonbinding" administrative materials has been a much-debated question since the articulation of the *Chevron* doctrine.[129] For courts construing the ADA, this has been an especially important issue, as both the EEOC and Department of Justice have relegated much of their interpretative content to informal guidelines and technical assistance manuals, as opposed to actual regulations.

The Third Circuit considered the problem in *Matczak v. Frankford Candy and Chocolate Co.*,[130] noting that the guidelines pertaining to mitigating measures appear only as an "appendix" to the regulations. Hence, the court concluded, guidelines are not entitled to full *Chevron* deference, although they would still be given "controlling weight" unless they were plainly erroneous. Likewise, the district court in *Sicard v. Sioux City*,[131] noted that the deference accorded to "mere interpretative regulations" is less than that offered to "true" regulations. Rather than simply accepting the guidelines as binding, the court suggested, the weight to be given to the EEOC's interpretation should depend upon a variety of factors, including the validity of the agency's reasoning, the consistency of the agency's position, and the temporal relationship between the statute's enactment and the articulation of the agency's position.[132] But after looking to all of those factors in the case before it, the court concluded that the EEOC's position was entitled to "substantial deference."[133]

In her majority opinion in *Sutton,* Justice O'Connor went even further in questioning whether deference should be given to the relevant administrative interpretations. According to Justice O'Connor, the EEOC's authority over the definition of disability was questionable because that definition appears in a portion of the text technically lying outside of Title I, the title over which the EEOC is granted regulatory authority.[134] In other words, even though the ADA's text specifically gives the EEOC authority to administer Title I, and the definition of disability clearly and explicitly applies to that title, Justice O'Connor felt free to disregard the agency's guidance on the subject because the definition of disability sits outside Title I.[135] This novel, clearly textualist reading of the agency's authority was reached even though the Court had relied heavily upon agency interpretations of that very definition just the prior term in *Bragdon v. Abbott,*[136] a point not discussed by the majority. Nevertheless, by questioning whether the agency had any authority over the issue, the Court was able to buttress its subsequent rejection of the agency's position.

Justice O'Connor, however, challenged more than just the agency's authority.[137] She also rejected the validity of its position. Employing textualist methodology, and in sharp contrast to Justice Breyer, O'Connor refused to accept that there could be inherent statutory ambiguity justifying deference to an administrative interpretation. To her, the statute clearly answered the mitigating measures question by requiring consideration of mitigating impacts. Because the statute was in her view "clear," deference to the EEOC would be inappropriate.[138]

## Statutory History and the Search for Congressional Intent

Several of the lower courts that had excluded the impact of mitigating measures from the determination of disability relied heavily on the ADA's legislative history. Courts that concluded that mitigating measures must be considered either ignored that history or declined to follow it, finding that the history contradicted the statute's plain meaning.[139]

In *Sutton,* for example, Justice O'Connor quickly dismissed reliance upon legislative history specific to the mitigating measures issue: "Because we decide that, by its terms, the ADA cannot be read in this manner, we have no reason to consider the ADA's legislative history."[140] Interestingly, however, she delved deeply into the legislative history of the preamble's reference to forty-three million Americans with disabilities.[141] Without explaining why that resort to legislative history was more appropriate than consideration of the specific committee reports discussing the mitigating measures issue, Justice O'Connor argued that the history of the preamble's reference to forty-three million people suggested that Congress assumed a functional definition of disability that was incompatible with coverage of the many tens of millions of individuals with controlled impairments.[142]

But perhaps even more revealing than a court's treatment of the parts of the legislative history pertaining to mitigating measures is a court's attitude toward a broader exploration of congressional intent. Should the issue of mitigating measures be understood narrowly, based upon the text of the definition of disability? Or, should the issue be considered in light of the general goals and purposes behind the ADA? In other words, should a court rely on intentionalist methodology, as Justice Brennan did in *Arline,* or should the court conduct a more limited inquiry, as textualism directs?

These questions were pivotal in the mitigating measures debate. Few courts openly adopted an intentionalist approach to the issue. But those that did usually excluded the impact of mitigating measures from the analysis.

Justice Stevens's dissent in *Sutton* provides the clearest example. His opinion began by noting that "in order to be faithful to the remedial purpose of the Act, we should give it a generous, rather than a miserly, construction."[143] He then went on to say that "[a]s in all cases of statutory construction, our task is to interpret the words of [the statute] in light of the purposes Congress sought to serve."[144]

With that directive in mind, Justice Stevens considered the mitigating measures issue in light of the congressional goal of ensuring that "individuals who now have, or ever had, a substantially limiting impairment are covered by the Act."[145] He noted that "[t]here are many individuals who have lost one or more limbs in industrial accidents, or perhaps in the service of their country in places like Iwo Jima."[146] If the aid of their prostheses was considered in determining whether they had a disability, the statute would not prohibit discrimination against such individuals, leading to the "counterintuitive conclusion that the ADA's safeguards vanish when individuals make themselves more employable by ascertaining ways to overcome their physical or mental limitations."[147] In other words, the statutory goal of ensuring that those individuals with a disability who can work not be thwarted by "irrational fear and stereotype"[148] would be defeated.

Justice Stevens's conclusion was buttressed by various legislative committee reports that were "replete with references to the understanding that the Act's protected class includes individuals with various medical conditions that ordinarily are perfectly 'correctable' with medication or treatment."[149] As for the statutory reference to forty-three million individuals with disabilities, Justice Stevens argued that while Congress may not have considered or contemplated the possibility that individuals, such as the plaintiffs, with severe myopia would fall within the protected class, it is a "familiar canon of statutory construction that remedial legislation should be construed broadly to effectuate its purposes."[150] So just as Title VII may be applied to whites, even though they were not the class Congress had in mind when the statute was enacted, the ADA should be applied to individuals with severe myopia, if they are the victims of irrational discrimination, even though they do not have the impairment Congress probably had in mind when the legislation was enacted.[151]

In reaching these conclusions, Justice Stevens employed reasoning quite similar to that used in the First Circuit's earlier opinion in *Arnold v. United Parcel Service, Inc.*[152] *Arnold,* which concerned an insulin-dependent diabetic, clearly proclaimed the validity and importance of legislative history, stating that if the text is "not unambiguously clear," the court is "obliged to look to other sources," including legislative history and administrative interpretations.[153] Moreover, like Justice Stevens, the *Arnold* court noted that the ADA is a "broad remedial statute," whose goal was to increase opportunities for individuals who are able to work and function.[154]

The District of Columbia used a similar approach in *Fallacaro v. Richardson,*[155] which, like *Sutton,* concerned a plaintiff with a correctable vision impairment.[156] Although that court found that the EEOC guidance was not entitled to substantial deference because it was not a proper regulation,[157] the court nevertheless noted, "It makes little sense to deprive an entire class of disabled individuals—the legally blind who have correctable vision—of the protections of the Act merely because it is so easy to accommodate their disability."[158] In other words, if the goal of the statute is to promote the employment and independence of individuals with impairments, it makes no sense to deny protection to those individuals whose impairments can be controlled and are simply kept out of the workplace because of irrational discrimination.

## Textualism

Given textualism's rise in the federal courts, its application to the ADA should come as no surprise. What is surprising is that the drafters of the ADA relied so heavily upon legislative history and administrative guidelines to ensure that the act would be interpreted in certain anticipated ways. With textualism ascending as the favored stance toward statutory interpretation, the assumption that courts would rely on the statute's legislative history and the EEOC's guidance should probably have been questioned more critically than it was.

Textualism's impact on the mitigating measures issue was apparent long before *Sutton*. In 1996, in *Ellison v. Software Spectrum, Inc.*,[159] for example, the Fifth Circuit quickly concluded that the EEOC's guidelines should not be followed because "had Congress intended that substantial limitation be determined without regard to mitigating measures, it would have provided for coverage under Sec. 12102(2)(A) for impairments that have the potential to substantially limit a major life activity."[160] Interestingly, in reaching this conclusion about congressional intent, the court did not look at the actual legislative history. Rather, following textualist methods, the court determined the "intent" of Congress by relying on the statute's text. To the court, the fact that the first prong of the ADA's definition of disability required a "substantial limitation" of a major life activity and not a "potential limitation" of a major life activity was itself dispositive of the issue.[161]

Justice O'Connor adopted a similar approach in *Sutton*. As has already been noted, she disregarded both the specific legislative history on point as well as the administrative guidance. Instead, she focused to a great degree on specific words in the ADA's text. Particularly important to Justice O'Connor was the fact that the statutory definition of disability refers to a physical or mental impairment that "substantially limits . . . one or more major life activities." Because the phrase, grammatically speaking, was "in the present indicative verb form," it could not, the Court concluded, be applied to those impairments that no longer substantially limit major activities because of the benefits of mitigating measures.[162] Similarly the Court noted that the definition of disability requires that disabilities "be evaluated 'with respect to an individual' and be determined based on whether an impairment substantially limits the 'major life activities of such individual.'"[163] This too, the Court concluded, required that the determination of disability be made based upon the current actual physical status of the plaintiff, with the impairment controlled, rather than on an analysis of how the plaintiff might fare in the absence of mitigation. To disregard the impact of mitigation, Justice O'Connor suggested, would be to consider individuals "as members of a group of people with similar impairments, rather than as individuals."[164] Finally, as discussed above, the Court considered the text's reference to forty-three million Americans with disabilities and determined that it, too, was incompatible with disregarding the mitigating impacts of medication or other devices.[165]

Left unconsidered in this analysis is the inherent ambiguity of the text the Court was construing. Despite the Court's reliance upon supposed textual clarity, the text is not clear at all. For example, the use of the present indicative tense in the first prong of the definition of disability is not absolutely incompatible with a decision to ignore the impact of mitigating measures. An interpreter, after all, could have concluded that the present verb form simply means that the court must determine the current status of the plaintiff without the mitigating measures (i.e., when the glasses are taken off). The present tense does not dictate the answer. Nor is the text's mandate to consider the impact of the impairment on "such individual" determinative of the question. Clearly a court must consider the status of the plaintiff, rather than of individuals not before the court. The mandate to look at "such individual" does not necessarily indicate whether the plaintiff's ability to engage in major life activities should be considered in the mitigated or unmitigated state. Finally, the preamble's reference to forty-three million Americans with disabilities can hardly be considered conclusive. Not only does the preamble not mention the definition of disability, but also, as Justice Stevens noted, the number cited is as poor a fit with the Court's interpretation as it is with the EEOC's.[166] Under the former interpretation, the number is too high, under the latter, too low. Neither fits, nor can either fit with any interpretation that encompasses the second and third prongs of the definition of disability, which assuredly add an inherent uncertainty to any attempt to identify a specific number of people with disabilities.

Thus, the purportedly clear text that the Court relied upon was actually not clear at all. The question then arises why those courts that have emphasized textual over extratextual sources consistently determined that the determination of disability should be made based on an impairment's mitigated state. To that issue, we now turn.

## The "Plain Meaning" of Disability

As we have seen, the application of textualist methodology led almost consistently to the conclusion that the effects of mitigating measures must be taken into account in determining whether a person is an "individual with a disability" within the meaning of the ADA. For the most part, those courts that decided to determine an individual's disability status without regard to mitigating measures did so by relying upon extratextual sources, particularly the EEOC's interpretative guidelines and the statute's legislative history. When courts rejected these sources, they usually concluded that the "plain meaning" of disability requires a determination of whether an impairment is substantially limiting despite the benefits provided by mitigating measures. In essence, these courts argued that the plain meaning of the statute demands that the first prong of the definition of disability apply only to individuals who are substantially limited in a major life activity despite any medication or devices they might use.

But why does reliance upon text require analysis of whether a plaintiff is substantially limited after the effects of mitigating measures are considered? After all, the text itself is silent on the issue. It does not explicitly say that a condition should be considered in its medicated or mitigated state. Given that ambiguity, it is tempting to suggest that textualism does not in fact necessitate the outcome adopted by textualist courts, that instead such courts use textualism to dispose of what they perceive to be nonmeritorious claims at the summary judgment stage. Hence, it might be argued, textualism simply serves as a useful device to enable courts to disregard the legislative history and EEOC guidelines that, if followed, would make summary judgment on the question of disability less frequent.[167] In other words, it is possible that conservative jurists, who are suspicious of ADA claims, adopt textualist rationales for the simple purpose of justifying a legal conclusion to which they are already predisposed.

While such a hypothesis cannot be rejected entirely, it still does not fully explain the courts' deep reluctance to accept that someone whose impairment is controlled could be a person with a disability. This reluctance was perhaps most vividly illustrated by the Fifth Circuit's opinion in *Washington v. HCA Health Services of Texas*.[168] In that case the court recognized that the statutory text was inherently ambiguous and that it was therefore appropriate for the court to consult legislative history and administrative guidance. But that did not end the matter. While the court realized that both the legislative history and administrative guidance supported the view that conditions should be assessed in their unmitigated state, it nevertheless stated that "the most reasonable reading of the ADA" would be one that considers mitigating impacts.[169] In other words, although the court was not honestly able to say that the text was unambiguous, thereby justifying the disregard of the legislative history and administrative interpretations that contradicted the text, it was still uncomfortable accepting the notion that an individual with a mitigated condition could have a disability. So, the court tried to split the difference, by adopting what it thought was a more "reasonable" conclusion, that only "serious" impairments would be considered in their unmitigated state.[170] In essence, the court determined that the text, as construed by traditional modes of statutory interpretation, included within the definition of disability people who should not be considered disabled.[171]

Most opinions were less candid. They never actually said that an individual with a mitigated condition does not fit within the common understanding of disability. Instead, like Justice O'Connor in *Sutton,* they point to various parts of the statute's text, without actually saying that what drove their conclusion was not the phrases in the text, but the word *disability* itself. To a textualist, it seems, textual fidelity is not the highest value; regardless of what the ADA's text says, *disability* has a clear meaning, and that does not include people with myopia or other controlled conditions.

Ultimately, these judges relied upon a common or plain meaning of disability, which does not encompass most of the conditions presented in the mitigating measures cases. For example, the dictionary, a favorite textualist source,[172] defines *disability* as "lack of adequate strength or physical or mental ability; incapacity."[173] Social scientists who have studied perceptions of disability have found a deep resonance between this definition, with its emphasis on "incapacity," and cultural attitudes toward people with disabilities. For example, in our culture it is widely understood that to have a disability is synonymous with needing help, with passivity and dependency.[174] People with disabilities, therefore, are "typically . . . seen as helpless and incompetent."[175] They are thought of as those who are unable to successfully negotiate the demands that contemporary life places upon its members.[176] People generally view individuals with disabilities as "damaged, defective, and less socially marketable than non-disabled persons."[177] As Marilynn J. Phillips has written:

> Commercial advertising and the popular media establish and reenforce such notions, powerfully influencing social attitudes and behavior toward persons with disabilities. Newspaper and magazine articles, as well as television interviews and editorial commentaries, abound with examples of disabled-as-damaged goods.[178]

This image of helplessness and incompetence is central to popular conceptions of disability. According to Anita Silvers,

> In contemporary Western culture, to be disabled is to be disadvantaged regardless of how much success one achieves individually. That is because costs are extracted if one is seen as a member of a poorly regarded group.[179]

This tendency to magnify the helplessness of individuals with disabilities may serve psychologically to distinguish disability as a state of "otherness" from the supposed norm of independence and capacity. Viewing those with disabilities as dependent and needy enables us to view those without impairments as strong and independent. By focusing on the dependency and incompetence supposedly associated with disability, we can forget, or at least try to forget, the universal vulnerability of the human state.[180]

The equation of disability with incompetence also helps explain why disability is widely accepted as creating affirmative societal obligations.[181] In contemporary Western culture, the individual with a disability is assumed to be a victim.[182] Because their assumed incapacity is attributed to factors thought to stem from beyond their individual control, people with disabilities are apt to be viewed as entitled to assistance from others.[183] Long before the modern welfare state emerged, government programs provided financial relief to a variety of individuals with disabilities.[184] Disability was a condition that excused one's inability to be self-sufficient and triggered obligations from others.

This cultural relationship between disability, dependency, and entitlement may have been strengthened by other uses of the term *disability* in the law outside of the civil rights context. In other areas of the law, disability signifies an inability to be self-sufficient and a need for the support of others. This is most clearly seen by the definition of disability used in the Social Security Act.[185] This act, which frequently forms the basis for litigation in the federal courts, defines a person with a disability as one who is unable "to engage in any substantial gainful activity by reason of any medically determinable physical or mental impairment."[186] A condition that can be controlled and does not prevent some one from working, therefore, is not a disability within the meaning of the Social Security Act. Indeed, the idea that a condition as common and easily treatable as myopia would justify payment under the Social Security Act appears ludicrous; surely the work ethic can have no meaning if disability and entitlement not to work is so widely dispersed.

The idea that disability means both inability and special entitlement is found in other areas of the law as well. The Individuals with Disabilities Education Act,[187] for example, defines "children with disabilities" as children who have particular listed impairments or conditions and "who, by reason thereof, *need special* education and related services."[188] Thus the act only applies to those children who require special services, the implication being that if the impairment is controlled and does not lead the child to need any additional services, the child does not have a disability. At the same time, the entitlement to special educational services comes along only with the label of disability. Again, disability here means not only difference; it means inability and entitlement.

The ADA, in contrast, employs a definition of disability that departs significantly from these legal ancestors. As an antidiscrimination statute, the ADA was not designed simply to provide benefits to those who are unable to be self-sufficient. Indeed, while the act does not completely reject the notion that disability creates entitlement (for the statute does require reasonable accommodations and other affirmative measures to assure equal access for individuals with disabilities), the ADA also prohibits differential and invidious treatment of individuals with disabilities, premised on the belief that such individuals, more often than not, can be economically independent. While it makes no sense to say that an individual whose impairment is completely controlled should be found to have a disability within the meaning of the Social Security Act, it is completely consistent with the goals of the ADA to find such an individual protected from invidious discrimination. Indeed, this individual—who has a condition that is controlled but may nevertheless be the target of invidious or irrational discrimination—is precisely among the classes for whom the ADA was enacted.

To the textualist judge, however, the common lay and legal meaning that denotes incapacity and entitlement is inconsistent with applying the statute to commonplace or controlled conditions. From a "common sense" perspective, individuals with conditions as frequently occurring as myopia do not have "true" or "real disabilities" because they are neither incapacitated nor deserving of forgiveness from the ethic of self-sufficiency.

This idea that disability must mean something quite different from what the ADA's legislative history and the interpretative guidelines (not to mention disability activists) say it means appears in the many cases in which the courts implicitly conclude that the plaintiff's condition is not "bad enough" to warrant treatment as a disability. For example, in *Cline v. Fort Howard Corp.*,[189] the court rejected the conclusion that an individual who was nearsighted and visually impaired had a disability within the meaning of the ADA. The court admitted that the plaintiff need not be "totally blind" to have a disability, but suggested that the plaintiff's impairments were not serious enough. A "visual impairment which hinders, or makes it more difficult for an individual to function at a full visual capacity, does not amount to a substantial limitation of one's ability to see where the evidence suggests the individual can otherwise conduct activities requiring visual acuity."[190] In other words, a condition as common and "normal" as the plaintiff's cannot be considered a disability.[191] Likewise, in *Schluter v. Industrial Coils, Inc.*, the court wrote that the ADA does not create a type of "job tenure for an employee with slightly impaired eyesight simply because she suffered insulin dependence and insulin reactions having no relation to the adverse employment action, while leaving unprotected employees with similar vision problems resulting from aging or generally poor eyesight."[192] In effect, the court assumed that the granting of disability status was the equivalent to an entitlement to the job ("tenure"), which surely should not be awarded to all individuals with conditions as common as the plaintiff's.

Similar sentiments help to explain the *Sutton* Court's concern with numbers. The forty-three million individuals in the statute's preamble was important to the Court because it suggested that disability was a minority phenomenon. As Justice Ginsburg said in her concurrence, the ADA applies only to a "confined" class.[193] If the statute applied to myopia, then "in no sensible way can one rank the large numbers of diverse individuals with corrected disabilities as a 'discrete and insular' minority."[194] Disability, it seems, is worthy of discrimination protection only if it is both rare and extreme.

## Textualism and Disability Rights

The rise of textualism and the increasing judicial insistence on interpreting statutes in light of their plain meaning creates a major dilemma for the disability rights movement. In order to confront and prohibit disability discrimination, that phenomenon must be named. Disability as an *identity* must be recognized, and the discrimination that targets it must be outlawed. In order to do that, the category must be reconceptualized. Disability must be redefined as capacity, rather than as incapacity; otherwise the discrimination that is to be prohibited would be justified.

But the very process of naming and identifying disability as a category is not, it seems, risk free. While Humpty Dumpty may have the luxury of saying that a word means only what he says it means, civil rights advocates and legislators are not so privileged. When they use a word such as *disability*, they invariably invite consideration of the conceptual baggage, including the stigma, associated with that word. Ironically, in the case of *disability*, the very stigma the ADA sought to dispel has influenced the interpretative process.

Are there ways out of this conundrum? The most obvious would be for Congress to amend the statute to make explicit the novel meaning intended. To an important extent, Congress did this in 1974 when it amended the definition of handicap in the Rehabilitation Act, to make absolutely clear that an individual can have a handicap even when he or she is not limited in the ability to work. Unfortunately, no definition can be all-encompassing. Ambiguities, such as whether the effect of an impairment is to be determined in the pre- or postmedicated state, are bound to arise.

Recognizing this inevitability, the ADA's drafters relied on other time-tested tools designed to guide the interpreter's hand. To ensure interpretation faithful to the idea of disability as a broad socially constructed phenomenon, the backers of the ADA provided the statute with a legislative history unusually rich in theoretical and practical detail. Moreover, they granted the EEOC and the Department of Justice explicit statutory authority to promulgate regulations[195] and to provide technical assistance to entities subject to the act.[196] With respect to the mitigation issue, all of these factors were critical to the willingness of many pre-*Sutton* courts to determine the existence of disability without regard to the effects of ameliorative measures.

The ADA's drafters did not foresee textualism's growing influence, or the corresponding reluctance of many federal courts, particularly the Supreme Court, to consider either legislative history or administrative interpretation in construing ambiguous statutory terms. To the textualist, the meaning of disability (or each of the prongs of its statutory definition) must be understood with reference to the term's "plain meaning," even if the statute was designed to alter that plain meaning. Thus the textualist clings closely to the preexisting images of disability that the statute identified and tried to change, ignoring the transformative images elucidated in the legislative history.

Given the rise of textualism, disability advocates must reassess their reliance on legislative history to guide statutory interpretation. While legislative history is useful, it can all too easily be disregarded. As much as possible, those who seek to transform social images must rely on textual devices to achieve their aims. Explicit statutory statements of intention (such as exist in the ADA's preamble) help, as do devices explicating that the statute should be interpreted in light of explicit extratextual standards. As was evident in *Bragdon,* specific statutory incorporations of extratextual references can be critical in inducing judicial departure from ostensibly "plain" meanings.

But can these devices suffice? *Sutton* suggests otherwise. The stigma and degrading images suffusing the disability category are both powerful and deep. And there may be no way a law enacted to change those images can avoid using the terms that conjure them.

In closing, consider the following hypothetical. What if the Americans with Disabilities Act had never used the term *disability?* What if the act had simply forbidden discrimination based upon the status of some absurd, meaningless word, like *conditionism?* And what if the statute defined *conditionism* as being "a physical or mental impairment that substantially limits a major life activity, the record of such impairment, or being regarded as having such impairment." Would that textual definition have made any difference? Would courts still find that plaintiffs are not "truly conditionistic"?

It is tempting to think that such an approach could have severed the statute from the stigma of disability, thereby preventing courts from falling back upon the plain meaning of that colloquial term. But before advocates for people with disabilities adopt such an approach in future legislative endeavors, some caution is in order. First, we may wonder if it is that easy to escape plain meaning. While we can dispense with the word *disability* in favor of the term *conditionism,* might we not find that the plain meaning of other terms such as *impairment* will infect the construction of *conditionism* as significantly as the plain meaning of the term *disability* now impedes the application of the ADA? In other words, is there any way to enact an intelligible statute without appending the baggage we wish to leave behind?

More disturbing is the possibility that a truly stigma-free statute could not be enacted. How was it in a conservative era, in a society that values independence and self-sufficiency as much as ours does, that a civil rights statute as broad and transformative as the ADA was enacted? One distressing and partial answer may be that the stigma of dependence and victimhood associated with the disability construct was an essential, albeit unrecognized, member of the ADA coalition. Thus the enactment of a statute designed to eradicate the stigma embedded in the popular disability construct may well have depended on disability's stigmatic association with dependency and entitlement. If so, using that statute to exorcise the demon that bore it will be exceedingly difficult. In this era of textualism, cultural change may have to precede legal change. Before we can alter legal interpretations, we may have to excise the stigma associated with popular conceptions of disability, for it is from these conceptions that judges draw the "plain meaning" of statutory terms.

NOTES

1. Pub. L. No. 101–336, 104 Stat. 328 (1990) (codified at 42 U.S.C. § 12101 (1994)).

2. *See* THE AMERICANS WITH DISABILITIES ACT: FROM POLICY TO PRACTICE,

at back cover (Jane West ed. 1991) [hereinafter West].

3. *Signing of the Americans with Disabilities Act by President George Bush,* FEDERAL NEWS SERV., July 26, 1990.

4. Jane West, *Introduction: Implementing the Act: Where We Begin, in* West, *supra* note 2, at xi.

5. *See* Ruth Colker, *Hypercapitalism: Affirmative Protections for People with Disabilities, Illness, and Parenting Responsibilities Under United States Law,* 9 YALE J.L. & FEMINISM 213, 222 (1997) (Courts in the United States have undermined the affirmative treatment principles underlying disability discrimination law, despite the clear statutory language to the contrary); Lisa Eichhorn, *Major Litigation Activities Regarding Major Life Activities: The Failure of the "Disability" Definition in the Americans with Disabilities Act of 1990,* 77 N.C. L. REV. 1405, 1434 (1999) (citing a study by the American Bar Association's Commission on Mental and Physical Disability Law concluding that a large number of cases have resulted in summary dismissal).

6. *See* Steven S. Locke, *The Incredible Shrinking Protected Class: Redefining the Scope of Disability Under the Americans with Disabilities Act,* 68 U. COLO. L. REV. 107, 124–25 (1997).

7. See 534 U.S. 181 (2002), holding that an individual with carpal tunnel syndrome was not "substantially limited" in the major life activity of performing manual tasks because she could perform many tasks of daily living, like bathing and brushing her teeth. Such reasoning leads to a great catch-22. If the plaintiff can demonstrate what she cannot do, she is in danger of being found to be "unqualified" for the job in a Title I action. *See* Robert Burgdorf Jr., *"Substantially Limited" Protection from Disability Discrimination: The Special Treatment Model and Misconstructions of the Definition of Disability,* 42 VILL. L. REV. 409, 425–26 (1997).

8. 527 U.S. 471, 119 S. Ct. 2139 (1999).

9. 527 U.S. 516, 119 S. Ct. 2133 (1999).

10. 527 U.S. 555, 119 S. Ct. 2162 (1999).

11. 42 U.S.C. § 2000e (1994).

12. Burgdorf chronicles how this came to be. *See* Burgdorf, *supra* note 7, at 415–51. In contrast, cases under Title VII of the Civil Rights Act of 1964, 42 U.S.C. 2000e, pay little attention to whether the plaintiff is of, or has, a certain race. Rather, the question is whether the plaintiff's treatment was based upon race. As a result, white plaintiffs can bring race discrimination claims, even though they are not, in a sense, in the protected class.

13. *See* Jonathan C. Drimmer, *Cripples, Overcomers, and Civil Rights: Tracing the Evolution of Federal Legislation and Social Policy for People with Disabilities,* 40 UCLA L. REV. 1341, 1359 (1993). Drimmer calls this the "social pathology" model of disability. *See id.* at 1348–49; *see also* JOSEPH P. SHAPIRO, NO PITY: PEOPLE WITH DISABILITIES FORGING A NEW CIVIL RIGHTS MOVEMENT 30–32 (1993); Anita Silvers, *Formal Justice,* in ANITA SILVERS ET AL., DISABILITY, DIFFERENCE, DISCRIMINATION 56–59 (1998).

14. *See* Drimmer, *supra* note 13, at 1347; Silvers, *supra* note 13, at 59–63; *see also* Mary Crossley, *The Disability Kaleidoscope,* 74 NOTRE DAME L. REV. 621, 649–53 (1999) (describing the medical model of disability).

15. See Sara D. Watson, A Study in Legislative Strategy: The Passage of the ADA, in Implementing the Americans with Disabilities Act: Rights and Responsibilities of All Americans 27 (Lawrence O. Gostin & Henry A. Beyer eds., 1993) [hereinafter Gostin & Beyer].

16. See Richard K. Scotch, Disability as the Basis for a Social Movement: Advocacy and the Politics of Definition, 44 J. Soc. Issues 159, 159–63 (1988); Joan Susman, Disability, Stigma, and Deviance, 38 Soc. Sci. Med. 15, 16 (1994); see also Crossley, supra note 14, at 653–65 (describing the social and minority group models of disability); Eichhorn, supra note 5, at 1414 (noting that the disability rights movement sees disability as a "socially-constructed phenomenon").

17. 38 Am. Scholar 412, 423 (1969). An important early legal analysis was by Jacobus tenBroek, The Right to Live in the World: The Disabled in the Law of Torts, 54 Cal. L. Rev. 841 (1966).

18. 42 U.S.C. §§ 4151–4157 (1994).

19. From the start, federal disability rights law has integrated conceptions of reasonable accommodation and disparate impact with a social conception of disability. See, e.g., Southeastern Comm. College v. Davis, 442 U.S. 397, 413 (1979).

20. 29 U.S.C. § 794 (1994).

21. Pub. L. No. 93–112, § 504, 87 Stat. 355, 394 (1973). The Rehabilitation Act originally used the term handicap. This was altered with the enactment of the ADA.

22. See S. Rep. No. 93–1297, at 38 (1974), reprinted in 1974 U.S.C.C.A.N. 6373, 6389; H. Rep. No. 101–485, pt. 2, at 52–53 (1990), reprinted in 1990 U.S.C.C.A.N. 267, 334–35.

23. The evidence of discrimination was chronicled throughout the hearings for the ADA. See, e.g., The Americans with Disabilities Act of 1989: Joint Hearing Before the Subcomm. on Select Educ. and Employment Opportunities of the Comm. on Educ. and Labor, House of Representatives, 101 Cong. 62 (1989) (Statement of Justin Dart Jr., Chairman, Task Force on the Rights and Empowerment of Americans with Disabilities). Evidence was also compiled in surveys and polls. See Louis Harris and Associates, Inc., The ICD Survey of Disabled Americans: Bringing Disabled Americans into the Mainstream (1986); National Council on Disability, On the Threshold of Independence: Progress on Legislative Recommendations, in Toward Independence (1988).

24. See Jane West, The Social and Policy Context of the Act, in West, supra note 2, at 4–5.

25. See id.

26. Robert L. Burgdorf Jr. & Christopher G. Bell, Eliminating Discrimination Against Physically and Mentally Handicapped Persons: A Statutory Blueprint, 8 Mental & Physical Disability L. Rep. 64 (1984).

27. Id. at 68.

28. See, e.g., National Council on the Handicapped, toward Independence (1986).

29. See id. at 12, 18.

30. See, e.g., Richard K. Scotch, Politics and Policy in the History of the Disability Rights Movement, 67 Milbank Q. 380 (1989) ("the disability rights movement has promoted the idea that prejudicial attitudes and exclusionary practices are far

greater barriers to societal participation for many disabled people than are their physical or mental impairments").

31. Chai R. Feldblum, *Definition of Disability Under Federal Antidiscrimination Law: Implications for People with AIDS and Asymptomatic HIV-Infection,* 21 BERKELEY J. EMP. & LAB. L. 91 (2000).

32. *See* 42 U.S.C. § 12201 (1994). This provision became very important to the Supreme Court's interpretation of the ADA in Bragdon v. Abbott, 524 U.S. 624, 118 S. Ct. 2196 (1998).

33. Some exceptions are Forrisi v. Bowen, 794 F.2d 931 (4th Cir. 1986); Jasany v. United States Postal Serv., 755 F.2d 1244 (6th Cir. 1985); E. E. Black Ltd. v. Marshall, 497 F. Supp. 1088 (D. Haw. 1980).

34. 480 U.S. 273 (1987).

35. *Id.* at 284.

36. *See* 42 U.S.C. § 12101(a)(1) (1994).

37. For example, the statute specifically excludes from the definition of disability "transvestitism, transsexualism, pedophilia, exhibitionism, voyeurism, gender identity disorders not resulting from physical impairments, or other sexual behavior disorders; compulsive gambling, kleptomania, or pyromania, or psychoactive substance use disorders resulting from current illegal use of drugs." 42 U.S.C. § 12211(b) (1994). The act also strikes a compromise with respect to homosexuality, declaring that "homosexuality and bisexuality are not impairments and as such are not disabilities under this chapter." *Id.* at 12201(a). This provision ensures that the statute does not prohibit discrimination on the basis of sexual orientation without treating sexual orientation as "an impairment."

38. *See, e.g.,* REPORT OF HOUSE COMMITTEE ON EDUCATION AND LABOR, H. R. REP. NO. 101–485, pt. 2, at 50–53 (1990) (discussing the definition of disability); REPORT OF SENATE COMMITTEE ON LABOR AND HUMAN RESOURCES, S. REP. 101–16, at 21–24 (1989) (same). Indeed, the legislative history also shows that in recognition of the potential breadth of the ADA, some members of Congress sought to explicitly exclude certain impairments. *See, e.g.,* 42 U.S.C. § 12208 (1994); 135 CONG. REC. 19864 (1989) (discussing exclusion of transvestites); 136 CONG. REC. 10911 (1990) (discussing proposed exclusion of individuals with infectious diseases from prohibition of discrimination by food industry).

39. Congress was aware of the need to address discrimination based on societal prejudices:

> For example, severe burn victims often face discrimination. In such situations, these individuals are viewed by others as having an impairment that substantially limits some major life activity (e.g., working or eating in a restaurant) and are discriminated against on that basis. Such individuals would be covered under the Act under the third prong of the definition.

H.R. REP. NO. 101–485, pt. 2, at 53 (1990), *reprinted in* 1990 U.S.C.C.A.N. 303, 335. The Supreme Court took notice of this legislative intent. "The amended definition reflected Congress's concern with protecting the handicapped against discrimination stemming not only from simple prejudice, but also from 'archaic attitudes and laws' and from 'the fact that the American people are simply unfamiliar with and insensitive to the difficulties confront[ing] individuals with handicaps.'" School Board of Nassau County v. Arline, 480 U.S. 273, 279 (1987) (quoting S. REP. No. 93–1297, at 50 (1974), *reprinted in* 1974 U.S.C.C.A.N. at 6400).

40. *See* Matthew Diller, *Dissonant Disability Policies: The Tensions Between the Americans with Disabilities Act and Federal Disability Benefit Programs,* 76 TEX. L. REV. 1003, 1023–25 (1998).

41. Disability theorist and activist Irving Kenneth Zola wrote in 1989, the year before the ADA was enacted, "What we need are more universal policies that recognize that the entire population is 'at risk' for the concomitants of chronic illness and disability." *See* Irving Kenneth Zola, *Toward the Necessary Universalizing of a Disability Policy,* 67 MILBANK Q. 401 (1989).

42. *See* 42 U.S.C. § 12101 (1994).

43. Sutton v. United Airlines, Inc., 527 U.S. 471, 119 S. Ct. 2139 (1999).

44. *See* Colker, *supra* note 5, at 231; *see also* Michael J. Puma, *Respecting the Plain Language of the ADA: A Textualist Argument Rejecting the EEOC's Analysis of Controlled Disabilities,* 67 GEO. WASH. L. REV. 123 (1998); Maureen R. Walsh, *What Constitutes a "Disability" Under the Americans with Disabilities Act: Should Courts Consider Mitigating Measures,* 55 WASH. & LEE L. REV. 917 (1998); William Brent Shellhorse, *The Untenable Stricture: Pre-mitigation Measurement Serves to Deny Protection Under the Americans with Disabilities Act,* 4 TEX. WESLEYAN. L. REV. 177 (1998); Catherine J. Lanctot, *Ad Hoc Decision Making and Per Se Prejudice: How Individualizing the Determination of "Disability" Undermines the ADA,* 42 VILL. L. REV. 327 (1997).

45. This view of disability helps to explain the stigma associated with disability. *See* ERVING GOFFMAN, STIGMA: NOTES ON THE MANAGEMENT OF SPOILED IDENTITY (1963). In this classic work, Goffman argued that stigma arises when an individual is perceived as deviant, i.e. different from the prevailing conceptions of normalcy.

46. Fine and Asch wrote that because disability evokes feelings of vulnerability and death, people without disabilities tend to focus on the helplessness and dependence of people with disabilities, thereby confirming the comforting (if false) view that those without disabilities are strong and independent. Michelle Fine & Adrienne Asch, *Disability Beyond Stigma: Social Interaction, Discrimination, and Activism,* 44 J. SOC. ISSUES 3, 16 (1988).

47. This argument is well presented by Erica Worth Harris in *Controlled Impairments Under the Americans with Disabilities Act: A Search for the Meaning of "Disability,"* 73 WASH. L. REV. 575, 596 (1998), where she argues that the reasonable accommodation provisions of the ADA should not apply to those whose conditions are controlled. Harris concedes that such a person may still have a disability under the second or third prongs of the definition, which apply to individuals who have a record of, or are perceived as having, such an impairment, see 42 U.S.C. § 121101, but she then goes on to argue for a narrow construction of those prongs, vitiating their impact. Fundamental to Harris's perspective, and to that of many of the courts that have considered the issue, is the idea that someone whose condition is controlled is not "really disabled." Disability, thus, is seen as a limited, almost pathetic category, a term that must be applied sparingly, to those upon whom nature has dealt a very cruel hand.

48. One may criticize the ADA for fostering an ideal of self-sufficiency that ignores the fact that dependency and vulnerability to both biological and social conditions are universal human traits. *See* Fine & Asch, *supra* note 46, at 16 (making the point that we are all interdependent).

49. *See* 42 U.S.C. § 12102(2)(C) (1994); Harris, *supra* note 47, at 596.

50. That was the case in *Sutton v. United Airlines, Inc.,* 527 U.S. 471, 119 S. Ct. 2139 (1999), and almost every other case that has considered the issue.

51. *See* Christian v. St. Anthony Med. Center, Inc., 1997 U.S. App. LEXIS 16288 (7th Cir. 1997) (arguing that discrimination due simply to irrational dislike of an impairment is not covered by the ADA). One can still argue that the plaintiff should qualify as having a disability within the meaning of 29 C.F.R. § 1630.2(*l*)(2), which states that the third prong applies when an individual is limited in major life activities only due to the "attitudes of others toward such impairment." However, the courts have seldom applied this provision, and it seems unlikely that a court would find that it applies to a mitigated condition without first assuming that the mitigated condition itself was a "real disability." Moreover, the *Sutton* Court's questioning of the authority of the EEOC to define the definition of disability creates serious doubt over the validity of this regulation. *See* 119 S. Ct. at 2145.

52. S. REP. No. 101–116, at 23 (1989).

53. *See* H.R. REP. No. 101–485, pt. 2, at 52 (1990), *reprinted in* 1990 U.S.C.C.A.N. 302, 334.

54. *Id.*

55. *See* H.R. REP. No. 101–485, pt. 3, at 28 (1990), *reprinted in* 1990 U.S.C.C.A.N. 445, 451.

56. *See* 42 U.S.C. § 12201(a) (1995).

57. *See* Feldblum, *supra* note 31, at 15.

58. *See, e.g.,* Davis v. Meese, 692 F. Supp. 505, 517 (E.D. Pa. 1988) ("An insulin-dependent diabetic is clearly a 'handicapped person' within the meaning of the Rehabilitation Act").

59. *See* Forrisi v. Bowen, 794 F.2d. 931, 932–33 (4th Cir. 1986); E. E. Black Ltd. v. Marshall, 497 F. Supp. 1088, 1099–1101 (D. Haw. 1980). These cases focused particularly on what it means to be "substantially limited" in the major life activity of working.

60. *See* Wallace v. Veterans Admin., 683 F. Supp. 758 (D. Kan. 1988) (finding rehabilitated drug addict an individual with a handicap without considering impact of rehabilitation); Trembczynski v. City of Calumet City, 1987 WL 1664 (N.D. Ill. 1987) (plaintiffs with myopia do not have a handicap within the meaning of the Rehabilitation Act; in reaching this conclusion court does not explicitly rely upon the fact that plaintiffs wear corrective lenses); *see also* Rezza v. United States Dept. of Justice, 1998 WL 48541 (E.D. Pa. 1998) (discussing whether recovering gambler has a handicap without explicitly considering whether recovery precludes a finding that plaintiff has a disability if mitigating measures are not considered); *but see* Stephanie P. Miller, *Keeping the Promise: The ADA and Employment Discrimination on the Basis of Psychiatric Disability,* 85 CAL. L. REV. 701, 712 (1997) (claiming that Rehabilitation Act cases did consider the impact of mitigating measures). All of the cases cited, however, appear to postdate the enactment of the ADA.

61. *See* Sutton v. United States Airlines, Inc., 527 U.S. 471, 119 S. Ct. 2139, 2147–49 (O'Connor, J.); *id.* at 2151 (Ginsburg, J., concurring).

62. The drafters were far more comfortable in assuming that the third prong pertained to purely social instances of disability, in other words, to situations in which social reactions are the only impediments to an individual's functioning. *See* H. R. REP. NO. 101–485, at 52–53 (1990), *reprinted in* 1990 U.S.C.C.A.N. 302, 335.

63. H. R. REP. NO. 101–485, at 28; *see also* S. REP. NO. 101–116, at 22 (1989) (making identical point to that in the text).

64. *See id.* at 23.

65. H. REP. NO. 101–485, pt. 2, at 52 (1990), *reprinted in* 1990 U.S.C.C.A.N. 303, 334. The committee went on to observe that an individual who "can walk for ten miles continuously is not substantially limited in walking merely because on the eleventh mile, he or she begins to experience pain because most people would not be able to walk eleven miles without experiencing discomfort." *Id.*

66. In her opinion for the Court in *Sutton,* Justice O'Connor focused heavily on the fact that the statute's preamble states "some 43,000,000 Americans have one or more physical or mental disabilities." 119 S. Ct. at 2147–49. For a further discussion of this issue, see *infra* text accompanying notes 141–43.

67. 42 U.S.C. § 12134 (1994).

68. 34 C.F.R. § 104 (1998).

69. 29 C.F.R. app. 1630.2(j) (1998).

70. U.S. DEPARTMENT OF JUSTICE, THE AMERICANS WITH DISABILITIES ACT: TITLE II TECHNICAL ASSISTANCE MANUAL 2 (1992).

71. *Id.*

72. *See* 42 U.S.C. §§ 12134, 12186(b) (1994).

73. U.S. DEPARTMENT OF JUSTICE, THE AMERICANS WITH DISABILITIES ACT: TITLE II TECHNICAL ASSISTANCE MANUAL 4 (1992); U.S. DEPARTMENT OF JUSTICE, THE AMERICANS WITH DISABILITIES ACT: TITLE III TECHNICAL ASSISTANCE MANUAL 9 (1992).

74. *See, e.g.,* 29 C.F.R. app. 1630.2(j) ("Determining whether a physical or mental impairment exists is only the first step in determining whether or not an individual is disabled").

75. Leading this debate on the bench has been Justice Antonin Scalia. *See generally* ANTONIN SCALIA, A MATTER OF INTERPRETATION: FEDERAL COURTS AND THE LAW (1997). Other federal judges to enter the fray are Judge Frank Easterbrook, *Symposium on Statutory Interpretation: What Does Legislative History Tell Us,* 66 CHI.-KENT L. REV. 441 (1990), former Judge Kenneth Starr, *American Civil Liberties Union v. FCC,* 823 F.2d 1554, 1583 (D.C. Cir. 1987) ("We in the judiciary have become shamelessly profligate and unthinking in our use of legislative history"), and Judge Patricia Wald, *The Sizzling Sleeper: The Use of Legislative History in Construing Statutes in the 1988–1989 Term of the United States Supreme Court,* 39 AMER. U. L. REV. 277 (1990); *see also* Richard J. Pierce Jr., *Justice Breyer: Intentionalist, Pragmatist, and Empiricist,* 8 ADMIN. L.J. AM. U. 747 (1995) (discussing the debate on the Supreme Court). Numerous academics have participated as well. *See, e.g.,* William N. Eskridge Jr., *The New Textualism,* 37 UCLA L. REV. 621 (1990); Martin H. Redish & Theodore T. Chung, *Democratic Theory and the Legislative Process:*

*Mourning the Death of Originalism in Statutory Construction*, 68 TUL. L. REV. 803 (1994).

76. *See* Eskridge, *The New Textualism*, 37 UCLA L. REV. at 625–26.

77. *See, e.g.*, Board of Educ. v. Rowley, 458 U.S. 176, 188 (1983) (construing the Education for All Handicapped Children Act, the Court stated, "Like many statutory definitions, this one tends toward the cryptic rather than the comprehensive, but that is scarcely a reason for abandoning the quest for legislative intent").

78. *See* Eskridge, *The New Textualism*, 37 UCLA L. REV. at 631.

79. *See id.* at 637.

80. This reliance is most prominently articulated in the so-called *Chevron* doctrine named after *Chevron U.S.A., Inc. v. Natural Resources Defense Council, Inc.*, 467 U.S. 837 (1984). For a discussion of *Chevron*, see Cass Diver, *Statutory Interpretation in the Administrative State*, 133 U. PA. L. REV. 549 (1985).

81. *See* Redish & Chung, *supra* note 75, at 815; Gregory E. Maggs, *Reconciling Textualism and the Chevron Doctrine: In Defense of Justice Scalia*, 22 CONN. L. REV. 393, 396–97 (1996). Intentionalism was probably most famously advanced in HENRY M. HART & ALBERT M. SAKS, THE LEGAL PROCESS: BASIC PROBLEMS IN THE MAKING AND APPLICATION OF LAW 1411 (10th ed., 1958).

82. 480 U.S. 273 (1987).

83. *See id.* at 277 (citing 123 CONG. REC. 13515 (1977) (statements of Sen. Humphrey)).

84. 480 U.S. at 280.

85. *Id.* at 279 (quoting S. REP. NO. 93–1297, at 50 (1974)).

86. *Id.* at 280. In footnote 5, Justice Brennan supported his broad reading of the regulations by citing a regulatory appendix that explained why the regulations do not provide for a comprehensive list of handicaps. *See id.* (citing 45 C.F.R. pt. 84 app. A at 310 (1985)).

87. *Id.* at 282.

88. *See* Eskridge, *The New Textualism*, 37 UCLA L. REV. at 641.

89. *See id.* at 641–42.

90. *See, e.g.*, Dunn & Delta Consultants, Inc. v. Commodity Futures Trading Comm., 519 U.S. 465, 480 (1996) (Scalia, J., concurring).

91. *See* Note, *Looking It Up: Dictionaries and Statutory Interpretation*, 107 HARV. L. REV. 1437, 1438–40 (1994).

92. *See* William Eskridge, *Textualism: The Unknown Ideal*, 96 MICH. L. REV. 1509, 1531 (1998) (reviewing ANTONIN SCALIA, A MATTER OF INTERPRETATION: FEDERAL COURTS AND THE LAW 1997) (discussing the approach of Scalia and fellow "new textualists").

93. *See, e.g.*, Thompson v. Thompson, 484 U.S. 174, 191–92 (1988) (Scalia, J., concurring) (stating that "committee reports, floor speeches, and even colloquies between congressmen . . . are frail substitutes for bicameral vote upon the text of a law and its presentment"); Hirschey v. Federal Energy Reg. Comm., 777 F.2d 1, 7–8 (D.C. Cir. 1985) (Scalia, J., concurring) (questioning use of committee reports).

94. *See* Eskridge, *The New Textualism*, 37 UCLA L. REV. at 649.

95. *See* ANTONIN SCALIA, A MATTER OF INTERPRETATION: FEDERAL COURTS AND THE LAW (1997) at 16–18.

96. *See, e.g.,* Mississippi Power Co. v. Mississippi, 487 U.S. 354, 381 (1988) (Scalia, J., concurring).

97. *See* Richard J. Pierce Jr., *The Supreme Court's New Hypertextualism: An Invitation to Cacophony and Incoherence in the Administrative State,* 95 COLUM. L. REV. 749, 751–52 (1995); Thomas W. Merrill, *Textualism and the Future of the Chevron Doctrine,* 72 WASH. U. L.Q. 351, 372 (1994); Michael Herz, *Textualism and Taboo: Interpretations and Deference for Justice Scalia,* 12 CARDOZO L. REV. 1663 (1991). For the argument that Justice Scalia applies the *Chevron* doctrine to no lesser extent than nontextualist judges, see Maggs, *supra* note 81, at 394.

98. Thus new textualists are particularly reluctant to defer to agency interpretations that do not appear in true regulations that have been promulgated pursuant to clear statutory authority to define statutory terms. *See* Public Employees Retirement Sys. of Ohio v. Betts, 492 U.S. 158 (1989).

99. *See* Chevron U.S.A., Inc. v. National Resources Defense Council, Inc., 467 U.S. 837, 844 (1984).

100. For a discussion of judicial attitudes toward the EEOC, see Rebecca Hanner White, *The EEOC, the Courts, and Employment Discrimination Policy: Recognizing the Agency's Leading Role in Statutory Interpretation,* 1995 UTAH L. REV. 51, 54–56 (arguing that the courts have given less deference to the EEOC than to other administrative agencies).

101. As Professor Eskridge notes, Justice Scalia's textualism has often been treated skeptically by his fellow justices. Moreover, it has been widely condemned by academics. *See* Eskridge, *supra* note 92, at 1513.

102. *See* Ellen P. Aprill, *The Law of the Word: Dictionary Shopping in the Supreme Court,* 30 ARIZ. ST. L.J. 275, 277 (1998) (discussing rise of textualism).

103. *See* Eskridge, *supra* note 92, at 1514.

104. For a discussion of the increasing influence of textualism on the Supreme Court, see Pierce, *supra* note 97.

105. 524 U.S. 624, 118 S. Ct. 2196 (1998). For a further discussion of *Bragdon,* see Wendy E. Parmet, *The Supreme Court Confronts HIV: Reflections on Bragdon v. Abbott,* 26 J.L. MED. & ETHICS 225 (1998).

106. The statute's goals are noted briefly only in the Court's rejection of the defendant's position that the direct threat defense should be based upon a good-faith standard. *See* 524 U.S. at 649.

107. *See id.* at 632.

108. *See id.*

109. 527 U.S. 471, 119 S. Ct. 2139 (1999).

110. The two other ADA cases decided at the same time relied heavily on the analysis contained in *Sutton. Murphy v. United Parcel Serv., Inc.,* 527 U.S. 516, 119 S. Ct. 2133 (1999), involved a UPS mechanic with high blood pressure. The Court in *Murphy* relied on its analysis in *Sutton* to determine that the plaintiff did not have a disability because his condition was controlled by medication and his employer did not believe that he was unable to perform a wide class of jobs. *See id.* at 2137–39. *Albertson's, Inc. v. Kirkingburg,* 119 S. Ct. 2162 (1999), concerned a truck driver with monocular vision. In that case the Court reiterated its holding in *Sutton* and emphasized that the determination of disability must be made on a case-by-case basis. *See id.* at 2169. In addition, the Court held that the employer's reliance on

Department of Transportation regulations setting forth the vision requirements of commercial drivers did not mean that the employer regarded the plaintiff as having "such impairment" within the third prong of the definition of disability. *See id.* at 2173–74.

111. *See id.* The Supreme Court noted that the plaintiffs failed to allege that the defendant regarded them as substantially limited in the major life activity of seeing. *See id.* at 2150. Thus, the Court did not decide whether the plaintiffs' complaint could have survived dismissal if they had raised such a claim.

112. Sutton v. United Airlines, Inc., 130 F.3d 893, 902–5 (10th Cir. 1997), *aff'd*, 119 S. Ct. 2139 (1999).

113. Most courts of appeals had held that the determination of disability should be made without regard to mitigating measures. *See* Arnold v. United Parcel Serv., Inc., 136 F.3d 854, 863 (1st Cir. 1998); Bartlett v. New York State Bd. of Law Exam'rs, 156 F.3d 321, 328–29 (2d Cir. 1998); Baert v. Euclid Beverage Ltd., 149 F.3d 626, 630 (7th Cir. 1997); Matczak v. Frankford Candy Chocolate Co., 136 F.3d 933, 937–38 (3d Cir. 1997); Holihan v. Lucky Stores, Inc., 87 F.3d 362, 363 (9th Cir. 1996). The Fifth Circuit's initial discussion of the issue, in dicta, appeared to favor consideration of mitigating measures. *See* Ellison v. Software Spectrum, Inc., 85 F.3d 187, 191 (5th Cir. 1996). In a later case, the court adopted an intermediate position, holding that some, but not all, mitigating measures should be considered. *See* Washington v. HCA Health Serv. of Texas, Inc., 152 F.3d 464, 470–71 (5th Cir. 1998), *vacated and remanded sub nom,* HCA Health Serv. of Texas v. Washington, 199 S. Ct. 2388 (1999).

114. 119 S. Ct. at 2146.

115. *See id.* at 2152 (Stevens, J., dissenting).

116. *See* Puma, *supra* note 44, at 127–28; Walsh, *supra* note 44, at 932–33.

117. 9 C.F.R. app. 1630.2(j) (1998).

118. 119 S. Ct. at 2155 (Stevens, J., dissenting).

119. *See id.* at 2161–62 (Breyer, J., dissenting). On this point, Justice Breyer explicitly disagreed with Justice O'Connor's conclusion that the EEOC lacked authority over the definition of disability.

120. 119 S. Ct. at 2161.

121. 57 F.3d 1446 (7th Cir. 1995).

122. *See id.* at 1454. Perhaps the court was able to bypass these issues because of the *Chevron* doctrine. Chevron U.S.A., Inc. v. NRDC, Inc., 467 U.S. 837 (1984). However, it may well be that the Seventh Circuit's acceptance of the EEOC's position in *Roth* was so quick and uncontested because the matter was not really outcome-determinative in the particular case before the court. Indeed, the Seventh Circuit cited the EEOC's interpretative guidelines primarily to buttress the conclusion that Roth (a physician with strabismus) did not have a disability, for the court noted that even if it disregarded the mitigating measures used by the plaintiff, he still could not show a substantial limitation to a major life activity. Hence the court's surprisingly uncritical acceptance of the EEOC's guidelines was simply dicta designed to demonstrate that even under the most generous pro-plaintiff approach, this particular plaintiff (whom the court clearly did not like) would not have a disability.

123. These cases include Arnold v. United Parcel Serv., Inc., 136 F.3d 854 (1st Cir.

1998); Matczak v. Frankford Candy & Chocolate Co., 136 F.3d 933 (3d Cir. 1997); Harris v. H.W. Contracting Co., 102 F.3d 516 (11th Cir. 1996); Liff v. Secretary of Transp., 1994 U.S. DIST. LEXIS 20970 (D.D.C. 1994); Wilson v. Pennsylvania State Police Dep't, 964 F. Supp. 898 (E.D. Pa. 1997). *Roth* was treated by the Seventh Circuit as authority in the later case of Baert v. Euclid Beverage, Ltd., 149 F.3d 626, 629 (7th Cir. 1998). Other cases to approve of the EEOC's guidelines without providing any real analysis are *Doane v. City of Omaha,* 115 F.3d 624 (8th Cir. 1997) and Sarsycki v. United Parcel Serv., 862 F. Supp. 336 (W.D. Okla. 1994).

    124. Harris, 102 F.3d at 520.

    125. Chevron, 467 U.S. at 844.

    126. *See* 102 F.3d at 521.

    127. *Id.* (citing Chevron, 467 U.S. at 843). A similar view was espoused in Wilson v. Pennsylvania State Police Dep't, 964 F. Supp. 898, 904–5 (E.D. Pa. 1997).

    128. Not surprisingly courts that rejected the position adopted by the guidelines have noted this deficiency. *See, e.g.,* Murphy v. United Parcel Serv., Inc., 141 F.3d 1185 (10th Cir. 1998); Schluter v. Industrial Coils, Inc., 928 F. Supp. 1437, 1445 (W.D. Wis. 1996); Moore v. City of Overland Park, 950 F. Supp. 1088 (D. Kan. 1996). The rejection of deference to the EEOC by these courts is considered below.

    129. *See, e.g.,* Robert A. Anthony, *The Supreme Court and the ADA: Sometimes They Just Don't Get It,* 10 ADMIN. L.J. Am. U. 1, 12–20 (1996).

    130. 136 F.3d 933 (3d Cir. 1997).

    131. 950 F. Supp. 1420 (N.D. Iowa 1996).

    132. *Id.*

    133. *Id.*

    134. *See* 119 S. Ct. at 2145. Justice O'Connor raised similar doubts in Toyota Motor Manufacturing, Kentucky, Inc. v. Williams, 534 U.S. 184, __ , 122 S.Ct. 681, 689 (2002).

    135. *See* 42 U.S.C. § 12116 (1994).

    136. 524 U.S. at 642.

    137. While no lower court denied that the EEOC had some authority over the definition of disability, the district court in Murphy v. United Parcel Serv., Inc., claimed that the agency's position itself was ambiguous and therefore not deserving of deference. *See* 946 F. Supp. 872, 881 (D. Kan. 1996), *aff'd,* 141 F.3d 1185 (10th Cir. 1998), *aff'd,* 527 U.S. 516, 119 S. Ct. 2133 (1999).

    138. *See* 119 S. Ct. at 2145–46.

    139. *See, e.g.,* Gilday v. Mecosta, Co., 124 F.3d 760, 767–68 (6th Cir. 1997); Gaddy v. Four B Corp., 953 F. Supp. 331, 337 (D. Kan. 1997); Schluter v. Industrial Coils, Inc., 928 F. Supp. 1437, 1445 (W.D. Wis. 1996).

    140. 119 S. Ct. at 2146.

    141. *See id.* at 2147–49.

    142. *See id.* Arguably, by making this claim, Justice O'Connor was herself engaging in a bit of intentionalism. However, her brand of intentionalism was far narrower than Justice Stevens's. Justice O'Connor focused solely upon Congress's intent in adopting the number cited in the preamble. She did not consider the goal of the statute as a whole or whether it could be effectuated with the interpretation she was giving it.

143. 119 S. Ct. at 2152 (Stevens, J., dissenting).

144. *Id.* at 2153 (quoting Chapman v. Houston Welfare Rights Org., 441 U.S. 600, 608 (1979)).

145. 119 S. Ct. at 2153.

146. *Id.*

147. *Id.* Justice Stevens also noted that the majority's reading means that individuals who have been completely cured of an impairment have a disability under the second prong of the definition, while those who have an ongoing, controlled impairment have no disability. *See id.*

148. *See id.* at 2158.

149. *Id.* at 2155.

150. *Id.* at 2157 (quoting Tcherenpnin v. Knight, 389 U.S. 332, 336 (1967)).

151. *See* 119 S. Ct. at 2157.

152. 136 F.3d 854 (1st Cir. 1998).

153. *Id.* at 858. In proclaiming the authority of legislative history, Judge Bownes acknowledged criticism of the "uncertainty about the value of legislative history." *Id.* at 860. From his perspective, however, the burden was clearly on those who would reject legislative history. The district court, Judge Bownes noted, provided no adequate explanation as to why it rejected the Senate report's clear pronouncements on the mitigating measures issue. *See id.*

154. *See id.* at 861.

155. 965 F. Supp. 87 (D.D.C. 1997). A similar analysis is evident in Ninth Circuit's decision in *Kirkingburg,* although the court there did not explicitly address its intentionalist analysis to the mitigating measures issue. *See* 143 F.3d 1228 (9th Cir. 1998).

156. Another case with similar facts is Wilson v. Pennsylvania State Police Dept., 964 F. Supp. 898 (E.D. Pa. 1997).

157. 965 F. Supp. at 92–93. The court erred in saying that the EEOC was not authorized by the ADA to promulgate regulations. The statute clearly gives the EEOC such authority, although as the Court noted in *Sutton,* the statutory authority does not specifically refer to the definition of disability. *See* 119 S. Ct. at 2145; 42 U.S.C. § 12116 (1994).

158. 965 F. Supp. at 93; *see also* Erjavac v. Holy Family Health Plus, 13 F. Supp. 2d 737, 744 (D. Ill. 1998) (finding that plaintiff with diabetes has a disability based upon *Arnold* and the statute's legislative history).

159. 85 F.3d 187 (5th Cir. 1996).

160. *Id.* at 191 n.3.

161. *See id.* Another example of a clearly textualist opinion on the subject is Schluter v. Industrial Coils, Inc., 928 F. Supp. 1437 (W.D. Wis. 1996).

162. *See* 119 S. Ct. at 2146 (citing 42 U.S.C. § 12102(2)(A) (1994)).

163. *Id.* at 2147.

164. *Id.* That the assessment must be individualized was also emphasized by Justice Souter in his opinion for the Court in Albertson's, Inc. v. Kirkingburg, 527 U.S. 555, 119 S. Ct. 2162, 2169 (1999).

165. *See* Sutton, 119 S. Ct. at 2147; *see also supra* text accompanying notes 193–94.

166. *See id.* at 2160 (Stevens, J., dissenting).

167.  *See, e.g.,* Michael J. Gerhardt, *A Tale of Two Textualists: A Critical Comparison of Justices Black and Scalia,* 74 B.U. L. REV. 25, 64–66 (1994); Nicholas S. Zeppos, *Legislative History and the Interpretation of Statutes: Toward a Fact-Finding Model of Statutory Interpretation,* 76 VA. L. REV. 1295, 1373–74 (1990).

168.  152 F.3d 464 (5th Cir. 1998), *vacated and remanded sub nom,* HCA Health Serv. of Texas v. Washington, 199 S. Ct. 2388 (1999).

169.  *See id.* at 469.

170.  *See id.* at 470–71.

171.  Legislative history aside, the court concluded that the term *disability* must be interpreted in accordance with common understanding.

172.  *See* Note, *Looking It Up, supra* note 91, at 1438–39.

173.  RANDOM HOUSE UNABRIDGED DICTIONARY 560 (2d. ed. 1997).

174.  *See* Fine & Asch, *supra* note 46, at 12.

175.  Scotch, *supra* note 16, at 161.

176.  *See* Victor M. Parachin, *Ten Myths About People with a Disability,* 13 VIBRANT LIFE 28, 30 (1997). These myths include that "[p]eople with disabilities always need help," and that "[t]here's nothing one person can do to help eliminate the barriers confronting people with disabilities." *Id.*

177.  Susman, *supra* note 16, at 18; *see also* Marilynn J. Phillips, *Damaged Goods: Oral Narratives of the Experience of Disability in American Culture,* 30 SOC. SCI. MED. 849, 850 (1990).

178.  Phillips, *supra* note 177, at 850.

179.  Silvers, *supra* note 13, at 54.

180.  *See id.* Ruth Colker notes that the belief that independence is the norm is critical in our individualistic and capitalistic culture. *See* Colker, *supra* note 5, at 215 ("America's version of capitalism needlessly relies on an individualistic philosophy without sufficiently considering the basic family and medical needs of workers in our society").

181.  *See* Silvers, *supra* note 13, at 17–18 (arguing that our culture stresses the importance of work, but permits benefits to people with disabilities as a safety net, recognizing the fundamental value of human life); John M. Vande Walle, Note, *In the Eye of the Beholder: Issues of Distributive and Corrective Justice in the ADA's Employment Protection for Persons Regarded as Disabled,* 73 CHI.-KENT L. REV. 897, 898 (1998).

182.  *See* Fine & Asch, *supra* note 46, at 10.

183.  *See* John M. Vande Walle, *supra* note 181, at 930–38.

184.  *See* Matthew Diller, *Entitlement and Exclusion: The Role of Disability in the Social Welfare System,* 44 UCLA L. REV. 361, 384–86 (1996).

185.  42 U.S.C. § 423(d)(1) (1994).

186.  42 U.S.C. § 423(d)(1)(A) (1994).

187.  20 U.S.C. § 1400 (1994).

188.  20 U.S.C. § 1401(a)(1)(A)(ii) (emphasis added).

189.  963 F. Supp. 1075 (E.D. Okla. 1997).

190.  *Id.* at 1080. The court in this case refused to preclude consideration of the plaintiff's corrective lenses. *See id.* at 1080 n.6.

191.  For a discussion of cases that assume that myopia is simply too common to

be considered a disability, see Carolyn V. Counce, *Corrective Devices and Nearsightedness Under the ADA,* 28 U. Mem. L. Rev. 1195, 1195–1205 (1998).

192. 928 F. Supp. 1437, 1447 (W.D. Wisc. 1996).

193. *See* Sutton, 119 S. Ct. at 2152 (Ginsburg, J., concurring).

194. *Id.*

195. 42 U.S.C. § 12117 (1994).

196. 42 U.S.C. § 12126 (1994).

*Kay Schriner and Richard K. Scotch*

# The ADA and the Meaning of Disability

For nearly a decade, the Americans with Disabilities Act (ADA)[1] has been the main protection for people with disabilities against discrimination in employment, public accommodations, public transportation, and telecommunications.[2] The act, approved in 1990 by bipartisan majorities of 377 to 28 in the House of Representatives and 91 to 6 in the Senate,[3] is a comprehensive statement of public policy: People with disabilities should not be unfairly excluded from employment, public accommodations, and other aspects of public life, and the federal government should act to protect them.[4]

One might expect that if the ADA represented a consensus in 1990, it would still enjoy widespread support today, and in fact, there have been no serious attempts in Congress to repeal or significantly limit the act. However, while popular criticism of the ADA persists,[5] the legal system has become the primary arena for challenges to the ADA's broad focus and underlying assumptions. Complaints filed under the ADA have been making their way through the administrative agencies responsible for implementation and the courts for several years now, and since 1999, the Supreme Court has issued several key decisions concerning the ADA, some of which involve the act's definition of disability. In this essay, we suggest that much of the larger disagreement over the Americans with Disabilities Act can be characterized as a clash of perspectives about the meaning of disability.

## Disability as a Sociopolitical Construct

Opinions about the Americans with Disabilities Act depend to a large extent on how one defines disability and the nature of the problems faced by people who have disabilities. The ADA was the culmination of a two-decade shift in federal disability policy.[6] For over a hundred years, disability has been defined in predominantly medical terms as a chronic functional incapacity whose consequence was functional limitations assumed to result from physical or mental impairment.[7] This model assumed that the primary problem faced by people with disabilities was the incapacity to work and otherwise participate in society. It further assumed that such incapacity was the natural product of their impairments, and to some extent their own "secondary" psychological reactions to their impairments.[8] The corollary to this assumption was that the role of government in assisting people with disabilities was both to provide financial support to this deserving group, who could not support themselves through no fault of their own, and to help in the repair and rehabilitation of their damaged bodies and minds and any psychosocial incapacity accompanying the damage.[9]

In the late 1960s, a fundamental transformation occurred in federal disability policy that rejected a primarily medical/clinical model of disability and substituted a sociopolitical or minority group model.[10] Under this model, people with disabilities may be seen as a minority group subject to unfair discrimination, and the role of government is to protect their civil rights to political, economic, and social participation by eliminating that discrimination.[11] In such a formulation, the opportunities accorded people with disabilities are limited far more by a discriminatory environment than by their impairments.

In the sociopolitical model, disability is viewed not as a physical or mental impairment, but as a social construction shaped by environmental factors, including physical characteristics built into the environment, cultural attitudes and social behaviors, and the institutionalized rules, procedures, and practices of private entities and public organizations. All of these, in turn, reflect overly narrow assumptions about what constitutes the normal range of human functioning.[12] Thus, the consequences of physical and mental impairments for social participation are shaped by the expectations and attitudes of the larger society. Michael Oliver, a leading British disability studies scholar, writes:

> All disabled people experience disability as social restriction, whether those restrictions occur as a consequence of inaccessibly built environments, questionable notions of intelligence and social competence, the inability of the general population to use sign language, the lack of reading material in Braille or hostile public attitudes to people with non-visible disabilities.[13]

Assumptions about how people perform everyday tasks, or about what people can and cannot do without assistance, are built into human environments in ways that can create barriers for those who do not conform to such expectations. If architecture and technology are based on limited images of "normal" physical functioning, they constrain individuals who must pursue alternative ways of performing various tasks. Stairs can limit the entry of people who use wheelchairs; printed words limit those who are blind. Similarly, organizational routines and public policies may limit participation through their assumptions about "normal" functioning. Fixed work schedules may exclude people whose conditions make it difficult for them to start work at 8:00 A.M., or who must take more frequent time off. Eligibility requirements for public assistance may assume that potential beneficiaries either are disabled and cannot work, or can work and therefore are not disabled. Thus, people with disabilities are frequently marginalized by the constraints of a constructed social environment in which assumptions of the inability to participate become self-fulfilling prophecies.

Building on this social model of disability is the assertion that, because they collectively occupy a stigmatized social position, people with disabilities occupy a social status analogous to that of racial and ethnic minorities.[14] People with disabilities share many of the stigmatizing experiences and characteristics of other groups commonly recognized as minorities. They are subject to prejudiced attitudes, discriminatory behavior, and institutional and legal constraints that parallel those experienced by African Americans and other disadvantaged and excluded groups.[15] People with disabilities are victimized by negative stereotypes that associate physical or mental impairment with assumed dependence on others and a general incapacity to perform social and economic activities.[16] Such stigmatizing assumptions can result in exclusion and social isolation through deprivation of access to employment, public facilities, voting, and other forms of civic involvement.[17] Because of these factors, people with disabilities are denied the opportunity to fully participate in society, a form of exclusion that public policy has defined as discrimination.[18] Using the Civil Rights Act of 1964 as its legislative model, the ADA seeks to eliminate this discrimination.[19] The sociologist Paul Higgins writes of the broad goals of the ADA:

> Rather than (primarily) looking to individual characteristics to understand the difficulties experienced by people with disabilities, rights encourage us, even require us, to evaluate our practices that may limit people with disabilities. Rights empower people with disabilities. With rights, people with disabilities may legitimately contest what they perceive to be illegitimate treatment of them. No longer

must they endure arrangements that disadvantage them to the advantage of nondisabled citizens.[20]

The ADA can be seen as more than a specific protection from discrimination—it is also a policy commitment to the social inclusion of people with disabilities. In 1986, the National Council of the Handicapped, a presidentially appointed advisory body, issued a report titled *Toward Independence* that helped lay the groundwork for the development of the ADA.[21] The report stated that

> [existing] handicap nondiscrimination laws fail to serve the central purpose of any human rights law—providing a strong statement of a societal imperative. An adequate equal opportunity law for persons with disabilities will seek to obtain the voluntary compliance of the great majority of law-abiding citizens by notifying them that discrimination against persons with disabilities will no longer be tolerated by our society.[22]

Similarly, in the introduction to her authoritative, edited volume written immediately after the ADA's passage, Jane West wrote:

> The ADA is a law that sends a clear message about what our society's attitudes should be toward persons with disabilities. The ADA is an orienting framework that can be used to construct a comprehensive service-delivery system. . . . The ADA is intended to open the doors of society and keep them open.[23]

## The Consequences of a Sociopolitical Model of Disability

Because of the ADA's reliance on a sociopolitical model of disability, it does not employ a simple conception of who is to be considered to have a disability and under what circumstances the treatment given a person with a disability should be considered discriminatory. The sociopolitical model provides a complex view of disability and disability-related discrimination by focusing upon the relationship between an individual's impairment and the nature of the environment in which that individual must function. For example, the employment provisions of the ADA define a qualified person with a disability in terms of her ability to perform the essential functions of a job with or without reasonable accommodation.[24] This definition relies on an analysis of the characteristics of the job as well as the characteristics of the person seeking the job.[25] As the statute is applied, the perceptions and expectations associated with disability and work help to shape judgments about the capacity of persons with a disability to perform adequately within specific environments.

Because of this reliance upon knowledge of the environment, the application of the ADA to specific situations may not embody a clear, abstract, behavioral standard of differential treatment. While the statute provides a number of specific examples of disability-related discrimination[26] and of reasonable accommodation,[27] the complexity of disability[28] and of workplaces[29] may mean that the ADA will lead to a wide variety of resolutions based on specific combinations of individual impairments, potential environmental obstacles, and possible adaptations by the person with the impairment. The application of ADA criteria will almost inevitably vary among individuals and across various social settings, and may pose unusual problems of interpretation for federal regulators and the courts. Paul Hearne, the director of the National Council on Disability from 1988 to 1989, writes, "The required type of accommodation will obviously vary with the individual employee, the requirements—and the purposes—of a particular job, and the environment of each workplace."[30]

The ADA was intended by its framers to change assumptions about how specific physical or mental impairments affect functioning.[31] Yet if the marginalization of people with disabilities is the result of social processes that are embedded in our culture, then it is not surprising that governmental and legal institutions as well have employed a traditional medical model of disability.[32] Public officials and the courts frequently mirror well-established limiting assumptions about people with disabilities.[33] The statute's broad definitions of who has a legitimate disability, what constitutes discrimination on the basis of disability, and what remedies are appropriate in countering such discrimination may be at odds with popular understandings of who should be treated as "truly" disabled, what their problems are, and what protections they deserve from regulators and the courts.

Further, the flexibility written into the statute may have led to a greater reliance on popular and limited conceptions of what people with various impairments can and should be allowed to do. Donald O. Parsons wrote shortly after the ADA's passage:

The human factor is likely to affect judicial behavior. . . . Cases that are either factually ambiguous or highly emotional are likely to be

determined primarily by judicial preference. . . . How a judge views
such cases will vary from judge to judge.[34]

## The Conservative Critique: Economic and Moral Dimensions of Disability

Critics in Congress, academia, and the media have attacked the ADA's
mandates, expressing skepticism over the validity of the claims of those
seeking protection from discrimination related to disability and the efficacy
of a civil rights (as opposed to a market) approach to improving the status
of people with disabilities.[35] To critics, the ADA is a case of ill-considered
social engineering in which an overly broad category of putative victims
claimed unreasonable accommodations from society. For example, Dick
Armey, Republican House Majority Leader since 1994, has called the ADA
"a disaster," predicting, "Under my majority leadership, the disabilities act
will be revisited and will be written properly so its focus and intent goes to
people with genuine disabilities."[36]

As discussed above, the medical model of disability characterizes people
with disabilities as having pathological individual attributes, typically
linked to incapacity and dependence, which in turn may lead to social and
economic isolation. This model can accommodate recognition of discrimination as a problem associated with disability, but it emphasizes that people with disabilities must "overcome" the limitations of their impairments
in order to function in society. By focusing on adaptations required from
people with disabilities, the medical model implies far less from employers
or other social gatekeepers in terms of accommodation since the environment is taken as given.[37] With regard to employment, the model suggests
that people with disabilities ought to adapt themselves to the demands of
productivity set in the marketplace. Efficiency concerns of firms should
outweigh claims of disabled job applicants, despite any social costs (or in
the language of economics, negative externalities) that might be generated
for society at large. One leading critic, Carolyn Weaver, has written of the
ADA:

> The legislation thus includes in the protected population people who,
> in an economic sense, are not as productive or do not make the same
> contribution to the profitability of the firm as other people with the
> same qualifications. (These are the people who can perform only the

essential functions of the job and who can do so only with accommodation.) While promoting the employment of this much broader group may be a highly desirable social goal, the antidiscrimination–reasonable accommodation approach is a costly and inefficient way of doing so and is likely to have highly undesirable distributional consequences.[38]

The conservative critique of the ADA is not solely based on grounds of economic efficiency, however. Beyond the issue of productivity is a recurrent concern about the moral legitimacy of claims made by individuals with disabilities on employers and public officials. The issue of moral basis for disability policy is a recurrent historical theme in American social welfare policy. Deborah Stone writes that the popular conception of disability "is best understood as a moral notion. . . . Disability . . . is an essential part of the moral economy."[39] Similarly, Theda Skocpol writes, "Institutional and cultural oppositions between the morally 'deserving' and the less deserving run like fault lines through the entire history of American social provision."[40]

Political conservatives have traditionally expressed concerns in social policy debates that "undeserving" people might benefit from public programs.[41] The ADA's legislative history establishes a broad and comprehensive definition of disability, including people with HIV/AIDS, most psychiatric conditions, and those with a history of substance abuse.[42] Conservative critics expressed great discomfort with this broad definition. For example, a publication of the Republican National Committee has included the ADA's regulations among those that are well intentioned but spiraling "out of control," at least in part because of their inclusion of "drug abusers, the obese and the 'emotionally disturbed'" among those protected.[43]

Frequently there is a moral dimension to this concern. Individuals who have conditions that are associated with engaging in morally questionable behavior or who are perceived as representing a lack of self-control or poor character may be seen as unworthy of public support. Even for some within the disability community, individuals with these conditions are not considered to be in the same moral category as people with visual or hearing impairments, or those who use wheelchairs. Some critics would even question the legitimacy of coverage for individuals with back problems, the impairment (along with spinal conditions) most often cited in early ADA complaints,[44] because the diagnosis of such problems is often based on self-reports of pain and the inability to perform certain tasks.[45]

Similar doubts may be raised about the moral legitimacy of the ADA by complaints that are based on conditions that some may perceive as frivolous expressions of self-indulgent victimhood such as obesity or chemical sensitivity. While people portrayed in media accounts as sad, angry, or troubled may have bona fide disabling conditions under the ADA's definitions, there may be little public sympathy for their claims. Media coverage of individuals claiming discrimination because they are fat, or phobic, or sensitive to environmental chemicals may color public perceptions of disability discrimination, regardless of the legal validity of the complaints or their ultimate disposition. The focus of criticism and stories in the media may create an image among the public about who benefits from the law that may overshadow the empirical reality of the great majority of disability discrimination and its victims.[46]

Do such concerns, based on perceptions shaped by the lenses of a limited, skeptical, and stigmatizing model of disability, constitute a backlash to the Americans with Disabilities Act? The act is still in place, unamended and intact, and there has been no serious attempt to repeal it, even at the zenith of conservative power in Congress. Similarly, there have been media accounts that cast a skeptical light on the act,[47] but these may be no worse than traditional coverage of disability rights issues. A few media horror stories have not led to any major public outcry against the ADA or people with disabilities. From a larger social standpoint, then, there may be a reservoir of good will toward the concepts underlying the ADA and toward protecting people with disabilities from discrimination and unfair treatment. Despite some high-profile grumbling from political conservatives, the Americans with Disabilities Act appears to enjoy strong support among the public and two of the three branches of government.

## The ADA and the Courts

The courts, however, are a different matter. The decade-long period of judicial interpretation of the ADA has raised serious doubts about its potential to accomplish the far-reaching results envisioned at its passage. Among other problems, we have seen many persons with disabilities refused coverage under the ADA and challenges mounted to the federal government's incursion into state affairs. To some degree, these events are part of a larger move to rebalance federal-state relations.[48] But they also reflect a deep and abiding misunderstanding of (and perhaps hostility toward) the ADA's formulation of disability discrimination and the nature of the remedies it would impose. The developments of the last ten years now suggest that the ADA is insufficient to accomplish the social change required to ensure equal opportunity for persons with disabilities, particularly in the contemporary legal climate.

A primary concern is the inability of disabled individuals to get their day in court. In case after case, courts have ruled that plaintiffs are not covered under the ADA's three-prong definition, which provides coverage to individuals with "a physical or mental impairment that substantially limits one or more of the major life activities," who have "a record of such an impairment," or who are "regarded as having such an impairment." Quite unexpectedly, courts have applied narrow interpretations of the definition, with the end result being what one commentator has referred to as "the incredible shrinking protected class."[49]

The instances of definitional narrowing are legion. Many of these cases involve the application of the ADA's first definitional prong. The presence of a serious physical or mental impairment often is insufficient to convince a court that the individual is covered by the act. Rather, courts are examining in great detail the effect such an impairment has on the individual's capacity to function. In contrast to case law under the Rehabilitation Act (on which the ADA's disability definition was based and under which individuals with impairments typically easily met the threshold definition), plaintiffs are routinely being carefully scrutinized to determine their status. In one instance, for example, a law firm that had terminated a legal secretary for poor performance was granted summary judgment on the basis that she was not a covered individual under the ADA. The court held that the secretary's condition (ulcerative colitis of the rectum that caused "frequent and painful diarrhea, stomach cramps, and rectal bleeding") was not an impairment that substantially limited a major life activity, despite the plaintiff's contention that her condition affected her ability to care for herself and eliminate bodily waste.[50] In another, a plaintiff with a serious arm injury that affected her ability to lift, hold, and manipulate objects was ruled not disabled because the effect of her impairment was not substantial.[51] Neither plaintiff was given the opportunity to have her case heard on the merits.

The failure of the courts to find plaintiffs covered by the ADA at times appears simply absurd. The Fifth Circuit court held in *Robinson v. Global Marine Drilling Co.* that a man whose lung capacity was 50 percent of normal due to asbestosis was not substantially limited in a major life activity, though the plaintiff experienced shortness of breath when climbing stairs or ladders. Breathing is a major life activity, said the court, but "[s]everal instances of shortness of breath when climbing stairs do not rise to the level of substantially limiting the major life activity of breathing."[52] The Fifth Circuit overturned a jury verdict in Robinson's favor because he was not covered by the ADA.

Often plaintiffs are denied coverage under the ADA because courts interpret the "substantially limited" provision as applied to the major life activity of working to mean that a plaintiff must be restricted in the ability to perform a *whole class* of jobs, not just the specific job at issue. This tendency started with a few cases decided under the Rehabilitation Act and intensified following passage of the ADA. Under this analysis, a plaintiff would have to show that he or she was "significantly restricted in the ability to perform either a class of jobs or a broad range of jobs in various classes as compared to the average person having comparable training, skills and abilities."[53]

A typical example is that of Allan Redlich, a law professor whose stroke in 1983 left him partially paralyzed. Redlich claimed that the law school had discriminated against him because of his disability when it granted him lower pay raises following his stroke. The court granted summary judgment to the university, holding that the professor was not substantially limited in working. Relying on the plaintiff's own evidence regarding his ongoing teaching, research, and service activities, the court ruled that he was not "significantly restricted in his ability to perform the class of job in which he was engaged, that of law professor."[54]

Other discrimination claims have foundered on the question of what constitutes a major life activity. Courts have placed great emphasis on the requirement that the life activity that is affected by an impairment is in fact *major*. One plaintiff diagnosed as mildly mentally retarded and learning disabled experienced a "breakdown" because of the stress caused when her employer required employees to reorganize into teams, with each member bearing new responsibility for the performance of all team tasks rather than the one discrete task each had been previously assigned. The company subsequently claimed that the employee, Denise Anderson, was not "disabled" as defined by the ADA because her impairment did not cause a substantial limitation in a major life activity—despite her claim that her mother tended to her business affairs because of her incapacity. The court ruled that taking care of one's business affairs "might be a sub-category of the major life activity of taking care of one's self" but "is not a stand-alone major life activity."[55]

In other instances, courts refuse to define a person as covered by the ADA by virtue of being "regarded as" having an impairment that substantially limits major life activities. One plaintiff with breast cancer alleged that her employer "regarded" her as having a disability based on statements made by her supervisor, including that her breasts were not worth saving and that she glowed in the dark.[56] The court disagreed, saying that while such comments were "beneath contempt," they did not prove that the employer considered the woman to have a substantially limiting impairment, and thus she was not covered under the ADA's "regarded as" prong. In another instance, Mayerson reports that her client, a man wearing a hearing aid, was not allowed to pursue his claim of discrimination because the court ruled that his employer did not regard him as disabled, even though the employer admitted that the plaintiff was not hired "because he wore a hearing aid."[57]

The Supreme Court has added to the problem with their decisions regarding the use of mitigating measures. The question of mitigating measures arises when an individual with an impairment uses medication, devices, or equipment to improve functioning. The use of mitigating measures was discussed during the writing of the ADA, and Congress indicated its intent that plaintiffs' disability status be determined without regard to the use of such measure.[58] But in three cases involving the use of mitigating measures, the Supreme Court held that the determination of whether plaintiffs are disabled under the ADA must take into account the use of such measures—in direct contradiction of congressional intent. In *Sutton v. United Airlines, Inc.,* the Court considered the case of twin sisters with severe myopia who wore corrective lenses but were denied employment as pilots by United Airlines because they failed to meet the visual acuity requirement. The Court held that they were not substantially limited in a major life activity—as determined in an individualized assessment of their status when wearing corrective lenses. In other words, "disability under the Act is to be determined with reference to corrective measures."[59] Two companion cases proceeded along similar lines. In *Murphy v. United Parcel Service,*[60] a mechanic who took medication for high blood pressure was determined not to have a disability because his medical condition was controlled. In *Albertson's, Inc. v. Kirkingburg,*[61] the Court held that an employer's reliance on federal regulations specifying vision requirements for commercial drivers should not be interpreted as meaning that the employer regarded an employee with monocular vision as having a disability under the "regarded as" prong of the definition.

Observers have interpreted these various rulings as related to more general trends within the federal courts and to the courts' experience with other federal disability legislation. Some courts are applying rules of textualism to their readings of the Americans with Disabilities Act in ways that effectively reduce its reach, contrary to the intent of Congress. This has been especially apparent in the disability definition cases. The training of defense attorneys following the passage of the ADA may partly account for this trend. Chai Feldblum argues that because many of these attorneys were unfamiliar with the more generous interpretation of the Rehabilitation Act's definition of disability (on which the ADA's definition was based), they were more likely to parse the three-prong definition—especially in light of the ADA regulations that emphasized individualized assessment and the importance of the substantial limitation and major life activity provisions.[62]

But the trend toward textualism—in which courts rely on the "plain meaning" of the statute itself with little or no regard for the explanations of statutory language likely to be found within the legislative history—exacerbates the problem by limiting the knowledge base on which courts can rely to understand the intentions of Congress when it passes broad remedial legislation such as the ADA. This no doubt has contributed to the poor showing of plaintiffs in the courts; a recent study by the ABA's Commission on Mental and Physical Disability Law shows that defendants prevailed in 92 percent of the cases.[63]

It may also be that courts' experience with disabled individuals themselves is a reason for the unexpected reactions some people with disabilities have encountered. The traditional disabled plaintiff appearing in federal court is the individual seeking disability insurance benefits where the evidence presented concerns that person's *inability to work*, which in turn secures an economic benefit from the insurance program. Courts' experience with this type of claim may explain their tendency to evaluate the disability status of a plaintiff in terms of work capacity. When courts are used to hearing plaintiffs proclaim their inability to work (a showing necessary to qualify for income from the program), they may be more likely to apply a work-based evaluation in ADA cases as well, and thus the tendency of the courts to assess the major life activity in terms of work ability.[64]

The courts' history with disability insurance applicants may also help account for the apparent hostility of some courts toward plaintiffs for rights-based claims under the Americans with Disabilities Act. Some plaintiffs, argues Fordham law professor Diller, have been seen as "whiners making excuses."[65] Rather than perceiving these issues as involving protections against disability-based discrimination in the workplace, courts have tended to view ADA cases as "requests for special benefits made by employees who are performing poorly."[66]

The upshot of case law over the last decade is that courts have a troubling proclivity to find that "no one has a disability."[67] At the very least, it is quite possible that an individual with say, epilepsy, will be considered as having a disability in one court but not another.[68] With these unforeseen applications of the ADA, plaintiffs face daunting challenges in proving that they are covered individuals under the act. We are thus left wondering how the ADA's other provisions would be interpreted in these cases. Given that civil rights statutes historically have been broadly interpreted by the courts, in part to ensure that the complaints of aggrieved persons will be heard, it is disappointing that disabled plaintiffs were not given the opportunity to prove their allegations of discrimination. Halting the process at the threshold question of coverage has kept many disabled persons from arguing their cases in the courts, despite Congress's intention that they be permitted to have their claims heard.

Arguing the cases on the merits would be far preferable to dismissing them outright on the basis of an overly narrow application of the ADA's definition of disability. Then we might be able to determine what workplace arrangements can and must be modified to accommodate a wider range of human characteristics. Is it not more relevant to debate the business necessity of say, vision requirements for airline pilots than whether applicants using corrective lenses are "disabled" under the ADA? Is it not more important that we contest the applicability of a blood pressure requirement for truck drivers than whether the driver who medicates his high blood pressure is "disabled"? The law professor's claim of discrimination may have been dismissed due to his failure to provide sufficient evidence, as Chai Feldblum has suggested,[69] but at least we would have to confront the professor's argument that the lower pay raises he received constituted disability discrimination. Similarly, Arlene Mayerson's deaf client should have had the opportunity to define the employer's decision to not hire him "because he wore a hearing aid" as discriminatory and thus illegal under the ADA.

In addition to the narrow issue of statutory interpretation regarding the class of individuals protected by the ADA, there is also the broader question of what conduct violates the constitutional guarantee to equal protection under the law. Recent shifts in constitutional interpretation are calling into question a basic premise of the ADA—that the failure to provide reasonable accommodations to persons with disabilities constitutes disability discrimination and thus violates the Fourteenth Amendment. In the 1985 *Cleburne* decision, the Supreme Court followed its practice of deferring to state legislatures in treating some groups of individuals differently than others, but held that such classifications must be "rationally related to a legitimate state interest."[70] Conduct reflecting "mere negative attitudes" and "vague, undifferentiated fears" would violate the Fourteenth Amendment's equal protection clause.[71]

In hearings on the ADA, Congress expanded on the analysis of disability-based discrimination. Hearing testimony from numerous sources, including the U.S. Commission on Civil Rights, the Advisory Commission on Intergovernmental Relations, and the congressionally appointed Task Force on the Rights and Empowerment of Americans with Disabilities, Congress accumulated an extensive record of discriminatory conduct based on discomfort and aversion, stigmatization, stereotyping, and paternalism.[72] Finally it fashioned a broad remedy that would affect both the private and public sectors.

The Americans with Disabilities Act thus was based on precedent and legislative fact-finding. Consistent with Fourteenth Amendment jurisprudence, Congress believed it had acted appropriately and constitutionally to remedy a long history of disability-based discrimination at the hands of the states and other actors. Recently, however, the ground of constitutional interpretation has shifted, with more emphasis placed on the rights of states to govern their own affairs without the heavy hand of federal interference. In a series of cases, the Supreme Court has reshaped the relationship between the national and state governments. Federal action is now constrained by requirements that, first, there be a showing of unconstitutional conduct by the states that justifies federal law, and, second, that federal action is congruent and proportional to the constitutional violation. Congress may enact legislation "both to remedy and to deter violation[s] of rights guaranteed [by the Fourteenth Amendment] by prohibiting a somewhat broader swath of conduct, including that which is not itself forbidden by the Amendment's text."[73] The congruence and proportionality test applies to the size of the swath; the "bigger the jelly center (constitutional violations), the bigger the donut (swath) can be."[74]

In *University of Alabama v. Garrett,* the Supreme Court applied these tests in deciding whether Congress had the authority to abrogate states' Eleventh Amendment immunity to private lawsuits for money damages brought under Title I of the ADA. The Court held that Congress had failed to compile a record of disability discrimination that would justify the imposition of the ADA's requirements on the states. The majority cited the small number of instances of states' employment-related discrimination in the legislative record and concluded that these failed to meet the standard it has set for demonstrating the presence of unconstitutional conduct by the states. The incidents considered by Congress "taken together fall far short of even suggesting the pattern of unconstitutional discrimination" required.[75] The Court went further. Even if it were to find the record satisfactory, there would still be questions regarding the congruence and proportionality of the ADA's requirements for reasonable accommodations. The provision of reasonable accommodations to ensure equal access to the workplace "far exceeds what is constitutionally required" because it "makes unlawful a range of alternate responses that would be reasonable but would fall short of imposing an 'undue burden' on the employer."[76] In the context of employment, states could "quite hard headedly—and perhaps hardheartedly" enforce job qualifications that "do not make allowance for the disabled."[77] It "would be entirely rational (and therefore constitutional) for a state employer to conserve scarce financial resources by hiring employees who are able to use existing facilities. . . ."[78]

The Court's decision in *Garrett* appears to depart from the formulation of unconstitutional state conduct found in *Cleburne* and related cases. *Cleburne* has emphasized that disability-based distinctions based on negative attitudes and fear raise concern about the rationality of such distinctions and thus their constitutionality, but *Garrett* strongly suggests that the current Court is less troubled by these attitudinal indicators. Negative attitudes and fear may *accompany* irrational conduct, but "their presence alone does not a constitutional violation make."[79] A claim of irrational distinction will have to "negative 'any reasonably conceivable state of facts that could provide a rational basis for the classification.' "[80]

This conclusion seems to indicate a misunderstanding of the nature and extent of disability discrimination. The "rationality" of job performance standards and other employment-related practices may be apparent only to those who possess the very attitudes and fears that the Court now says are constitutional. Arguing for the presence of, for example, rigid physical examination requirements that are entirely irrelevant to job performance of the jobs in question may be justified as rational by those who believe myths about the incapacities of persons with impairments. A requirement that individuals with amputated limbs wear prostheses before they can be hired, even when it might not be required to meet job demands, may appear rational to an observer who finds negative reactions to the absence of limbs unobjectionable.[81] The majority does not deny that there is discriminatory behavior. Indeed, the opinion notes that Congress's general findings regarding the presence of disability discrimination were supported by the record assembled during debate on the ADA.[82] The Court simply refuses to elevate it to its proper place as unconstitutional inequality before the law.

By apparently retreating from *Cleburne,* the *Garrett* Court seems to grant a pass to states to make distinctions that might be justified before an uninquisitive court. The rational basis test requires the Court to be deferential toward the people's legislative representatives who consider a range of facts and views in their policy deliberations. But in *Cleburne,* a city's denial of a special use permit for a group home for individuals with intellectual impairments was subjected to a close inspection to determine the motives of city officials. Finding that their conduct rested on irrational prejudice, the denial was found to be an unconstitutional violation of the Fourteenth Amendment.

In *Garrett,* the Court directed its deference differently, showing considerably more deference to *state* legislatures than it did to the *federal* legislature. The double standard did not go unnoticed by the minority, who said that "it is difficult to understand why the Court, which applies minimum rational-basis review to statutes that *burden* persons with disabilities . . . subjects to far stricter scrutiny a statute that seeks to *help* those same individuals."[83] In any event, the *Garrett* decision suggests that the judiciary will be less likely to scrutinize the motive of states than it was under *Cleburne.*

The *Garrett* decision is perhaps an unfortunate harbinger of legal things to come. If abandoning "hardheaded" and "hard-hearted" conduct that may also reflect negative attitudes and fear is not required to accommodate people with disabilities, the likelihood is that the lives of people with disabilities will not be much improved, at least not at the behest of the courts under the Americans with Disabilities Act. This conduct is precisely the sort Congress meant to address by the ADA, and the courts' narrowing of its scope renders it less effective. Clearly, raising the consciousness of the current Court about the nature and extent of disability-based discrimination is an unfinished task.

## The Policy Implications of the Human Variation Model

The potential utility of the Americans with Disabilities Act to improve the lives of people with disabilities depends on its full and faithful interpretation by the courts, but, with or without that, we must also consider the potential of the ADA to reach all the barriers encountered by individuals with disabilities in their quest for equality and integration. Resting our collective hopes on a civil rights strategy could have paid off—in theory at least. The ADA's disparate impact prohibition and reasonable accommodation requirement, properly understood, offer the possibility for significant reconstruction of social attitudes and practices as well as the built environment. But for it to accomplish the far-reaching change that is necessary would require a much more receptive judiciary than currently exists and, given the difficulty of using the law to produce a change of heart, probably a more receptive public as well. Moreover, the inherent limitations of the sociopolitical/civil rights model—as applied in the context of American political and legal tradition—pose conceptual and practical obstacles to the transformation of society.

The limitations of the sociopolitical model of disability and its predecessors suggest that approaches such as the human variation model may be necessary for us to fully understand and address the obstacles of participation and integration faced by people with disabilities. The human variation model, as we have already indicated, may help us find a way out of the conceptual morass of disability by starting from the assumption that person-environment relationships and interactions are complex and in constant flux. An individual with an impairment may be disabled at one moment and not the next depending on the environment in which she finds herself. Impairments themselves can be temporary, permanent, or cyclical.[84] The relationship between impairment and life roles such as working also may vary from individual to individual. Two individuals with the same "objective" condition such as, say, arthritis may respond very differently, with one continuing to work and the other not. Systemic conditions too are varied and variable. Family structures and resources differ; one community may offer more support to individuals who need it than another, and some employers are more responsive to the needs of their employees and their families than are others. Macrosystem conditions such as the economic cycle can dictate patterns of unemployment and underemployment that more indirectly affect the ability of individuals with various impairments to participate in the workforce. When the labor market offers fewer full-time permanent positions and more contingent and part-time positions, the relative ability of the individual with a disability to work will be affected.[85]

A singular reliance on prohibitions to discrimination will almost certainly fail to reach all of the nooks and crannies where disadvantage is lodged in these complex person-environment relationships. Not every barrier is the result of prejudice and discrimination, or even unintentional differential treatment that creates an obstacle; impairments themselves often cause differences in functional abilities that are relevant to considerations of possible public policy responses. Even the broad definition of disability discrimination that requires reasonable accommodations and modifications and that prohibits disparate impact could not address all of the impediments faced by persons with impairments. In many cases, the less advantaged life circumstances of individuals with disabilities are caused by multiple factors that no doubt include these forms of discrimination but also include atypical physical and mental functioning. Responding to these many causal factors will require several coordinated approaches to address the full range of variables that might contribute to an optimal person-environment fit.

The ADA's reasonable accommodation and modification requirements are clearly among the approaches that are required to broaden the range of environmental niches for individuals. The ADA's essential message is that social institutions can and should embrace more flexibility in arranging workplaces and other environmental settings. When employers allow individuals with health conditions flexible work schedules to pursue medical treatment while still performing the essential functions of a job, it increases the probability that such persons can maintain employment. If employers were to permit persons with limited intellectual abilities to perform a specific job even when other employees were required to perform a wide range of jobs, it would create a niche in which those individuals could function and be valued. But when achieved by virtue of a legal mandate, such accommodation may come at a high price by creating confrontation where cooperation would be preferred. As we have stated elsewhere:

> A human variation perspective on employment suggests that lack of access to employment by persons with disabilities be resolved by cooperatively maximizing each individual's productivity rather than by staking out and defending legal entitlements to employment based on membership in a minority group. The perspective defines the problem of employing people with disabilities as one of having employers view individuals as potential contributors rather than as members of groups whose legal status threatens the autonomy of business judgments.[86]

We also may need to consider the possibility that there are limits to environmental flexibility.[87] Of course, the ADA recognizes this in its requirement that a disabled person be "otherwise qualified" and able to perform the essential functions of the job with reasonable accommodations if necessary. Employers are not required to employ individuals who cannot meet the needs of the firm.

There are numerous impairments that, in the context of the workplace, may so seriously interfere with an individual's ability to perform a particular job that no reasonable accommodation will suffice. Some conditions may so inhibit an individual's work performance that the person is unable to perform a job's essential functions. The determination of whether individuals are "otherwise qualified" when those individuals have mental illness are illustrative in this regard. Employers have not been required by the courts to continue to employ

a programmer with depression whose workplace stress could not be controlled sufficiently by reducing her overtime and avoiding deadline-intensive work; a man with recurrent depression who had difficulty completing tasks on time, getting along with his boss, and supervising other people; a field representative with a bipolar disorder who acted inappropriately with co-workers and had requested a second extended medical leave of absence for treatment; a restaurant manager with depression who could only work the day shift and no more than 40 hours a week; a customer service representative whose panic attacks prevented her from using the telephone.[88]

In each case, the individual's ability to do the job (with reasonable accommodations if necessary) was the issue. Employers were not required to alter the workplace so much with respect to those particular jobs that it could accommodate the differences of these individuals.

When viewed from this perspective, the ADA's inherent limitations (quite apart from its interpretation by the courts) become starkly apparent. Employers and other covered entities are not required to make changes in their normal course of business that would pose undue burdens or fundamentally alter programs or activities. Indeed, the evidence thus far strongly suggests that not only are defendants winning many more ADA cases than would be expected, but also that those individuals who are benefiting are those whose impairments are less severe, not those persons whose more severe disabilities (such as mental illness and intellectual disability) make them among the most vulnerable members of the disability community.[89]

Improving the opportunities for integration and participation for these more severely impaired individuals will require social welfare policies of the type more traditionally thought of as disability policy. Though these must be reformed to reflect more contemporary notions about the *capabilities* of persons with disabilities (as in the new work incentives that may help disability insurance beneficiaries return to work) and the importance of the *environment* (as in programs to further integration by subsidizing home ownership among persons with intellectual disabilities), they are nonetheless an integral part of a modern disability policy agenda.

Approaches that would "incentivize" employment and other desirable outcomes may also be required. Burkhauser[90] has proposed tax credits for employers' and individuals' accommodation expenses to encourage the provision of accommodations in the workplace, as well as income subsidies for persons with disabilities who are in the labor force. These are possible policy choices that are conceptually independent of rights-based claims and thus have the advantage of avoiding the disputes such claims provoke (though they admittedly have disadvantages all their own).

## Civil Rights and Social Change

The Americans with Disabilities Act is a potentially crucial protection for people with disabilities. Beyond the specific outcomes of legal proceedings, the ADA's mandates have led to significant expansion of access to the social, economic, and political mainstream by raising awareness about disability issues and by providing incentives to businesses and other covered entities to do the right thing. However, whatever legal protection from discrimination has been gained, it would be very difficult to argue that people with disabilities have achieved social or economic parity as the result of the ADA, or that having a disability is no longer a relevant factor in the life chances of many individuals.

But that might be far too much to expect from a civil rights law. People with disabilities face a variety of barriers to social participation, including limited human capital, social isolation, and cultural stereotypes.[91] While all of these can be directly linked to discrimination, none of them will be easily changed by an act of Congress. Fundamental and far-reaching social change will be necessary for people with disabilities to enjoy full access to American society.

The experience of African Americans has implications for the potential of civil rights statutes to serve as vehicles for overcoming social disadvantage. While Jim Crow laws and legal segregation have been abolished, the research community is divided on the effects of equal opportunity policy for African Americans' incomes and access to employment.[92] Poorly educated African Americans as a group are relatively worse off in terms of earnings or employment than they were thirty years ago, and the state of black-white relations remains far short of the goals of the civil rights movement of the 1960s.[93] In fact, one of the most contentious issues in the current debate over race relations is affirmative action. The concept of affirmative action requires employers and others to take positive steps to overcome the historic disadvantages experienced by members of minority groups and women. In some ways, the concept is analogous to the positive accommodations needed to make employment, education, public accommodations, and other institutional spheres truly accessible to Americans with disabilities.

Just as the economic and social challenges facing many African Americans are not likely to be resolved by civil rights laws alone, the social exclusion of people with disabilities will not be resolved by the ADA on its own. Access to good jobs, health insurance, personal assistance, community-based services, and accessible technologies will be enhanced, but not guaranteed, by laws such as the ADA. Antidiscrimination laws may be necessary, but not sufficient, for major institutional change.

Might we then expect that the ADA can at least end overt discrimination committed on the basis of disability? If the sociopolitical model of disability is correct, even this may be too great a burden to place on the legal system. The stigma associated with disability is so embedded and reinforced within our culture and social structure that only tremendous efforts will root it out.[94] As we have experienced in race and gender equity issues, changing cultural values and social relationships that have become institutionalized in the informal patterns of everyday life may be beyond the capacity of statutory mandates. As Donald L. Horowitz has pointed out, the courts have a built-in emphasis on formal relationships, and may lack the capacity to alter informal patterns of behavior.[95] Such an effort may be a more appropriate task for a broadly based social and political disability movement than for a law dependent on judicial and regulatory enforcement. Interpersonal contacts may help to break down pernicious stereotypes and arbitrary limitations on people with disabilities. Grassroots advocates may be better able to educate communities about the nature of the barriers faced by people with disabilities and how the participation of people with disabilities can be achieved with beneficial results. Legal protections from discriminatory practice are probably indispensable, but such guarantees cannot be the only strategy toward ending the discrimination and social exclusion faced by Americans with disabilities.

NOTES

1. 42 U.S.C. § 12101 (1994).

2. A brief overview of the impact of the ADA is provided in FRED PELKA, THE ABC-CLIO COMPANION TO THE DISABILITY RIGHTS MOVEMENT 18–22 (1997).

3. *See id.* at 20.

4. *See* Jane West, *The Social and Policy Context of the Act, in* THE AMERICANS WITH DISABILITIES ACT: FROM POLICY TO PRACTICE 3, 21 (Jane West ed., 1991).

5. *See, e.g.,* Cary LaCheen, *Achy Breaky Pelvis, Lumber Lung, and Juggler's Despair: The Portrayal of the Americans with Disabilities Act on Television and Radio,* 21 BERKELEY J. EMP. & LAB. L. 223 (2000).

6. For a discussion of this transformation, see RICHARD K. SCOTCH, FROM GOOD WILL TO CIVIL RIGHTS: TRANSFORMING FEDERAL DISABILITY POLICY (1984).

7. *See* Harlan Hahn, *Towards a Politics of Disability: Definitions, Disciplines, and Policies,* SOC. SCI. J., Oct. 1985, at 87, 88–89 [hereinafter Hahn, *Towards a Politics*]. For a discussion of the historical roots of disability as a clinical concept in public policy, see DEBORAH A. STONE, THE DISABLED STATE 90–117 (1984). For an extended summary and critical discussion of the medical model of disability, see GARY L. ALBRECHT, THE DISABILITY BUSINESS: REHABILITATION IN AMERICA 67–90 (1992).

8. *See, e.g.,* ROBERT A. SCOTT, THE MAKING OF BLIND MEN 6–8 (1969).

9. For a history of the federal vocational rehabilitation system, see EDWARD D. BERKOWITZ, DISABLED POLICY: AMERICA'S PROGRAMS FOR THE HANDICAPPED (1987).

10. *See* Scotch, *supra* note 6, at 8–9. For a general discussion of the minority group model, see Harlan Hahn, *Introduction: Disability Policy and the Problem of Discrimination,* 28 AM. BEHAV. SCIENTIST 293 (1985) [hereinafter *Disability Policy*].

11. *See* Hahn, *Towards a Politics, supra* note 7, at 93–96.

12. For a discussion of the consequences of a mismatch between natural human variation and the limited expectations built into social environments, see Richard K. Scotch & Kay Schriner, *Disability as Human Variation: Implications for Policy,* 549 ANNALS AM. ACAD. POL. & SOC. SCI. 148, 154–57 (1997).

13. MICHAEL OLIVER, THE POLITICS OF DISABLEMENT: A SOCIOLOGICAL APPROACH at xiv (1990), *quoted in* Len Barton et al., *Disability and the Necessity for a Socio-Political Perspective, in* 51 WORLD REHABILITATION FUND MONOGRAPH 5 (International Exchange of Experts and Information in Rehabilitation eds., 1992).

14. *See* Hahn, *Disability Policy, supra* note 10, at 300–301.

15. *See generally* FRANK BOWE, HANDICAPPING AMERICA: BARRIERS TO DISABLED PEOPLE (1978); JOHN GLIEDMAN & WILLIAM ROTH, THE UNEXPECTED MINORITY (1980); LOUIS HARRIS AND ASSOCIATES, INC., THE ICD SURVEY OF DISABLED AMERICANS: BRINGING DISABLED AMERICANS INTO THE MAINSTREAM (1986); NATIONAL COUNCIL ON THE HANDICAPPED, TOWARD INDEPENDENCE: AN ASSESSMENT OF FEDERAL LAWS AND PROGRAMS AFFECTING PERSONS WITH DISABILITIES—WITH LEGISLATIVE RECOMMENDATIONS (1986) [hereinafter TOWARD INDEPENDENCE].

16. For an extensive review of stereotypes commonly associated with disability and their consequences, see IMAGES OF THE DISABLED, DISABLING IMAGES (Alan Gartner & Tom Joe eds., 1987).

17. *See id.*

18. For a discussion of how the civil rights framework became associated with the status of people with disabilities, see RICHARD K. SCOTCH, FROM GOOD WILL TO CIVIL RIGHTS: TRANSFORMING FEDERAL CIVIL RIGHTS POLICY (1984).

19. *See id.* at 51–52.

20. PAUL C. HIGGINS, MAKING DISABILITY: EXPLORING THE SOCIAL TRANS-FORMATION OF HUMAN VARIATION 199–200 (1992).

21. *See* TOWARD INDEPENDENCE, *supra* note 15, at 18–21; *see also* NATIONAL COUNCIL ON DISABILITY, EQUALITY OF OPPORTUNITY: THE MAKING OF THE AMERICANS WITH DISABILITIES ACT (1997) (providing an account of the policy development process culminating in the enactment of the ADA).

22. TOWARD INDEPENDENCE, *supra* note 15, at 18.

23. Jane West, *The Social and Policy Context of the Act, in* THE AMERICANS WITH DISABILITIES ACT: FROM POLICY TO PRACTICE 3, 22 (Jane West ed., 1991).

24. 42 U.S.C. § 12111(8) (1994).

25. *See, e.g.,* Chai R. Feldblum, *Employment Protections, in* THE AMERICANS WITH DISABILITIES ACT: FROM POLICY TO PRACTICE 81, 88–90 (Jane West ed., 1991).

26. *Id.* at 90.

27. *Id.* at 93.

28. *See* Scotch & Schriner, *supra* note 12, at 154–57.

29. *Id.* at 157–58.

30. Paul G. Hearne, *Employment Strategies for People with Disabilities: A Prescription for Change, in* THE AMERICANS WITH DISABILITIES ACT: FROM POLICY TO PRACTICE 111, 124 (Jane West ed., 1991).

31. *See* Jane West, *Introduction—Implementing the Act: Where to Begin, in* THE AMERICANS WITH DISABILITIES ACT: FROM POLICY TO PRACTICE xi, xi–xii (Jane West ed., 1991).

32. *See* Robert L. Burgdorf Jr., *"Substantially Limited" Protection from Disability Discrimination: The Special Treatment Model and Misconstructions of the Definition of Disability,* 42 VILL. L. REV. 409, 561 (1997).

33. For a discussion of the need for a reconsideration of the assumptions built into law and public administration, see Hahn, *Disability Policy, supra* note 10, at 315.

34. Donald O. Parsons, *Measuring and Deciding Disability, in* DISABILITY & WORK: INCENTIVES, RIGHTS, AND OPPORTUNITIES 72, 73 (Carolyn L. Weaver ed., 1991).

35. *See generally* DISABILITY & WORK: INCENTIVES, RIGHTS, AND OPPORTUNITIES (Carolyn L. Weaver ed., 1991) [hereinafter DISABILITY & WORK]; *see also* LaCheen, *supra* note 5; *infra* text accompanying note 40.

36. Barbara Vobejda, *Disabled People See Budget-Cutting Fervor as Threat, New Attitude,* WASH. POST, Aug. 3, 1995, at A12.

37. *See* Hahn, *Towards a Politics, supra* note 7, at 89.

38. Carolyn L. Weaver, *Incentives versus Controls in Federal Disability Policy, in* DISABILITY & WORK, *supra* note 35, at 6–7.

39. Stone, *supra* note 7, at 143.

40. THEDA SKOCPOL, PROTECTING SOLDIERS AND MOTHERS: THE POLITICAL ORIGINS OF SOCIAL POLICY IN THE UNITED STATES 149 (1992).

41. *See, e.g.,* EDWARD BERKOWITZ & KIM McQUAID, CREATING THE WELFARE STATE: THE POLITICAL ECONOMY OF TWENTIETH-CENTURY REFORM 12 (2d. ed. 1988).

42. *See* Feldblum, *supra* note 25, at 85–87.

43. Vobejda, *supra* note 36.

44. *See* Nancy R. Mudrick, *Employment Discrimination Laws for Disability: Utilization and Outcome,* 549 ANNALS AM. ACAD. POL. & SOC. SCI. 53, 67 (1997).

45. For a discussion of the difficulty of scientifically measuring pain and subjective accounts of incapacity as eligibility criteria, see Stone, *supra* note 7, at 134–39.

46. For an analysis of employment discrimination complaints under the ADA and comparable state statutes, see Mudrick, *supra* note 44.

47. *See* LaCheen, *supra* note 5.

48. Michael H. Gottesman, *Disability, Federalism, and a Court with an Eccentric Mission,* 62 OHIO ST. L.J. 31 (2001).

49. Steven S. Locke, *The Incredible Shrinking Protected Class: Redefining the Scope of Disability Under the Americans with Disabilities Act,* 68 U. COLO. L. REV. 107 (1997).

50. Chai R. Feldblum, *Definition of Disability under Federal Anti-Discrimination Law: What Happened? Why? And What Can We Do About it?* 21 BERKELEY J. EMP. & LAB. L. 149 (2000) (*quoting* Ryan v. Grae & Rybicki, 135 F.3d 867 (2d Cir. 1998)).

51. *Id.* at 148.

52. Quoted in *id.* at 156.

53. *Id.* at 142 (*citing* 29 C.F.R. § 1630.2(j)(3)(i) (1995)).

54. Redlich v. Albany Law School, 899 F.Supp. 100, 106, 107.

55. Anderson v. General Motors, 1997 U.S. Dist. LEXIS 7829, at *15.

56. Ellison v. Software Spectrum, Inc., 85 F.3d 187 (5th Cir. 1996).

57. Arlene B. Mayerson, *Restoring Regard for the "Regarded as" Prong: Giving Effect to Congressional Intent.* 42 VILL. L. REV. 587, 593 (1997).

58. Feldblum, *supra* note 50.

59. 527 U.S. 471, 488 (1999).

60. 199 S. Ct. 2133 (1999).

61. 119 S. Ct. 2162 (1999).

62. Feldblum, *supra* note 25.

63. Matthew Diller, *Judicial Backlash, the ADA, and the Civil Rights Model,* 21 BERKELEY J. EMP. & LAB. L., 19, 20 (2000).

64. *Id.*

65. *Id.* at 50.

66. *Id.*

67. *Id.* at 25.

68. Feldblum, *supra* note 50, at 152.

69. *Id.* at 142.

70. Cleburne v. Cleburne Living Center, Inc., 473 U.S. 432, 440 (1985).

71. *Id.* at 448, 449.

72. Gottesman, *supra* note 48, at 79–80.

73. Arlene B. Mayerson & Silvia Yee, *The ADA and Models of Equality,* 62 OHIO ST. L.J. 535, 539 (2001) (*quoting* Kimel v. Fla. Bd. of Regents, 528 U.S. 62, S. Ct. 631 (2001)).

74. *Id.* at 539.

75. Bd. of Trustees of the University of Alabama v. Garrett, 121 S. Ct. 955, 965 (2001).

76. *Id.* at 967.

77. *Id.* at 964.

78. *Id.* at 966.

79. *Id.* at 964.

80. *Id.*

81. Cited in respondents' brief in *Garrett,* 21–22 .

82. *Garrett,* 121 S. Ct. at 965, citing the act's findings.

83. *Id.* at 975.

84. Irving K. Zola, *Disability Statistics: What We Count and What It Tells Us: A Personal and Political Analysis,* 4 J. DISABILITY POLICY STUDIES 9 (1993).

85. Edward H. Yelin, *The Employment of People With and Without Disabilities in an Age of Insecurity,* 549 ANNALS OF THE AMERICAN ACADEMY OF POLITICAL AND SOCIAL SCIENCE 117 (1997).

86. Richard K. Scotch and Kay Schriner, *Disability as Human Variation: Implications for Policy,* 549 ANNALS OF THE AMERICAN ACADEMY OF POLITICAL AND SOCIAL SCIENCE 158 (1997).

87. Adrienne Asch, *Critical Race Theory, Feminism, and Disability: Reflections on Social Justice and Personal Identity,* 62 OHIO ST. L. J. 391 (2001).

88. American Bar Association Commission on Mental and Physical Disability Law, MENTAL DISABILITIES AND THE AMERICANS WITH DISABILITIES ACT (2d ed. 1997)( footnotes omitted).

89. Nancy R. Mudrick, *Employment Discrimination Laws for Disability: Utilization and Outcome,* 549 ANNALS OF THE AMERICAN ACADEMY OF POLITICAL AND SOCIAL SCIENCE 53 (1997).

90. Richard V. Burkhauser, *Post-ADA: Are People with Disabilities Expected to Work?* 549 ANNALS OF THE AMERICAN ACADEMY OF POLITICAL AND SOCIAL SCIENCE 71 (1997); Richard V. Burkhauser, *An Economic Perspective on ADA Backlash: Comments from the BJELL Symposium on the Americans with Disabilities Act,* 21 BERKELEY J. EMP. & LAB. L. 367 (2000).

91. For a discussion of the barriers faced by people with disabilities, see Hahn, *Disability Policy, supra* note 10, at 304–9. For a discussion of barriers related to expanding employment for people with disabilities, see generally Edward H. Yelin, *supra* note 85, and William G. Johnson, *The Future of Disability Policy: Benefit Payments or Civil Rights?* 549 ANNALS AM. ACAD. POL. & SOC. SCI. 160 (1997).

92. *See, e.g.,* PAUL BURSTEIN, DISCRIMINATION, JOBS, AND POLITICS: THE STRUGGLE FOR EQUAL EMPLOYMENT OPPORTUNITY IN THE UNITED STATES SINCE THE NEW DEAL 182 (1985).

93. Among the best recent overviews of the persistence of economic and social disadvantage among African Americans are WILLIAM JULIUS WILSON, THE TRULY DISADVANTAGED: THE INNER CITY, THE UNDERCLASS, AND PUBLIC POLICY (1987) and WILLIAM JULIUS WILSON, WHEN WORK DISAPPEARS: THE WORLD OF THE NEW URBAN POOR (1996).

94. *See* Scotch & Schriner, *supra* note 12, at 152.

95. *See* DONALD L. HOROWITZ, THE COURTS AND SOCIAL POLICY 255–98 (1977).

*Vicki A. Laden and Gregory Schwartz*

# Psychiatric Disabilities, the Americans with Disabilities Act, and the New Workplace Violence Account

A few years ago, a new video game hit computer stores, promising killing "[s]o freakin' real, your victims actually beg for mercy and scream for their lives!"[1] The game is called "Postal" and is based on a disgruntled, psychotic postal worker arming himself to the teeth and systematically shooting his way through several different scenarios, including a schoolyard, a construction site, and a marching band. The victims, primarily innocent, unarmed bystanders, do not die immediately. Instead, the player must decide whether to let victims beg for mercy or execute them immediately. The disgruntled postal worker periodically complains, "[O]nly my weapon understands me."

The makers of the game did not create this image out of whole cloth. The image of the disgruntled postal worker who explodes in senseless, random violence had already entered popular culture, symbolizing the potential lethality of the psychotic worker. So embedded in popular discourse is this account that newspapers, television programs, movies, attorneys, and schoolchildren refer to episodes of unexplained, individual violence as "going postal."[2] The threat of occupational injury or death, once represented by dangerous machinery or hazardous environments, has now become discursively located in conceptions of the "pathogenic worker," lurking unnoticed in the workplace, poised to explode in lethal violence against his supervisors or coworkers. We might refer to the set of stories, images, attributions, and prescriptions associated with this imagery as the *new workplace violence account.*

This new workplace violence account, we will argue, plays a role in attempts to delegitimize the Americans with Disabilities Act (ADA). Deploying vivid media representations of volatile, psychotic employees, ADA critics suggest that the act has deprived employers of the ability to protect employees from criminal assault by dangerous coworkers. Riding the coattails of this account, and in circular fashion both lending authority to and deriving epistemological authority from it, is a burgeoning workplace violence prevention industry composed of employment defense law firms, security experts, and consultants who counsel employers on how to identify and remove potentially violent workers in the "hands-tied" era of the ADA.[3] This rapidly expanding violence prevention industry advances bold claims about the enormity and severity of the problem, reinforcing a key premise of ADA critics that the ADA unreasonably subordinates public safety interests to the "special rights" of the disabled.

This fear-inducing account is predicated on two assumptions: first, that worker-on-worker violence is a significant problem; and second, that it can be reduced or prevented through the identification and exclusion of "high risk" workers. Significantly, however, data collected on workplace violence and empirical research on prediction of violence contradict both of these claims.[4] The incidence of worker-on-worker violence is infinitesimally small.[5] Violent acts by "pathogenic" employees are trivial contributors to workplace morbidity and mortality, in stark contrast to injuries and deaths caused by environmental conditions, from which attention is diverted by the new workplace violence account.[6]

Undeterred by a lack of empirical support for the claim that worker-on-worker violence constitutes an important social problem, the workplace violence industry advertises its technical prowess in identifying potentially dangerous workers.[7] In doing so, it ignores a large body of empirical research establishing that prediction of violence, even by skilled clinicians in highly controlled in-patient settings, is dubious at best.[8] In the hands of employers, the "tools" for predicting violence by individuals operating within a wide array of uncontrolled situational contexts have even less prognostic validity or reliability.

Given the crude methods available for purported prediction of violence, it is unsurprising that individuals with psychiatric disabilities face intensified scrutiny and efforts based on diagnostic categories. Claims that individuals with psychiatric disabilities harbor the potential for violence tap into a deep reservoir of transhistorical fear and stigma-induced stereotyping that enactment of the ADA did little to drain.[9] That individuals with psychiatric disabilities find themselves at the center of the political/judicial debate over the ADA owes as much to this historical legacy as it does to the discursive influence of the new workplace violence prevention industry. One can observe these old fears and stereotypes, and the junk science they animate, operating in a variety of legal contexts, including trends toward permitting the introduction of propensity evidence in sexual assault cases, the enactment of notification schemes such as "Megan's Law," and capital sentencing standards that permit introduction of expert testimony predicting future dangerousness.

The heightened fear of employee violence that permeates the new workplace violence account is aggressively marketed to employers, freighting interactions between employers and employees. For example, in 1998 a postal worker was fired merely for telling coworkers about his nightmares that involved a shooting at work—a shooting in which *he, himself, was a victim*.[10] This same fear of lurking violence has prompted companies to hire consultants as surrogates to notify employees of termination.[11] In this social climate, cases alleging mistreatment, discrimination, and outright exclusion based on fear of violence are beginning to find their way into the courts. On the whole, ADA claims arising out of these situations have received a chilly reception. Predictably, courts have proved hospitable to employers, mirroring conventional biases against individuals with psychiatric disabilities, and reflecting the new workplace violence account.

Part 1 of this article examines the cultural emergence of the archetype of the disgruntled postal worker. Part 2 discusses its appropriation by the new workplace violence prevention industry. Part 3 presents an account of the reality of workplace violence. The conclusion comments on the contribution of these discursive trends to the backlash against the ADA. In sum, this essay argues that the claim that potentially dangerous workers can be identified and excluded from the workplace is a sham. The "tools" employed by the new workplace violence industry operate not to identify and exclude potentially dangerous individuals, but rather to identify and exclude individuals with psychiatric disabilities.

## I. The Social Construction of Workplace Violence

Workplace violence, now frequently identified as "epidemic," received scant attention until 1987.[12] Indeed, the phrase *violence in the workplace* did not appear in major media outlets until 1986.[13] In the past, occupational health and safety professionals focused on detecting and correcting unsafe conditions.[14] The Occupational Health and Safety Act of 1970 was largely enacted in response to increasing injury rates in manufacturing industries in the 1960s. Thus, regulations promulgated under the act address myriad environmental dangers, from unsafe equipment[15] to exposure limits for toxic substances,[16] but omit workplace violence as a locus of concern. Similarly, the National Institute for Occupational Safety and Health (NIOSH) did not begin to address assault-related injuries in the workplace until the late 1980s.[17] These regulatory priorities accurately reflected the dominant contribution of environmental factors to death, injury, and disease on the job, from asbestos-induced deaths from mesothelioma to repetitive injuries caused by poor ergonomic design.[18] Unsafe conditions resulted in 2,516 deaths[19] and roughly three million injuries in 1997.[20] That workplace violence was not on the Occupational Safety and Health Administration's or NIOSH's radar screen is therefore understandable.

In the late 1980s and early 1990s, however, a series of sensational murders at U.S. Postal Service branches seized the national headlines. In August 1986, part-time postal worker Patrick Sherrill killed fourteen coworkers at a post office in Edmond, Oklahoma. In the words of one workplace violence consultant: "This watershed event fixed a seemingly unalterable course toward increased violence in the working environment."[21] Interestingly, however, media coverage of the post office killings initially focused on harsh conditions and abusive management in the agency itself. But after another sensational incident at a post office in Royal Oak, Michigan, in 1991, and a set of incidents occurring on a day in 1993, the "disgruntled" or "deranged" worker became the focus of media accounts. At congressional hearings following these events, the Postal Service promised to begin screening applicants in order to prevent violence.[22]

Following these incidents, the "dangerous coworker" emerged as a progressively distinct and increasingly recognizable category in the taxonomy of social violence. Rather than drawing attention to the dehumanizing conditions and speedups that already exacted a huge toll from postal employees, injuring vast numbers of them, the post office killings fueled a growing focus on worker-on-worker violence. This in turn led to an implicit construction of the individual worker, rather than the conditions in which work was conducted, as the primary locus of occupational risk.

In the late 1980s and early 1990s government agencies such as NIOSH, as well as individual epidemiologists at a variety of universities and research institutes, began directing resources and attention to the study of workplace violence.[23] During the early 1990s, congressional hearings were held on the post office incidents.[24]

At the same time, the popular media began assimilating the post office incidents into movies, sitcoms, and other narratives. Newspapers and television portrayals featured employees with grudges who suddenly erupted in murderous rages.[25] An episode of *King of the Hill* broadcast in April 1998, for example, depicts a fired drug addict returning to his former job.[26] Someone rushes into the office and announces, "Leon's in the parking lot . . . and he looks disgruntled." Expecting a volley of bullets, everyone cowers under desks or behind other pieces of office furniture. Notably, instead of a gun, Leon returns with a social worker, and the show proceeds to focus on the demands for accommodation the social worker makes. The episode is but one example of the sheer evocative power of the postal worker incidents that generated the term *going postal*.[27]

After the major motion picture *Clueless* popularized the phrase *going postal*,[28] it gained increasing currency in newspapers across the country. The video game Postal further extends its cultural influence. Through repetition, sensational reports of isolated incidents, and incorporation into a wide variety of entertainment media, the image of the violent coworker, poised to explode into a homicidal rage, came to function as a leitmotif in discussions of violence at the workplace.

Who "goes postal"? Media accounts of workplace violence construct varying profiles of the employee with a strong predisposition toward violence. This individual "overreacts" to perceived injustice; he has few friends or apparent interests and seems "strange"; he is a loner with poor social skills, some form of mental illness, and a fascination with weapons.[29] Through this stereotype, specific demographic and personality traits and more broadly, certain psychiatric conditions, are tightly linked to violence.

## 2. The Emergence of the Workplace Violence Prevention Industry

The stereotyped image of the disgruntled, potentially violent worker has not remained confined to media depictions. A simple Internet search turns up myriad websites sponsored by lawyers, consultants, and other professional service providers specializing in the supposed prevention of workplace violence.[30] Large defense-side labor and employment law firms conduct trainings on workplace violence and advertise their availability for consultation on prevention strategies, appropriating popular accounts in their literature, with seminar titles such as "Slackers, Hackers and Pistol Packers."[31] Practice guides and continuing legal education materials introduce attorneys to the "growing problem" of workplace violence, and advise on strategies for navigating among ostensibly conflicting obligations, such as protecting employees from violence by coworkers versus compliance with the ADA.[32] A newly constituted army of workplace violence "experts" market specialized tools for identifying dangerous workers.[33] Lending support to the clamor are organizations ranging from NIOSH[34] to state and local law enforcement agencies.[35] Through their publications, these organizations lend an aura of governmental validation to the claim that worker-on-worker violence represents a problem of epidemic proportions.

Many of these professional services recommend the use of particular checklists of behavioral indicators of future employee violence. For example, one recent review listed the following indicators of violence potential: "(i) erratic behavior; (ii) behaving as if upset or under stress; (iii) making threats or engaging in threatening behaviors; (iv) bringing a dangerous instrumentality to the work premises; or (v) an off-duty commission of a violent act."[36] Suggested tools for identifying dangerousness, a state assumed to be hypostatic and context-independent, include such traditional tools as clinical assessments and psychological profiling tests, but also less familiar methods, including handwriting analysis.[37] With the advent of less costly DNA testing, the ability to perform testing on biological specimens such as hair and saliva, and the proliferation of behavioral genetic research linking genetic loci to impulsive and aggressive behavior,[38] the arsenal of tools hawked to employers for imagined uses is likely to expand.

The literature, advertising, and services provided by the new workplace violence prevention industry reveal several distinct themes. First, much of the literature disseminated by the industry begins by framing the problem as an epidemic. As one workplace violence consulting firm recently claimed, "Violence in the workplace has become the occupational health and safety issue of the 1990s. As a problem, it only will worsen as sweeping social and economic changes take the nation into the next century."[39] A recent survey by a security company concluded that "executives are realizing it's the employees themselves who increasingly are the threat."[40]

Second, in these accounts, workplace violence is depicted as an employee "going postal."[41] For example, one website asserts that a "disgruntled employee may return to his or her former place of employment after being terminated and commit murder."[42] Such marketing materials transform accounts of random violence by disgruntled workers into apparently commonplace occurrences for which every employer should prepare. For example, another website focusing on workplace violence notes that after the Oklahoma post office incident, "workplace violence became a problem that could occur anywhere and anytime."[43] The commodity value of disseminated fear is obvious. Reshaping perceptions of extraordinary events by representing them as commonplace increases the perceived need for professional services, if only to address liability concerns.[44]

Third, the literature relies on a particular constitutive construction of the potentially violent employee. Such employees are generally male, white, over thirty-five years old, and have psychiatric or substance abuse problems, poor social skills, and a fascination with weapons.[45] Another account presents a similar profile of the dangerous employee:

> A middle-aged man who is a chronic complainer, distrustful and rigid, is the typical disgruntled employee, studies have shown. Other signs of danger are: constantly blames problems on others; carrying a concealed weapon or flashing a weapon to test other employees' reactions; paranoid behavior; seems desperate due to recent family, financial or other personal problems; interest in semiautomatic or automatic weapons; moral righteousness and the belief that the company is not following its rules and procedures.[46]

Often, the profiling is more reductionist, directly inviting surveillance of individuals with psychiatric conditions.[47] The informal checklists of violence indicators offered by workplace violence "experts" often degenerate into a focus on behaviors assumed to indicate underlying mental health problems. For example, one organization posted the following description on a website: "The physiological causes of workplace violence are also the result of employees who have experienced emotional, physical, or sexual abuse from childhood. Employees may bring their 'baggage' into the workplace. The manager or supervisor assumes the parental role and the co-workers may resemble siblings."[48]

Fourth, violence prevention entrepreneurs offer classifications and heuristic strategies for screening out the potentially violent employee. These range from the unsophisticated and intuitive, such as anecdotal stories told by retired police officers from which lists of informal indicators are extracted,[49] to the ostensibly sophisticated, such as clinical assessments by psychologists or psychological personality tests.[50]

In summary, following a small number of incidents in the late 1980s and early 1990s, sensational news stories and the subsequent assimilation of the stories into a wide range of media narratives generated a particular account of workplace violence. The vividness of the post office incidents and their commercial fictionalization have led people to perceive that worker-on-worker violence poses a high level of occupational risk. The fear accompanying this heightened perception of risk has in turn been exploited by an industry whose advertisements and advice to employers not only capitalized upon but accentuated and further disseminated the new workplace violence account. The account drew and continues to draw attention away from other more significant sources of occupational mortality and morbidity while generating a perceived need for the specialized services of the new workplace violence entrepreneurs. As the conclusion to this essay discusses, this account also plays a role in the weakening and delegitimizing of the Americans with Disabilities Act.

## 3. The Reality of Workplace Violence

Characterizations of workplace violence by the new workplace violence entrepreneurs frequently begin with statistical references reflecting the scope or scale of workplace violence. For example, these descriptions may begin by noting that homicide has become the second leading cause of workplace death for men, and the leading cause of workplace death for women.[51] Other accounts may refer to the costs associated with workplace violence.[52] These statistics are often accompanied by images or apocryphal accounts of a current or former worker "going postal."[53] The juxtaposition of the statistics with particular images or stories thus creates an impression in the mind of the reader that the statistics cited refer specifically to worker-on-worker violence. This, however, is not the case.

### The Reality of Workplace Homicide

The category of "homicide" reflected in the statistics cited by the new workplace violence entrepreneurs includes not only deaths caused by coworkers, but also deaths caused by customers, intruders, and other outsiders. It includes, for example, deaths of convenience store clerks and taxicab drivers in connection with armed robberies.

Despite the breadth of this category, the actual number of homicides at the workplace is small, particularly given the significant and increasing amount of time that employees spend at work. Statistics from 1996 reveal that there are slightly more than 20,000 homicides per year nationally.[54] In 1997, the most recent year for which detailed statistics are available, workplace homicides accounted for only 856 homicides, or roughly 4.25 percent of the total.[55]

More importantly, however, workplace homicide accounts for only 14 percent of all deaths related to employment.[56] The leading cause of work-related mortality, accounting for 42 percent of the total, is vehicular accidents—not surprising when one considers that traffic accidents accounted for roughly 44,000 deaths in 1996.[57] Deaths during crimes perpetrated by nonemployees accounted for the overwhelming majority of those roughly 856 work-related homicides.[58] The most recent figures indicate that fully 85 percent of workplace homicides occur in connection with robberies or other crimes perpetrated by outsiders.[59] Only 7 percent of all workplace homicides are perpetrated by current or former employees.[60] Accordingly, in 1997, only 56 of the 856 work-related homicides, or even more starkly contextualized, only 56 of the approximately 20,000 nationwide homicides, were perpetrated by employees or former employees at work.[61]

Thus, these statistics reveal that workplace homicide is an uncommon occurrence. Homicides by employees or former employees are vastly less common still. Customer and stranger violence presents a far greater homicide risk than does violence by employees or former employees. Moreover, these risks are concentrated in certain industries, with retail, service, transportation, and public utilities industries accounting for over 75 percent of workplace homicides in 1997.[62] Measures directed at protecting employees against crime by customers, intruders, and other strangers would have the greatest likelihood of reducing the toll from work-related homicide. In fact, Southland Corporation (the operator of 7-Eleven stores) and Roy Rogers restaurants, both establishments at high risk for crime victimization, have experienced great success in reducing workplace homicide by focusing efforts on preventing robbery.[63] In spite of this evidence, the new workplace violence account locates the source of homicide risk in workers themselves, not in customers or strangers.

## The Reality of Assault in the Workplace

One can observe in the new workplace violence account a similar misconstruction of the sources of risk of assault.[64] The Bureau of Labor Statistics logged 18,538 nonfatal workplace assaults in 1997.[65] This should first be compared to the 1.91 million aggravated assaults and 1.24 million simple assaults with an injury reported by the Bureau of Justice Statistics for 1997.[66] Moreover, the number of assaults specifically attributable to current and former employees is even smaller, accounting for only 7 percent of employment-related assaults.[67] Visitors and intruders, such as robbers, inflicted 33 percent of these assaults, and health care patients were responsible for another 45 percent.[68] As one might expect, service sector employees, such as those working as nurses' aides and security guards, were the victims of 52 percent of assaults.[69] Managerial and professional employees chiefly in professions such as nursing and social work were victims of 21 percent of the assaults.[70]

Most current accounts of workplace violence fail to address these facts. They attempt instead to bolster their claims by relying on the Bureau of Justice Statistics Criminal Victimization Survey that reported approximately 1.5 million workplace assaults per year.[71] The high estimate of total assaults that this survey obtained is explained by the inclusion of simple assault *not* resulting in any injury and from the inclusion of many forms of sexual harassment.[72] While high rates of low-level aggression and sexual harassment have undeniable importance and reveal much about the daily lives of employees and the appropriate targets of prevention strategies, they plainly constitute different phenomena than those represented in the new workplace violence account.

As might be expected, none of the studies of violence that measure deaths or injuries included violence inflicted by employers that might be properly classifiable as homicide or assault. The 1999 immolation of four employees at Tosco's Avon, California refinery, which appears to have resulted from high-level managers' refusal to permit workers to shut down an unsafe operation involving volatile chemicals, is one example of uncounted corporate homicide.[73] Also omitted in these estimates of "assault" are injuries caused by managers who force employees to work with dangerous equipment or machinery.[74]

In summary, these depictions reveal that the new workplace violence account is premised on the claim that workplace violence, specifically worker-on-worker violence, is "epidemic" in the United States. The claim is bolstered by statistics reflecting apparently high levels of such violence and promotional literature generally associating these statistics with apocryphal accounts of worker-on-worker violence. This presentation obscures the fact that worker-on-worker violence represents but a minute portion of total workplace mortality or morbidity risk, and draws attention away from more substantial sources of risk, such as traditionally defined unsafe working conditions. Indeed, even the official reports that the workplace violence industry cites to support its claims are careful to specify that the problem of workplace violence derives overwhelmingly from companies failing to protect workers from outsider crime. A recent NIOSH report observed, "Unfortunately, sensational acts of co-worker violence (which form only a small part of the problem) are often emphasized by the media to the exclusion of the almost daily killings of taxicab drivers, convenience store clerks and other retail workers, security guards, and police officers. These deaths often go virtually unnoticed, yet their numbers are staggering."[75]

Nevertheless, in typical fashion the new workplace violence entrepreneurs frequently claim that, through the use of their psychological profiling and related products, they can help employers identify and exclude those employees or applicants who pose a heightened risk of future violence.[76] For example, one top personality testing service proclaims: "Inappropriate aggressive behavior and employee violence have become major concerns for employers throughout the United States. The IS2™ is used to aid in the identification of individuals who may tend to disregard rules and/or societal norms."[77] Another employment consultant offers to "identify early warning signs and potentially dangerous personalities" and to "[a]ssess violent employees or managers."[78] Still another offers the services of its "Hostile Employee Suppression Unit."[79] These services confidently present profiles of violent employees:

> Individuals who commit violence tend to fit a pattern. . . . Often, they are loners and the main focus of their life is their job. Perpetrators may exhibit a fascination with weapons and the occurrence of violence in other workplaces. Other warning signs may include: previous threats or violent behavior; verbal abuse, intimidation of co-workers and harassing phone calls; holding grudges, inability to handle criticism, and wishing harm upon others; romantic obsession with a co-worker or manager; marital problems, psychological disorders, alcohol or drug abuse.[80]

While some profiles of the dangerous employee include behavioral factors such as past violence and threats, they are fundamentally based on the assumption that people with mental disturbance are potentially violent. Thus, almost all of the profiles include the general category of "psychological disorders" as a major indicator of potential violence and often simply focus on traits and behaviors assumed to be associated with mental disturbance, such as "paranoid *style of thinking.*"[81]

### Lack of Data That Can Predict Workplace Violence

In spite of the many claims made by workplace violence entrepreneurs, research has identified few verifiable correlates of future violence. Those that have been identified—primarily history of violence, substance abuse, and demographic factors—are largely exogenous;[82] that is, they lie primarily outside the individual. Even this limited body of actuarial correlates of violence bears little relation to the kinds of behavioral or diagnostic markers of the supposedly violent "personality types" generally included in the instruments advertised by the new workplace violence entrepreneurs. In particular, available research presents no valid basis for concluding that an individual who "act[s] strangely" or who has diagnosed psychiatric conditions poses any greater risk of future violence than others in the general population.[83]

Research has failed to establish that psychiatric disorder per se is a dominating risk factor for future violence.[84] The existing limited research on this issue indicates that only serious psychiatric disorder is linked to violence and then, only in combination with substance abuse.[85] Only certain psychiatric conditions, such as schizophrenia, major depression, and bipolar disorder—in combination with the additional factor of substance abuse—appear associated with a heightened risk of violence.[86] It must be emphasized that even in this narrow class of diagnostic categories linked to small increases in risk of violence, the increased risk is confined to individuals whose psychiatric conditions are severe.[87] Individuals with mild or moderate symptomology do *not* differ significantly from the normal population in their rate of violence.[88] Thus, only when particular psychiatric disorders of particularly high severity are combined with substance abuse does psychiatric disorder correlate significantly with violent behavior. Such individuals are exceedingly unlikely to have gained employment or even to live in unsupervised settings.

One of the preeminent researchers on the prediction of violence recently summarized the state of this evidence as follows:

By all indications, the great majority of people who are currently disordered . . . are not violent. None of the data give any support to the sensationalized caricature of the mentally disordered served up by the media, the shunning of former patients by employers and neighbors in the community, or "lock 'em all up" laws proposed by politicians pandering to public fears. The policy implications of mental disorder as a risk factor for violent behavior can be understood only in relative terms. Compared to the magnitude of risk associated with the combination of male gender, young age, and lower socioeconomic status, for example, the risk of violence presented by mental disorder is modest. Compared to the magnitude of risk associated with alcoholism and other drug abuse, the risk associated with "major" mental disorders such as schizophrenia and affective disorder is modest indeed. Clearly, mental health status makes at best a trivial contribution to the overall level of violence in society.[89]

Moreover, if even moderate levels of psychiatric disorder are not associated with an increased likelihood of future violence, behavioral *traits* can be expected to have even less predictive acuity. Nonetheless, undesirable behavioral traits prompt most referrals of workers to industrial psychologists for fitness-for-duty evaluations.[90] Assessment of behavioral traits is also recommended by many of the new workplace violence entrepreneurs as a screening device.[91] Neither specific behavioral traits nor histories of psychiatric diagnosis or treatment have heuristic value in predicting future violence in a workplace environment.

The connection between psychiatric disability and the propensity for violence remains poorly understood and so lacking in clinical utility that studies of clinical predictions have demonstrated these indicators to be accurate less than half the time.[92] These dismal figures have not improved in the past thirty years.[93] In fact, the inaccuracy of clinical predictions of dangerousness received widespread attention in *Barefoot v. Estelle*,[94] a 1983 Supreme Court case challenging the admissibility of predictions of dangerousness in capital sentencing in Texas. In its amicus curiae brief for *Barefoot*, the American Psychiatric Association contended that "two out of three predictions of long-term future violence made by psychiatrists are wrong," and that "a layman with access to relevant statistics can do at least as well and possibly better" than psychiatrists in making such predictions.[95]

A highly influential 1988 article in the journal *Science*[96] presented an equally troubling picture of clinical predictions of violence. The study revealed that predictions of this sort were riddled with error. The errors derived from serious disagreement among clinicians regarding the assessment of subjects' current status, "overpathologization," and the subsequent failure of clinicians to achieve superior results to either laypersons or actuarial methods.[97]

Furthermore, a 1994 study of forensic violence prediction by Robert Menzies and his colleagues[98] demonstrated similar results. Despite the use of an "intensified and diversified assembly of prediction indices and outcome measures over an extended six-year time frame," Menzies determined that the accuracy of predictions concerning 162 persons remanded for forensic evaluations was "decidedly unimpressive."[99] In a typical finding, laypersons using a psychometric instrument outperformed chief psychiatrists in predicting future violence.[100] Expanding on findings from a prior study, Menzies concluded that the overwhelming body of empirical evidence remains highly equivocal as to the ability to distinguish between individuals who are potentially violent and those who are not.[101] Using "the best methods that we could muster," stated Menzies, "we were in general not able appreciably to elevate the accuracy of forensic forecasts" over those achieved in an earlier study published in 1985.[102] Pessimistic about the possibility of gains in accuracy, Menzies and his colleagues struck a decidedly mordant tone in concluding that abandonment of the dangerousness construct is unlikely. In so doing, they cited recent trends toward the construct's rehabilitation, "second generation work aimed at the scientification of dangerousness" and the construct's "continuing discursive power."[103]

These critiques encourage the conclusion that even the use of referral to a clinical psychologist for a fitness-for-duty exam is unlikely to provide information that would identify potentially violent employees with any reliable degree of accuracy except, perhaps, in instances of severe disability unlikely to be present in the employment context. Rather, they suggest that prediction of violence is tenuous at best, even in highly controlled contexts, with institutionalized subjects diagnosed with one or more of a narrow set of severe psychiatric disorders. The claim that an individual worker's propensity for future violence can be predicted in the employment environment, using *any* tools, let alone the crude "tools" offered by the new workplace violence entrepreneurs, is both spurious and dangerous.

## The Judicial Response

As we have seen, conspicuously missing from the new workplace violence account is any meaningful empirical support for its central assumptions: that workplace violence is "epidemic," that violence-prone workers are legion, and that future dangerousness can be predicted in the employment setting. The pseudoscience, reliance on stereotypes, and "intuitive epidemiology" underlying the account encourage fear-driven responses. Employers persuaded by the account can be expected to embrace and deploy screening, surveillance, and preemptive exclusion, sweeping up individuals with psychiatric disabilities and even those whose behavior invites suspicion of psychiatric disability.

The legislative history and statutory purposes of the ADA stand in express conflict with the approach encouraged by this popular account. Mythology and stereotyping, such as the belief that psychiatric disability is associated with a propensity for dangerousness, were explicitly denounced in the congressional debate preceding the passage of the act,[104] and have been repudiated in the EEOC's interpretive guidance to its implementing regulations.[105] In contrast to the employer response encouraged by the popular account, the ADA calls for rational, scientific decision-making in the assessment of risk. It requires that an employer seeking to exclude an employee because of safety concerns demonstrate that the individual poses a direct threat to the health or safety of other individuals in the workplace.[106] In the same respect, the EEOC has adopted the position taken by the Supreme Court in the 1987 Rehabilitation Act case, *School Board of Nassau County v. Arline*.[107] According to the EEOC, in determining whether an individual constitutes a direct threat, an employer must make a reasonable medical judgment that relies on the most current medical knowledge and/or the best available objective evidence.[108] Specific factors that must be addressed include "(i) the duration of the risk, (ii) the likelihood that the potential harm will occur, (iii) the nature and severity of the potential harm, and (iv) the imminence of the potential harm."[109]

The confrontation between the popular account and the rational scientific model upon which the ADA and its regulations are predicated can readily be discerned in judicial decisions interpreting the direct threat defense, as well as in cases that wrestle with issues raised by employees perceived as threatening. When a popular account is at odds in crucial respects with a prescribed judicial duty, it can be expected that judicial responses will be modulated by the popular account, particularly where, as in this area, the popular account has a strong valence and taps into a wellspring of fears.

In reconciling such dissonance in the context of psychiatric disabilities, courts have sought to recast or reinterpret case narratives in order to accommodate the pragmatic and normative concerns embedded in the new workplace violence account. They have also restructured the legal inquiry in ways that more readily accommodate and conform to the new social construction of workplace violence. In the process of performing these rearrangements, the scientific approach to risk advanced by the ADA has frequently been subordinated to a less rigorous approach characterized by overgeneralization, stereotyping, and other forms of heuristic thinking.

Perhaps the best example of these two judicial devices—recasting the case narrative and manipulating the required legal analysis, is *Cody v. Cigna Healthcare*.[110] In *Cody*, a nurse with depression and anxiety complained to a high-level manager that her symptoms were being exacerbated by her assignment to work in parts of St. Louis that she viewed as dangerous. Her direct supervisor and coworkers did not respond well to news of her disability and complaints. A cup, labeled with the phrase "alms for the sick" appeared on Cody's desk, and she was warned that if she complained to a higher-level supervisor, she would suffer negative consequences.[111]

Cody became upset in response to the cup incident and, at her supervisor's suggestion, left work for the day. After she left, a coworker informed the manager to whom Cody had complained that Cody had been "behaving strangely" and had spoken about carrying a gun. The coworker expressed fear that Cody might be violent. The next morning, other coworkers told the manager that Cody had been observed "sprinkling salt in front of her cubicle to keep away evil spirits," staring into space for lengthy periods, and "drawing pictures of sperm." Her coworkers also reported that Cody had talked about a gun.[112]

When Cody arrived for a scheduled meeting with the manager, he claimed to have seen "a noticeable bulge in her purse."[113] A local security specialist was summoned, and Cody's purse was searched. No weapon was found. Nevertheless, the manager ordered her to see a psychologist. When Cody left the meeting to go home, she was unable to open either the exit door or the parking lot gate because, while the meeting was in progress, her security card had been deactivated. On instructions from the manager, the parking lot attendant confiscated the card. Subsequently, the manager denied Cody's request for a transfer, causing her to decline to return to her job. She then brought claims under the Americans with Disabilities Act and the Missouri Human Rights Act for workplace harassment and constructive discharge based on mental disability.[114]

In its analysis, the Eighth Circuit began by examining whether Cody was a "qualified individual with a disability" entitled to protection under the act.[115] In order to establish that she met this threshold, Cody had to demonstrate that she had a substantially limiting impairment or was regarded by her employer as having one.[116] The court concluded that Cody failed to meet either of these definitions. It found that Cigna's offer of paid medical leave and its imposition of the requirement that she see a psychologist did not indicate that Cigna believed her to be substantially impaired.[117] The court interpreted security measures to which she was subjected on the day of the meeting as not indicating such belief either. Rather, according to the court, these actions provided evidence only that Cigna regarded Cody as a threat, not as disabled. "Employers," the Eighth Circuit opined, "need to be able to use reasonable means to ascertain the cause of troubling behavior without exposing themselves to ADA claims under Sections 12112(a) and 12102(2)(C)."[118]

The *Cody* court's presentation of the facts obscures a remarkable subtext: an individual with serious psychiatric disabilities aggravated by her job assignment was demonized by her coworkers after she requested an accommodation. Her coworkers seem to have banded together in an effort to oust her by tormenting her and by portraying her to her supervisor as lethal. Rather than a deliberate distortion, this may have been an accurate expression of their assumptions about her. Interestingly, however, it was the coworkers, not Cody, who committed aggressive, menacing acts directed at others. In the judicial domain, the story that emerges about an employer's need to address legitimate workplace safety concerns created by a psychiatrically disabled employee buries this account of virulent stereotyping and group harassment.

Under the ADA, in order to justify the security measures taken to exclude Cody from the workplace, her employer should have been required to present scientific and/or objective evidence that she posed a "significant risk of substantial harm to the health or safety of . . . others that cannot be eliminated or reduced by reasonable accommodation."[119] The EEOC has argued, and many courts have agreed, that employers bear the burden of proving the existence of a direct threat, or any other affirmative defenses to liability.[120] In contrast, the Eighth Circuit reconfigured the legal terrain to Cody's detriment. The Court relocated the nature of the potential threat emanating from Cody from the issue of direct threat to the question of statutory coverage. Since Cody could not make the initial showing that she was disabled or regarded as disabled—rather than regarded as a threat—she was simply excluded from protection under the act.[121] In this way, not only was the burden of proof shifted to Cody, but more importantly, the standard for examining the employer's response was substantially relaxed and adjusted so as to accommodate the perception of threat portrayed in the popular account.

That the legal topography has become more difficult for ADA plaintiffs in circumstances similar to Cody's is highlighted by juxtaposing *Cody* with *Lussier v. Runyon*.[122] In *Lussier*, an earlier Rehabilitation Act case, the plaintiff was a postal worker who suffered from post-traumatic stress disorder. He was targeted by his supervisors as a violence risk in the wake of the 1991 Royal Oak and Ridgewood post office violence incidents.[123] As the Court noted, "On November 15, 1991, the Postmaster General responded to the Royal Oak tragedy by issuing a news release announcing that Postal Service personnel files would be reviewed to uncover Postal Service workers with dangerous propensities."[124] The supervisor placed a copy of this news release in Lussier's file. Later Lussier was terminated for complaints about his temper and inability to get along with subordinates, as well as for concealing information about arrests on his application.[125] Sifting through the evidence presented in support of Lussier's termination, the court rejected as pretextual the postal service's reasons for termination, concluding that his termination was based on unfounded fears "that Lussier could be violent . . . based on [the supervisor's] understanding of Lussier's medical and military background."[126]

Another common strategy for reconfiguring the legal landscape has appeared in recent ADA cases. When employees' actual or perceived psychiatric disabilities cause conflict with coworkers or supervisors, this conduct may be characterized as violating company rules or judicial expectations of appropriate workplace behavior. In these circumstances an employer need not prove that the employee's behavior constitutes a direct threat, since misconduct may be deemed inconsistent with the ADA's requirement that an individual with a disability demonstrate that "with or without reasonable accommodation" she or he "can perform the essential functions of the job."[127] Compliance with all rules and behavioral expectations is regularly seen as an essential function of any job.[128] While previously some courts had found that if conduct were causally related to a disability—so that the disability manifested itself in the conduct—such conduct would not render the employee unqualified,[129] currently only the Second Circuit maintains this position. This represents a significant narrowing of the protections accorded employees with psychiatric disabilities under the ADA.

A consensus has emerged that misconduct, however intertwined with disability, can be punished.[130] Courts have not yet confronted claims by individuals with disabilities such as Tourette's syndrome, in which many symptoms might constitute misconduct, if conduct and disability are seen as separable. However, a student's challenge to his exclusion from mainstream education under the Individuals with Disabilities Education Act prompted just such a result. In *Clyde K. v. Puyallup School District, No. 3*,[131] the Ninth Circuit treated a Tourettic student's sexually explicit exclamations as the equivalent of sexual harassment for which he could be excluded. This case illustrates that in cases where disability and conduct are connected but conceptually distinguishable, courts have little difficulty upholding punishment of conduct.[132]

Although the EEOC regulations and interpretive guidelines defining essential job functions call for an individualized assessment of whether particular functions are essential requirements of a specific job,[133] the ability to get along with coworkers or comply with supervisors, and other such behavioral standards, are assumed to be unvarying and universal. In this vein, an additional consensus has emerged in opposition to earlier case law. In *Nisperos v. Buck*,[134] a 1989 case, the court found that remaining drug-free was not an essential function of the job of an Immigration and Naturalization Service attorney, despite the agency's jurisdiction over drug smuggling. Such a result would be highly unlikely in the current judicial climate, where termination for trivial transgressions, including those resulting from serious provocation, is upheld.[135]

Under the ADA, a court considering whether a particular employee presents a direct threat or is able to perform the essential functions of a job must consider whether reasonable accommodation would reduce the threat or enable the employee to successfully perform the job. However, accommodations likely to enable individuals with psychiatric disabilities to meet these requirements are routinely deemed per se unreasonable by reviewing courts.[136] Courts frequently find modifications in the environment, including work at home, transfer away from stressful coworkers or an abusive supervisor, or modification of conduct standards, to be unreasonable as a matter of law.

For example, in *Gaul v. Lucent Technologies Inc.*,[137] significant conflict with a coworker caused an employee with depression and anxiety disorders to express concern that he would "pop"—that is, suffer another nervous breakdown. He sought transfer away from the "prolonged and inordinate" stress that had precipitated his crisis. By framing the request as one for a low-stress environment that would require continuous monitoring, the court had no difficulty finding his request unduly burdensome.[138] It framed such a request as an unwarranted intrusion into personnel matters. In couching modification of environmental stressors as beyond reach, the court further narrowed the ADA's protection of individuals with psychiatric disabilities.

Just as there is dissonance between the ADA and the Rehabilitation Act in the case law interpreting "direct threat" and "qualifications," crucial differences emerge between cases regarding the accommodation of psychiatric disabilities under the ADA and analogous cases under the Rehabilitation Act. In 1991 the court in *Kent v. Derwinski*[139] did not hesitate to order a supervisor to employ "soft approach" discipline methods in correcting the deficiencies of a developmentally disabled laundry worker. Now, with few exceptions,[140] courts increasingly deny the very accommodations that would enable employees with psychiatric disabilities to succeed.

In summary, while earlier cases decided under the Rehabilitation Act characteristically applied a rigorous analysis to employer decisions to exclude workers based on fears of future dangerousness, more recent decisions display far more deference to employers' judgment, even when patently based on stereotyping and other forms of heuristic thinking. This deferential approach is reconciled with the analytical strictures of disability discrimination laws in two ways. First, courts adjudicating ADA cases are increasingly removing the analysis of potential dangerousness from the "direct threat" defense. The direct threat analysis requires an exacting analysis, objective and individualized medical and risk-related evidence. By relocating analysis to other more flexible parts of the statute, courts are more easily influenced by fears, stereotypes, and "intuitive epidemiology" that characterize the new workplace violence account.

Second, courts are increasingly analyzing reasonable accommodation issues in mental disability cases not within the framework of the undue hardship defense, but rather under the threshold question of statutory coverage. By holding certain types of accommodations to be per se unreasonable, a plaintiff's claims can be rejected at the outset, on the grounds that she or he is unable to perform the essential functions of the job, with or without reasonable accommodation. In this respect, courts are founding critical legal analysis not on those portions of the statute that impose high burdens on employers and limit opportunities for heuristic analysis, but rather on sections that permit more ready influence by the myths, fears, and stereotypes perpetuated by the new workplace violence account.

Additionally, as seen in *Cody v. Cigna Healthcare,* where the specter of workplace violence is raised, courts tend to structure a case's factual narrative in a manner that reflects the popular account of workplace violence.[141] Once the events giving rise to the case are recast in this manner, the employer's decision to exclude the plaintiff appears reasonable, prudent, and nondiscriminatory. In short, judges, along with employers, appear to have been captured by the popular account of workplace violence. A substantial set of recent mental disability cases reveal that the result of this trend is a weakening and a rhetorical delegitimation of the mental disability provisions of the ADA.

## Conclusion

People, including judges, can be expected to respond to the hazards they perceive. Laws that appear to constrain or prohibit prudent responses to perceived risk will naturally generate resistance, resentment, or even ridicule. Unfortunately, the ability to accurately perceive the existence or seriousness of a risk is constrained by a variety of subconscious factors. Indeed, the severity of a risk is often estimated based on the ease with which one can bring to mind situations in which that risk materialized.[142] The more vividly and frequently a particular disaster scenario is portrayed, the more serious the risk it represents is perceived to be. In similar fashion, the more closely a class of aversive events conforms to popular conceptions about the way things are, the more likely their occurrence will seem and the more serious any risks associated with their occurrence will appear.[143]

The ADA was enacted, in large measure, to prevent subjective and irrational perceptions of risk from limiting the opportunities of people with disabilities to participate fully in all aspects of society. Unfortunately, to the extent that cultural forces reinforce exaggerated perceptions of risk, people will perceive laws like the ADA, which require a more scientific and less heuristic approach to risk, as ill-conceived obstacles to prudent risk reduction efforts.

The new workplace violence account, conceived and perpetuated largely for commercial gain, is providing just this type of reinforcement. The account posits that worker-on-worker violence is a serious problem and suggests that potentially violent workers can be identified and removed from the workplace before disaster descends. Furthermore, it portrays the ADA as an unfortunate obstacle around which a prudent employer must navigate to protect employees.

This representation influences judicial construction of the ADA. One can reasonably expect that if a law is viewed as an impediment to prudent action, it will be interpreted as narrowly as possible. Further, this perception and this narrowing interpretation may not remain confined to workplace violence cases. Instead, precedents originating in these cases have the potential to affect the disposition of other cases as well. In this way, the discursive power of the new workplace violence account extends far beyond the fear of workplace violence and psychiatric disabilities. It ultimately operates to weaken and, we suggest, rhetorically to delegitimize the act as a whole.

NOTES

1. *Postal,* Ripcord Games (Running with Scissors 1997).

2. *See* Karl Vick, *Violence at Work Tied to Loss of Esteem,* St. Petersburg Times, Dec. 17, 1993, at 1A ("in some circles excessive stress is known as 'going postal'"); Michael Lopez, *Passive Aggression Typical in America's Workplace,* Desert News, Jan. 17, 1999, at M4 (describing the term *going postal* as almost a cliché).

3. *See infra* notes 32–33, 35.

4. *See infra* part 3.

5. *See infra* part 3A–B.

6. *See infra* notes 75–76 and accompanying text.

7. *See infra* notes 35, 37–38 and accompanying text.

8. *See infra* part 3C.

9. *See generally* Deviance and Medicalization: From Badness to Sickness 38–72 (Peter Conrad & Joseph W. Schneider eds., 1992).

10. *See generally* Georgia Pabst, *Man Fired over Dreams Presaging Shooting, Postal Service Says His Dreams, Gestures Threatened Others*, MILWAUKEE J. SENT., Dec. 15, 1998, at A1. Ironically, the dreams turned out to be correct; another worker did in fact attack that office.

11. *See* Gilbert Chan, *Veteran Cop Teaches Employers How to Recognize Warning Signs*, SACRAMENTO BEE, Nov. 15, 1998, at E1.

12. *See* Jess F. Kraus & David L. McArthur, *Epidemiology of Violent Injury in the Workplace*, 11 OCCUPATIONAL MEDICINE: STATE OF THE ART REVIEWS 201, 202, nn.1, 19 (Apr.–June 1996). The first mention of assault-related deaths actually appeared in 1982, but no report appeared in a peer-reviewed journal until 1987.

13. *See* Marcida Dodson, *Expert Says Job Stress Can Result in Violence*, L.A. TIMES, Apr. 1, 1986, at B1 (covering a multiple homicide at the California Employment Development Department Office in Garden Grove, California). This was the earliest mention of the phrase located through a search of the LEXIS/NEXIS ARCNWS database. Newspapers appear not to have used the phrase again until the 1989 post office shooting incident in Escondido, California, and then only in the context of Postal Service management policies and work conditions contributing to suicides and employee violence; *see also* Robert W. Welkos & H. G. Reza, *Workers Say Postal Jobs Take a Terrible Toll; Many Blame Stress on Hard-Driving Bosses*, L.A. TIMES, Aug. 11, 1989, at A1. It is highly unlikely that the phrase appeared anytime before 1986, since studies of assault related injury appeared in peer-reviewed journals for the first time in 1987; *see* Kraus & McArthur, *supra* note 12.

14. *See* ALICE HAMILTON, EXPLORING THE DANGEROUS TRADE (1985).

15. *See* 29 C.F.R. §§ 1910.66–68 (1998) (prescribing standards for powered platforms, manlifts, and vehicle-mounted work platforms).

16. *See* 29 C.F.R. § 1910.1000 (1998) (establishing exposure limits for air contaminants).

17. *See* Kraus & McArthur, *supra* note 12, at 201–2.

18. *See, e.g.,* NIOSH, MORTALITY BY OCCUPATION, INDUSTRY, AND CAUSE OF DEATH (1997); NIOSH, ATLAS OF RESPIRATORY DISEASE MORTALITY, UNITED STATES: 1982–1993 (1998).

19. *See* BUREAU OF LABOR STATISTICS, NATIONAL CENSUS OF FATAL OCCUPATIONAL INJURIES, 1997 Table 1, *available at* <http://www.bls.gov/special.requests /ocwc/oshwc/cfoi/cfnr0004.txt> (visited Jan. 19, 1999). We estimated the figure of 2,516 occupational deaths by subtracting the 2,599 traffic-related and 1,103 assault- and violence-related workplace deaths from the 6,218 total occupational deaths in 1997.

20. *See* BUREAU OF LABOR STATISTICS, SAFETY AND HEALTH STATISTICS, OCCUPATIONAL INJURIES AND ILLNESSES (1997), *available at* <http://www.bls.gov /news.release/osh.nws.htm> (visited Jan. 19, 1999).

21. *See* S. Anthony Baron, *Organizational Factors in Workplace Violence: Developing Effective Programs to Reduce Workplace Violence*, 11 OCCUPATIONAL MEDICINE: STATE OF ART REVIEWS 335 (Apr.–June 1996).

22. *See Postal Operations and Services Violence in the United States Postal Service, 1993: Before the Joint Hearing of the U.S. House of Representatives Subcomm. on Census, Statistics and Postal Personnel and the Subcomm. on Postal Operations and Services, Comm. on Postal Operations and Civil Service* (1993) (statement of Marvin

Runyon, Chief Executive Officer and Postmaster General of the United States). In fact, the homicide rate for postal workers from 1980 to 1989 was lower than the national average. *See* NIOSH, U.S. Dep't of Health & Human Serv's Current Intelligence Bulletin, Violence in the Workplace (1996) (visited Feb. 29, 2000) <http://www.cdc.gov/niosh/violintr.html> [hereinafter NIOSH, Violence in the Workplace]. The comparatively low homicide rate for Postal Service employees is even more noteworthy given that the agency employs roughly 840,000 people nationwide. *See* George Watson, *Signs Were There Despite Indications of Medical Illness, Suspect in Shootings Received No Help,* HARTFORD COURANT, Sept. 19, 1998, at A1. It is even more remarkable in light of the fact that many of Postal Service positions involve risk factors for attacks from nonemployees, such as robberies. *See* discussion *infra* part 2A.

23.  *See* Kraus & McArthur, *supra* note 12, at 202.

24.  *See Joint Hearings, supra* note 22 (statement of Marvin Runyon); Bill McAllister, *Runyon Vows Efforts to Curb Violence at Post Offices,* WASH. POST, Aug. 6, 1993, at A19.

25.  *See generally* Lopez, *supra* note 2, at M4 ("Workplace violence has become such a powerful concern in recent years that a phrase, now almost a cliché, has been added to the office lexicon: 'going postal'"); De Tran, *Slayings Latest in Workplace Assaults Violence,* L.A. TIMES, July 9, 1993, at A26 ("'More people in general in the country are using the workplace as a site to vent out their rage,' said Michael Mantell, a San Diego specialist in police psychology"); Chan, *supra* note 11, at E1 ("a series of bone chilling headlines: 'Terror at 1 Market Plaza . . .' 'Insurance Agent shoots 5 . . .' 'Postal Worker kills 14'").

26.  *King of the Hill: Junkie Business* (FOX television broadcast, Apr. 26, 1998).

27.  The term first appears in newspapers in 1993. *See* Vick, *supra* note 2. But the term has gained wide usage since that time. *See* Lopez, *supra* note 2.

28.  CLUELESS (Paramount Studio 1995).

29.  *See* Watson, supra note 22, at A1 ("After Premo was shot and arrested, a portrait emerged of a delusional loner who talked about being abducted by aliens and vague plots to 'get him'"); Jolie Soloman & Patricia King, *Waging War in the Workplace,* NEWSWEEK, July 19, 1993, at 30 (describing profile of those who target the workplace as a site of violent actions); Raymond Smith, *Looking to Head Off Violence in the Workplace,* PRESS ENTERPRISE, Dec. 20, 1998, at B3; *Struggling To Understand Causes of Workplace Violence,* CHICAGO TRIB., Dec. 17, 1993, at Bus. 1 ("The typical workplace killer is a middle-aged man, probably a loner with few relationships away from the job, who is frustrated by problems at work"); Debora Vrana, *Careers: Madder Than Ever,* L.A. TIMES, Nov. 2, 1998, at C28 ("But what signals an employee is in danger of a violent meltdown? A middle-aged man who is a chronic complainer, distrustful and rigid is the typical disgruntled employee, studies have shown"); Megan Mulholland, *Biggest Threat of Workplace Violence Is from Other Workers, Expert Says,* KNIGHT RIDDER TRIB. BUS. NEWS., Oct. 15, 1998 ("The most likely perpetrator is a middle-aged white man who is withdrawn and questions his self worth. . . . He blames others and may have drug dependencies and mental problems. Characteristics include a history of violent behavior, obsession with weapons, direct or veiled threats, obsession with work, unwanted romantic interests, grudges and difficulty accepting criticism"); Roland Maiuro, *We Must*

*Reduce Violence in Workplace,* NEWSDAY, Sept. 29, 1998, at A37 ("The most common 'profile' of a violence-prone employee is a white male, 35 or older, who has few interests and social supports outside of work, an affinity for guns, a history of family problems, and a tendency to harbor resentments and grudges, verbalize extremist opinions and abuse drugs or alcohol during times of stress").

30. *See e.g.,* Guardsmark, *Guardsmark Home Page* (visited Mar. 6, 1999) <http://www.guardsmark.com> (advertising, "Workplace violence is a heart-stopping reality. If you want the best protection for your employees . . . depend on Guardsmark"); Workplace Violence Research Institute, *Workplace Violence Research Institute Home Page* (visited Oct. 10, 1998), <http://www.noworkviolence.com> (promoting its services as a "full-service provider in workplace violence prevention programs: Consulting, Training, Incident Prevention, Crisis Response and Program Maintenance"); Joan Hill, *Business School Study Uncovers Workplace Violence Warning Signs,* U.S.C. CHRON., Aug. 29, 1995 (visited Oct. 10, 1998), *available at* <http://www.usc.edu/extrelations/news_service/chronicle_html/1995.10.02.html> (outlining study of "danger signs that employers should look for to prevent potential violence in the workplace"); Janet L. Robinson, *10 Facts Every Employer and Employee Should Know About Workplace Violence* (visited Jan. 14, 1999), *available at* <http://www.smartbiz.com /sbs/columns/robin1.htm> (providing statistics, profiles, and prevention suggestions for employers); Crisis Solutions, *Introduction to Crisis Solutions* (visited Oct. 15, 1998), <http://www.crisissolutions.com /about/html> ("Whether the violence results during the commission of a crime, is caused by a disgruntled or deranged present or former employee, or is perpetrated as a result of domestic discord or abuse, 'at work' has become a more dangerous place." "The odds are that within the next 3 years, if your company has not already experienced a crisis or critical incident in the workplace—you will"); Peerless Video, *Peerless Video Home Page,* <http://www.peerless-video.com/> (offering training videos to manage violence in the workplace, suggesting that "workplace violence rarely comes without warning signs").

31. Landels Ripley and Diamond, Slackers, Hackers, and Pistol Packers: How to Avoid Hiring the Wrong Person, Working Breakfast Series (Sept. 18, 1998); *see also* Law Offices of Rebecca A. Speer, What Employers Need to Know About Workplace Violence (visited Feb. 20, 2000), available at <http://www.workplacelaw.com> (providing information to "encourage employers to learn about workplace violence and the positive strategies they can adopt to meet critical legal obligations and business objectives related to the problem").

32. *See generally* Louis P. DiLorenzo & Darren J. Carroll, *The Growing Menace: Violence in the Workplace,* NEW YORK ST. B.J., Jan. 1995, at 24, 26; William E. Pilchak, *Employment Issues Arising from Employee Violence,* 1998 National Institute on the Americans with Disabilities Act (Las Vegas); Darrell S. Gay, *Defending a Mental Disability Case,* 586 PLI/LIT 383, 399–402 (1998); Kimberlie K. Ryan, *Work Zone or War Zone? An Overview of Workplace Violence,* 26 COLORADO LAWYER 19 (1997); Stephen F. Befort, *Pre-employment Screening and Investigation: Navigating Between a Rock and a Hard Place,* 14 HOFSTRA LAB. L.J. 365 (1997).

33. *See generally* Safe@Work, *Safe@Work Home Page* (last modified Sept. 25 1999), <http://www.careerlab.com/safework.htm> ("Things we can do for you: . . . Identify early warning signs and potentially dangerous personalities. Assess violent

employees or managers"); Crisis Solutions, *supra* note 30; International Security Services, Inc., available at <http://www.intlsec.com/welcome.html> (offering a "Hostile Employee Suppression Unit"); George Barford & Kaiwen Tseng, *Psychological Tests and Work Place Violence—a Review*, 68 FLA. B.J. 76 (1994).

34. *See* NIOSH, Violence in the Workplace, supra note 22, at 5; *see also* OSHA, U.S. Department of Labor, Workplace Violence Awareness and Prevention: Facts and Information (visited Jan. 19, 1999), *available at* <http://www.osha-slc.gov /workplace_violence/workplaceViolence.PartI.html>. Importantly, NIOSH carefully distinguishes coworker violence from the "epidemic" of general assaults and homicide. "Unfortunately, sensational acts of co-worker violence (which form only a small part of the problem) are often emphasized by the media to the exclusion of the almost daily killings of taxicab drivers, convenience store clerks and other retail workers, security guards, and police officers. These deaths often go virtually unnoticed, yet their numbers are staggering. . . ." *Id.* at <http://www.cdc.gov/niosh /violintr.html>.

35. *See generally* Illinois State Police, *Characteristics of Persons Who Commit Acts of Violence in the Workplace* (last modified Aug. 25, 1997) <http://www.state.il .us/ISP/viowkplc/vwpp4.htm>; University of California at Irvine, *Workplace Violence Prevention and Response* (visited Mar. 1, 1999), <http://www.abs.uci.edu/ depts/police/workplaceviolence.html> (characterizing holding a grudge and inability to take criticism as signals of violence potential).

36. Janet E. Goldberg, *Employees with Mental and Emotional Problems*, 24 STETSON L. REV. 201, 234 n.231 (1994); Baron, *supra* note 21, at 338–41.

37. *See, e.g.*, KIMON S. IANNETTA ET AL., DANGER BETWEEN THE LINES, RESOURCE MANUAL FOR PREDICTION OF VIOLENCE (1998).

38. *See* Brunner et al., *Abnormal Behavior Associated with a Point Mutation in the Structural Gene for Monoamine Oxidose A*, SCIENCE 578, 578–80 (Oct. 22, 1993).

39. Mark Braverman & Susan R. Braverman, *Seeking Solutions to Violence on the Job*, USA TODAY MAGAZINE, May 1, 1994.

40. Vrana, *supra* note 29 (referring to survey by Pinkerton).

41. *See generally id.*

42. Robinson, *supra* note 30, at <http://www.smartbiz.com/sbs/columns /robin1.htm>.

43. Ella W. Van Fleet & David D. Van Fleet, *Workplace Violence: Moving Toward Minimizing Risks* (visited Oct. 9, 1998), <http://www.minerva.org/models /cm96_02.html>. The statement is followed by descriptions of high-profile incidents, escalating through the bombings of the World Trade Center and the Oklahoma City Federal Building, as evidence of the dangers of workplace violence.

44. *See, e.g.*, John Sample, *Workplace Violence Training and Liability Prevention*, 2 HRD LIABILITY UPDATE (Mar. 1997) *available at* <http://www.sampleassociates.com/newsletters/mar97.html> (discussing the "most relevant theories" of employer liability with respect to violent employees).

45. *See, e.g.*, Robinson, *supra* note 30, at <http://www.smartbiz.com /sbs /columns/robin1.htm>; Illinois State Police, *supra* note 35, at <http://www.state .il.us/ISP/viowkplc/vwpp4.htm> (listing psychosis, depression, and personality disorders, including personality traits, as indicators of violence potential). The Illinois State Police exempts "hunters or gun hobbyists" from characteristics of "inter-

est or obsession with weapons." *Id.* at <http://www.state.il.us/ISP /viowkplc /vwpp4.htm>.

46. Vrana, *supra* note 29.

47. *See generally* Sentry Insurance, *Workplace Violence* (visited January 1, 1999), <http://www.sentry.com/workviol.htm> ("psychological disorders"); Illinois State Police, *Violence in the Workplace: Abnormal Behavior* (last modified Aug. 25, 1997), <www.state.il.us/isp/viowkplc/vwpp5.htm> (suggesting looking for emotional difficulties as indicator of abnormal behavior, and listing mental illness as a cause for abnormal behavior). *See, e.g.,* Sample, *supra* note 44, at <http://www.sampleassociates.com/newsletters/mar97.html> (listing "[s]ignificant changes in behavior (mood swings, outbursts, insubordination, paranoia)); Baron, *supra* note 21, at 339–40 (listing "[s]evere personality disorders" and "psychotic and/or paranoid behavior" as indicators); Goldberg, *supra* note 36, at 234 n.231.

48. *See* Robinson, *supra* note 30, at <http://www.smartbiz.com/sbs /columns/robin1.htm> .

49. *See* Chan, *supra* note 11, at E1.

50. *See generally* Workplace Violence Research Institute, *supra* note 30 (offering "Symptom Recognition Workshop" as an element of workplace violence prevention program); Hilson Research, Inc., 1999 Catalog 4 (1999).

51. *See, e.g.,* Maiuro, *supra* note 29, at A37 ("murder has become the No. 1 cause of death for women on the job. For men, who traditionally suffer much mightier rates of death due to accidental injuries associated with physical labor, it is now ranked third, after machine-related deaths and driving accidents"); *see also* Robinson, *supra* note 30, at <http://www.smartbiz.com/sbs/columns/robin1.htm>.

52. Workplace violence marketing materials frequently cite total costs to the national economy in the billions of dollars per year. *See, e.g.,* Guardsmark advertisement, N.Y. TIMES, available at <http://www.guardsmark.com>; Peerless Video, *Call to Action: Managing Violence in the Workplace* <http://www.peerless-video.com/call.htm>; Crisis Solutions, *supra* note 30 at <http://www.crisissolutions.com>. Such exaggerated claims rarely cite any support, but in all likelihood come from definitions of workplace violence broad enough to cover personal and property theft. *See infra* part 3A.

53. *See supra* notes 1–2 and accompanying text.

54. The National Center for Health Statistics reported 20,738 homicides for 1996, based on Vital Statistics Reports. *See* National Center for Health Statistics, *FASTATS: Homicide* (visited Nov. 8, 1998), <http://www.cdc.gov/nchswww/fas-tats/homicide.htm>.

55. *See* BUREAU OF LABOR STATISTICS, *supra* note 19, at <http://www.bls .gov/special.requests/ocwc/oshwc/ cfoi/cfnr0004.txt>. This figure is down from the average of 1,032 from 1992 to 1996.

56. *See id.* at table 1.

57. *See* National Center for Health Statistics, *Leading Causes of Death,* <http://www.cdc.gov/nchswww/ datawh/statab/pubd/leadcod.htm>.

58. *See* BUREAU OF LABOR STATISTICS, *supra* note 19, at <http://www.bls.gov /special.requests/ocwc/oshwc/cfoi/cfnr0004.txt>. BLS statistics count death at the hands of a coworker or former coworker separately from death by robbery or other

crimes *even if* the incidents overlap. Telephone Interview with Guy Toscano, BLS Census of Fatal Occupational Injuries (January 1999).

59. *See* BUREAU OF LABOR STATISTICS, *supra* note 19, at <http://www.bls.gov /special.requests/ocwc/oshwc/cfoi/cfnr0004.txt>. This figure is up from 1995 when crimes perpetrated by outsiders accounted for 75 percent of workplace homicides. *See* Guy Toscano, *Workplace Violence: An Analysis of Bureau of Labor Statistics Data*, 11 OCCUPATIONAL MEDICINE: STATE OF THE ART REVIEWS 227 (Apr.–June 1996). NIOSH also estimated that 73–82 percent of workplace homicides are due to robbery and crimes by outsiders. NIOSH, *supra* note 34.

60. *See* BUREAU OF LABOR STATISTICS, *supra* note 19, at <http://www.bls.gov /special.requests/ocwc/oshwc/cfoi/cfnr0004.txt>.

61. *See id.*

62. *See* NIOSH, Violence in the Workplace, *supra* note 22. Workplace homicides by industry and sex are distributed as follows: for male workers, 36.1 percent occur in retail trade, 16 percent in the service industry, 10.5 percent in public administration, and 10.6 percent in transportation/public utilities. The percentage of homicides for women in the same sectors are 45.5 percent, 22.2 percent, 2.9 percent, and 3.8 percent. *Id.*

63. *See* Francis J. D'Addario, *Improving Workplace Security*, 11 OCCUPATIONAL MEDICINE: STATE OF THE ART REVIEWS 349 (Apr.–June 1996).

64. *See* Braverman & Braverman, *supra* note 39 (after recognizing that worker-on-worker violence is only a fraction of the problem, the article transitions to a discussion of the dangerous coworker, citing the NW Insurance Survey); Vrana, *supra* note 29 ("Although deaths are relatively rare, reports of anger and hostility in the workplace are on the rise").

65. *See* BUREAU OF LABOR STATISTICS, NATIONAL CENSUS OF NON-FATAL OCCUPATIONAL INJURIES. As with workplace homicides, this figure is down from 21,255 in 1993. *See* Toscano, *supra* note 59, at 233. NIOSH similarly estimated 22,400 nonfatal assaults in 1992. NIOSH, *supra* note 34, at <http://www.cdc.gov/niosh /violintr.html>. The Bureau of Labor Statistics ("BLS") nonfatal assault figures cannot be directly compared to workplace homicide rates in the Census of Fatal Occupational Injuries since nonfatal assaults exclude self-employed and government workers and the figures are compiled from entirely distinct sources. BLS compiles nonfatal assault figures from reports required under OSHA, and therefore the statistics include only assaults resulting in days away from work. By omitting minor, non-injury-causing incidents, the data may not be an accurate representation of all assaults. They do, however, provide data on the injury-causing assaults that motivate the new workplace violence account. Toscano, *supra* note 59.

66. *See* BUREAU OF JUSTICE STATISTICS, CRIMINAL VICTIMIZATION 1997: CHANGES 1996–97 WITH TRENDS 1993–97, *available at* <http://www.ojp.usdoj.gov /bjs/cvictgen.htm>. BJS reported 8.6 million total assaults in 1997. *Id.* This figure includes any type of verbal assault as well as the type of injury-producing attack that the workplace violence model posits.

67. *See* BUREAU OF LABOR STATISTICS, *supra* note 20, at <http://www.bls.gov /news.release/osh.nws.htm>; NIOSH, *supra* note 34 at <http://www.cdc.gov /niosh/violintr.html>.

68. *See* BUREAU OF LABOR STATISTICS, *supra* note 20, at <http://www.bls.gov /news.release/osh.nws.htm>; *see also* NIOSH, *supra* note 34 at <http://www.cdc .gov /niosh/violintr.html> (health care patients account for 45 percent of assaults). The category of health care patient includes any injury received by a hospital emergency room worker or acute psychiatric institution.

69. *See* BUREAU OF LABOR STATISTICS, *supra* note 20, at <http://www.bls.gov /news.release/osh.nws.htm>.

70. *Id.*

71. *See id.* at <http//www.ojp.usdoj.gov/bjs/pub/ascii/cv97.txt>. For examples of marketing material using the Department of Justice figures, *see* Sample, *supra* note 44 at <http://www.sampleassociates.com/newsletters/mar97.html>; Law Offices of Rebecca A. Speer, *supra* note 31, at <http://www.workplacelaw.com>; Sentry Insurance, *supra* note 47, at <http://www.sentry.com/workviol.htm>.

72. Toscano, *supra* note 59; *see also* Joseph T. Hallinan, *Workplace Not as Dangerous as Government Might Have You Believe,* SAN DIEGO SOURCE (Aug. 28, 1998), *available at* <http://www.sddt.com/ files/librarywire/98/08/28/la.html>.

73. *See* Christopher Heredia et al., *Deadly Blast at Tosco Plant; Fireball Possibly Caused by Gas Leak Leaves One Worker Dead, Four Injured,* S.F. CHRON., Feb. 24, 1999, at A1; Cathleen Sullivan, *Whistleblower at Tosco,* S.F. EXAMINER, Feb. 26, 1999, at A1.

74. *See* Braverman & Braverman, *supra* note 39 ("Most of the recent work on workplace violence has not explored this issue. Instead, attention has been directed to three areas: hiring and firing policies; security strategies and work design for high-risk occupations; and constructing a 'profile' of the potentially violent worker. . . . Although these are important issues and deserve attention, they bypass the crucial system dimension").

75. NIOSH, *supra* note 34, at <http://www.cdc.gov/niosh/violintr.html>

76. *See, e.g.,* Guardsmark, *supra* note 30, at <http://www.guardsmark.com>; Sample, *supra* note 44, at <http://www.sampleassociates.com/newsletters /mar97.html> (offering to train supervisors to identify potentially violent employees).

77. Hilson Research, Inc., 1999 CATALOG 4 (1999). The catalog also assures employers that the Inwald Survey 2 ("IS2™") "is in compliance with the Americans with Disabilities Act (ADA) and the Civil Rights Act (CRA). It can be administered prior to a conditional job offer." *Id.* Only in the *IS2 ™ Sample Report,* does the company clarify the limitations of the test. "This report is intended to be used as an aid in assessing an individual's suitability for employment. It is not intended as a substitute for a pre-employment interview, as a final evaluative report regarding a candidate's ultimate job suitability, or as a sole source for denying employment to an applicant." Hilson Research, Inc., IS2™ Sample Report (Nov. 11, 1994).

78. Safe@Work, *supra* note 33, at <http://www.careerlab.com/safework.htm>.

79. International Security Services, *supra* note 33, at <http://www.intlsec.com /welcome.html>.

80. Sentry Insurance, *supra* note 47, at <http://www.sentry.com /workviol.htm>.

81. *See* Sample, *supra* note 44, at <http://www.sampleassociates.com/newsletters/mar97.html> (pointing to "significant changes in behavior (mood swings, outbursts, insubordination, paranoia)" as indicators of potential violence); Crisis

Solutions, *supra* note 30, at <http://www.crisissolutions.com> ("Whether violence results during the commission of a crime, is caused by a disgruntled or deranged present or former employee." Sentry Insurance, *supra* note 47, at <http://www.sentry.com/workviol.htm> ("warning signs may include . . . marital problems, psychological disorders, alcohol or drug abuse").

82. *See* John Monahan, *Dangerous and Violent Behavior,* 1 Occupational Medicine: State of the Art Reviews 559, 566 (Oct.–Dec. 1986). Monahan notes that mental disorder does *not* in the aggregate correlate with violent behavior. Rather the correlates of crime among the mentally disordered appear identical to those among any other group. They include (1) age, (2) gender, (3) race, (4) social class, and (5) prior criminality. Similarly, the correlates of mental disorder among criminal offenders mirror those in other populations: they tend to be (1) age, (2) social class, and (3) previous disorder.

83. The relevance of such indicators *to the individual* in question is precisely the issue under the ADA. *See infra,* part 4, discussing direct threat standard under the ADA articulated in *School Board of Nassau v. Arline,* 480 U.S. 273 (1987).

84. *See* John Monahan, *The Scientific Status of Research on Clinical and Actuarial Predictions of Violence,* in Social and Behavioral Sciences (1998). In the past few years, a few studies have indicated that there may indeed be some connection between mental disturbance and violence potential. *Id.* Monahan points out, however, that "demonstrating the existence of a statistically significant relationship between mental disorder and violence is one thing, demonstrating the legal and policy significance of the magnitude of that relationship is another." *Id.*

85. *See* Jeffrey W. Swanson et al., *Mental Disorder, Substance Abuse, and Community Violence: An Epidemiological Approach,* Violence and Mental Disorder 109–10 (John Monahan & Henry J. Steadman eds., 1994) ("since violence itself was a statistically rare event, the *absolute risk* of violence in the presence of mental illness remained low—about 7 percent in the course of a year—even while the *relative risk* was about three times as high as in the nondisordered population. On the other hand, having a substance abuse diagnosis was associated with a much higher risk of violence in both absolute and relative terms"). *Id.* at 112.

86. *See* Monahan, *supra* note 85. But as the authors of this preliminary study note, the association of these symptoms with violence, "both in an absolute sense and compared with other known causes and correlates of violence . . . is also modest. . . . Finally, our results and their theoretical underpinnings challenge the unfortunate stereotyping of mental patients. Most mental patients do not experience the specific psychotic symptoms we identified as risks for violent behavior"; *see also* Bruce G. Link & Ann Stueve, *Psychotic Symptoms and the Violent/Illegal Behavior of Mental Patients Compared to Community Controls,* Violence and Mental Disorder 156 (John Monahan & Henry J. Steadman eds., 1994).

87. *See id.* at 149–50.

88. *Id.* at 150.

89. Monahan, *supra* note 84.

90. *See* Carrol M. Brodsky, *Psychiatric Aspects of Fitness for Duty,* 11 Occupational Medicine: State of the Art Reviews 719 (Oct.–Dec. 1996).

91. *See generally* William D. Hooker, *Psychological Testing in the Workplace,* 11 Occupational Medicine: State of the Art Reviews 699 (Oct.–Dec. 1996).

92. *See* Monahan, *supra* note 84.

93. *Id.*

94. 463 U.S. 880 (1983).

95. Brief Amicus Curiae for the American Psychiatric Association at 8–9, Barefoot v. Estelle, 463 U.S. 880 (1983) (No. 82–6080).

96. *See* David Faust & Jay Ziskin, *The Expert Witness in Psychology and Psychiatry*, 241 SCIENCE 31 (1988).

97. *Id.*

98. *See* Robert J. Menzies et al., *The Dimensions of Dangerousness Revisited: Assessing Forensic Predictions About Violence*, 18 LAW AND HUMAN BEHAVIOR 1 (1994).

99. *Id.* at 18.

100. *Id.* at 19.

101. *Id.* at 25.

102. *Id.* (referring to Robert J. Menzies et al., *The Dimensions of Dangerousness: Evaluating the Accuracy of Psychometric Predictions of Violence Among Forensic Patients*, 9 LAW AND HUMAN BEHAVIOR 49 (1985)).

103. *Id.* at 25–26.

104. The House Judiciary Report, for instance reads:

> For example, an employer may not assume that a person with a mental disability, or a person who has been treated for a mental disability, poses a direct threat to others. This would be an assumption based on fear and stereotype. The purpose of creating the "direct threat" standard is to eliminate exclusions which are not based on objective evidence about the individual involved. Thus, in the case of a person with mental illness there must be objective evidence from the person's behavior that the person has a recent history of committing overt acts or making threats which caused harm or which directly threatened harm.

H.R. Rep. No. 101–485 (III) at 30 (1990), *reprinted in* 1990 U.S.C.C.A.N. 445, 453 (footnotes omitted).

105. *See,* 29 C.F.R. app. § 1630(2)(r). The EEOC's Interpretive Guidance to the ADA states, "Such consideration [of direct threat] must rely on objective, factual evidence—not on subjective perceptions, irrational fears, patronizing attitudes, or stereotypes—about the nature or effect of a particular disability, or of disability generally."

106. *See* 42 U.S.C. § 12111(3) (1994).

107. 480 U.S. 273, 284 (1987).

108. 29 C.F.R. § 1630.2(r); *see also* Bragdon v. Abbott, 118 S. Ct. 2196, 2210 (1998).

109. 29 C.F.R. § 1630.2(r).

110. 139 F.3d 595 (8th Cir. 1998).

111. *Id.* at 597.

112. *Id.*

113. *Id.*

114. *Id.*

115. *Id.* at 598.

116. *Id.* at 598–99.

117. *Id.* at 599.

118. *Id.*

119. 29 C.F.R. § 1630.2(r).

120. The EEOC made this argument, with which the court disagreed, in *EEOC v. Amego, Inc.,* 110 F.3d 135, 137 (1st Cir. 1997). *See also* Nunes v. Wal-Mart, 164 F.3d 1243, 1247 (9th Cir. 1999) (finding that defendant bears the burden of proving that plaintiff was a direct threat because it is an affirmative defense); Rizzo v. Children's World Learning Centers, 84 F.3d 758, 764 (5th Cir. 1996) (stating that "as with all affirmative defenses the employer bears the burden of proving that the employee was a direct threat").

121. The court never reached the issue of whether Cody had experienced dis-ability-based harassment. However, it should be noted that courts have been dis-inclined to find coworker and supervisor harassment sufficiently severe or perva-sive to be actionable. For example, in *McClain v. Southwest Steel Co., Inc.,* 940 F. Supp. 295, 300–302 (N.D. Okla. 1996), the plaintiff's coworkers called him "crazy" and a "lunatic," queried him about Prozac and hospitalization, and asked him "what the f***'s wrong with you," without violating the plaintiff's rights under the ADA.

122. Lussier v. Runyon, 3 A.D. Cases 223 (D. Me. 1994).

123. *Id.* at 225–26.

124. *Id.* at 226.

125. *Id.* at 226–28.

126. *Id.* at 231.

127. 42 U.S.C. § 12111(8).

128. *See* Grenier v. American Cyanamid Plastics, Inc., 70 F.3d 667, 674–75 (1st Cir. 1995) (listing cases setting out conduct-related essential functions including: Pesterfield v. Tennessee Valley Auth., 941 F.2d 437, 441–42 (6th Cir. 1991) (getting along with supervisors and coworkers); Mancini v. General Electric Co., 820 F. Supp. 141, 147 (D. Vt. 1993) (following orders); Pickard v. Widnall, 1994 WL 851282, *9 (S.D. Ohio 1994) (mental and emotional stability); Johnson v. Morrison, 849 F. Supp. 777, 778 (N.D. Ala. 1994) (handling pressures and stresses)).

129. *See* Teahan v. Metro-North Commuter Railroad Co., 951 F.2d 511, 516–17 (2d. Cir. 1991), *cert denied,* 113 S. Ct. 54 (1992).

130. *See* Nielsen v. Moroni Feed Co., 162 F.3d 604, 608 n.8 (10th Cir. 1998).

131. 35 F.3d 1396 (9th Cir. 1994).

132. *See also* Palmer v. Circuit Court of Cook Cty., 117 F.3d 351 (7th Cir. 1997), *cert. denied,* 1998 U.S. LEXIS 761 (1998).

133. *See* 29 C.F.R. § 1630.2(n); 29 C.F.R. pt 1630, app § 1630.2(n).

134. 720 F. Supp. 1424, 1428–29 (N.D. Cal. 1989).

135. For example, in a recent case, *Keil v. Select Artificials,* 1999 U.S. App. LEXIS 3411 (8th Cir. 1999), a deaf employee had been repeatedly denied any permanent accommodation, such as an interpreter or TDD, isolating him in his workplace. After the owner purchased a new car, and she again denied him a TDD, he upbraided her for selfishness in front of several coworkers, and slammed a desk drawer. The court upheld termination based on these seemingly excusable infrac-tions.

136. *But see* Bultemeyer v. Fort Wayne Community Sch., 100 F.3d 1281, 1285 (7th

Cir. 1996) (holding that reasonable accommodation of individual with serious psychiatric disabilities was required).

137. 134 F.3d 576, 578 (3d Cir. 1998).

138. *Id.* at 581.

139. *See* Kent v. Derwinski, 790 F. Supp. 1032, 1040 (E.D. Wash. 1991) (holding that avoiding direct criticism and undue stress on an employee constituted appropriate accommodation).

140. *See* Wood v. County of Alameda, 1995 U.S. Dist. LEXIS 17513 (N.D. Cal. 1995) (ordering transfer away from a stress-inducing coworker); *see also* Bultemeyer v. Fort Wayne Community Sch., 100 F.3d 1281 (7th Cir. 1996) (requiring employer to account for employee's mental disability in interactive accommodation process).

141. *See supra* notes 112–22 and accompanying text.

142. This tendency is referred to as the "availability heuristic." *See* Amos Tversky & Daniel Kahneman, *Availability: A Heuristic for Judging Frequency and Probability*, 5 Cognitive Psychology 207 (1973).

143. This phenomenon is known as the "representativeness heuristic." *See* Daniel Kahneman & Amos Tversky, *Subjective Probability: A Judgment of Representativeness*, 3 Cognitive Psychology 430 (1972).

*Anita Silvers and Michael Ashley Stein*

# From *Plessy* (1896) and *Goesart* (1948) to *Cleburne* (1985) and *Garrett* (2001)

## A Chill Wind from the Past Blows Equal Protection Away

What are the standards of care and conduct, of risk and liability, to which [the disabled] are held and to which others are held in respect to them? Are the standards the same for them as for the [nondisabled]?

—JACOBUS tenBROEK, 1967

In its 1948 decision in *Goesart v. Cleary,*[1] the United States Supreme Court upheld the constitutionality of a Michigan statute that prohibited women from working as bartenders, unless they were the spouse or daughter of the establishment's male owner. While the Court acknowledged that the preceding years had wrought vast social and legal changes in women's status and roles, it nonetheless held that Michigan had acted "reasonably" in excluding women lacking on-site male patronage from bartending jobs. Because the statute had a "rational basis," the Court held, it did not violate the Fourteenth Amendment's guarantee of equal protection of the laws. In the Court's view, the equal protection clause did not require the states to accord equal treatment to members of different groups whose situations were "different in fact or opinion."[2]

No matter how skilled a woman might be at pouring drinks or tallying sums, to the Court, her situation was self-evidently different from a man's. For the justices, the mere thought of a female serving drinks evoked the image of a "sprightly and ribald" Shakespearean alewife. So, they believed, the mere presence of a female dispensing intoxicating beverages behind the bar could not help but trigger the very "moral and social problems" that the state intended to prevent by excluding women from bartending jobs in the first place.

Because, in the Court's view, the distinction between men and women drawn by the Michigan legislature was not wholly lacking in reason, the disadvantage it imposed on women did not violate the Constitution. However exclusionary the law might be, equal protection considerations could not upend it, the Court concluded, because the state had a "rational interest" both in protecting women from the limitations of their ability to maintain the peace and in protecting the public from the raucous disruptions that would no doubt be provoked by their presence.[3]

More than fifty years later, in *University of Alabama v. Garrett*,[4] the Supreme Court, in eerily similar fashion, upheld the constitutionality of a state university's demotion of a nursing supervisor to a poorer paying job because she had undergone treatment for breast cancer. Patricia Garrett had sued the University of Alabama, an arm of the state, under Title I of the Americans with Disabilities Act. Title I prohibits disability discrimination in employment, and it provides a private right of action for injunctive and monetary relief for a person who claims that his or her rights under the ADA have been violated by a covered employer. The University's Board of Trustees responded to Garrett's suit by claiming that, as a sovereign state, it was accorded immunity from private suits for money damages by the Eleventh Amendment to the United States Constitution.

The Supreme Court agreed. It held, by a now familiar five-to-four margin,[5] that in providing a disabled individual with a private ADA claim for money damages to remedy disability discrimination in state employment, Congress had accorded disabled persons rights beyond those to which they were constitutionally entitled under Section 1 of the Fourteenth Amendment's equal protection clause.[6] With a logic chillingly similar to that applied in *Goesart* almost half a century earlier, the *Garrett* majority held that, so long as a state had some "rational basis" for treating persons with disabilities less favorably that members of the nondisabled public, its action would not deprive the disabled of the equal protection of the laws.

Affirming its earlier decision in *City of Cleburne v. Cleburne Living Center*,[7] the *Garrett* majority held that disability does not constitute a "suspect classification" for equal protection purposes. Accordingly, states may pass legislation or take other action disadvantaging persons with disabilities without running afoul of the equal protection clause, so long as they have a "rational basis" for doing so. By prohibiting "rational" discrimination against persons with disabilities, and by requiring state employers to accommodate an employee's disability, the ADA provided remedies that were, in the Court's language, "incongruent and disproportional" to disabled people's negligible equal protection rights. So, concluded the Court, in applying Title I of the ADA to state employers Congress had exceeded its constitutional authority under Section 5 of the Fourteenth Amendment.[8]

In supporting the State of Alabama, the Court found that the ADA called for "incongruent" and "disproportionate" remedies for the ways state employers treat disabled applicants and employees. Stating that "it would be entirely rational (and therefore constitutional) for a state employer to conserve scarce financial resources by hiring employees able to use existing facilities," the Court found the ADA's requirement that employers make their facilities "readily accessible to and usable by individuals with disabilities" disproportionate to any constitutionally cognizable damage inflicted by the state's past discriminatory policies.[9]

Notably, in assessing congruence and gauging proportionality, the Court referred to the ADA's reasonable accommodation provisions. But curiously, there was no accommodation issue at stake in Garrett's case. It was a garden variety dispute over disparate treatment. This digression, in and of itself, suggests that the Court was concerned with far more than merely insulating the states from a congressionally imposed duty to accommodate persons with disabilities. In finding even Title I's disparate treatment provisions to be incongruent with and disproportional to disabled persons' rights under the equal protection clause, the Court essentially held that the states could well have a "rational interest" in excluding disabled people from state employment altogether.[10]

The judicial logic reflected in *Garrett* is distressingly reminiscent of that employed in the now discredited *Goesart* decision. For example, in his *Garrett* concurrence, Justice Kennedy admitted that the past several years had ushered in more enlightened attitudes about and public policies toward persons with disabilities. He went on to suggest that these more enlightened stances might discourage the exclusion of people with disabilities from state and private employment. Nonetheless, Justice Kennedy concluded, failure to apply this improved understanding to state personnel policy does not violate the Constitution. As sovereign entities, the states are free to discriminate against persons with disabilities, either through disparate treatment or through failure to make reasonable accommodations, so long as they have some rational basis for doing so.[11]

According to Chief Justice Rehnquist, who delivered the Court's judgment in *Garrett,* the equal protection clause does not actually require equal treatment if a group has "distinguishing characteristics" upon which a state bases a decision to treat members of the group differently.[12] Thus, no matter how capable Ms. Garrett might have been in directing nurses or otherwise executing her administrative responsibilities, to the Court her situation could not help but be different from those of identically qualified employees who had no present or past record of disability.

Although the decision in *Garrett* directly affected a relatively narrow class of actions,[13] its political and theoretical implications are broad. In *Garrett,* the Court made explicit a position at which its previous ADA decisions had merely hinted. The Court declared that the legal standard of treatment for Americans with disabilities need not be the same as for nondisabled citizens, because disabled people are fundamentally "different." Thus, four decades after Jacobus tenBroek asked whether legal standards are the same for the disabled as for other people,[14] the Supreme Court unequivocally answered "no."

The Court's analysis in *Garrett* is especially chilling because it so closely resembles that deployed by courts decades earlier in sustaining state sponsored discrimination against women and people of color. In those early cases, as in *Garrett,* the Court took the mere fact of a group's biological difference as demonstrating the rationality of denying ordinary opportunities to the group's members.

It is inconceivable that today's Court would uphold state statutes imposing exclusionary treatment on anyone "belonging to the colored race" or argue, as did an earlier Court in *Plessy v. Ferguson,* that "[l]egislation is powerless to eradicate racial instincts, or to abolish distinctions based upon physical differences."[15] For more than half a century, between its announcement of the notorious "separate but equal" doctrine in *Plessy* in 1896 and its renunciation of that same doctrine in *Brown v. Board of Education* in 1954,[16] the Court insisted that states had a "rational interest" in the differential treatment of people, based on "any visible admixture of black blood."[17] Since *Brown,* the Court has acknowledged that separation from others of similar age and qualifications solely because of one's race generates a feeling of inferiority as to one's status in the community that can affect a person "in a way unlikely ever to be undone."[18]

Similarly, half a century after *Goesart,* very little, if anything, strikes us as justifying sex-based occupational segregation. It is inconceivable that the Court would uphold a state's overt refusal to hire qualified females because its work sites had no ladies' restrooms. There is simply no way that a state policy of hiring only men because they could use existing facilities would survive equal protection scrutiny. More likely, the state would be ordered to modify the plumbing.

In short, fifty years after *Goesart,* very little if anything strikes us as justifying sex discrimination. We are far more likely to agree with the Supreme

Court's 1973 statement in *Frontiero v. Richardson*[19] that sex "frequently bears no relation to ability to perform or contribute to society."[20] Indeed, in *Mississippi University for Women v. Hogan,* the Court went even further, observing that most forms of state-sponsored sex discrimination were not so much means of achieving important government interests as they were codifications of normatively and empirically discredited social conventions.[21] In all the years since passage of the 1964 Civil Rights Act, the Court has only once upheld state-sponsored sex discrimination in employment.[22]

Social norms assigning women certain roles and denying them access to others have been replaced by a broad consensus that individual women and men should be presumed equally qualified to perform a particular job, unless proven otherwise. Thus, over the past century, judicial decisions turning on governmental claims about associations between social group membership and job-related characteristics have increasingly insisted on the presentation of empirically sound statistical analysis. The "naive social science" of popular myth and stereotype no longer suffices to justify state-sponsored disparate treatment.

Unfortunately, no similar transformation has advanced judicial thinking with respect to government classification of people with disabilities. A medicalized account of disability, which strongly resembles the outdated, pseudoscientific accounts of the inherent frailty of women or the cognitive inferiority of African Americans, still dominates legal analysis[23] despite mounting evidence that biological nontypicality does not equate to inherent limitation or inability. Myths and stereotypes about people with disabilities are perpetuated by, among other things, legal categories derived from social welfare laws, which cast people with disabilities as social incompetents dependent upon public or private assistance. This "impairment" or "welfarist" model has kept disability classifications mired in out-of-date notions rooted in empirically unsubstantiated stereotypes and subordinating social conventions.

Our purpose in this paper is to trace the Court's revival of the regressive logic of *Plessy* and *Goesart* in its opinions concerning the civil rights of disabled Americans. First, we examine the Supreme Court's definition of the disability classification, arguing that it is an artificial construction based on social convention rather than empirical fact. Then, focusing on one particularly salient example of this flawed judicial approach, we introduce the *Cleburne* doctrine, derived from the Court's decision in *City of Cleburne v. Cleburne Living Center,* and explore its implications for people with disabilities. We continue by explicating Congress's response to *Cleburne,* as expressed in the preamble to the Americans with Disabilities Act (ADA), and then explain how and why post-ADA Supreme Court cases, culminating in *Garrett,* have reinforced rather than repudiated *Cleburne's* legacy. In conclusion, we describe the logical errors embedded in the currently misdrawn disability classification and propose a reconceptualized taxonomy.

## Constitutional Classifications and Natural Kinds

One frequently voiced critique of the Court's equal protection jurisprudence is that it illegitimately converts legal categories into "natural kinds." The Court, in this view, takes as natural fact the inferiority of certain groups of people who are subject to disadvantageous statutory classification, and supposes that these groups are of a kind naturally deserving subordinating treatment. The Court's assumptions in this regard, the critique points out, do not derive from actual fact, but are simply reflections of popular social constructions. Anthony Amsterdam and Jerome Bruner, for example, observe that a

> "cripple" becomes a less natural category to the extent that prosthetic technologies become available; it is a particularly natural category when a culture not only lacks technological resources but regards physical afflictions as punishments for one's misbehavior in a prior life.[24]

The "natural kinds fallacy," we propose, results from mistakenly believing that what *is* the case must, in fact, *be* the case. Suppose, for example, that empirical studies in the late 1940s, when *Goesart* was decided, demonstrated that the typical American woman was unable to defend herself in a bar fight. Suppose as well that some *Plessy* era empirical study showed that a high proportion of African Americans were unable to read. These deficits are indisputably contingent. Women could not fight, and African Americans could not read, because the social roles to which they were then assigned gave them little opportunity to learn or hone these skills. These deficits are undeniably remediable through social changes that provide women with personal defense training and African Americans with public education. It is obviously false to attribute these deficits to women's or African Americans' biological natures.

A category or kind is natural if it exists independent of constitutive human processes. That is, a natural category is *described* by people rather than *constructed* by people. The properties of any natural kind are a matter of fact, to be discovered through the empirical study of that kind. Yet the Court's regressive methodology in cases such as *Plessy* and *Goesart* was the opposite of what we would expect if the classifications at issue were being approached as natural kinds.

The Court in these cases viewed legislative or administrative stipulation, not empirical investigation, as the proper way to identify the attributes of the categories under construction. As we shall see, the Court has characterized the larger group of people with disabilities in terms of properties drawn from the definition of disability embedded in welfarist legislation, rather than in terms of properties verified by empirical study. Thus, the Court's error is not only that it mistakes what is contingently true of disabled people for what is naturally definitive of them, but also that it accords state legislative stipulations about disabled people logical and discursive priority over empirically verifiable truth.

We realize that it will be no easy task to reconceive the disability category by presuming the essential competence of disabled individuals and by requiring that any presumptions to the contrary be based on empirical study of persons whose biological anomalies have historically been associated with disabilities. The first step in achieving this goal, however, is simple: the Court needs to commit itself to the idea that, in matters pertaining to the civil rights of disabled persons, empirically verifiable fact must override stipulative convention.

The Court's failure to make this commitment imposes two sets of costs. The first involves costs to the legal process itself. The more courts shape classifications by deferring to stipulative definitions, the more they invite confusion and contradiction. For example, in a series of cases that preceded and are cited in *Brown*, courts ruled both that the tangible resources of racially separated educational systems must be made equal, and that African Americans had to be admitted to facilities previously reserved for whites, because equal opportunities to pursue certain courses of study would be otherwise unavailable to them.[25] All of these cases involved situations in which opportunities believed to be equal in principle were empirically shown to be unequal in fact. Because access to state-sponsored opportunities was segregated by race, the resources allocated by the majority group to the minority group were, not surprisingly, systematically inferior to the resources arrogated by the majority to itself.

Cumulatively, the facts of these cases strongly controverted the claim made in *Plessy* that people with the biological difference of deeply pigmented skin could enjoy equal opportunity while relegated to separate facilities. In these cases, the claim that separate could be equal increasingly strained credulity; courts tied themselves into ever more tortured knots attempting to respond within *Plessy*'s doctrinal bounds to the factual record before them. Finally, the Court's decision in *Brown v. Board of Education* relieved the strain.

A second set of costs is imposed on the many individual people burdened by the Court's empirically unjustifiable disability classification. The *Plessy* Court's sacrifice of empirical reality to stipulative convention imposed upon African Americans substantial costs in humiliation and lost opportunity. Women incurred similar costs as a result of cases like *Goesart v. Cleary.* In hindsight, the nature and injustice of these costs are easy to see. But neither the courts nor the public seem able to recognize that the same costs are presently being imposed on people with disabilities by the Court's disability discrimination jurisprudence.

## The Costs of *Cleburne*

A clear illustration of Supreme Court reliance upon stipulative convention in shaping the disability classification can be found in *Cleburne v. Cleburne Living Center,*[26] one of the few pre-ADA cases to succeed in deploying the Fourteenth Amendment to disabled people's benefit. Although the *Cleburne* plaintiffs prevailed, the Court took the case as an opportunity to emphasize how different disabled people are from other citizens, and how these purported differences circumscribe the rights of disabled persons to equal protection of the laws.

The defendant in *Cleburne* was a Texas town that required a special use permit be obtained by anyone seeking to open a housing facility for people with mental retardation. No similar requirement was imposed on persons wishing to open, for example, boarding homes for unimpaired persons, fraternity houses, or convalescent homes. The Cleburne Living Center (CLC) wanted to open a home for people with mild to moderate cognitive limitations. The special permit process required that it secure agreement from all neighbors living within two hundred feet of the proposed site. Not all of CLC's prospective neighbors acceded, so a permit was not approved. Even had it been approved, the permit was good for only one year. After making remodeling investments, CLC would have had to repeat the application process every twelve months. CLC sued in federal district court, arguing that the permit system violated the rights of its mentally retarded prospective residents to the equal protection of the laws, as secured by the Fourteenth Amendment to the United States Constitution.

Stating that the zoning ordinance was rationally related to the state's legitimate interests, District Judge Porter rejected CLC's claim in an unpublished memorandum opinion. On appeal, a three-judge panel of the Fifth Circuit unanimously disagreed. Writing for the court, Judge Goldberg presented four reasons why the city's zoning requirement bore no rational relationship to the policy it purported to effectuate. First, the city could have no legitimate interest in responding to the private biases of the proposed group home's neighbors. Second, the city's claim that the classification helped rather than harmed mentally retarded people was not credible. Third, despite the city's claim that the site's location in a flood plain constituted a danger to the mentally retarded prospective residents of the group home, other groups of people who might have difficulty escaping from a flood—including the elderly and the infirm—were not required to seek special permits. Fourth, held the district court, the city's voiced concern with the density of occupancy of the proposed residence lacked merit, as the proposal met federal standards for group homes. Moreover, the city never adequately explained why the ordinance explicitly permitted other unrelated people, such as fraternity brothers, to live under "crowded" conditions, but not the mentally retarded. In sum, the four reasons given by the city to justify imposing a prohibitively high barrier on the mentally retarded were adjudged not rationally related to the proffered public interest in protecting a putatively weak and incompetent group.[27]

The city, however, argued that in addition to its interest in safeguarding retarded people, the zoning system protected the public against disruptions occasioned by their presence in a particular neighborhood. In an attempt to justify the permit requirement, the city voiced concerns with street congestion, fire hazards, and neighborhood serenity, and pointed to the possibility that the city might be held liable for harms CLC's mentally retarded residents might inflict. The appellate court was unconvinced, and it struck down the special permit requirement on equal protection grounds.[28]

The Supreme Court affirmed one aspect of the Fifth Circuit's reasoning and rejected another. Writing for the majority, Justice White held that the special permit requirement "rest[s] on an irrational prejudice against the mentally retarded." The Court affirmed the Fifth Circuit's decision invalidating the special permit law, but only insofar as the law applied to the particular disabled individuals in this particular case. In contrast to race and gender, stated the Court, mental retardation was not, in Fourteenth Amendment parlance, a "suspect classification." Thus, the city's use of the mental retardation classification in treating some of its residents less favorably than others would be constitutional, so long as it had some rational basis for doing so. There was, held the Court, no general presumption that legislative action employing the disability classification would result in a constitutional violation, even if the legislation systematically disadvantaged individuals who fell within that classification.[29]

Although the Court explicitly limited its finding that irrational prejudice against people with mental retardation lay behind the special permit requirement in the particular case before it, the program as a whole could hardly have another motivation. The various decisions in *Cleburne* raise a number of interesting and important issues.

Unlike the Supreme Court, the Fifth Circuit did not approach the *Cleburne Living Center* case assuming that the city's differential treatment of mentally retarded persons was subject only to rational basis review. Because this issue was as yet unresolved when the case went before the appellate court, the city was compelled to delineate precisely what interests it claimed were being furthered by the special permit system. Had the Court of Appeals not so closely scrutinized the city's purported justifications, the program's essential illogic might not have become so patently apparent. By deciding that statutory classifications disadvantaging mentally retarded people need not prompt heightened scrutiny, the Court made it prospectively much more difficult to challenge claims that a state's interests are rationally served by excluding disabled people from civic and commercial opportunities.

A second point is worthy of note. In analyzing *Cleburne Living Center,* the Court relied on provisions of the Developmental Disabilities Act and the Education of All Handicapped Children Act,[30] providing that mentally retarded children have a right to a public education that does not exceed their abilities, rather than the same education accorded nonretarded children, as demonstrating that states are permitted to treat the mentally retarded differently than they treat other people. In essence, the Court concluded that these statutes proved the point that the states can treat the mentally retarded in restrictive ways without running afoul of the Fourteenth Amendment.

Third, the *Cleburne* decision requires each group of disabled plaintiffs to litigate anew. In his partial dissent, Justice Marshall identified this as a "novel" approach, to leave intact "a legislative Act resting on 'irrational prejudice,' thereby forcing individuals in the group discriminated against to continue to run the Act's gauntlet."[31]

This problem is endemic to disability discrimination law. In statute after statute, case after case, the same issues concerning access and exclusion must be litigated individually, victim by victim, program provider by program provider, and may have to be revisited whenever the management of a program or facility changes hands. Ironically, the volume of litigation invited by the Court's reluctance to generalize disability discrimination findings is often cited as evidence of the burdensomeness and fundamental unfeasibility of providing equal opportunity for the disabled.[32] As we have seen, however, this problem is not endogenous to the disability classification itself. Rather, it emerges as an artifact of the courts' approach to disability discrimination.

Disability discrimination rulings resist extrapolation because of how both the courts and Congress have constructed the disability category. The *Goesart* Court characterized women in terms of socially undesirable dependence and incapacity. The *Cleburne* Court characterized mentally retarded people in the same terms. As in *Goesart,* the *Cleburne* Court relied on stereotypes and various other forms of flawed inference, rather than requiring clear evidence that the classification's members could accurately be characterized as inherently and uniquely vulnerable, disruptive, and otherwise problematic.

Close examination of the *Cleburne* Court's reasoning elucidates the problem. The *Cleburne* Court held that no heightened level of judicial review is demanded when mentally retarded people are singled out for differential treatment. This result is justified, in the Court's view because mentally retarded people are *different* from other people. So, states have wide latitude to treat them differently.

The *Cleburne* Court enunciated a five-part test for determining whether differential treatment survives equal protection scrutiny under a rational basis standard:

1. Is there a real difference between the group's members and other people?
2. Does the difference affect people's ability to cope with and function in the every day world?
3. In this regard, is the difference's impact immutable?
4. Is the challenged differential treatment rationally related to a legitimate state interest?
5. On balance, has the difference elicited more beneficial than burdensome statutory treatment?

With respect both to cognitive impairment specifically, and to disability generally, the majority declared, the answers are, generally speaking, "yes." The differential treatment of persons with disabilities is generally permissible because there are real, immutable differences between disabled and nondisabled people. These differences affect the ability of disabled people to function, and generally have elicited more favorable than unfavorable treatment.

But sometimes, the *Cleburne* Court allows, the answer to the fourth question may be "no." In the *Cleburne Living Center* case, for example, the Court could identify no legitimate state interest served by prohibiting individuals with mental retardation from living in the particular neighborhood where CLC wanted to locate its new group home. The lesson here is that a statute may, on its face, pass the rational basis test, but fail the test with respect to its application to a particular situation.[33] Analyzing cases in this way, however, means that each allegation of disability discrimination will have to be litigated de novo, with little aid from precedent. For this reason, civil litigation generally fails to stimulate broad reform in social policy on disability issues.

The *Cleburne* Court acknowledged that people who fall within the mental retardation category differ from each other as much or more than some of them differ from nonretarded people. Nevertheless, it treated mental retardation as a nonproblematic classification for equal protection purposes. The classification is necessary, the Court said, to enable the government to pursue policies designed to *assist* retarded people in realizing their full potential. Thus, there can be no presumption that legislative action treating mentally retarded people differently is "rooted in considerations that the Constitution will not tolerate." This is so even if, incidentally, the action disadvantages some retarded individuals.[34]

The *Cleburne* doctrine calls out for critical response. Martha Minow offers an instructive analysis by articulating several different accounts of the values at issue in Justice White's majority opinion and in the separate opinions of Justices Stevens[35] and Marshall.[36] While we admire the sweep of her approach, we think it may overlook or obscure a central disagreement over the logic of validly constructing constitutionally protected classes.

According to Minow, three different understandings of the disability classification emerge from the various opinions in *Cleburne*.[37] Writing for the Court, Justice White constructed the mentally retarded as a class of naturally inferior people characterized by "a reduced ability to cope with and function in the every day world." As a group, in White's view, the mentally retarded are "different, immutably so, in relevant respects." These "immutable differences" legitimate the state's interest in providing for their welfare. In sum, the Court validated the classification because of its usefulness in "a wide range of decisions."[38]

As Minow describes the lead opinion in *Cleburne,* the Court divides society into two classes, the normal and the abnormal, and presumes the abnormal, in this case the mentally retarded, to be more like each other than like the rest of the community.[39] This essential "otherness," then, justifies treating mentally retarded people differently. In a concurring opinion joined by Chief Justice Burger, Justice Stevens took a different approach. He emphasized the essential similarity of retarded and non-retarded people. In his view, the mentally retarded were entitled to equal treatment unless an "impartial lawmaker" or a mentally retarded person "could rationally vote in favor of a law" providing for special treatment.[40] Thus, far from presuming a law justified, Justice Stevens would require that statutory provisions limiting the opportunities of mentally retarded people be carefully scrutinized to assure that they serve not only a legitimate state interest, but also the interests of the mentally retarded people whose opportunities the law may restrict.

Minow observes that this way of thinking abstracts away retarded people's real differences by assimilating them to the "rational man" standard that forms a community norm.[41] It is, however, a mistake to equate mental retardation with nonrationality or irrationality. As even Justice White agreed, the classification ranges over "those whose disability is not immediately evident to those who must constantly be cared for."[42]

Being rational requires no great intelligence—especially when one is being rational about one's self-interest. When Sandra Jensen, a woman with Down syndrome, fought for a place on a heart transplant list, she clearly understood that securing a new heart was in her rational self-interest. Moreover, she argued compellingly that she deserved this opportunity by referencing the similarity of her situation to that of the nonretarded patients admitted without controversy to the list.[43] She used, in short, a definitively rational form of argument. When, as they often do, people with mild mental retardation object to being treated less favorably than nonretarded people, they appeal to consistency and thereby demonstrate their grasp of a basic technique of rational argument.

For the sake of argument, however, let us assume that retarded people, as a class, are different in some meaningful way from nonretarded people. Even granting that the classification has some meaningful reference, its boundaries and gradations would remain subject to controversy. In *Cleburne,* however, the Court spoke as if the boundary could accurately be described as "a reduced ability to cope with and function in the everyday world."[44] But this characterization applies as well to absent-minded professors and unworldly *religieuses,* who can behave so incompetently and disruptively as to be burdensome. They nevertheless benefit from constitutional protections denied to mentally retarded people.

In an alternative formulation, the *Cleburne* Court draws the relevant category boundary as the limited ability "to meet the standards of maturation, learning, personal independence, and social responsibility expected for an individual's age level and cultural group."[45] Surely this characterization is too vague.

In justifying its construction of a constitutionally unproblematic mental retardation category, the *Cleburne* Court leaned heavily on the notion that retarded people's limitations are immutable. But this characterization is called into serious question by new educational techniques that help mentally retarded individuals achieve far beyond outdated, conventional expectations. A nineteen-year-old with Down syndrome who is a high school graduate, enrolled in a community college, and earning a wage surely falls within a "normal" range by societal standards. In her case, her trisomy may be immutable, but her limitations in regard to social achievement are not. To be rational, therefore, policy decisions about whether the states may exclude or disadvantage her should not be transfixed by the immutability of chromosomal trisomy. Rather, they should be shaped by recognition of the transformability of social conditions.

The Court also proposed that the fact of legislative response to "the plight" of the mentally retarded itself "demonstrate[d] their unique problems." This reasoning is patently tautological. It fails to establish that the problems confronted by mentally retarded people arise from immutable impairments rather than mutable social conditions—including legislative classification and accompanying disparate treatment. In asserting that special measures directed at the retarded reflected their "real and undeniable differences," the Court neglects the extent to which these differences are reified when legislatures or other social actors single out the mentally retarded for differential treatment. Thus, even currently "real" social differences between retarded and nonretarded people may prove mutable, depending on how cultural practices address them.

As stated in Justice Marshall's partial dissent, the emergence in the nineteenth century of a state-mandated regime of "segregation and degradation," which warehoused the retarded for life, rivaled "in its virulence and bigotry . . . the worst excesses of Jim Crow."[46] According to Minow, Marshall's account verges on a "social relations" approach through which differences between groups are acknowledged, but valued. The meaning of such differences is always contextual: their import must be assessed in light of power differentials and other relationships that exist between the relevant groups. Attributions of difference that fuel exclusionary practices are especially condemnable as self-serving mechanisms for preserving the power of dominant classes. In their place, the social relations approach emphasizes interconnectedness and the multiplicity of avenues open to people wishing to contribute to the collective good. The social relations approach calls for the transformation of marginalizing practices so as to cultivate everyone's freedom to participate in both the rewards and responsibilities of social interaction.[47]

In sum, the *Cleburne* majority presumed that retarded people's differences (and by extrapolation, the differences from species-typical biology displayed by other persons with disabilities) can serve as legitimate proxies for social limitations. Unless proven otherwise on a case-by-case basis, these differences can be assumed to be rationally related to legitimate state interests. Justice Stevens's concurrence presumed exactly the opposite, namely, that disabled people's differences do not justify disparate treatment, until the converse is affirmatively established. Finally, Justice Marshall's partial dissent used the history of oppression of disabled people as a kind of lens through which society's tendencies to distort their attributes could be clearly perceived.

Illuminating as Justice Marshall's analysis might be, it addressed the assessment rather than the construction of the relevant class. It assumed that the disabled are different, but it did not inquire as to which of these differences could responsibly be characterized as traits defining the class. People can differ from one another biologically or socially. Biological traits, such as the absence or impairment of a corporeal component, are essential to the disability classification, but they are not socially relevant unless they are linked to social limitations that render individuals burdensomely dependent or disruptive. All who are subject to a particular classification may share certain biological characteristics, but not all of that classification's members are necessarily socially burdensome or disruptive. Only a minority may be so.

Let us now assume not only that retarded people are different from non-retarded people in some respects, but also that a subset of the class differs in ways strongly linked to dependency and social disruption. Even if this were so, the classification employed by the City of Cleburne would be both over- and underinclusive. It would be underinclusive because it would not encompass groups or individuals fairly characterized as dependent or disruptive. It would be overinclusive because it would encompass individuals who could not fairly be characterized in either way.

Tussman and tenBroek pointed out that overinclusiveness more grievously violates normative standards of classification than does underinclusiveness, because "over-inclusive classifications reach out to the innocent bystander, the hapless victim of circumstance and association."[48] To the *Cleburne* justices, both the underinclusiveness and the overinclusiveness of the sex-based classification embraced by their predecessors in *Goesart* were recognized as reflecting "outmoded notions" that violated standards of reasonable classification.[49] In *Cleburne,* however, these same justices were troubled by the potential underinclusiveness of a disability-related classification, but found its overinclusiveness unproblematic.

The *Cleburne* Court was able to answer the second, third, and fourth questions of its doctrinal test in the affirmative because it was willing to endorse the use of an overinclusive classification scheme. This renders the *Cleburne* doctrine highly suspect. Overinclusiveness is a salient marker of constitutionally defective classification schemes.

The Court's affirmative response to its fifth question, concerning the balance of beneficial and burdensome statutory treatment, is equally problematic. An affirmative answer is justified only if the Court's inquiry is limited to the small minority of the class's members who benefit from special services made permissible by a constitutional standard permitting differential treatment. Considering the impact of an overinclusive classification on the class as a whole, on balance, the scheme does more harm than good.

## *Cleburne*'s Post-ADA Legacy

In drafting the preamble to the Americans with Disabilities Act,[50] Congress specifically attempted to repudiate the *Cleburne* doctrine. In response to *Cleburne*'s assertion that the benevolent federal legislative response to "the plight of the mentally retarded"[51] belies the existence of any "continuing antipathy or prejudice" against the developmentally disabled, Congress wrote:

> [I]ndividuals with disabilities continually encounter various forms of discrimination, including outright intentional exclusion, the discriminatory effects of architectural, transportation, communication, barriers, overprotective rules and policies, failure to make modifications to existing facilities and practices, exclusionary qualification standards and criteria, segregation, and relegation to lesser services, programs, activities, benefits, jobs, or other opportunities.[52]

Answering the *Cleburne* Court's assertion that even the disability sub-class consisting of mentally retarded persons was too "large and amorphous"[53] to constitute a quasi-suspect classification for equal protection purposes, Congress characterized the *entire category* of people with disabilities as "a discrete and insular minority."[54] Moreover, rebutting *Cleburne*'s assertion that the record of federal protective legislation "benefiting" the mentally retarded "negates any claim that the mentally retarded are politically powerless in the sense that they have no ability to attract the attention of the lawmakers,"[55] Congress asserted that people with disabilities "have been faced with restrictions and limitations, subjected to a history of purposeful unequal treatment, and relegated to a position of political powerlessness in our society."[56]

These direct efforts notwithstanding, Congress ultimately failed to uproot the regressive jurisprudence that animated the *Cleburne* Court's analysis of the disability category. Thus, the methodological flaws assumedly buried with a discredited *Goesart*, disinterred in *Cleburne*, then ostensibly reburied in the ADA's preamble, reemerged in post-ADA Supreme Court cases, most particularly, its recent decision in *Garrett*.

The ADA, like the social model of disability on which it was premised, challenges *Cleburne*'s presumptive underpinnings in three important ways. To begin with, the *Cleburne* Court viewed legislative applications of the disability category as generally benign, even beneficial, to people with disabilities. Indeed, as earlier noted, the Court saw the very existence of such specially targeted efforts as compelling evidence of mentally retarded people's substantial political power.

In contrast, when Congress investigated the question of disability and the sociopolitical power imputed to the disabled by the *Cleburne* majority, it found a landscape characterized far more by subordination than by empowerment. Through a comprehensive, nationwide survey conducted by Louis Harris and Associates,[57] the Independent Commission on Disability (IDC) found that two-thirds of working-age individuals with disabilities were unemployed, and that two-thirds of unemployed disabled individuals wanted to work. Many were able to work, but were denied access or transportation to work sites, or to equipment once there. Many could not find employers who would hire them or pay them on an equal basis with similarly situated nondisabled employees.[58] Having amassed evidence contradicting the *Cleburne* Court's presumption, Congress declared in the ADA's preamble that the disability category had historically been used to deny liberty and opportunity to the people assigned to it, not to help disabled people reach their full potential.[59]

Moreover, Congress cited the "continuing existence of unfair and unnecessary discrimination and prejudice," which denied disabled people equal opportunities in society. This discrimination, Congress noted, persisted in state-controlled activities such as education, transportation, public services, and voting. To counteract these continuing disadvantages, Congress explicitly defined "public entity" in Title II of the ADA to mean "any State or local government," including all their departments and agencies.[60] As was well documented by Justice Breyer's dissent in *Garrett*, state-legislated policies denying equal opportunity to disabled employees continue to the present.[61] Moreover, as many as one-third of the country's 120,000 polling places are inaccessible to people with disabilities.[62] Evidence like that compiled by Congress in establishing the need for the ADA has long been viewed as more than sufficient to justify constitutional protections in the areas of race and gender.[63]

The ADA challenges *Cleburne* in a second way, by announcing a sweeping antidiscrimination directive by the federal government on behalf of disabled Americans. Congress declared that the statute's main purpose was "to provide a clear and comprehensive national mandate for the elimination of discrimination against individuals with disabilities," by promulgating "clear, strong, enforceable standards," addressing both individual and systematic forms of discrimination. Clearly, through passage of the ADA, Congress explicitly intended to bring about broad-based changes in social policy.

Congress stated that part of its purpose in enacting the ADA was "to ensure that the Federal Government plays a central role in enforcing the standards" contained within it.[64] This language indicates that policies and practices are to be enjoined if they constitute or facilitate discriminatory actions. By contrast, *Cleburne* (and later *Garrett*) found constitutionally permissible discriminatory state policies or practices, so long as they could fairly be characterized as rationally related to a legitimate state interest.

Third, and perhaps most significantly, the *Cleburne* doctrine is premised on the notion that disability immutably diminishes people's capacity to "cope with and function in the world."[65] The ADA, however, is grounded in the principle that the effects of disability are mutable and can often be mitigated or relieved through changes in the built environment.[66] Here again, the ADA's legislative history reveals that Congress accumulated a prodigious body of evidence—case after case in which being disabled resulted in capable citizens being denied opportunity and excluded from social participation.[67]

One might reasonably question whether any accumulation of facts about the competence of people with disabilities could persuade either the *Cleburne* or the *Garrett* Court to embrace a social model of disability. In this regard, we might recall that, while acknowledging the enormous changes in women's social status, the *Goesart* Court stated that "the fact that women may now have achieved the virtues that men have long claimed as their prerogatives and now indulge in vices that men have long practiced, does not preclude the States from drawing a sharp line between the sexes."[68] The *Cleburne* Court permitted benefits and burdens to be distributed differently to disabled and nondisabled persons based on presumed differences in their inherent and immutable capabilities. In reaffirming *Cleburne,* the *Garrett* Court held that the states could continue to draw sharp lines between species-typical and species-atypical people, regardless of technological, social, and legal changes. In essence, *Garrett* solidifies *Cleburne*'s equation of disability and dysfunctionality.

Even before *Garrett,* the Supreme Court labored to press the disability category into the mold from which *Cleburne* was cast. For example, in finding for the HIV-positive plaintiff in *Bragdon v. Abbott,* the Court stipulated that she was severely limited in her ability to reproduce. As the Court itself acknowledged, nothing about the plaintiff's HIV infection made it physically impossible, or even very difficult, for her to conceive, carry, and deliver a child. Rather, the Court identified the burdensomeness of such an action on other people (for instance, the social cost of caring for a child whose mother has died) as constituting a disabling factor that substantially limited the plaintiff's participation in the major life activity of reproduction.

The next year, the Court found that the plaintiff in *Cleveland v. Policy Management Systems Corporation*[69] might in fact be a "qualified person with a disability," even though she had applied for and been granted benefits under the Social Security Disability Insurance (SSDI) program, which requires applicants to establish that they are unable to work in any gainful employment. *Cleveland,* however, represents only a partial victory for people with disabilities, because the Court placed the burden on the ADA plaintiff to establish, as a condition of getting her case to trial, that with reasonable accommodation she could have overcome the employment-related dysfunction on which her SSDI application was premised. In this way, the Court applied a key aspect of the ideology underpinning *Cleburne:* it assigned to the disability classification a presumption of incompetence, and signaled that individuals classified as disabled would have to prove themselves exceptions to this rule before they could establish entitlement to the range of opportunities afforded other Americans. Moreover, the *Cleveland* Court structured the showing required of the plaintiff in this way despite explicitly acknowledging that the conception of disability applied by the Social Security Administration and the understanding of disability that informs the ADA are so different that one can presume no contradiction when a person claims both to be unable to work for purposes of Social Security Disability entitlement and to be "qualified" to perform a particular job within the meaning of the ADA.

In the same year that *Cleveland* was decided, ADA plaintiffs Sutton, Kirkingburg, and Murphy all were excluded from protection against disability discrimination because, in the eyes of the Court, the limitations occasioned by their impairments, unlike Abbott's, could be overcome.[70] The one other ADA case decided that year, *Olmstead v. L.C.*, upheld the claims of plaintiffs with both mental retardation and psychiatric illness who had been certified by health care professionals as able to live in the community. The ruling conformed perfectly to *Cleburne*'s embrace of paternalism as a constitutionally permissible approach to state treatment of the disabled. It repeatedly emphasized that whether people like the plaintiffs could exercise their right to be in the community required that "treatment professionals have determined that community placement is appropriate . . . and the placement can be reasonably accommodated, taking into account the resources of the State." In so holding, the Court reaffirmed its "as applied" approach to deciding whether policies that segregate disabled people are constitutional.[71]

*Garrett* made clear that the *Cleburne* doctrine would apply not only to situations involving mental retardation, but to all disability discrimination cases. In *Garrett,* the Court invoked the *Cleburne* Doctrine to strip away much of the protection against disability discrimination the ADA had granted to state employees. Citing *Cleburne* with approval, the Court imposed on disabled plaintiffs the burden of demonstrating that no rational state interest could have been served by excluding them from the workplace.

The Court's description of disabled people as requiring "allowances" and "special accommodations"—terms that appear nowhere in the ADA—unmasks the Court's assumption that disabled people are less competent than nondisabled people.[72] By characterizing disabled people as being in need of special protective treatment (exactly as women were wrongly characterized in *Goesart*), it was easy for the Court to presume that their exclusion from the workplace could be rational. This presumption effectively closed the door on empirical investigation that could show the fundamental reasonableness of inclusion and the fundamental illogic of exclusion. In effect, *Garrett* imposes on disabled people, individual by individual, the burden of showing why it is impermissible for a state to segregate and exclude them. Apparently, no accumulation of empirical evidence, however massive, would suffice to shift the burden to the states to show why these citizens can be marginalized without running afoul of the equal protection clause.

It is now well established that people tend to form categories around prototypical category exemplars.[73] This cognitive tendency may be magnified when we imagine the most salient members of a category to be the most in need or otherwise deserving of attention. The *Garrett* Court's discussion illustrates how the salience of instances of great neediness captures attention, even when they do not relate to a particular case before the Court. In *Garrett*, the Court stipulated that it is rational to hire employees who can use existing facilities and to hold to "job-qualification requirements which do not make allowance for the disabled."[74] The Court thus made remodeling facilities and revising job qualifications emblematic of what it means to provide disabled people access to the workplace.

However, when Director of Nursing Patricia Garrett attempted to return to work after treatment for breast cancer, she was told that she would have to give up her director position, even though having had breast cancer in no way diminished her qualifications or competence, and even though her illness did not prevent her from using the hospital's existing facilities. Indeed, Patricia Garrett requested no accommodation of any kind. She simply wanted to be protected from "old fashioned" disparate treatment discrimination. Somehow, this fact managed to elude the *Garrett* majority, which seemed automatically to equate disability discrimination with refusal to make "special" accommodations.[75]

After *Garrett*, it is unclear whether any level of empirical demonstration would sway the current Court to hold state action toward the disabled unconstitutional under the equal protection clause. Writing for the majority, Chief Justice Rehnquist stated that biases and "negative attitudes" never rise to the level of constitutional discrimination, so long as the prejudicial attitude "rationally furthers the purpose identified by the state." One permissible purpose, he noted, was the preservation of scarce state funds. Under this reasoning, if a state formerly practiced exclusion (for instance, by constructing buildings without level entrances or by developing electronic forms incompatible with screen readers), remedying the resulting exclusion of people with disabilities could always be characterized as irrational, because making alterations comes at a cost.[76] In this account of rational policymaking, neglect of past wrongs will generally be viewed as more rational than remedying them.[77]

Extrapolating the Court's thinking about disability discrimination to racial discrimination, this approach would have enabled states with racially segregated schools to resist integration on the ground that it would cost more to integrate students of color into the white schools than to continue educating them separately. Projecting the Court's logic into cases involving sex-based discrimination, the approach taken in *Garrett* would have justified state refusals to include female physicians in its hospital staffs on the ground that the physical facilities for physicians had been constructed only for males.

Under the logic of *Garrett,* those seeking to end to the exclusion of people of color or women from public programs or workplaces would have borne the burden of proving that states practicing segregation had no need to conserve fiscal resources. As no state possesses surplus funds for very long, this constitutes an impossibly high bar. More generally, had the Court imposed the presumption, put forward in *Goesart* and revived in *Garrett,* that the status quo presumptively serves some state interest and for that reason is rational, it is unclear what empirical research could have been marshaled to end segregation. Had the Warren Court applied this sort of reasoning in *Brown v. Board of Education,* one has to wonder whether it would have been swayed by the famous empirical studies demonstrating the psychological harm segregation necessarily inflicted on black children.

It may be that nothing Congress might have done in drafting the ADA could have prevented the Supreme Court from using *Garrett* to reaffirm the *Cleburne* doctrine. Indeed, the content of the ADA's preamble indicates that Congress was well aware of this problem and specifically attempted to override the *Cleburne* Court's holding that disability did not constitute a suspect classification for equal protection purposes. In *Garrett,* the Court ignored Congress entirely, and arrogated to itself the sole constitutional authority to declare which social groups are, and are not, entitled to heightened Fourteenth Amendment protection. Nevertheless, we would argue, the manner in which Congress drafted the ADA's coverage provisions rendered the statute particularly vulnerable to the reassertion of the particular theory of disability on which *Cleburne* was premised.

Congress defined "the disabled" as that group of people who have a physical or mental impairment that substantially limits one or more major life activities, who have a history of such an impairment, or who are regarded as having had such an impairment.[78] This tripartite definition was imported into the ADA from the Rehabilitation Act of 1973. Congress imported the Rehabilitation Act's disability definition as a matter of expediency. Regulations issued in 1977 by the Department of Health, Education, and Welfare (HEW) specifically enumerated who was considered "handicapped" under the Rehabilitation Act's definition. The extensive HEW regulations were utilized, fairly uniformly, by both agencies and courts enforcing the Rehabilitation Act.[79]

In the Rehabilitation Act context, of course, limitation of major life activities is associated with the very dependency that income replacement and rehabilitation services are designed to mitigate. But beyond the Rehabilitation Act context, this association between disability and incapacity may be neither apt nor accurate. Contrary to the *Cleburne* Court's presumption, one cannot soundly assume that variation in people's abilities to perform various life activities equates to an inability to function or cope in the world. By defining the disability category in terms of the inability to perform a major life activity, the ADA reinforces the equation of disability and incapacity characterizing the old medical or impairment model on which the Rehabilitation Act was based.

Along with the wholesale importation of the definition of disability from the Rehabilitation Act, Congress, in drafting the ADA, also imported the act's definition of disability-based discrimination. This was neither an obvious, nor an unopposed choice. Dissatisfied with the scope of pre-ADA civil rights statutes affecting the disabled,[80] many academic commentators[81] and disability rights groups[82] advocated amending the 1964 Civil Rights Act through addition of the term *handicapped* to the prohibited bases of discrimination. The result of this emendation would have been protection against discrimination "based on" disability—a formula utilized in some other disability-related antidiscrimination statutes,[83] and in civil rights statutes like Title VII, which protect members of other historically subordinated groups.

By contrast, the Rehabilitation Act required that those individuals defined as having a disability must satisfy a second requirement, that they be "qualified" individuals with disabilities.[84] This formulation was incorporated into Titles I and II of the ADA. The implications of this standard are significant, both legally and discursively; the standard's inclusion as part of the definition of statutory coverage requires disabled individuals to commence a Title I or Title II claim from a de facto presumption of incompetence.

In sum, having first imported into the ADA's definition of disability the Rehabilitation Act's welfarist conception of the nature of the disability category, Congress then reinforced the *Cleburne* framework by incorporating into the ADA the Rehabilitation Act's requirement that Title I and II claimants also prove their qualifications, not in connection with the merits of a claim, but rather on the threshold issue of statutory coverage. In drafting the ADA Congress very clearly intended to repudiate the assumption of incapacity underlying the *Cleburne* doctrine, but the statute's actual language unintentionally bolsters it.

## Redrawing the Disability Classification

Much as the "separate but equal" doctrine of *Plessy v. Ferguson* had to be repudiated before racial segregation could be legally delegitimated, so must the *Cleburne* doctrine be rejected before the full inclusion of people with disability can be achieved. In connection with our attempts to undermine *Cleburne,* we must learn from the legal and rhetorical strategies successfully deployed to destabilize *Plessy. Plessy*'s central notion, that the policy of separate but equal benefited all citizens equally, and the state as well, was undermined by empirical investigations demonstrating that segregating people on the basis of skin pigmentation caused unavoidable harms—harms that half measures, pursued within a segregationist framework, could not mitigate.[85]

Using social science research, the *Brown* appellants convinced the Supreme Court that even when financial resources were allocated equally between racially segregated educational systems, "colored" children did not, and could not, flourish. This research included the now-famous "doll studies," which demonstrated that segregation inflicted feelings of inferiority and humiliation on black children, and injured their sense of personal dignity and self-worth. These negative feelings were in turn shown to engender self-hatred and rejection, accompanied by self-destructive, antisocial behavior. The ultimate harms of state-enforced segregation thus extended far beyond those inflicted upon black children. By diminishing segregated children's motivation to learn, by stifling their educational and mental development, and by provoking interracial tensions and antisocial behavior, racial segregation damaged the collective interests of the general polity.[86]

Analogous factors militate against the state-enforced exclusion of people with disabilities from mainstream society generally, and from the workplace in particular. Commenting in 1967 on the nation's new policy of racial integration, Jacobus tenBroek pointed out how a parallel system of segregation damaged disabled people. He described how the state, and especially the courts, denied disabled people the simple right "to be in the world." He pointed out that disabled people had, for example, no enforceable right to open a bank account, or to enter vehicles offering public transportation, or to be served in a restaurant. Under these conditions of personal humiliation and squelched opportunity, it was not surprising, tenBroek observed, that disabled people's will to be self-sufficient and productive was slowly sapped, or even extinguished.[87]

The marginalized status of America's disabled population has improved little in recent years, even since passage of the ADA. A recent survey conducted by Harris Interactive and the National Organization on Disability illustrates the point.[88] Surveying 535 people with disabilities, and 614 people without disabilities,[89] the 2000 NOD/Harris Survey found that only 32 percent of working-age (sixteen to sixty-four) people with disabilities were employed in either a full-time or part-time capacity, as compared to 81 percent of working-age people without disabilities. Twenty-nine percent of disabled households lived in poverty, in contrast with 10 percent of nondisabled ones. Twenty-two percent of the disabled population failed to complete high school, as opposed to only 9 percent of nondisabled society. Twelve percent of people with disabilities graduated from college, as compared to 23 percent of those without disabilities. Twenty-eight percent of the disabled, compared to 12 percent of the nondisabled, did not seek health care services because they could not afford to pay for them.[90]

In light of these findings, the 2000 NOD/Harris Survey concluded that having a disability resulted in increased social isolation and decreased community participation. People with disabilities, the survey found, were more than twice as likely to feel "not at all satisfied" with their level of community involvement, were more likely than their nondisabled peers to feel strongly that they were not contributing members of their communities, and felt "isolated from other people" at a rate twice that of nondisabled respondents. Similarly, people with disabilities were less likely than those without disabilities to go to restaurants, to socialize with friends and family, to participate in religious services, to shop, or to attend sporting or other entertainment events.[91]

As late as the 1996 presidential electoral year, 16 percent fewer disabled than nondisabled eligible adults were registered to vote. In that year, only 30 percent of disabled voting age people went to the polls, as compared to 49 percent of nondisabled, voting age people.[92] These statistics should not be surprising for, as we have seen above, some one-third of the nation's polling places are not fully accessible to disabled people.[93]

People, both those with and those without present disabilities, achieve a keen sense of equality and citizenship in society from paid work. Our identities are fundamentally shaped by our employment status.[94] An important article by Yale law professor Vicki Schultz elegantly makes the point:

> Our historical conception of citizenship, our sense of community, and our sense that we are of value to the world all depend importantly on the work we do for a living and how it is organized and understood by the larger society. In everyday language, we are what we do for a living.[95]

Writing about the dialogical constitution of identity, Princeton philosophy professor Kwame Anthony Appiah reaches a similar conclusion:

> In the modern world, a life with neither job nor money cannot be a life of dignity. We have also learned that a life of handouts is not dignified either, and we are struggling to find a reasonable middle way between demeaning handouts and forced labor. People with severe . . . disabilities have taught us in recent years that we need to reshape public space if they are to enter it with the dignity they deserve.[96]

In *Garrett,* the Court reasserted not only the *Cleburne* doctrine, but also the welfarist conception of disability on which it was premised. In reaffirming that the exclusion of people with disabilities from the workplace was constitutionally permissible, the Court perversely suggested that a policy of including disabled people in the workplace is less rational than a policy that systematically relegates them to dependency on social welfare.[97]

Contrary to the Court's faulty logic in *Garrett,* the exclusion of workers with disabilities frustrates rather than furthers state interests. This claim is sound from a strictly economic perspective: disability-related public assistance obligations exceed $120 billion annually.[98] Conversely, employing disabled workers reduces state obligations by a commensurate amount. One report, for example, estimated that employing one million disabled people would result in a $21.2 billion annual increase in earned income, a $2.1 billion decrease in means-tested cash income payments, a $286 million annual decrease in food stamp usage, a $1.8 billion decrease in Social Security payments, 284,000 fewer people using Medicaid, and 166,000 fewer people using Medicare.[99] In other words, society is collectively damaged not only by the stigma associated with the outmoded welfarist approach to disability, but also by its economic cost.[100]

While more difficult to quantify, the social costs of excluding disabled people from the labor market are equally significant. Educating and employing people with disabilities has social utility, just as educating and employing African Americans, ethnic minorities, and women has social utility. As is the case with respect to other historically marginalized groups, employment brings disabled individuals into contact with their nondisabled counterparts. Interaction between workers who already have disabilities and their currently nondisabled peers facilitates their mutual socialization. Frequent and ordinary contact with disabled people can transform them from a salient and threatening (because unfamiliar) group into individuals whose familiarity makes them both less salient and less threatening.[101]

Employment-based interaction between members of historically marginalized outgroups and members of the dominant social group decreases the perception of "otherness" associated with outsider status and facilitates the acceptance of members of previously stigmatized and marginalized social groups by the dominant majority. When presently able-bodied workers become disabled and remain in the workplace, this socialization process is accelerated and enhanced. Existing personal ties ease the transition from perceived otherness to perceived essential sameness.[102] In this way, the state's economic interests, as well as its interest in promoting ties of affection and solidarity among its citizens, are strengthened by the full inclusion in the workforce of people with disabilities.

Earlier, we showed how *Cleburne's* construction of the disability category perpetuates state action that subordinates people with disabilities. We now turn to the categorical reconstruction that would be required to facilitate the integration of people with disabilities not only into the workplace, but into other social venues as well. First, we suggest, when examining challenged statutes or practices affecting the disabled as a group, a court should proceed from the same baseline assumptions it applies when assessing the rights of women or people of color. As a matter of simple justice and judicial consistency, courts must stop deferring to unsubstantiated, stereotype-driven conceptions about disabled people's capabilities, characteristics, and preferences. As a practical matter, this would require courts to presume, as an initial matter, that most people with a particular disability would be competent to perform the specific social function or functions at issue in a given case. This initial presumption of competence should be rebuttable only by empirical evidence demonstrating that the classification being employed by the defendant is not overinclusive. This, after all, is the standard that would be applied in actions challenging racial or gender classifications. There is no sound reason why the equal protection clause should countenance stereotype-driven, overinclusive disability classifications, while prohibiting similarly stereotype-driven, overinclusive classifications based on race or sex.

We are not arguing for the abolition of all forms of disability-based differential treatment. We take issue only with the use of disability as a proxy for some other characteristic, particularly when based on empirically unfounded stereotypes[103] that lead to broad generalizations supporting the exclusion of all or many people with disabilities, regardless of competence or qualifications.[104] Adopting a neutral disability classification,[105] which neither presumes that people with disabilities are incompetent nor assumes that differential state treatment of the disabled is beneficial or benign, would bring disability discrimination jurisprudence into line with the modern approach to race and gender classification. Without such a reconstruction of the disability classification, judicial consideration of disabled people's claims to inclusion will be mired in circularity.

The reconceptualization we propose would ensure that judicial determinations of whether disabled individuals are competent to perform particular social functions are based on empirically verifiable fact, not on myths, stereotypes, or constrictive social conventions. This new analytical framework will not result in the institution of "special protections" for the disabled. Rather, it will simply extend to people with disabilities the same safeguards against derogating state action based on myths and stereotypes that have been extended to other historically subordinated social groups.

NOTES

The authors wish to express their deep appreciation to editor Linda Hamilton Krieger, whose advice and editing decisions improved both the intelligibility and the readability of this chapter.

1. 335 U.S. 464 (1948).

2. Writing for the Court, Justice Frankfurter opined that the issue raised "need not detain us long," for it "is one of those rare instances where to state the question is in effect to answer it." *Id* at 465. Illustrative of the Court's perspective is the use of the term *barmaid* in contrast to the statute's gender neutral language. See Pub. Acts Mich. 1945, No. 133, Sec. 19a.

3. *See* Goesart, 334 U.S. at 464. For an account of the role of women in the labor force during World War II, *see* PENNY COLMAN, ROSIE THE RIVETER: WOMEN WORKING ON THE HOME FRONT IN WORLD WAR II (1995).

4. 531 U.S. 356 (2001).

5. In a high proportion of cases, conservative Justices Rehnquist, Scalia, Thomas, Kennedy, and O'Connor vote together, over the dissent of Justices Souter, Ginsburg, Breyer, and Stevens.

6. "All persons born or naturalized in the United States, and subject to the jurisdiction thereof, are citizens of the United States and of the state wherein they reside. No state shall make or enforce any law which shall abridge the privileges or immunities of citizens of the United States; nor shall any state deprive any person of life, liberty, or property, without due process of law; nor deny to any person within its jurisdiction the equal protection of the laws." U.S. Const. amend. XIV § 1.

7. City of Cleburne v. Cleburne Living Center, 473 U.S. 432 (1985).

8. "The Congress shall have power to enforce, by appropriate legislation, the provisions of this article." U.S. Const. amend. XIV § 5.

9. Garrett, 531 U.S. at 966.

10. The Immigration and Naturalization Service follows precisely such a policy when it excludes aliens on "health-related grounds," a category that includes certain types of "physical or mental disorder." *See* 8 U.S.C. § 1182 (a)(1).

11. Garrett, 531 U.S. at 375 (Kennedy, J., concurring).

12. *Id.*

13. Garrett restricts only ADA Title I claims for monetary damages brought in federal court by state employees or applicants for state employment. Suits for injunctive relief are not affected. Claims for money damages can still be brought in federal court by federal government agencies on behalf of state applicants or employees, or in state courts by aggrieved persons themselves—so long as the state in which the suit is brought has consented to being sued in cases of this type.

14. Jacobus tenBroek, *The Right to Be in the World: The Disabled in the Law of Torts,* 54 CAL. L. REV. 841 (1967).

15. 163 U.S. 537, 551 (1896).

16. 347 U.S. 483 (1954).

17. Plessy, 163 U.S. at 552.

18. Brown, 347 U.S. at 494.

19. 411 U.S. 677 (1973).

20. *Id.* at 686.

21. 458 U.S. 718 (1982). Ironically, Hogan concerned a policy of the state-sponsored university limiting enrollment in its nursing program to women.

22. Dothard v. Rawlinson, 433 U.S. 321 (1977) involved a woman's application for a position as a correctional counselor in a state penitentiary system.

23. Particularly notable among the literature describing this model of disability are the writings of Paul K. Longmore and Harlan Hahn. A succinct exegesis is provided in Jonathan C. Drimmer, *Cripples, Overcomers, and Civil Rights: Tracing the Evolution of Federal Legislation and Social Policy for People with Disabilities,* 40 UCLA L. REV. 1341 (1993).

24. ANTHONY AMSTERDAM & JEROME BRUNER, MINDING THE LAW: HOW COURTS RELY ON STORYTELLING, AND HOW THEIR STORIES CHANGE THE WAYS WE UNDERSTAND THE LAW AND OURSELVES 50, 247 (2000).

25. Brown, 347 U.S. at 491–94.

26. 473 U.S. 432 (1985).

27. *See* Cleburne Living Center v. City of Cleburne, 726 F.2d 191, 194, 200–202 (5th Cir. 1984).

28. *Id.* at 200–202.

29. Cleburne, 473 U.S. at 450.

30. 42 U.S.C. § 6010 (1977); 20 U.S.C. § 1400 (1975) (now called the Individuals with Disabilities Education Act).

31. Cleburne, 473 U.S. at 474 (Marshall, J., concurring in part and dissenting in part).

32. *Id.*

33. Cleburne, 473 U.S. at 442–43, 446.

34. *Id.* at 442–46.

35. *Id.* at 451 (Stevens, J., concurring).

36. *Id.* at 455 (Marshall, J., concurring in part and dissenting in part).

37. *See* Martha Minow, *When Difference Has Its Home: Group Homes for the Mentally Retarded, Equal Protection, and the Legal Treatment of Difference,* 22 HARV. C.R.-C.L. L. REV. 111, 120–31 (1987) [hereinafter Minow, *When Difference Has Its Home*]. *See also* MARTHA MINOW, MAKING ALL THE DIFFERENCE: INCLUSION, EXCLUSION, AND AMERICAN LAW 106 (1990) [hereinafter Minow, MAKING ALL THE DIFFERENCE].

38. Cleburne, 473 U.S. at 442, 444, 446.

39. *See* Minow, MAKING ALL THE DIFFERENCE, *supra* note 37 at 106.

40. *Id.* at 454. For instance, Justice Stevens thought that both an impartial legislator and a self-interested retarded person could support preventing retarded people from operating hazardous equipment. *Id.*

41. *See* Minow, MAKING ALL THE DIFFERENCE, *supra* note 37 at 115, bearing in mind her treatment, *id.* at 341–49, of In re Phillip B., 92 Cal. App. 3d. 796, 156 Cal. Rptr. 48 (1979), *cert. denied sub nom.* Bothman v. Warren B., 445 U.S. 949 (1980), in which a trial judge used a similar device to introduce the "standpoint" of a mentally retarded fourteen-year-old.

42. Cleburne, 473 U.S. at 442. The record established that nearly 90 percent of the individuals falling into the classification were only mildly retarded, and another 6 percent were moderately retarded. *Id.* at 442 n.9.

43. *See* Celeste Fremon, *"We Do Not Feel That Patients with Down Syndrome Are Appropriate Candidates for Heart-Lung Transplantation": These Words Were a Death Sentence for Sandra Jensen, and That, She Decided, Just Wasn't Going to Happen,* L.A. TIMES, Apr. 14, 1996, at 18. Jensen become "the first seriously retarded person in the United States to receive a major transplant." *New Heart for Retarded Woman,* N.Y. TIMES, January 24, 1996, at A16.

44. Cleburne, 473 U.S. at 442.

45. *Id.* at 443 n.9 (citing brief for American Association on Mental Deficiency to define "deficits in adaptive behavior").

46. *Id.* at 443, 444, 462.

47. *See* MINOW, MAKING ALL THE DIFFERENCE, *supra* note 37 at 119, 211–24.

48. Joseph Tussman and Jacobus tenBroek, *Equal Protection of the Laws,* 37 CAL. L. REV. 341, 349–51 (1949).

49. Cleburne, 473 U.S. at 441.

50. 42 U.S.C. § 12101(a).

51. 473 U.S. at 443.

52. 42 U.S.C. § 12101(a)(5).

53. 473 U.S. at 445.

54. 42 U.S.C. § 12101(a)(7).

55. 473 U.S. at 445.

56. 42 U.S.C. § 12101(a)(7).

57. Louis Harris and Associates, The ICD Survey of Disabled Americans: Bringing Disabled Americans into the Mainstream (1986) [hereinafter ICD Survey]. The results of this poll were summarized to Congress by the president of Louis Harris and Associates during hearings on the ADA. *See* Senate Subcommittee on the Handicapped, S. Hrg. 166, pt. 2, at 9 (1987) (statement of Humphrey Taylor); *quoted in* S. Rep. No. 116, 101st Cong., 1st Sess. 8 (1989); *also quoted in* H.R. Rep. No. 485, 101st Cong., 2d Sess., pt. 2, at 31 (1990). See also H.R. Rep. No. 485, 101st Cong., 2d Sess., pt. 3, at 25 (1990).

58. See ICD Survey at 47, 50–51.

59. 42 U.S.C. § 12101(5), stating that "individuals with disabilities continually encounter various forms of discrimination," including those arising from "overprotective rules and policies." *See generally* Richard K. Scotch, From Good Will to Civil Rights: Transforming Federal Disability Policy (1984).

60. *See* 42 U.S.C. § 12101 at (a)(9), (a)(3); *id.* at § 12131(A)–(B).

61. *See* Appendix to *Garrett,* 531 U.S. at 389 (Breyer, J., dissenting).

62. As a result, in 1996 only 30 percent of voting-age disabled people cast ballots, compared to 49 percent of the nondisabled voting population. *See* David Cracy, Disabled Voters Roused to Action (AP National Wire November 2, 2000).

63. For examples, see Pamela S. Karlan, John C. Jeffries Jr., Peter W. Low, & George A. Rutherglen eds., Civil Rights Actions: Enforcing the Constitution (2000).

64. 42 U.S.C. § 12101(b)(1)–(3).

65. Cleburne, 473 U.S. at 442.

66. Thus, ironically, the Supreme Court's holdings in *Sutton, Murphy,* and *Albertson* can be interpreted to mean that, for ADA purposes, the use of mitigating measures by disabled people transmutes them into "normal," nondisabled people bereft of antidiscrimination protection. *See generally* Aviam Soifer, *The Disability Term: Dignity, Default, and Negative Capability,* 47 UCLA L. Rev. 1279 (2000).

67. The evidence referred to is compiled in S. Rep. No. 116, 1st Sess. 6 (1989).

68. Goesart, 335 U.S. at 466.

69. 526 U.S. 795 (1999).

70. *See* Sutton v. United Airlines, Inc., 527 U.S. 471 (1999); Albertson's, Inc. v. Kirkingburg, 527 U.S. 555 (1999); Murphy v. United Parcel Serv., 527 U.S. 516 (1999).

71. Olmstead v. L.C., 527 U.S. 581, 587 (1999).

72. *Garrett,* 121 S. Ct. at 964.

73. Eleanor Rosch, *Principles of Categorization* in Cognition and Categorization 27–48 (E. Rosch & B.B. Lloyd eds. 1978).

74. *See Garrett,* 121. S. Ct. at 964.

75. *See id.*

76. *See id.*

77. *See* Harlan Hahn, *Disputing the Doctrine of Benign Neglect: A Challenge to the Disparate Treatment of Americans with Disabilities* in Americans with Disabilities: Exploring Implications of the Law for Individuals and Institutions 269 (Leslie Pickering Francis & Anita Silvers, eds. 2000).

78. 42 U.S.C. Sec § 12102(2)(A)–(C).

79. Now reorganized as the Department of Health and Human Services (HHS).

80. Of note are two articles by Janet Flaccus: *Discrimination Legislation for the Handicapped: Much Ferment and Erosion of Coverage,* 55 U. CIN. L. REV. 81 (1986); *Handicap Discrimination Legislation: With Such Inadequate Coverage at the Federal Level, Can State Legislation Be of Any Help?* 40 ARK. L. REV. 261 (1986).

81. *See, e.g.,* Robert L. Burgdorf & Christopher Bell, *Eliminating Discrimination Against Physically and Mentally Handicapped Persons: A Statutory Blueprint,* 8 MENTAL & PHYSICAL DISABILITY L. REP. 64 (1984).

82. Most prominent was the National Council on the Handicapped's strong opposition to the Rehabilitation Act model: "Proof of class membership is not required under other types of nondiscrimination laws, and statutes guaranteeing equal opportunity for persons with disabilities need not have such a requirement either." National Council on the Handicapped, Toward Independence A-25 (1988).

83. Examples include the prohibition of discrimination on the basis of disability for the purposes of Foreign Service employment, *see* 22 U.S.C. § 3905(b)(1) (1988); participation in any pursuit funded under the Full Employment and Balanced Growth Act, *see* 15 U.S.C. § 3151(a) (1988); activities of labor organizations, *see* 5 U.S.C. § 7116(b)(4) (1988); and the sale or rental of housing, *see* 42 U.S.C. § 3604(f)(1)–(2) (1988).

84. 29 U.S.C. § 794 (1974).

85. *Brown,* 347 U.S. at 495 n.11.

86. *Id.* at 494.

87. *See* tenBroek, *The Right to Be in the World: The Disabled in the Law of Torts, supra* note 14.

88. The survey was performed in conjunction with the National Organization on Disability. *See* 2000 N.O.D./Harris Survey of Americans with Disabilities ("2000 NOD/ Harris Survey"), available online at <http://www.nod.org/hs2000.html>.

89. *Id.*

90. *Id.*

91. *Id.*

92. *Id.*

93. *See supra* notes 62–63.

94. *See* JUDITH N. SHKLAR, AMERICAN CITIZENSHIP: THE QUEST FOR INCLUSION 63–101 (1991).

95. Vicki Shultz, *Life's Work,* 100 COLUM. L. REV. 1881 (2000).

96. Kwame Anthony Appiah, *Liberalism, Individuality, and Identity,* 27 CRITICAL INQUIRY 305, 331–32 (2001).

97. *See Garrett, supra* note 4.

98. *See* David I. Levine, *Reinventing Disability Policy* (Institute of Industrial Relations Working Paper no. 65) 1 (June 11, 1997).

99. *See People with Disabilities Show What They Can Do,* HR MAGAZINE, June 1998, at 144 (citing Rutgers economist Douglas Kruse).

100. Joan Susman, *Disability, Stigma, and Deviance,* 38 SOC. SCI. MED. 15 (1994).

101. The socially beneficial effects of bringing disabled and non- (or not yet) disabled persons together in the workplace are discussed in Michael Ashley Stein, *Employing People with Disabilities: Some Cautionary Thoughts for a Second Genera-*

*tion Civil Rights Statute, in* EMPLOYMENT, DISABILITY, AND THE AMERICANS WITH DISABILITIES ACT: ISSUES IN LAW, PUBLIC POLICY, AND RESEARCH 51 (Peter David Blanck ed., 2000).

102. *Id.*

103. Unfounded assumptions about the productivity of disabled employees are discussed in Michael Ashley Stein, *Market Failure and ADA Title I* in AMERICANS WITH DISABILITIES: EXPLORING IMPLICATIONS OF THE LAW FOR INDIVIDUALS AND INSTITUTIONS, *supra* note 77 at 193. The body of research on accommodation costs originates with Peter Blanck. *See, e.g.,* Peter David Blanck, *The Economics of the Employment Provisions of the Americans with Disabilities Act: Part I—Workplace Accommodations,* 46 DEPAUL L. REV. 877 (1997).

104. We object to this use of disability as a proxy for other characteristics even where the disability classification is ostensibly used to "benefit" people with disabilities. *See, e.g.,* Scott A. Moss & Daniel A. Malin, *Public Funding for Disability Accommodations: A Rational Solution to Rational Discrimination and the Disabilities of the ADA,* 33 HARV. C.R.-C.L. L. REV. 197 (1998).

105. For some of the properties of a neutral disability classification, *see* Anita Silvers, *A Neutral Ethical Framework for Understanding the Role of Disability in the Life Cycle,* AM. J. BIOETHICS (forthcoming).

*Marta Russell*

# Backlash, the Political Economy, and Structural Exclusion

The Americans with Disabilities Act (ADA)[1] is both a civil rights bill passed by Congress with the intent of ending employer discrimination and a labor economics bill, intended to increase the relative wages and employment of disabled persons by "leveling the playing field."[2] However, just as the Civil Rights Act of 1964 produced a backlash by those who feared that minorities and women would take jobs away from whites and men, the ADA has been subject to backlash by the public, our elected officials, and the courts.

The most pronounced hostility toward the ADA has come from business. Of course, one might not think of this as a "backlash," given that organized business interests opposed the act from the start. The National Association of Manufacturers, the Chamber of Commerce, the American Banking Association, and the National Federation of Independent Businesses all publicly voiced opposition to the ADA.[3] Ongoing resistance from business interests is nonetheless significant, in that it exposes the economic nature of opposition to effective ADA enforcement.

The year the ADA was signed, the Cato Institute, a Libertarian think tank, called on President George Bush to ask Congress to reconsider the ADA, since from the standpoint of free enterprise, it represented a reregulation of the economy that, in their view, was harmful to business.[4] Paul Craig Roberts, a supply-side economist at the Center for Strategic and International Studies in Washington, warned on the day the act was signed that "[the ADA] will add enormous costs to businesses that will cut into their profits."[5] Rick Kahler opined in a piece entitled "ADA Regulatory Black Hole" that "the ADA make[s] getting out of business look more profitable all the time,"[6] while Trevor Armbristor wrote that the ADA "has produced spectacular injustice and irrationality."[7] In 1995, the director of regulatory studies at the Cato Institute wrote, "If Congress is serious about lifting the regulatory burden from the economy, it must consider major changes in, if not outright repeal of, the ADA. And if Congress is to undo the damage already done by the act, it should consider paying reparations to cover the costs that individuals, private establishments, and enterprises have suffered under the ADA's provisions."[8]

This paper explores the backlash against and hostility toward the ADA by examining the relationship between politics, policy, and economics—particularly with regard to the interests of business. I argue that the backlash against the ADA is a product of capitalist opposition. This opposition has not only stifled the many benefits that might have resulted from effective ADA enforcement, it has promoted negative attitudes toward the ADA among groups of workers who have become fearful that their own interests will be jeopardized by the act's employment provisions.

In making this argument, I claim that liberal policy proscriptions will necessarily fail to create the conditions required to achieve economic and social justice. Moreover, I argue, explanatory theories based in social or economic liberalism cannot adequately account for this failure. To account for the ADA backlash phenomenon, one must look to radical theory, which analyzes the sociohistoric process of the political economy under capitalism and asserts that capitalism cannot be directed toward social-ethical ends. To effectuate economic and social justice, an economic system must be redistributive and collectivist in nature.[9] Discrimination in general, and discrimination against disabled people in particular, will not be eliminated until the economic system itself is changed.

The capitalist economic system, I will argue, is a crucial contributing factor to a backlash against civil rights laws in general and the ADA in particular, to the poor enforcement of those laws, and to the lack of economic advancement of the various groups the laws aim to protect. Despite an expanding U.S. economy, the neoliberal era has brought rising inequality, a decline in workers' standards of living, greater job insecurity, and growing economic anxiety. Income and wealth disparities are at their highest levels since the Great Depression. Poverty and hardship remain a persistent blight on the American landscape. This paper will detail how the structurally flawed political economy, sustained by a self-serving decision-making class, perpetuates poverty, inequality, underemployment, and systematic, compulsory unemployment. It will demonstrate that this flawed economy, which does not provide for the material needs of all, engenders divisions among groups of workers locked in intense competition over a scarcity of decent paying jobs, health care, and shrinking benefits. Lastly, it aims to delineate why a different approach is vital to remedying the predicament in which we find ourselves.

## Equal Opportunity Ideology and Persistent Wage and Employment Gaps

In the United States, civil rights laws have been enacted to remove obstacles faced by subordinated groups, such as women, people of color, and disabled people. Historically, such groups have experienced vast negative disparities in pay, income, and employment opportunities.[10] In the United States, seventeen million working-age people are identified as disabled.[11] The ADA was enacted amid broad expectations that it would vastly increase economic opportunities for disabled workers. To consider whether these expectations were realistic at the outset, or are realistic today, it is useful to examine whether more than thirty years of civil rights protection has brought about similar income equality and economic parity for minorities and women.

Women, minorities, and disabled persons have all experienced both employment and wage discrimination, resulting in their confinement to the bottom of the socioeconomic pyramid. Discrimination occurs when two groups of workers with equal average productivity earn different average wages[12] or have different levels of opportunity for employment. Poverty is disproportionate among the fifty-four million Americans who have some level of disability. Census Bureau data from 1997 estimates that 28 percent of those ages twenty-five and older with severe disabilities lived in poverty, compared with 10 percent of those with disabilities considered not severe, and 8 percent of people with no disability.[13] A 1998 National Organization on Disability/Harris Survey found that disabled persons are almost three times as likely as nondisabled persons to live in households with total incomes of $15,000 or less (29 percent compared to 10 percent).[14] Furthermore, the gap between disabled and nondisabled persons living in very low income households has remained virtually constant since 1986, four years before passage of the ADA.[15]

But the NOD/Harris Survey annual income cutoff at $15,000 does not paint a complete picture of the depth of poverty many disabled persons endure. For example, since $759 is the average per month benefit that a disabled worker received in 2000 from Social Security Disability Insurance (SSDI), and $373 is the average federal income for the needs-based Supplemental Security Income (SSI), the real income of persons[16] on these programs is more likely to be between $4,500 and $10,000—far below the $15,000 mark.

Most analysts attribute these gaps largely to discrimination and seek to provide a remedy based on "equal opportunity," or equal access (but not a right) to employment and pay. The Civil Rights Act of 1964,[17] affirmative action requirements included in various federal regulatory schemes, the Equal Pay Act of 1963,[18] and the Americans with Disabilities Act[19] were enacted to eradicate sex, race, and disability discrimination in wage-setting and employment procurement systems.

Yet what does the data show had occurred at the end of the century? The U.S. Census Bureau's Current Population Survey (March 1998) shows that the income gap was altered for the black population between 1993 and 1997, when black median family incomes rose from 57 to 61 percent of white levels, and the bottom 80 percent showed wage gains relative to the rest of the population.[20] But the gap widened for Hispanic workers, who saw their median family incomes fall from 69 to 60 percent of white levels between 1979 and 1997.[21]

Studies show that there were periods of substantial progress after passage of the Civil Rights Act of 1964 and adjunct affirmative action programs, leading to declining racial discrimination between 1965 and 1975.[22] But the movement toward racial equality stagnated and eventually weakened after the mid-1970s.[23] From 1972 (earliest year available) to 1999, the unemployment rate for blacks has fluctuated between 7.1 percent and levels as high as 21.7 percent of the population.[24] During the same period, white unemployment ranged from a high of 8.1 percent to a low of 3.3 percent, while Hispanic unemployment ranged from 16.9 percent to 6.4 percent.[25] Blacks and Hispanics continue to experience higher levels of unemployment and receive lower wages than whites. While the median white worker earned $19,393, the median black earned only $15,348 and the median Hispanic even less, $13,150.[26]

Although the wage gap between men and women did shrink, this change cannot be attributed to equal pay laws. Since 1973, much of the change in the wage gap has resulted from the fall in men's real earnings; white and black men's earnings have gradually moved down, while white women's earnings have gradually risen, exceeding the earnings of black men in 1991.[27] The U.S. Department of Labor reports that after the recession in the early 1990s, women's earnings failed to show the steep gains exhibited during the 1980s in comparison to wages earned by men.[28] Young women workers had come to within 95 percent of their male counterparts in 1993, helping to narrow the overall gap significantly, but by 1999, the ratio of young women's earnings to young men's had slipped back to 92 percent.[29] Narrow or wide, the wage gap has persisted for over forty-five years, during which equal pay laws were active for thirty-six.[30]

Wage gap studies do not traditionally trace comparable data for disabled people, but unpublished data from John McNeil of the Census Bureau suggest a negative association between earnings and disability. In 1995, workers with disabilities holding part-time jobs (disabled persons are more likely to work part time) earned on average only 72.4 percent of the amount nondisabled workers earned annually.[31] Such wage differentials were observed for disabled persons working full time. Median monthly income for people with work disabilities averaged about $1,511 and $1880 in 1995—as much as 20 percent less than the $1,737 to $2,356 earned by their counterparts without disabilities.[32]

Of greater significance is the chronic unemployment of disabled people. Studies show that disabled persons experience lower labor force participation rates, higher unemployment rates, and higher part-time employment rates than nondisabled persons.[33] The U.S. Current Population Survey suggests that in 1998, only 30.4 percent of those disabled people between ages 16 and 64 were in the labor force, while 82.3 percent of same age nondisabled persons were either employed or actively seeking work for pay.[34] A 2000 NOD/Harris Survey found that only 32 percent of disabled people of working age (eighteen to sixty-four) work full or part time, compared to 81 percent of the nondisabled population, a gap of forty-nine percentage points. More than two-thirds of those not employed say they would prefer to be working.[35]

Material progress for women and minorities appears to be incremental at best. Wage inequality among similarly skilled workers, vast income disparities, wage gaps, and poverty persist. More than thirty years after the passage of federal antidiscrimination legislation, we can soundly conclude that, although the Civil Rights Act of 1964 did make a difference in the *extent* of racial and gender discrimination, neither civil rights laws nor affirmative action programs have produced the conditions of complete economic equality desired by employment rights advocates.[36] Proponents of affirmative action say only that, if affirmative action is eliminated, gains made will be *eroded,* not that affirmative action has ushered in an era of economic parity for minorities and women. Affirmative action has not proven to be a major solution to poverty or a sufficient means of effectuating economic or social equality.[37]

Though only ten years have passed since the passage of the ADA, there is no reason to believe that disabled people will fare better post-ADA than did women and minorities following the passage of civil rights laws and the broad-scale implementation of affirmative action programs. The reasons are both similar and distinct.

Every redistributive measure, including civil rights laws, involves politi-

cal compromise between the public and the powerful interests of big business and big government. The ADA in particular faces some extraordinary
limitations as a direct result of the political climate in which it was produced and enacted.[38] The philosophical momentum for social justice that
spurred the Civil Rights Act and subsequent progressive court decisions in
the 1960s and 1970s was well into decline by the 1990s. For example, in the
era following passage of civil rights laws in 1957, 1960, 1964, and 1968, the
Republicans made dramatic inroads into Democratic victories that forged
the civil rights movement, established the Office of Economic Opportunity,
and initiated the War on Poverty during the Great Society. Presidents Reagan and Bush dismantled the entire Community Services Administration,
responsible for driving much of the 1960s social change agenda by advancing human services, occupational safety, consumer protection, and environmental protection laws.[39]

On the way out were civil rights and economic entitlements, replaced by
a conservative thrust to reduce "big bad government." The dominant
agenda of the late 1970s and 1980s was bolstered by corporate goals that
emphasized globalization and political dominance of government.[40]
Increased international capital mobility and liberalized international trade
have resulted in the transfer of more power to management, at the expense
of labor.[41] Conservative forces targeted protective regulations for repeal or
rollback, which, in their view, interfered with business.[42] Economic policy
in the post-1979 period moved decisively toward a more laissez-faire,
deregulated approach.[43] Industries like transportation and communications have been largely deregulated. Social protections, including safety,
health, and environmental regulations, the minimum wage, government
transfer payments (welfare), and the unemployment insurance system all
have been weakened.[44] The ADA was no exception. It was watered down
substantially to achieve congressional consensus and Bush's presidential
approval in 1990.[45]

A 1997 comparative study between the pre-ADA state and federal disability antidiscrimination laws shows that civil rights laws have not produced
the gains in employment rates, wage rates, or employment opportunities for
disabled people that advocates expected.[46] One study suggests that the proportion of working-age adults with disabilities who are employed has
declined since 1986, when one in three (34 percent) were working.[47] Historical disability employment data from census data (1991 to 1997) show no statistically meaningful changes.[48] Another study suggests that while many
Americans reaped higher incomes from an economy that created a record

number of new jobs during seven years of continuous economic growth (1992–98), the employment rates of disabled men and women continued to fall so that by 1998, they were still below the 1992 level.[49]

Efforts to advance the civil rights of disabled people are further hampered by the absence of affirmative action programs for the disabled. Though the extent to which affirmative action contributed to the gains made by women and minorities remains controversial, there is little doubt that, when accompanied by adequate enforcement, affirmative action requirements have a positive impact.[50] The absence of affirmative action programs for disabled persons is particularly significant, given ADA plaintiffs' overall lack of success in the courts. In the first eight years after the ADA's passage, defendant employers prevailed in ADA employment cases over 90 percent of the time, at both the trial and appellate court levels.[51] Professor Ruth Colker of the Ohio State University College of Law states that this pattern of outcomes is "worse than results found in comparable areas of the law; only prisoner rights cases fare as poorly."[52]

For true equality to be achieved, all forms of bias must be eradicated. Aside from the traditional biases or social influences that determine one's access to social goods, such as where one was educated, one's family economic status, and the environment in which one was raised,[53] disabled workers (as distinct from women and minorities) face economic bias and labor market discrimination due to business accounting practices, which weigh standard (nondisabled) costs of labor against nonstandard (disabled) costs of labor. Such business accounting calculations foreshadow the continuation of a gap in pay and employment opportunities for disabled individuals.

Despite over thirty years of liberal reform through federal equal opportunity laws, substantial race-, gender-, and disability-based inequities remain in the American labor economy. Both racial and gender employment and earnings inequalities have diminished since the enactment of civil rights legislation in the 1960s, but such reductions have been uneven, incomplete, and unstable.[54] On balance, the extent of inequality suffered by women, people of color, and disabled persons can be viewed as a measure of the political success of liberal ideology, where the activities of the courts and government enforcement agencies either serve to advance or to roll back formal legal rules promoting equality.

## Competition: Labor Market and Structural Inequality

Mainstream economists commonly explain inequality of wages and employment opportunities between races and genders in two ways. First, individual workers differ with respect to productivity-linked characteristics. The resulting condition is referred to as a human capital gap. Second, workers experience differences in treatment due to discrimination. The dominant or human capital view holds that individuals exhibit skill and educational differences due to skill-biased technological changes. These differences, the account proceeds, cause the widening gap in pay. By increasing education and technological training, these differentials will be overcome.[55]

Neoclassical supply-and-demand models posit that the labor market will equalize pay and employment differentials. Pay inequality is explained as a natural result of the spread of information technologies (the computer revolution), which creates differences in marketable skills. Those best trained in these new fields reap the benefits in pay from the transformation in the workplace, while those without such training fall behind.[56] Supply-and-demand theory asserts that this result obtains because the pressures of the marketplace, what Adam Smith called the "invisible hand," direct the activities of individuals and serve as a self-regulating mechanism for wages, prices, and production. In practice, the demand for workers trained in technological fields will encourage more workers to seek such training, eventually equalizing wage differentials over the long run.

In direct contradiction to this neoclassical model, a substantial body of research challenges the notion that differences in human capital, quality of education, and years of work experience can adequately explain the wage differentials and employment patterns that remain prominent in the economy.[57] For instance, research by economists Jared Bernstein and Lawrence Mishel shows that skill-biased technological change cannot account for existing wage disparities. Throughout the 1990s, average starting wages for college graduates, the most technically advanced and computer-literate workers in the labor market, fell by 7 percent.[58] New engineers and computer scientists were offered 11 percent and 8 percent less respectively in 1997 than their counterparts received entering the market in 1989.[59] This flatly contradicts claims that more education and skill training will equalize pay differentials. Furthermore, productivity rates, which should be exploding if the computer revolution were generating huge returns for high-tech skills, grew no faster in the 1990s than in the 1980s.[60] Economists James Galbraith, Claudia Goldin, and Lawrence Katz show that a readjustment of incomes to a wider and more equal distribution of skill levels for the overall workforce failed to happen in the past and is not happening in today's economy.[61]

Competitive market forces obviously did not eliminate discriminatory practices in the decades leading up to the passage of the Civil Rights Act of 1964. In fact, discrimination managed to sustain itself, both in the United States and elsewhere, for generations at a time.[62] Research by Martin Carnoy published in 1994 demonstrated that while blacks narrowed the educational gap separating them from whites, they slid further behind economically after the mid-1970s.[63]

Some analysts attribute inequality not to individual ineptitude but in large measure to labor segregation. Estimates of the hard figures on inequality by James L. Westrich of the Massachusetts Institute for Social and Economic Research show that there is a hierarchical division of labor within the labor force. For example, women are numerous at the bottom of the economic pyramid and scarce at the top: while 23.7 percent of women earn less than ten thousand dollars a year (a result of both low pay and part-time status), just 12.8 percent of men earn so little. While 58.7 percent of women earn under twenty-three thousand dollars a year, only 36.3 percent of men do; and 9.9 percent of men earn over seventeen thousand dollars a year, compared to only 2.6 percent of women.[64]

A study by Donald Tomaskovic-Devy for the U.S. Department of Labor's Glass Ceiling Commission at Cornell University found that while part of the wage gap results from differences in education, experience, or time in the workforce, a significant portion can not be explained by any of those factors.[65] His findings revealed that "differences in human capital, investments in education and training by individuals explain a small proportion of the gender gap and about a third of race/ethnic earnings inequalities, but that substantial earnings inequalities are not a function of gender or race/ethnic differences in education, labor market experience or firm tenure.[66] Instead, these gaps are attributable to the social division of labor, a systematic underpayment and occupational segregation of people because of their sex or race.[67]

Tomaskovic-Devy shows that "not only is there racial and gender discrimination against individuals, but as a result of employment segregation, jobs that become associated with particular racial or gender categories tend to be organizationally stereotyped and valued accordingly."[68] As jobs become stereotypically female or minority, there is a tendency in many workplaces to provide lower wages and less opportunity for skill training and promotions. He concludes that the confinement of "many women of all ethnic backgrounds and minority men to lower quality jobs *than they can perform*" is a direct cause of gender and race/ethnic earnings inequalities.[69]

Economist James Galbraith challenges the theory that people are, in fact, paid in proportion to the value of what they produce. Galbraith shows that power, and particularly market or monopoly power, changes with the general level of demand, the rate of growth, and the rate of unemployment.[70] He explains that "in periods of high employment, the weak gain ground on the strong; in periods of high unemployment, the strong gain ground on the weak."[71] In this view, inequality is a product of differential power, rather than differential skill. This concept is consistent with Adam Smith, who observed that "masters [capitalists] are always and everywhere in a sort of tacit, but constant and uniform combination, not to raise the wages of labour above their actual rate."[72] Smith keenly perceived the tendency toward monopoly power of capital, writing that "masters too sometimes enter into particular combinations to sink the wages of labour even below this rate."[73] Smith understood capitalists generally to have greater power over wages than workers, but saw that the relationship changes with the employment rate. For example, Smith asserts that "the scarcity of hands occasions a competition among masters, who bid against one another in order to get workmen, and thus voluntarily break through the natural combination of masters to not raise wages."[74] A shortage of labor forces capitalists to raise wages.

Marxist economic theory provides further insight. Marx's theory of surplus value posits that profit lies in the ability of capitalists to pay less for labor power than the actual value the worker will impart to the commodities they help to produce.[75] Profit, as such, essentially resides in underpaid labor. Marx defines competition as a tendency toward equalization of profit margins, leading to monopolies as the consequence of competition rather than its antithesis.[76]

Marxist interpretations link economic competition to discrimination in the workplace. Economists William Darity and Patrick Mason explain that "race and gender exclusion are used to make some workers less competitive for the higher paying positions. This approach emphasizes that the major elements for the persistence of discrimination are racial or gender differences in the access to better paying jobs within and between occupations."[77] Racial inequality, then, can be traced to the economic system that generates it.[78]

Disabled persons encounter similar power differentials in the labor market. Richard Epstein, a leading economist in the law-and-economics movement, admits that disabled persons "have been subject to unfair treatment in the marketplace" but holds that this is due to government interference with the control of their labor in the competitive process.[79] Epstein argues that "the disabled should be allowed to sell their labor at whatever price, and on whatever terms, they see fit" and sees the free market as the appropriate mechanism. He states that "the minimum wage laws and various kinds of ostensible safety and health regulations can impose a greater burden on them [disabled persons] than on others. Repeal those laws as well."[80] Epstein believes that in a deregulated, competitive market, disabled people's labor would fall below minimum wage because it is worth less.

This idea is not novel. Section 504 of the Rehabilitation Act of 1973 provided that federally financed institutions are required to pay a "fair" or "commensurate" wage to disabled workers, but under the act, employers are not required to meet even minimum wage standards.[81] The traditional sheltered workshop is the prototype for below-minimum-wage work for disabled persons. The sheltered workshop model is based on the notion that disabled workers are not able to keep up with the average widget sorter. Under federal law, any nonprofit employer is allowed to pay a subminimum wage to disabled employees, so long as the employer can show that the disabled worker has "reduced productive capacity."[82]

Republican legislator Scott Baugh latched onto the subminimum wage concept for disabled workers by drafting legislation in 1996 that would allow employers to hire disabled workers at a "special minimum wage" without the minimal and very subjective "protection" of having to show that the prospective employee is "less productive" than a nondisabled one.[83] Any disabled person could be considered "less productive," and theoretically, a subminimum wage or wage below nondisabled in any pay category could be used to lower the wage floor, as women and minorities are used to hold it down.

In the neoclassical view, markets are efficient, ethical generators and distributors of wealth. According to this theory, blame for the wage gap falls on the individual worker himself. If one fails to keep up with changes in the economy, the argument goes, it is because of his or her shortcoming rather than the functioning of the labor market. If a worker is less productive, it is her fault, and she does not deserve a minimum wage (and certainly not a living wage) for her labor. A materialist analysis, in contrast, posits that the labor market is a social construct, where marginalization of certain groups works to the advantage of the business class.

In the next three segments, I will examine some structural mechanisms that permit or encourage discriminatory practices. Specifically, I explore how "disability" is socially created, that is, how workers with disabilities are made less competitive by capitalist business practices, how the capitalist system reproduces unemployment, and how workers competing in such a labor market are pitted against one another in ways that undermine the collective power of labor.

## The Business Backlash, Labor, and Profits

Two years after the ADA was signed into law, Richard Epstein devoted an entire chapter of his neoclassical analysis *Forbidden Grounds* to opposing the concept of civil rights for disabled persons.[84] Starting from the premise that the ADA constitutes redistributive interference with the market, he concludes that the ADA should be repealed.[85] Epstein's sentiments echo those emanating from the business sector at large.

In a report on the performance of the Equal Employment Opportunity Commission, charged with enforcing ADA Title I, which prohibits discrimination in employment, the U.S. Commission on Civil Rights concludes that enforcement of the ADA has fallen short in several important areas.[86] The commission's explanations for the difficulties include high workloads, insufficient resources, huge backlogs of cases, lack of staffing, failure to monitor underling agencies, and lack of policy clarification of heavily disputed clauses in the ADA. The commission also pointed out that successful implementation has been inconsistent and in some instances, elusive.

A 1998 study by the American Bar Association's Commission on Mental and Physical Disability Law shows that disabled workers bringing discrimination suits are unlikely to succeed in court. Of the more than twelve hundred cases filed under Title I of the ADA since 1992, employers prevailed 92 percent of the time.[87] By 2000 employers prevailed more than 95 percent of the time.[88] Another study by Law Professor Ruth Colker shows similar results, finding that employers successfully defend more than 93 percent of reported ADA employment discrimination cases at the trial court level and succeed in 84 percent of cases appealed.[89]

The U.S. Commission on Civil Rights reports that one of the most persistent criticisms of the ADA has been that employers are forced to pay too high a price to comply with the statute's employment provisions.[90] While it is clear that disabled workers should not be denied civil rights simply because employers may incur costs while attempting to comply with the ADA, business objections are informative and reveal labor market mechanisms endemic to capitalism. Business practices demonstrate that the economic structure does generate obstacles to the employment of disabled people. Equal opportunity law has failed in this aspect to provide a sufficient remedy for economic discrimination.

The goal of business is to make a profit. The basis of capitalist accumulation is the business use of surplus labor, extracted from the workforce of skilled labor in a way that generates profits.[91] Typical business accounting practices weigh the costs of employment against the profits to be made. Productive labor, or exploitation of labor, means simply that labor is used to generate a surplus value based on what business can gain from the worker productivity against what it pays in wages, health care, and benefits (the standard costs of having an employee).[92] The surplus value created in production is then appropriated by the capitalist.[93] The worker receives wages, which in theory cover socially necessary labor, or what it takes to reproduce labor power every working day.[94]

Operating within this system, an employer will resist any operation cost that is viewed as extraordinary or nonstandard. From a business perspective, the hiring or retaining of a disabled employee represents nonstandard additional costs when calculated against a company's bottom line. Epstein endorses this view, stating that the employment provisions of the ADA constitute a disguised subsidy[95] and that "successful enforcement under the guise of 'reasonable accommodation' necessarily impedes the operation and efficiency of firms."[96]

Whether real or perceived in any given instance, employers continue to express concerns about increased costs in the form of providing reasonable accommodations,[97] anticipate extra administration costs when hiring nonstandard workers, and speculate that a disabled employee may increase worker's compensation costs in the future.[98] Employers, if they provide health care insurance at all,[99] anticipate elevated premium costs for disabled workers.[100] Insurance companies and managed care health networks often exempt "preexisting" conditions from coverage, or make other coverage exclusions based on chronic conditions, charging extremely high premiums for the person with a history of such health care needs.[101] Employers, in turn, tend to look for ways to avoid providing coverage to cut costs.[102] In addition, employers characteristically assume that they will encounter increased liability[103] and lowered productivity from a disabled worker.[104]

Prejudice-based disability discrimination, stemming from employers' assumptions that a disabled person cannot do the job or from a generalized aversion to hiring a blind, deaf, mobility or otherwise impaired person, undoubtedly contributes to the high unemployment rate of disabled people.[105] Disabled workers, however, also face inherent economic discrimination within the capitalist system, stemming from employers' expectations of encountering additional nonstandard production costs when hiring a disabled worker as opposed to hiring a worker with no need for accommodation in the form of interpreters, environmental modifications, or readers, extra liability insurance, maximum health care coverage (inclusive of attendant services), or even health care coverage at all.

Using this analysis, the prevailing rate of exploitation determines who is "disabled" and who is not. Disability thus represents a social creation, which defines who is offered a job and who is not. An employee who is too "costly" (significantly disabled) will not likely become (or remain) an employee at all. Census data tends to support this view. For working-age persons with no disability, the likelihood of having a job is 82.1 percent.[106] For people with a nonsevere disability, the rate is 76.9 percent. The rate drops to 26.1 percent for those with a significant disability.[107] In today's highly competitive business climate, it can fairly be asserted that business managers and owners will not cut into their profits for moral, noble, or socially just purposes in order to lower the disabled unemployment rate.

In liberal capitalist economies, redistributionist laws that, if enforced, will cost business, are necessarily in tension with business interests, which resist such cost-shifting burdens. Writing for the Seventh Circuit in 1995, Judge Richard Posner related the business schematic of cost-benefit analysis to the ADA:

> If the nation's employers have potentially unlimited financial obligations to 43 million disabled persons, the Americans with Disabilities Act will have imposed an indirect tax potentially greater than the national debt. We do not find an intention to bring about such a radical result in either the language of the Act or its history. The preamble actually "markets" the Act as a cost saver, pointing to "billions of dollars in unnecessary expenses resulting from dependency and nonproductivity." §12101(a)(9). The savings will be illusory if employers are required to expend many more billions in accommodation than will be saved by enabling disabled people to work.[108]

Civil rights laws traditionally demand equal treatment. In the case of employment and disability, however, civil rights laws, operating within a capitalist paradigm, envision equal treatment, while failing to acknowledge the full nature and extent of economic discrimination. This fatal oversight ensures that laws such as the ADA will fall short of accomplishing their employment-related goals. For equal opportunity to be *truly* equal, biases (including economic biases) must be eradicated. A government committed to providing such opportunities could "level the playing field" to compensate for economic discrimination by employers. It could ensure ongoing health care for disabled persons (preferably within a disability sensitive universal health care system not linked to employment status), subsidize job accommodations, and allow other subsidies to reimburse businesses that hire or retain employees with disabilities. Government enactment of severe and immediate penalties on employers (including government employers) who balk at providing job accommodations in a timely manner could serve as a backup measure to further advance disabled workers' access to jobs.

There exist strong ideological tensions between laws that grant subsidies and civil rights–based remedies, which legally mandate that employers comply with antidiscrimination principles. Under the ADA, employers are required to provide access and accommodations as a matter of individual right.[109] By contrast, subsidies provide a government offset to business costs based on the notion that it is in the government's (and society's) interest to see that disabled persons are employed. Disability rights groups and activists (myself included) have favored the civil rights approach over subsidies, but given the economic discrimination inherent in capitalism, can we afford to remain fixed in our belief that civil rights will provide timely relief for those disabled persons seeking employment redress in the courts? Will the courts initiate an economic revolution that forces employers to provide accommodations?

So far, disabled plaintiffs have faced great difficulty prevailing in court on key issues. The U.S. Commission on Civil Rights notes that many disability experts ascribe the problem in judicial and administrative confusion over interpretation of Title I's provisions.[110] Legal and policy experts within the disability rights movement have observed that ADA enforcement is proving problematic. Arlene Mayerson, an attorney with the Disability Rights Education and Defense Fund, characterizes ADA case law as "hypertechnical, often illogical interpretations of the ADA" that have generated a "disturbing trend" of court precedents.[111]

Robert Burgdorf Jr., one of the ADA's drafters, concludes that "legal analysis has proceeded quite a way down the wrong road."[112] Burgdorf points to a judicial tendency to view ADA plaintiffs as seeking *special benefits and treatment* instead of equal rights.[113] Whatever the reasons for this judicial backlash, courts are clearly thwarting congressional intent by turning away disabled persons who seek judicial remedies. The interests of business and conservative, antiregulatory factions appear to have the upper hand.

It is reasonable to view consistently negative court outcomes as an extension of the business backlash against the ADA. The American Bar Association's Commission on Mental and Physical Disability Law reports that, while employers have complained the most of unfair treatment under the ADA, "the facts strongly suggest the opposite: employees are treated unfairly under the Act due to myriad legal technicalities that more often than not prevent the issue of employment discrimination from ever being considered on the merits."[114] Ruth Colker concludes that the courts are deploying strategies that result in "markedly pro-defendant outcomes under the ADA" by "abusing the summary judgment device. In other words, judges are making decisions that should be made by a jury."[115] This, Colker explains, results in proemployer outcomes because juries, traditionally more hospitable to civil rights, are not deciding the cases.[116] Legitimate claims are systematically being thwarted, as medical conditions found not to constitute "disabilities" within the meaning of the ADA, and as courts fail to understand how the concept of equality maps onto the problem of disablement and the provision of reasonable accommodations.

Workers pay a heavy personal price when employers contest disablement or refuse badly needed access modifications, reasonable accommodations, or removal of work barriers, and choose instead to put up a fight in court. When, for example, an employee cannot work without an accommodation and the employer does not readily provide one, the worker is often unable to perform her job and is fired.[117] Common sense would dictate that when the worker has a protracted court battle ahead of her to enforce her right to an accommodation but no paycheck in the mail, the last practical resort is to go onto disability benefits. Yet frequently, employers use a worker's application for disability benefits to undermine discrimination cases against them. Under the Social Security Administration's (SSA) definition of disablement, a worker is qualified for benefits if he/she cannot work; SSA does not consider whether the employee could continue to work if the employer provided a reasonable accommodation. The employer, contesting the worker's discrimination suit, holds that if the worker claims he or she cannot work for purposes of claiming disability benefits, he or she is not qualified within the meaning of the ADA.[118]

In the spring of 1999, this issue was brought before the Supreme Court in *Cleveland v. Policy Management Systems Corp.*[119] There, the plaintiff became disabled, asked for but was denied a reasonable accommodation, then lost her job due to failure to perform. The plaintiff subsequently successfully applied for Social Security disability benefits. The plaintiff sued the employer for failure to comply with the ADA. The Supreme Court granted certiorari to decide

> whether an ADA plaintiff 's representation to the [Social Security Administration] that she was "totally disabled" created a rebuttable

presumption sufficient to judicially estop her later representation that, for the time in question, with reasonable accommodation, she could perform the essential functions of her job.[120]

The Court ruled in *Cleveland* that application for and receipt of SSDI benefits does not automatically estop a recipient from pursuing an ADA claim or erect a strong presumption against the recipient's ADA success. However, it held that to survive a summary judgment motion an ADA plaintiff cannot ignore her SSDI contention that she was too disabled to work, but must explain why that contention is consistent with her ADA claim that she can perform the essential functions of her job, at least with reasonable accommodation.[121] Under this holding, therefore, both parties will have the opportunity to present or contest the plaintiff's explanation. Furthermore, a plaintiff may argue that her SSDI statement of total disability was made in a forum that does not consider the effect that a reasonable workplace accommodation would have on ability to work. She may also argue that statements were reliable at the time they were made.[122]

If *Cleveland* was a step forward, the Supreme Court took a few steps back with its rulings in the next four ADA employment cases: *Sutton v. United Airlines*,[123] *Murphy v. United Parcel Service*,[124] *Albertson's v. Kirkingburg*,[125] and *Board of Trustees of the University of Alabama v. Garrett*.[126] At issue in the first three cases was the meaning of disability under the ADA, and in the last, whether workers can file employment discrimination suits for damages against state governments under ADA's Title I.

Significantly narrowing the scope of the law in the first three cases, the Court ruled that correctable physical limitations (such as monocular vision, nearsightedness, or high blood pressure) do not qualify as disabilities under the ADA and do not entitle plaintiffs to sue under Title I, regardless of whether they were fired because of such conditions. The Court distinguished between workers whose disabilities can be mitigated through corrective equipment or medicine and those workers whose disabilities cannot.

But what does "mitigated" imply? The dissenting justices in *Sutton* did not overlook the possibility that the majority's opinion in that case could be read to include the very people the Court maintained that the ADA protected.[127] Joined by Justice Breyer, Justice Stevens suggested that under the majority's ruling, the act would not even protect people who had lost limbs in industrial accidents or while in armed service to their country.

With the aid of prostheses, coupled with courageous determination and physical therapy, many of these hardy individuals can perform all of their major life activities just as efficiently as an average couch potato. . . . [But if] the Act were just concerned with their present ability to participate in society, many of these individuals' physical impairments would not be viewed as disabilities . . . [and] many of these individuals would lack statutory protection from discrimination based on their prostheses.[128]

The dissenters accused the Court of making the ADA's safeguards "vanish when individuals make themselves more employable by ascertaining ways to overcome their physical or mental limitations," adding that "many of these individuals would lack statutory protection from discrimination based on their prostheses."[129]

Indeed, the majority opinion in *Sutton* presents workers with an exasperating catch-22. If one is not disabled because one's condition is "correctable" with medication, wheelchairs, prostheses, hearing aids, insulin, and so on, how can one expect to receive a reasonable accommodation that depends on being defined as "disabled"? Yet employers can continue to fire workers because of performance limitations caused by such unaccommodated "nondisabilities." Additionally, employers may still conclude that a person is too disabled to work, even though under the law they are not disabled enough to be protected by the ADA. Here is the catch-22 for ADA plaintiffs: if one is disabled enough to sue, one is too disabled to work. If one is not too disabled to work, one does not have a disability within the meaning of the ADA and is denied statutory protection from discrimination.

The United States Chamber of Commerce called the decision "an incredibly significant victory for the business community." Business groups filing amicus curiae briefs urged the Court to consider "the impact its decision in this case may have beyond the immediate concerns of the parties to the case."[130] The National Association of Manufacturers asserted that "like sexual harassment last year, disability discrimination is the major employment law issue on the Supreme Court's docket this year. Manufacturers should not be forced to pay damages, including punitive damages, to individuals who can lead normal lives with medication or corrective lenses."[131] The American Trucking Association and the Equal Employment Advisory Council (a nonprofit association made up of more than 315 major companies) joined the amicus brief.

By far, the ruling that most clearly reveals where the Supreme Court conservative majority stands of a disabled person's right to be treated equally under the Fourteenth Amendment's equal protection clause is *Trustees of the University of Alabama v. Garrett,* decided in the early months of 2001.[132] Usurping congressional authority to address and provide remedies for discrimination, the Court in *Garrett* barred state employees from suing a state for damages for disability discrimination in employment. After *Garrett*, states are immune to private civil actions seeking damages for disability discrimination under ADA, Title I.

Refusing to defer to congressional judgment that a state pattern of employment discrimination against the disabled population in fact existed, the *Garrett* Court found the ADA's employment provision unconstitutional, as an abridgment of the State of Alabama's right to sovereign immunity under the Eleventh Amendment. The Court's opinion, which completely avoids any consideration of the merits of the plaintiff's claim against the state, held that whatever state discrimination did exist did not meet the test of being "irrational," and the remedy provided by Congress, suits for damages, was not proportional to the harm such discrimination inflicts.

In so holding, the Court elevates institutional economic concerns over an individual's civil rights. Though the Court suggests that disabled workers still have a remedy through injunctive relief,[133] if the Court's logic is followed, injunctive relief may not be worth much to the disabled state worker. There is no constitutional right of action under the Fourteenth Amendment's equal protection clause for "rational" disability discrimination. If disability discrimination is economically rational, excluding disabled people from state employment could be used to save funds that would otherwise be spent to modify state facilities. Indeed, the *Garrett* majority wrote that while "it would be entirely rational (and therefore constitutional) for a state employer to conserve scarce financial resources by hiring employees who are able to use existing facilities," the ADA requires employers to "make existing facilities used by employees readily accessible to and usable by individuals with disabilities."

Further, the *Garrett* majority questions the constitutional foundation for Congress having provided disabled workers a remedy under the ADA's "reasonable accommodation" provision. Writes Justice Rehnquist:

> The ADA does except employers from the "reasonable accommodation" requirement where the employer can demonstrate that accommodation would impose an "undue hardship" upon it, Section 12112(b)(5)(A), but, even with this exception, the accommodation duty far exceeds what is constitutionally required.[134]

Since Congress specifically found substantial discrimination against disabled persons "costs the United States billions of dollars in unnecessary expenses resulting from dependency and nonproductivity[135] and sought through the ADA to reduce unnecessary dependency and unrealized productivity, the *Garrett* decision stands at direct odds with congressional intent. *Garrett* not only weakens the disabled worker's position in securing or retaining state employment, it also opens the door to private-sector employer challenges to the ADA. This illustrates the contradiction that disablement exposes in capitalism: the same decision-making class that desires to end disability "dependency," as they define it, does not want to do what it takes to bring disabled people into the workforce. The governing elite cannot offer solutions to the problem in anything but the liberal terms of equal rights, but in capitalist economies, redistributionist laws like the ADA run head-on into conservative cost-efficiency rationales.

The *Garrett* decision amplifies the political economy of disability antidiscrimination legislation and raises substantial concerns about this conservative Supreme Court's political agenda. Justice Breyer underscores the political issues, stating, "The Court . . . improperly invades a power that the Constitution assigns to Congress."[136] The Court seems to have adopted a careful incremental approach to returning the nation to the *Lochner* era, when no legislation could be passed that would actually constrain corporate power or fight discrimination. The five-to-four majority is steeped in core conservative economic cost-efficiency theory and intent upon undoing existing legislation as it relates to the Fourteenth Amendment's equal protection clause. The evidence: the weakening of the ADA in *Garrett, Sutton, Murphy,* and *Albertson's* discussed here; the striking down of the Age Discrimination Act in *Kimel v. Florida Board of Regents;*[137] and the invalidation of portions of the Violence against Women Act in *United States v. Morrison.*[138]

The favoritism the Court exhibits toward employers is also evident in *Circuit City Stores, Inc. v. Adams,*[139] which held that workers have no right to sue for on-the-job discrimination and harassment if the employer includes a boilerplate arbitration provision in the employment application. The decision, in effect, assigns private lawsuits to compulsory arbitration, removing the worker's right to a jury trial. The present political reality underscores the dangers of relying on legislative remedies to assure social and economic justice, when they are subject to conservative court intervention. Unlike the Warren and, to a lesser extent, the Burger Courts, the current Rehnquist Court cannot be relied upon to be the main guarantor of liberal rights.

For these reasons, greater nonjudicial government intervention in this precarious period is not only justified but essential to achieve positive outcomes for workers with disabilities. Government provision of ongoing health care, reasonable accommodation costs, and other subsidies would remove some of the added cost from the employer's calculus when deciding to hire or retain disabled workers. Successful intervention promises to lessen the burden on disabled workers otherwise forced to litigate in courts that are hostile to the rights of disabled individuals. Mandated affirmative action as a follow-up to the ADA seems ever more necessary to change the present course.

However, these proposals come with two qualifiers. First, such reforms would, at most, constitute stopgap measures that could yield more job placement for disabled persons in the short run but, as the next segments will show, cannot alone significantly affect disability unemployment in the overall labor economy. Second, subsidies risk augmenting acrimony and division within the labor force.

## The Job Gap: Compulsory Unemployment

Traditionally, disabled people have been placed in that unemployable category of people James O'Connor refers to as the "surplus population," irrelevant to the current political-economic system.[140] Now that more disabled people can work, provided that economic employment disincentives and Social Security work penalties are removed and adequate quality health care made available, there exists the potential for many to join what Marx calls the "reserve army of labor."[141] This includes the official unemployed and all those parts of the population, whether part of the workforce at a given time or not, who might become part of the workforce if the demand for them grew. The surplus population and reserve army overlap; the slums of Mexico City are part of the U.S. reserve army of labor—and they are also a surplus population.

The liberal notion of "equal opportunity" presents the illusion that it can resolve the unemployment issue; if civil rights can rid the world of discrimination, then everyone can get a job, work hard, and make it to the top. But the American capitalist paradigm creates the reserve army of labor and the surplus population by design, leaving large numbers of people unemployed and in poverty. Economists believe that a threshold of unemployment is necessary to avoid inflation and maintain the health of the American economy. Nobel laureate William Vickrey, in his presidential address to the American Economics Association in 1993, called this "one of the most vicious euphemisms ever coined, the so-called 'natural' unemployment rate."[142]

The theory of a natural rate of unemployment, or nonaccelerating inflation rate of unemployment (NAIRU) has dominated macroeconomics for nearly twenty-five years.[143] Its effects can also be observed on Wall Street. When news of the creation of 705,000 jobs in February 1996 hit the press, the Dow Jones industrial average tumbled 3 percent in a matter of hours.[144] The *Wall Street Journal* explained that "fears that employment data will confirm that the economy is growing at a faster rate than central bankers find acceptable continue to weigh on the market."[145]

The number of people affected by the "natural unemployment rate" must be made a significant part of the discussion about unemployment. The Bureau of Labor Statistics puts official unemployment at 5.5 million (2000),[146] but another 3.1 million people work part-time when they would rather have a full-time job, and 4.4 million who need jobs are omitted from the analysis entirely because they have given up looking for work and are therefore, not counted.[147] The real jobless rate is closer to 13 million, or 8.9 percent of the population—more than twice the official rate.[148]

How many disabled persons are poised to join the active reserve army?[149] The Economic and Social Research Institute finds that, with accommodations, 2.3 million unemployed disabled people could be working.[150] But this figure appears to underestimate the disabled reserve army. There are 17 million working-age disabled persons, 5.2 million of whom are working.[151] This leaves 11.8 million either officially unemployed or not in the labor force. Seven out of ten disabled persons ages sixteen to sixty-four who are not employed say that they would prefer to be working.[152] Thus, as many as 8.3 million workers could be enlisted in the active reserve army. Further, there are indications that disabled persons may be significantly underemployed, preferring to work full-time when they are only employed part-time. Between 1981 and 1993, the proportion of disabled persons working full-time declined by 8 percent, while the number working part-time for both economic and noneconomic reasons increased disproportionately.[153]

Essentially, about 20 million working people are condemned by federal anti-inflation policy either to compulsory unemployment or to employment at low wages. Keynesian scholars such as Robert Eisner, William Vickrey, and James Galbraith argue, however, that a policy of full employment is necessary to equalize the wealth of society. In *Created Unequal: The Crisis in American Pay,* Galbraith shows that the less-than-full-employment strategy has resulted in greater inequality (low wages)[154] and a dangerous polarization within society. Galbraith concludes that, while many commitments are necessary to maintain full employment, maintenance of low, stable interest rates is fundamental. As long as the Federal Reserve sees interest rates as a weapon in the war against inflation, full employment will be sacrificed.[155] In order to reduce inequality, Galbraith argues for "sustained full employment, stable and low interest rates, a higher minimum wage, and reasonable price stability,"[156] all of which he (and others) believe can be accomplished by means other than the current Federal Reserve strategy.[157]

For our purposes, it suffices to understand that whether the unemployment rate is at 4 percent, 6 percent, or 10 percent, the capitalist system necessarily produces joblessness: the reserve army of labor buoys, or provides an underpinning of support, for those who are employed. Radical theory maintains that this can only cause, directly or indirectly, greater job insecurity, and divisions among the working class, because the economy fails to meet people's material needs.[158]

## Job Insecurity and the Fixed-Pie Syndrome

According to a 1998 quarterly nationwide survey of U.S. workers conducted by Rutgers University's Heldrich Center for Workforce Development and the University of Connecticut's Center for Survey Research and Analysis, some 59 percent of respondents say they are very concerned about job security for "those currently at work."[159] An additional 28 percent indicate they are "somewhat concerned."[160]

Reports on U.S. job trends show that workers have reason for concern. Workers appear less likely to be able to count on long-term employment, which in the past provided steady wage growth, fringe benefits, and long-term job security. Jobs grew increasingly insecure in the 1990s, as the share of workers in "long-term jobs" (those lasting at least ten years) fell from 41 percent in 1979 to 35.4 percent in 1996, with the worst deterioration having taken place since the late 1980s.[161] Corporate mergers and downsizing have contributed to job cuts or company shutdowns that cost nearly 30 percent of U.S. workers their jobs from 1990 to 1995.[162] Merger-related layoffs soared in 1998 to nearly double the level of 1997, reflecting a slew of high-priced mergers and acquisitions.[163] Job cuts resulting from mergers totaled 73,903 in 1998, up 99.6 percent from the 1997 total of 37,033.[164]

A new round of layoffs began in 2000. According to the Bureau of Labor

Statistics, the total number of people laid off that year was more than 1.8 million. In January 2001, the BLS reported that the unemployment rate rose to 4.2 percent, the highest level in 15 months.[165] Further, as of this writing, more mass layoffs are planned by blue-chip companies.[166] General Electric is promising to shed 75,000 workers; Verizon is eliminating 10,000 jobs; DaimlerChrysler is getting rid of 20 percent of its workforce;[167] Disney is cutting 4,000 jobs worldwide;[168] Delphi Automotive Systems Corporation plans to eliminate 11,500 jobs;[169] and DuPont is cutting 4,000 jobs, or about 4 percent of its workforce, as well as 1,300 contract workers.[170] Amazon.com is laying off 15 percent of its workforce, BarnesandNoble.com 16 percent, CNET Networks 10 percent. Xerox, JCPenney, Textron, Lucent Technologies, Toshiba America, and AOL Time Warner are all firing workers.[171]

To understand job-loss anxiety, it is necessary to know what happens to a worker's material reality when he or she loses a job. Workers have difficulties finding new employment, with more than one-third still out of a job when interviewed one to three years after their displacement.[172] Workers rarely regain their old wage and are often forced to take jobs paying about 13 percent less than the old job.[173] An increasing percentage of workers are working part-time jobs, from 13 percent of all jobs in 1957 to more than 19 percent, or nearly 20 million people, in 1993.[174] Others try to make ends meet with two or more part-time jobs. In 1997 more than 7.9 million people worked more than one job.[175]

In the 1990s the "contingent" workforce grew substantially; almost 30 percent of workers in 1999 were employed in situations that were not regular full-time jobs—including independent contracting and other forms of self-employment, such as temporary agency labor or day labor.[176] The number of workers employed by temporary agencies almost doubled, rising from 1.3 percent in 1989 to 2.4 percent in 1997.[177] Temporary workers on average earn less than workers with comparable skills and backgrounds who work in regular full-time jobs and are less likely to receive health or pension benefits.[178]

Displaced workers are facing increased job insecurity, lowered career expectations, lowered wages, and less control over their financial futures. Such economic trends have been linked to intergroup tensions. Increased intergroup disparities and divisiveness arise out of worsening economic conditions and increased competition for scarce resources.[179] Job insecurity can convert to a scarcity mentality, the thinking that "there is not enough to go around."

Although employers are not required to hire disabled people under affirmative action programs, disabled persons seeking work and those potentially coming off public benefit programs under the Social Security Return-to-Work program represent an influx of new competition joining the ranks of labor. Women on welfare transitioning into jobs[180] are similarly positioned, both as a group of potential workers moving from the surplus population to work and as an undereducated workforce.[181]

The Personal Responsibility and Work Opportunity Reconciliation Act of 1996, which ended federal welfare entitlements and ensconced welfare-to-work as a primary goal of federal welfare policy, illuminates the backlash phenomenon. Welfare reform can be viewed through the zero-sum game paradigm: under U.S. capitalism, one group benefits absolutely at the expense of the other. When some workers gain, others will lose; when some workers get jobs, others will be displaced. Radical or Marxist theory asserts that employers deliberately exploit the least powerful workers (minorities) to increase profits and to divide workers and keep the wage floor down.[182]

Two years after the enactment of welfare reform, both worker displacement and increased worker exploitation are already having an impact. Jon Jeter reported that women coming off welfare are competing with and in some cases displacing other low-wage workers under the "subsidized employment" plan.[183] Under this plan, the state pays a company to hire someone in the program at minimum wage. At the Omni Inner Harbor Hotel in Baltimore, for instance, social service workers placed thirteen jobless women into welfare-to-work jobs. During her ninety-day probation period, each woman wipes, dusts, and vacuums on eight-hour shifts, five days a week, just as regular housekeepers paid $6.10 per hour. In return, she receives $410 a month in welfare benefits from the state and a $30 weekly stipend from the Omni Inner Harbor Hotel. The hotel saves the difference.[184]

According to Jeter, the entry of subsidized workers has increased coworker tension at the hotel, where regular low-wage employees have formed a union among the three hundred bellmen, housekeepers, doormen, and kitchen workers to improve their wages and benefits.[185] Jeter explains the twofold threat to coworkers: not only can subsidized welfare workers undercut regular worker's wages and possibly interfere with union goals of better wages and benefits, but they raise the question of whether management will hire the welfare recipient as a permanent worker and displace a regular employee.[186] The welfare-to-work program has added even more uncertainty to an uneasy coexistence between groups of working poor in Maryland and across the nation, who fear the loss of their jobs to a cheaper workforce.

Welfare advocate Laura Riviera explains the effect of subsidized employment under the Wisconsin welfare-to-work program, called a model for welfare reform by the Clinton administration. "Women are introduced to other employees as 'the W-2 participant.' Knowing that this person is required to work at the company for free, employees automatically feel threatened by this person," says Riviera. "This sets up a situation where it is very difficult for that person to get along well with other employees no matter how hard she tries."[187]

Riviera reports that she has heard from many women who were working and barely making ends meet until welfare reform began. "They were pushed out of their minimum wage jobs by these less expensive employees provided by the state and are now in the W-2 program."[188]

Similar job displacement has occurred under the workfare grant program in New York City, where the recipient receives a predetermined amount of money and in turn must work in a "volunteer" position assigned by the caseworker. When Steven Greenhouse conducted interviews with more than fifty workfare workers and visited more than two dozen work sites, he found that many workfare participants had taken the place of city workers.[189]

> In many municipal agencies, the city has shrunk its regular work force and increased the number of workfare participants. The Sanitation Department's work force slid from 8,296 in 1990 under Mayor David N. Dinkins to 7,528 in early 1994, when Mr. Giuliani took office, then down 16 percent more last year, to 6,327. Today, the department employs more than 5,000 workfare laborers, who wear bright orange vests, sweeping streets and doing other tasks around the city.[190]

According to Greenhouse, workfare recipients are doing much of the work once performed by departed city employees. The 34,100 people in the city's Work Experience Program constitute a low-cost labor force that does a substantial amount of work that had been done by municipal employees before Mayor Rudolph W. Giuliani reduced the city payroll by about 20,000 employees, or about 10 percent.[191]

Jeter reported similar conflicts in the *Washington Post*. In Baltimore, officials at Patterson High School decided last year not to renew the contract with the janitorial company that cleaned the building and looked for welfare recipients to do the work, in part because "their rates would be cheaper."[192] A job-training program in Alabama requires some welfare recipients to work for more than four months without pay for employers such as Continental Eagle, a cotton gin manufacturer near Montgomery.[193]

Other sources of workfare labor were sought as well. New York City rules introduced by the Giuliani administration in 1995 extended workfare to homeless shelters, making workfare and other requirements a conditon of shelter for the 4,600 families and 7,000 single adults in New York City's homeless shelter system. The poor and homeless receive their subsistence benefits only on condition that they accept workfare jobs at the equivalent of minimum wage rates in city clerical jobs and other positions which would normally be filled by civil service workers earning two or three times their wage, plus benefits.[194]

While the stated intent of welfare reform is to move those on welfare into work and thereby lower federal and city welfare outlays, participating businesses receive a net gain from welfare reform: having a captive workforce that can be pushed into lower-wage jobs, whether permanently or temporarily, keeps wages low and increases business profit margins. An insidious fiscal benefit to government has also emerged—undercutting regular worker salaries cuts city service budgets and generates a surplus at the expense of the poorest parts of the workforce.[195]

Welfare reform may result in an overall lowering of the cost of labor. The Economic Policy Institute warns that the low-wage labor market is already suffering greatly; proposals to put welfare recipients to work will drive the wages of the working poor down further. It estimates that to absorb all the welfare workers, the wages of the bottom third of the labor force would have to fall by 11 percent nationally.[196] Former labor secretary Alexis Herman explained that disabled workers can be put to such a purpose as well: "As President Clinton has said: The last big group of people in this country who could keep the economy going strong with low inflation are Americans with disabilities . . . who are not in the workforce."[197] President Clinton made the macroeconomic link between welfare workers and disabled people when he told CNBC that "you can bring more people from welfare or from the ranks of the disabled into the workforce [to keep inflation (wages) down]."[198]

While the majority of reports focus on the initial success of welfare reform in terms of numbers of people dropped from the rolls, there is a growing realization among state and county officials that placing all recipients into jobs is unrealistic for myriad reasons. There is also evidence that those dropped from the rolls may not be faring so well. A Wisconsin study of the transition period conducted by John Pawasarat of the University of Wisconsin at Milwaukee found that 75 percent of those hired lost their jobs within nine months.[199] Only 28 percent sustained projected annual earnings of $10,000 for two consecutive quarter. Such work was often part-time, low-paying, and quick to end.[200] When the Children's Defense Fund and the National Coalition for the Homeless reevaluated the status of former welfare recipients in 1998, they found that only about 50 to 60 percent of those who left welfare were working, and that those who worked typically earned less than $250 per week—too little to lift a family out of poverty.[201]

There are not enough living wage jobs available for women being forced off welfare, and there will not be enough jobs for disabled persons wishing to work or to transition from public benefits into a job. The welfare reform experience indicates that subsidies to business can elevate coworker tension, yet, in the case of disability and employment, subsidies for reasonable accommodations and health care *will be necessary* to level economic discrimination inherent in business accounting practices. Just as women coming off AFDC create increasing competition for jobs and increasing job insecurity, disabled job seekers must be aware that they too can generate resentment among those lacking job security, who may view subsidies to disabled workers as a threat to their employment.

Though many disabled people will be entering the workforce at lower pay levels, akin to the welfare-to-work population (due in part to the fact that large numbers of disabled people lack access to higher education), the global economy makes job insecurity a factor in the traditionally more secure, educated class as well. Evidence of change can also be found in the incidence of displacement within the elite workforce. The President's Council of Economic Advisers reported that "analysis shows that job displacement rates rose for more educated workers, so that while blue collar and less educated workers remain more likely to be displaced than others, displacement rates have clearly risen among those workers who had been previously immune from the threat of job dislocation."[202]

Economists are beginning to see trends indicating that white-collar workers are no longer immune to neoliberal policies that emphasize free market production and increase the labor pool. As economists Anne Colamosca and William Wolman explain, globalization has produced an economy in which "the rapid worldwide spread of available skilled labor" puts foreign workers "in head-to-head competition with their American counterparts."[203] Furthermore, the globalization of financial markets has served to lower the wage floor, as employers search for low labor costs in far corners of the globe and American workers' wages shrink in response. "Capital migrates to low wage areas and the only way that it can be kept in the developed world is if wages in the developed world are kept low."[204]

## Some Unresolved Problems

In part, backlash against the ADA stems from the design of our economic system. Differentials in pay, income, and employment opportunities persist in the labor market, despite antidiscrimination laws. Civil rights, though still necessary to counter individual acts of prejudice and discrimination, have only the power to randomly and partially redress the maladies of unemployment, income, and wage inequality existing throughout the labor market. If everyone were equally educated and trained for jobs, and if civil rights laws were strictly enforced, millions would remain unemployed and underemployed in any capitalist system. Antidiscrimination laws cannot bridge the systemic employment gap, and individual rights cannot reach the root of the parity predicament created by capitalism. Neither the market nor civil rights laws can undermine the structure of inequality nor prevent its reproduction.

After years of dedicated civil rights activism, Dr. Martin Luther King Jr. came to a similar conclusion. At the 1967 Southern Christian Leadership Conference convention Dr. King implored the movement to "address itself to the question of restructuring the whole of American society. There are 40 million poor people here. And one day we must ask the question, 'Why are there 40 million poor people in America?' And when you begin to ask that question, you are raising questions about the economic system, about a broader distribution of wealth. When you ask that question, you begin to question the capitalistic economy."[205]

To be effective, any solution to the ADA backlash problem must address the very nature of social relations. Any workable solution must wrestle with the following question: What is work, who controls it, and what is its purpose? If work is controlled by the Federal Reserve Bank, by investors and Wall Street, all looking to make ever higher profits from people's labor rather than trying to make the system work for all, the paradigm itself must be challenged. It then becomes imperative to ask what an economy is for— to support market-driven profits, or to sustain community bonds and elevate human experience?

To stem the tide of the larger civil rights backlash, which promises to grow as more workers are displaced in the global economy,[206] it is essential to reassert the basic, radical theoretical principle that an economy is only working if it works *for people,* if it delivers health care, a living wage, and a secure livelihood and income for every person. The exclusion of even 3 percent of the population from employment in the liberal definition of "full employment" is simply intolerable.[207] Since private industry views unemployment as an integral part of the "normal" capitalist system (which keeps wages and inflation low and makes unemployment compulsory), people must bypass private industry and insist that government recognize the fundamental right of each person to a livelihood, meaning both full employment at a minimum living wage and quality, disability-sensitive universal health care. This must be the cornerstone of our economic policy.

A government guarantee of full employment would require reorganizing the economy to allow everyone free choice among opportunities for useful, productive, and fulfilling paid employment or self-employment. Base compensation must be set at a living real wage, below which no remuneration for disabled or nondisabled workers should be allowed to fall.

The wide range of disablement means that some disabled persons may never be hired by businesses, but would nevertheless like to be productive in their communities. In order to bring more excluded persons into the workforce, it will be necessary to expand the work environment beyond the bounds set by the capitalist profit motive and ensure that federal and state governments act as the employers of last resort. In addition, those unable to work for pay or to find employment must have a government entitlement to an adequate standard of living, which rises with increases in the wealth and productivity of society.

## Problems of Power

Gregory Mantsios writes that "the class structure in the United States is a function of its economic system—capitalism, a system that is based on private rather than public ownership and control of commercial enterprises, and on the class division between those who own and control and those who do not. Under capitalism, these enterprises are governed by the need to produce a profit for the owners, rather than to fulfill collective needs."[208] Inequality is traceable both to the economic system[209] and to the interaction between private interests and government. Liberal remedies that seek change by requiring government to enact sustained full employment, raise the minimum wage, lower interest rates, and initiate price stability still rely on the premise that these controls can occur with capitalism intact in a democratic society, when hierarchical power relations remain a crucial impediment to realizing such positive outcomes.

Many have questioned the relationship between political power, monetary policy, and wealth inequality in our representative democracy. There is consensus among these theorists (some liberal, some radical) that government has failed to stop rising inequality and has contributed to the decline of labor power, because it has been derelict in its duty to exercise power over private capital. The degradation of workers occurs in this age of mergers and acquisitions, bolstered by the power of speculative capital and unregulated by government precisely *because capital has control of government.*[210] The enormous power of private capital over government is evident in business's backlash against the ADA, in Federal Reserve inflation management strategies primarily aimed to benefit Wall Street, in the millions of dollars spent by the insurance industry to prevent the development of a universal health care program, and in both the passage and content of welfare reform legislation passed by Congress and signed by President Clinton in 1996.

After several centuries of capitalism, our society still shows no signs of allowing sustained full employment. If history provides any guide, it is safe to assume that the decision-making class will *never* allow it. In the 1940s the United States experienced the lowest unemployment rate in its history (1 percent); directly on its heels came McCarthyism, an organized attack on socialist ideals of equitable distribution. In the 1970s, drops in wages and the standard of living coincided with a regressive decline in the power of unions, noticeable over the past few decades.[211] Economist Michel Kalecki's observation that labor must be kept weak to preserve profits and the class dictatorship of capital seems undeniable. Government enactment of full employment under capitalism can only result in an even greater crushing of labor, so as to reinstate "stability" and reassert control over the economic lives of workers.[212]

Capitalist measures—whether the type promoted by free market conservatives or by welfare liberals—fail to respond to the discrimination faced by millions of disabled Americans. Only measures that address systemic and long-standing economic inequality will provide the necessary protections against further workplace discrimination. The present reality, however, is that disabled people are the last legally protected class to enter the workforce. They seek economic equality at a time when unemployment levels are low, and when downsizing and labor market globalization are in full force. It is in such a "positive" economic environment, when business has obtained both the legal and political legitimacy necessary to discriminate in the name of workplace and market efficiency, that our battle for distributive justice becomes the toughest of all.

NOTES

1. 42 U.S.C. §§ 12101–12213 (1994).

2. "[T]he Nation's proper goals regarding individuals with disabilities are to assure . . . economic self-sufficiency[.] Discrimination. . . costs the United States billions of dollars in unnecessary expenses resulting from dependency and nonproductivity." 42 U.S.C. § 12101(a)(8)–(9) (1994).

3. *See Nursing Homes, Others Want Exemptions from ADA Access,* DISABILITY RAG, July–Aug. 1991, at 8; *Disability Issues Could Become Political Footballs,* REP. DISABILITY PROGRAMS, June 22, 1995, at 104; *It Could Happen,* DISABILITY RAG, Jan.–Feb. 1991, at 17, 18. For a fuller discussion of the ADA and business, see MARTA RUSSELL, BEYOND RAMPS: DISABILITY AT THE END OF THE SOCIAL CONTRACT 109–43 (1998).

4. *See Read 'Em and Weep,* DISABILITY RAG, July–Aug. 1992, at 28.

5. Robert Shogun, *Halt Bush's Tilt to Left, Conservatives Tell GOP,* L.A. TIMES, July 14, 1990, at A26.

6. Rick Kahler, *ADA Regulations Black Hole,* RAPID CITY J., Apr. 2, 1995, at C10. Kahler later published a retraction to this piece.

7. Trevor Armbrister, *A Good Law Gone Bad,* READER'S DIG., May 1998, at 145, 155.

8. Edward L. Hudgins, *Handicapping Freedom: The Americans with Disabilities Act,* 18 REGULATION MAGAZINE, 2 CATO REVIEW OF BUSINESS AND GOVERNMENT (1995).

9. *See* HOWARD BOTWINICK, PERSISTENT INEQUALITIES: WAGE DISPARITY UNDER CAPITALIST COMPETITION (1993); *see generally* ROBERT CHERRY ET AL., EDS., THE IMPERILED ECONOMY: MACROECONOMICS FROM A LEFT PERSPECTIVE (1987); PAUL BARAN & PAUL M. SWEEZY, MONOPOLY CAPITAL: AN ESSAY ON THE AMERICAN ECONOMIC AND SOCIAL ORDER (1966).

10. *See* 42 U.S.C. § 12101(a) (1994) (delineating, in introducing the purpose of the Americans with Disabilities Act, congressional findings regarding the historical isolation and segregation of disabled persons).

11. LOUIS HARRIS & ASSOC., NATIONAL ORGANIZATION ON DISABILITY/1998, *Harris Survey of Americans with Disabilities* (1998) (commissioned for the National Organization on Disability) [hereinafter NOD/1998 HARRIS SURVEY].

12. The wage gap is a statistical indicator often used as an index of the status of women's earnings relative to men's. It is also used to compare the earnings of people of color to those of white men. Wage gap statistics can be found in the study by the U.S. Bureau of the Census, MONEY INCOME IN THE UNITED STATES: 1997, <http://www.census.gov/hhes/www/income.html> (last modified Oct. 28, 1999) or from Census Bureau Current Population Reports, Series P-60, U.S. Commerce Department.

13. 1997 is latest year available, <http://www.census.gov>.

14. NOD/2000 HARRIS SURVEY.

15. Other census data confirms that there has been no improvement in the economic well-being of disabled persons. In 1989, for instance, 28.9 percent of working-age adults with disabilities lived in poverty; in 1994, the figure climbed slightly to 30.0 percent. H. Stephen Kaye, *Is the Status of People with Disabilities Improving?* DISABILITY STATISTICS ABSTRACT (Disability Statistics Center, San Francisco), May 1998, at 2.

16. A total of 6,212,000 persons receive Supplemental Security Income, and 4 million receive Social Security Disability Insurance. Social Security Administration Basic Facts About Social Security, <http://www.ssa.gov/pubs/10080.html> (visited February, 8, 2000); 1998 SSI Annual Report, available through the Social Security Administration's website by searching for the "1998 Annual Report" at <http://www.ssa.gov/search/index.htm> (visited Feb. 8, 2000).

17. Title VII of the Civil Rights Act of 1964 prohibits wage and employment discrimination on the basis of race, color, sex, religion, or national origin. 42 U.S.C. § 2000e-2 (1994).

18. Pay equity demands that the criteria used by employers to set wages must be sex and race neutral. The Equal Pay Act of 1963 prohibits unequal pay for equal or "substantially equal" work performed by men and women. 29 U.S.C. § 206(d) (1994). Title VII of the Civil Rights Act of 1964 prohibits wage and employment discrimination on the basis of race, color, sex, religion, national origin. 42 U.S.C. § 2000e-2 (1994). In 1981, the Supreme Court made it clear that Title VII is broader than the Equal Pay Act and prohibits wage discrimination even when jobs are not identical. *See* County of Washington v. Gunther, 452 U.S. 161, 177–81 (1981).

19. Title I of the Americans with Disabilities Act prohibits disability discrimination in employment. 42 U.S.C. § 12101–12117 (1994).

20. U.S. CENSUS BUREAU, CURRENT POPULATION SURVEY (March 1998) (visited Feb. 8, 1999), <http://www.census.gov/hhes/www/income98.html> [hereinafter U.S.C.B., CURRENT POPULATION SURVEY]; HISTORICAL INCOME TABLES— FAMILIES, TABLE F-5, RACE AND HISPANIC ORIGIN OF HOUSEHOLDER—FAMILIES BY MEAN AND MEDIAN INCOME, 1947–1998 (last modified Nov. 10, 1999) <http://www.census.gov/hhes/income/histinc/f05.html> [hereinafter U.S.C.B., HISTORICAL INCOME TABLES]. For a discussion of empirical evidence on earnings gaps and discrimination for Hispanics, see GREGORY DEFREITAS, INEQUALITY AT WORK: HISPANICS IN THE U.S. LABOR FORCE (1991).

21. U.S.C.B., CURRENT POPULATION SURVEY, *supra* note 20; U.S.C.B., HISTORICAL INCOME TABLES, *supra* note 20.

22. For a time-series discussion of black/white earnings ratios, see John Donohue III & James Heckman, *Continuous Versus Episodic Change: The Impact of Civil Rights Policy on the Economic Status of Blacks,* 29 J. ECON. LITERATURE 1603 (1991); Peter Gottschalk, *Inequality, Income Growth, and Mobility: The Basic Facts,* 11 J. ECON. PERSP. 21, 28–29 (spring 1997). Gottschalk demonstrates that the earnings gap between blacks and nonblacks narrowed between the early 1960s and 1975, but progress ceased after this point.

23. William A. Darity Jr. & Patrick L. Mason, *Evidence on Discrimination in Employment: Codes of Color, Codes of Gender,* 12 J. ECON. PERSP. 63, 76 (spring 1998).

24. *See* U.S. Bureau of Labor Statistics, Labor Force Statistics from the Current Population Survey (last modified Feb. 1, 1999), <http://www.bls.gov/webapps/legacy/cpsatab.2.htm> [hereinafter U.S.B.L.S., Labor Force Statistics]. The Census Bureau does not count the prison population as unemployed. Seventy percent of the prison population is black. Adding in the incarcerated population as unemployed—almost 8 percent of all black adult males—changes the unemployment rate for black men from the reported 6.7 percent in December 1998 to 16.5 percent. Angela Davis, Speech at California State University, Fullerton (Mar. 23, 1999); *cf.* Robert Cherry, *Black Men Still Jobless,* Dollars and Sense 43 (Nov.–Dec. 1998).

25. *See* U.S.B.L.S., Labor Force Statistics, *supra* note 24.

26. *See* U.S. Census Bureau, Historical Income Tables—People, Table P-4: Race and Hispanic Origin of People (both sexes combined) by Median and Mean Income: 1947 to 1998 (last modified Nov. 10, 1999), <http://www.census.gov/hhes/income/histinc/p04.html>.

27. *See* Women's Bureau, U.S. Dep't of Labor, Facts on Working Women: Earnings Differences Between Women and Men (visited Dec. 28, 1999), <http://www.dol.gov/dol/wp/public/wb_pubs/wagegap.2.htm>.

28. *Id.* Between 1980 and 1990 the ratio of hourly earnings climbed by 13.1 percentage points; between 1990 and 1997 it climbed by only 2.9 points. Between 1980 and 1990 the annual ratio climbed by 11.4 points, but between 1990 and 1996 the ratio climbed by only 2.2 percentage points. "Between 1980 and 1990 the weekly earnings ratio climbed by 7.5 percentage points; between 1990 and 1997 the ratio climbed 2.5 percentage points." *Id.*

29. Heather Boushey, Economic Policy Institute economist, *quoted in* Lisa Girion, *Wage Gap Continues to Vex Women: The Disparity Is Growing Despite Gains in Education, Employment,* L.A. Times, February 11, 2001 at W1.

30. *See* Women's Bureau, *supra* note 27.

31. H. Stephen Kaye, *supra* note 15, at 2.

32. *Id.*

33. Edward Yelin, *The Employment of People with and Without Disabilities in an Age of Insecurity,* 549 Annals Acad. Pol. & Soci. Sci. 117, 117–28 (1997); R.L. Bennefield & J.M. McNeil, *Labor Force Status and Other Characteristics of Persons with a Work Disability: 1981 to 1988,* Current Population Reports, Series P-23, No. 160, Washington, D.C.: U.S. Bureau of the Census (1989).

34. Individuals are considered to be in the labor force if they are employed or are not employed but are actively seeking work for pay. United States Current Population Survey (1998), at <http://www.census.gov /hhes/www /income98 .html>.

35. NOD/2000 Harris Survey at http://nod.org/hsevent.html#Harris2000; *see generally* Laura Trupin et al., *Trends in Labor Force Participation Among Persons with Disabilities, 1983–1994,* Disability Statistics Report (June, 1997) (Disability Statistics Ctr., San Francisco).

36. *See* Jonathan S. Leonard, *The Impact of Affirmative Action Regulation and Equal Employment Law on Black Employment,* J. Econ. Persp. at 47, 47–63 (fall 1990); John Donohue & James Heckman, *supra* note 22.

37. *See, e.g.,* Cornel West, Race Matters 95 (1993).

38. For conservative opposition to government regulation, see R. P. O'Quinn, *The Americans with Disabilities Act: Time for Amendments,* Cato Institute Policy Analysis No. 158 (Aug. 9, 1991); Brian Doherty, *Unreasonable Accommodation,* REASON MAGAZINE 18 (Aug.–Sept. 1995).

39. *See* NICHOLAS LEMANN, THE PROMISED LAND 218 (1992); MICHAEL PARENTI, DEMOCRACY FOR THE FEW 99–119, 271 (1995).

40. RUSSELL, *supra* note 3, 109–16.

41. These objectives were accomplished, in part, through the promotion of policies such as the North American Free Trade Agreement (NAFTA) and General Agreement on Tariffs and Trade (GATT). *See* PARENTI, *infra* note 43, at 67–75, 80. *See generally* JEFF MCMAHAN, REAGAN AND THE WORLD: IMPERIAL POLICY IN THE NEW COLD WAR (1984).

42. *See generally* LAWRENCE MISHEL ET AL., THE STATE OF WORKING AMERICA, 1998–1999 (Economic Policy Institute 1999); WILLIAM WOLMAN & ANNE COLAMOSCA, THE JUDAS ECONOMY: THE TRIUMPH OF CAPITAL AND THE BETRAYAL OF WORK (1997).

43. *See generally* MICHAEL PARENTI, DEMOCRACY FOR THE FEW (1995); Hudgins, *supra* note 8.

44. MISHEL ET AL., *supra* note 42, at 25.

45. *See* RUSSELL, *supra* note 3, at 113–21.

46. *See* Walter Y. Oi, *Employment and Benefits for People with Diverse Disabilities: Disability, Work, and Cash Benefits,* 103 (J. L. Mashaw, V. P. Reno, R.V. Burkhauser, & M. Berkowitz eds., 1996); S. A. Moss & D.A. Malin, Note, *Public Funding for Disability Accommodations: A Rational Solution to Rational Discrimination and the Disabilities of the ADA,* 33 HARV. C.R.-C.L. L. REV. 197 (1998); For an analysis on the impact of state and federal civil rights legislation on the employment and wages of disabled persons, see Nancy Mudrick, *Employment Discrimination Laws for Disability: Utilization and Outcome,* 549 ANNALS AM. ACAD. POL. & SOC. SCI. 53 (1997).

47. NOD/1998 HARRIS SURVEY, *supra* note 11; *see also* NATIONAL INSTITUTE ON DISABILITY AND REHABILITATION RESEARCH, U.S. DEP'T OF EDUCATION, TRENDS IN LABOR FORCE PARTICIPATION AMONG PERSONS WITH DISABILITIES, 1983–1994 (Disability Statistics Report 10).

48. U.S. Census Bureau, *Disability Employment, Earnings, and Disability Tables* from the Survey of Income and Program Participation, at http://www.census.gov/hhes/www/disable/dissipp.html.

49. Peter Budetti, Richard Burkhauser, Janice Gregory, & H. Allan Hunt, *Ensuring Health and Security for an Aging Workforce,* W.E. Upjohn Institute for Employment Research (2001).

50. An important study revealing the near unanimous opinion among economists of the positive impact of government antidiscrimination programs on income of African Americans can be found in John Donohue & James Heckman, *supra* note 22, at 1603–43. Richard B. Freeman's paper, *Changes in the Labor Market for Black Americans,* 1948–72, 1 BROOKINGS PAPERS ON ECON. ACTIVITY 67, 67–120 (1973), was among the first to identify government antidiscrimination programs as a source of progress.

51. *See* Ruth Colker, *The Americans with Disabilities Act: A Windfall for Defendants*, 34 Harv. C.R.-C.L. L. Rev. 99, 100 (1999).

52. *Id.*

53. *See* Gregory Mantsios, *Class in America: Myths and Realities,* in Paula S. Rothenberg, Race, Class, and Gender in the United States 210–13 (1998).

54. *See* Donald Tomaskovic-Devy, *Race, Ethnic, and Gender Earnings Inequality: The Sources and Consequences of Employment Segregation* (visited Dec. 29, 1999), <http://www.ilr.cornell.edu/GlassCeiling/14/14front.html>.

55. Scholars such as Robert J. Samuelson, William E. Becker, Donald A. Hicks, and William J. Baumol are representative of this point of view.

56. *See* Robert Topel, *Factor Proportions and Relative Wages: The Supply-Side Determinants of Wage Inequality,* J. Econ. Persp. 55, 69 (1997). Topel states, "Wage inequality has risen in modern economics because rising demands for skills have made talented people more scarce. As in other market situations, this 'problem' of a demand-driven rise in price contains the seeds of its own solution. Supply is more elastic in the long run than in the short run. Rising returns to skill encourage people to invest in human capital, which in the long run will increase the proportion of skilled workers in the labor force"; *see also* Robert Z. Lawrence, Single World, Divided Nations? International Trade and OECD Labor Markets 129 (1996).

57. *See, e.g.,* Darity & Mason, *supra* note 23, at 2; James K. Galbraith, Created Unequal: The Crisis in American Pay (1998); *see generally* Jared Bernstein, *Where's the Payoff? The Gap Between Black Academic Progress and Economic Gains* (Economic Policy Institute 1995); For an economist's explanation of why blacks have narrowed the human capital gap between blacks and whites, yet slid further behind in average earnings, see Martin Carnoy, Faded Dreams: The Politics of Economics and Race in America (1994).

58. *See* Mishel et al., *supra* note 42, at 162.

59. *Id.* at 30.

60. *Id.* at 26–27, 198.

61. Galbraith, *supra* note 57, 50–88 (1998). There was no systematic change in skill premiums within industries during the period 1920 to 1947, despite a large increase in the supply of educated labor during this time; *see* Claudia Goldin & Lawrence Katz, The Decline of Non-competing Groups (1995); Claudia Goldin & Lawrence Katz, The Origins of Technology-Skill Complementarity (1996).

62. Darity & Mason, *supra* note 23, at 83–84.

63. Carnoy, *supra* note 57, at 14–15.

64. Letter from James L. Westrich, Massachusetts Institute for Social and Economic Research, to Marta Russell 1 (Apr. 23, 1999) (on file with author).

65. Tomaskovic-Devy, *supra* note 54.

66. *Id.*

67. *Id.*

68. *Id; see also* Paula S. Rothenberg, Race, Class, and Gender in the United States 234–35 (1998).

69. Tomaskovic-Devy, *supra* note 54 (emphasis added).

70. GALBRAITH, *supra* note 57, 37–49.

71. *Id* at 266. Two mainstream economists have produced evidence that—all things being equal—unemployment depresses wages. *See* DAVID BLANCHFLOWER & ANDREW OSWALD, THE WAGE CURVE (1994); *see also* Heather Boushey, *Unemployment, Pay, and Race*, LEFT BUS. OBSERVER 3, 3 (July 1998).

72. ADAM SMITH, AN INQUIRY INTO THE NATURE AND CAUSES OF THE WEALTH OF NATIONS 28 (J. Shield Nicholson ed., 1901) (1776).

73. *Id.*

74. *Id.*

75. *See* KARL MARX, 1 CAPITAL 270–80 (Ben Fowkes trans., Vintage Books 1st ed. 1977) (1867).

76. *Id.* at 929.

77. Darity & Mason, *supra* note 23, at 86–87.

78. *See* West, *supra* note 37; OLIVER CROMWELL COX, CASTE, CLASS, AND RACE: A STUDY IN SOCIAL DYNAMICS (1948).

79. RICHARD EPSTEIN, FORBIDDEN GROUNDS: THE CASE AGAINST EMPLOYMENT DISCRIMINATION LAWS 484 (1992).

80. *Id.* at 484.

81. *See* RICHARD K. SCOTCH, FROM GOOD WILL TO CIVIL RIGHTS: TRANSFORMING FEDERAL DISABILITY POLICY 102 (1984).

82. The Fair Labor Standards Act (i.e. 29 U.S.C. § 214(c)) allows DOL to issue certificates authorizing rates below the statutory minimum wage. The program is described in 29 C.F.R. Part 525.

83. RUSSELL, *supra* note 3, at 137.

84. EPSTEIN, *supra* note 79, at 480–94.

85. *Id.* at 494.

86. UNITED STATES COMMISSION ON CIVIL RIGHTS, HELPING EMPLOYERS COMPLY WITH THE ADA: AN ASSESSMENT OF HOW THE UNITED STATES EQUAL EMPLOYMENT OPPORTUNITY COMMISSION IS ENFORCING TITLE I OF THE AMERICANS WITH DISABILITIES ACT III (1998).

87. Study Finds Employers Win Most ADA Title I Judicial and Administrative Complaints, 22 MENTAL AND PHYSICAL DISABILITY L. REP. 403, 404 (May–June 1998). They concluded that of the 760 decisions in which one party or the other prevailed, employers prevailed in 92.1 percent of those cases. *Id.*

88. As reported in the MENTAL AND PHYSICAL DISABILITY L. REP. (May–June 2000.)

89. Ruth Colker, *supra* note 51, at 99–100.

90. U.S. COMMISSION ON CIVIL RIGHTS, *supra* note 90, at 4–5.

91. *See* Marx, *supra* note 75, at 270–80.

92. *See id.* at 293–306.

93. *See id.* at 293.

94. *See id.* at 274–75.

95. EPSTEIN, *supra* note 79, at 485.

96. *Id.* at 484.

97. Sixty-nine percent of employers that provided accommodations spent nothing or less than $500, 19 percent spent between $500 and $2,000, 9 percent spent between $2,001 and $5,000, and 3 percent spent over $5,000. PRESIDENT'S

Committee on Employment of People with Disabilities, Costs and Benefits of Accommodations (last modified July 1996), <http://www50.pcepd.gov ./pcepd/pubs/ek96/benefits.htm>. However, only a few persons have won reasonable accommodations lawsuits against employees; 80 percent of all title I cases have been thrown out on summary judgment. See Ruth O'Brien, Crippled Justice 163 (2001).

98. See Marjorie Baldwin, *Can the ADA Achieve Its Employment Goals?* 549 Annals Am. Acad. Pol. & Soc. Sci. 42, 49 (Jan. 1997).

99. One out of every five workers is uninsured. The primary reason workers are not insured is because health care benefits are not offered by employers. The coverage rate has decreased in the past decade, dropping from 73 percent in 1989 to 67 percent in 1996. Kaiser Family Foundation, "Employer Health Benefits 1999 Annual Survey," 30.

100. See U.S. Commission on Civil Rights, *supra* note 90, at 134–35.

101. See William Johnson, *The Future of Disability Policy: Benefit Payments or Civil Rights?* 549 Annals Am. Acad. Pol. & Soc. Sci. 171 (Jan. 1997); *see also* Baldwin, *supra* note 98, at 47.

102. Employers have been abandoning responsibility for providing health care. See Olveen Carrasquillo et al., *A Reappraisal of Private Employer's Role in Providing Health Insurance,* 1999 New Eng. J. Med. 109, 109–14.

103. Disabled persons may be classified and written up as a "risk" in private insurance. See 42 U.S.C.A. § 12111(c) (1994). Disabled persons may be deemed a "direct threat," or a significant risk to the health or safety of others that cannot be eliminated by reasonable accommodation. The direct threat defense is spread out over several sections of the ADA, and can be used as a defense to certain Title I (employment discrimination) and Title III claims (for discrimination by public accommodations).

104. See Baldwin, *supra* note 98, at 46–47.

105. The ADA is patterned on the minority group model of prejudice. See Chai R. Feldblum, *Employment Protections,* 69 Milbank Q. 82 (winter 1991); 42 U.S.C.A. § 12101(a)(7) (1994) and Harlan Hahn, *Towards a Politics of Disability: Definitions, Disciplines, and Policies,* 22 Soc. Sci. J. 87 (1985).

106. John M. McNeil, *Americans with Disabilities: 1994–95* > (visited Dec. 29, 1999), <http://www.blue.census.gov/hhes/www/disable /sipp/disab9495 /oldasc .htm>; *see also* National Institute on Disability and Rehabilitation Research, Chartbook on Work and Disability in the United States (1998) (visited Dec. 29, 1999), <http://www.infouse.com/disabilitydata/workdisability_ 1_2.html>.

107. See McNeil, *supra* note 106.

108. Vande Zande v. State of Wisconsin Dep't of Admin., 44 F.3d 538, 543 (7th Cir. 1995) (ruling in favor of employer-defendant).

109. There are exceptions, such as when compliance would create an "undue hardship" on the business's finances. 42 U.S.C. § 12112(b)(5)(a).

110. U.S. Commission on Civil Rights, *supra* note 87, at 5–6.

111. Arlene B. Mayerson, *Restoring Regard for the "Regarded as" Prong: Giving Effect to Congressional Intent,* 42 Vill. L. Rev. 587, 612 (1997).

112. Robert Burgdorf Jr., *"Substantially Limited" Protection from Disability Dis-*

*crimination: The Special Treatment Model and Misconstructions of the Definition of Disability,* 42 VILL. L. REV. 409, 585 (1998).

113. *See id.* at 413–14.

114. *Study Finds Employers Win Most ADA Title I Judicial and Administrative Complaints,* 22 MENTAL & PHYSICAL DISABILITY L. REP. 403, 404 (1998).

115. Ruth Colker, *supra* note 51, at 101.

116. *Id.* at 101–2.

117. *See, e.g.,* Matthew Diller, *Judicial Backlash, the ADA, and the Civil Rights Model,* 21 BERKELEY. J. EMP. & LAB. L. 19 (2000). See Toyota Motor Manufacturing, Kentucky, Inc. v. Williams, No. 00–1089 decision of the Supreme Court.

118. *See* Matthew Diller, *Dissonant Disability Policies: The Tensions Between the Americans with Disabilities Act and Federal Disability Benefit Programs,* 76 TEX. L. REV. 1003, 1007–8 (1998).

119. 526 U.S. 795 (1999).

120. *Id.* at 974.

121. *Id.* at 977–78.

122. *Id.* at 977.

123. 527 U.S. 457 (1999) (corrective lenses and myopia).

124. 527 U.S. 516 (1999) (medication-controlled hypertension).

125. 527 U.S. 555 (1999) (monocular vision).

126. 531 U.S. 356, 121 S. Ct. 955 (2001).

127. 527 U.S. 457, 471 (Stevens, J., dissenting).

128. *Id.* at 473.

129. *Id.*

130. Brief Amici Curiae of the Equal Employment Advisory Council, the U.S. Chamber of Commerce, and the Michigan Manufacturers Association in support of respondents, at 4.

131. *NAM Urges Court Not to Expand the Americans with Disabilities Act,* NAM NEWS RELEASE (Nat'l Ass'n Mfrg., Wash., D.C.), Mar. 24, 1999, at 1.

132. 531 U.S. 356, 121 S. Ct. 955 (2001).

133. *Id* at 968 n.9.

134. *Id* at 967.

135. 42 U.S.C. § 12101(9).

136. 121 S. Ct. at 975 (Breyer, J., dissenting).

137. 528 U.S. 62 (2000).

138. 529 U.S. 598 (2000).

139. 532 U.S. 105, 121 S. Ct. 1302 (2001).

140. JAMES O'CONNOR, THE FISCAL CRISIS OF THE STATE 161 (1973).

141. MARX, *supra* note 75, at 589–92, 600–601; *see also* KARL MARX, THE GRUNDRISSE 491 (Martin Nicolaus, trans., 1973) (1858). The reserve army of labor has historically included women and minority workers.

142. SHEILA D. COLLINS ET AL., JOBS FOR ALL, A PLAN FOR THE REVITALIZATION OF AMERICA 10 (1994) (quoting Vickrey).

143. *See* Milton Friedman, *The Role of Monetary Policy,* AM. ECON. REV. 1, 1–17 (Mar. 1968); *see also* MICHAEL PERELMAN, THE PATHOLOGY OF THE U.S. ECONOMY: THE COSTS OF A LOW-WAGE SYSTEM 40 (1993).

144. Suzanne McGee, *Anxiety That Jobs Data Will Show Economy Is Growing at*

*Healthy Clip Weighs on Traders,* WALL ST. J., June 5, 1996, at C22 (quoting a U.S. Bureau of Labor Statistics Report).

145. *Id.*

146. *See* Davis, *supra* note 26.

147. The figure is adjusted for the official definition of "employed." Under current U.S. definitions of employment, one must be actively looking for work to count as unemployed. People are classified as unemployed if they meet all of the following criteria: they had no employment during the reference week; they were available for work at that time; and they made specific efforts to find employment sometime during the four-week period ending with the reference week. If one has given up the search for work as hopeless, one is not counted as jobless. In addition, U.S. unemployment statistics may tend to undercount the poor and unemployed more than most European statistics. The BLS uses a head count rather than full-time equivalent (FTE) to account for employment. Since a person who is employed only ten hours a week counts the same as one who is employed forty hours a week, significant numbers of the underemployed can skew the employment rates upward as compared to the FTE approach. *See* DAVID DEMBO & WARD MOREHOUSE, THE UNDERBELLY OF THE U.S. ECONOMY: JOBLESSNESS AND THE PAUPERIZATION OF WORK IN AMERICA 13 (1995).

148. In 1997, 16.8 million worked full-time year-round, yet earned less than the official poverty level for a family of four. This represents 18 percent of full-time workers. Roughly one in four women and one in seven men who had full-time jobs year-round earned less than the poverty level for a family of four. These estimates are calculated from the U.S. Census Bureau, *supra* note 12, at 38–41.

149. Workers only marginally attached to the labor force—such as the ten million disabled persons on disability benefits—don't enter into the unemployment calculation. The Current Population Survey focuses on the civilian noninstitutional population over age sixteen. If a person fits this criterion, CPS determines if they are in the labor force or not in the labor force (NLF). If they are in the labor force, then they are employed or unemployed. If they are neither employed nor unemployed (but still in the civilian noninstitutional population over age sixteen) they are considered NLF. The NLF population is not, however, separately identified on the basis of their disability status, so the only estimate available of how many disabled people might join the labor force comes from a survey such as NOD/Harris.

150. Jack A. Meyer & Pamela J. Zeller, Kaiser Comm'n on Medicaid and the Uninsured, Profiles of Disability: Employment and Health Coverage 9 (1999).

151. 10.8 million people with disabilities are not currently in the labor force. Trupin et al., *supra* note 35.

152. NOD/1998 HARRIS SURVEY, *supra* note 11.

153. Edward Yelin & Patricia Katz, *Making Work More Central to Work Disability Policy,* 72 MILBANK Q. 593 (1994).

154. When unemployment is high, inequality rises; when unemployment is low, inequality tends to fall. GALBRAITH, *supra* note 57, at 148; *see generally* DOUG HENWOOD, WALL STREET: HOW IT WORKS AND FOR WHOM (1997); DEAN BAKER, THE IMPACT OF MIS-MEASURED INFLATION ON WAGE GROWTH (Economic Policy Institute, 1998).

155. *See* Henwood, *supra* note 154, at 219; WOLMAN & COLAMOSCA, *supra* note 42, at 141–66.

156. *See* Henwood, *supra* note 154, at 213.

157. For Galbraith's solutions, which are too involved to outline here, *see id.,* at 263–70.

158. For insecurity and polarization of the working class, see generally O'CON- NOR, *supra* note 140; MICHAEL PERELMAN, THE PATHOLOGY OF THE U.S. ECONOMY: THE COSTS OF A LOW-WAGE SYSTEM (1993); SHELDON DANZIGER & PETER GOTTSCHALK, AMERICA UNEQUAL (1996).

159. Gene Koretz, *Economic Trends: Which Way Are Wages Headed?* BUS. WK, Sep. 21, 1998, at 26.

160. *Id.*

161. *See* MISHEL ET AL., *supra* note 42, at 7.

162. *Cognetics Annual Report on Job Demographics,* COUNCIL ON INTERNA- TIONAL AND PUBLIC AFFAIRS, 2 (winter 1997).

163. Aaron Bernstein, *Is the Job Engine Starting to Sputter?* BUS. WK. (Oct. 5, 1998).

164. *Id.*

165. Press Statement of Katherine G. Abraham, Commissioner Bureau of Labor Statistics, Feb. 2, 2001.

166. BLS Daily Report, Wednesday, Feb. 21, 2001.

167. George Szamuely, N.Y. PRESS, Feb. 13, 2001.

168. http://www.nytimes.com/2001/03/28/business/28DISN.html.

169. Keith Bradsher, *11,500 Jobs Are Being Cut at Big Maker of Auto Parts,* N.Y. TIMES, March 30, 2001.

170. Claudia H. Deutsch, *DuPont to Cut 4,000 Jobs,* N.Y. TIMES, Apr. 3, 2001.

171. Szamuely, *supra* note 167.

172. MISHEL ET AL., *supra* note 42, at 8.

173. *Id.*

174. *Id.*

175. Thomas Amirault, *Characteristics of Multiple Jobholders,* 120 MONTHLY LAB. REV. ONLINE (Mar. 1997) (visited Feb. 8, 2000), <http://www.bls.gov/opub /mlr/1997/03/art2exc.htm>.

176. Ken Hudson, *No Shortage of Nonstandard Jobs,* briefing paper from the Economic Policy Institute, Dec. 1999 at http://fog.lights.com:8765/epinet /static.html.

177. MISHEL ET AL., *supra* note 42, at 21.

178. *See generally* U.S. GEN. ACCOUNTING OFFICE, GAO REPORT NO. HRD- 91–56, WORKERS AT RISK: INCREASED NUMBERS IN CONTINGENT EMPLOYMENT LACK INSURANCE, OTHER BENEFITS (1991).

179. *See* Sheryl L. Lindsley, Communicating Prejudice in Organizations, in COMMUNICATING PREJUDICE 187–205 (Michael L. Hecht et al. eds., 1998).

180. Since January 1993, the number of people on welfare rolls has fallen 48 per- cent to 7.3 million nationally, with three-quarters of the drop coming since the measure became law in 1996. *Clinton Asks Business to Hire More from Welfare Rolls,* Aug. 3, 1999 (visited Feb. 8, 2000), <http://cnn.com/ALLPOLITICS/stories /1999/08/03/welfare/>.

181. 42.7 percent of disabled persons enrolled in high school do not graduate. U.S. Dept. of Education, H. Stephen Kaye, *Education of Children with Disabilities,*

Disability Statistics Abstract, July 19, 1997, at 2. Only 6.3 percent of all students enrolled in undergraduate postsecondary institutions (1992–93) had a disability. Of these, 46.3 percent were attending school full time (compared to 52.9 percent of nondisabled students. *See* Thomas D. Snyder, *National Center for Education Statistics,* 96 Dig. of Educ. Stat. 133 (1996).

182. John E. Roemer, *Divide and Conquer: Microfoundations of a Marxian Theory of Wage Discrimination,* 10 Bell J. Econ. 695, 695–96 (1979).

183. Jon Jeter, *Room for Working Poor in Welfare's New Deal?* Wash. Post, Mar. 15, 1997, at A01.

184. *Id.*

185. *Id.*

186. *See id.*

187. Electronic mail from Laura L. Riviera to Thomas Kruse (June 1, 1998) (on file with author).

188. *Id.*

189. Steven Greenhouse, *Many Participants in Workfare Take the Place of City Workers,* N.Y. Times, Apr. 13, 1998; *see also* Steven Greenhouse, *Union to Sue Giuliani Administration over Use of Welfare Recipients in Jobs,* N.Y. Times, Feb. 4, 1999.

190. *See* Greenhouse, *Many Participants, supra* note 189.

191. *Id.*

192. Jon Jeter, *Room for Working Poor in Welfare's New Deal?* Wash. Post, Mar. 15, 1997, at A1 (referring to statement by the building's custodian).

193. *Id.*

194. In early 2000, the New York State Supreme Court ruled that New York may not force homeless adults to accept workfare jobs in exchange for city shelter, and increasingly city workfare contractors which place welfare recipients into private-sector jobs have come under scrutiny for questionable practices. Nina Bernstein, *City's Rules for Shelters Held Illegal,* N.Y. Times, Feb. 23, 2000 at B1. See Nina Berstein, *New Problems with Welfare-to-Work,* N.Y. Times, April 14, 2000 at B6.

195. One example: the Pataki administration has quietly built up a $500 million surplus in federal welfare money over the last two years as a result of the dramatic decline in the number of people on public assistance, and expects that sum to grow to $1.4 billion. Raymond Hernandez, *New York Gets Big Windfall from Welfare,* N.Y. Times, Feb. 9, 1999. The surplus can then be converted into tax breaks for special interest lobbies such as housing developers.

196. Lawrence Mishel & John Schmitt, Cutting Wages by Cutting Welfare: The Impact of Reform on the Low-Wage Labor Market 1 (Economic Policy Institute 1995).

197. Alexis M. Herman, U.S. Secretary of Labor, Remarks Before the National Council on Independent Living, the National Association of Protection and Advocacy, and the National Council on Disability (June 24, 1999).

198. Interview by Ron Insana, CNBC, with President Bill Clinton, Waterfield Cabinet Company, Clarksdale, Miss. (July 6, 1999).

199. Jason DeParle, *Flaws Emerge in Wisconsin's Welfare-to-Work Plan,* N.Y. Times, Oct. 18, 1998, at A1.

200. *Id. See generally* Joel Dresan, *W-2 Work or Else; Food Charities Face Bigger Loan Under Wisconsin Works,* Milwaukee J. Sentinel, July 21, 1988, at 2.

201. CHILDREN'S DEFENSE FUND, AFTER WELFARE, MANY FAMILIES FARE WORSE (visited Nov. 19, 1999) <http://www.childrensdefense.org /release981202.html>.

202. Council of Economic Advisors, Job Creation and Employment Opportunities: The United States Labor Market, 1993–1996 (visited Feb. 8, 2000), <http://whitehouse.gov/WH/EOP/CEA/html/labor.html>.

203. WOLMAN & COLAMOSCA, *supra* note 42, at 87–138 (1997).

204. *Id.* at 53, 141–66; *see generally* BENNETT HARRISON, LEAN AND MEAN: THE CHANGING LANDSCAPE OF CORPORATE POWER IN THE AGE OF FLEXIBILITY (1994).

205. A TESTAMENT OF HOPE: THE ESSENTIAL WRITINGS OF MARTIN LUTHER KING, JR. 245, 250 (James M. Washington ed., 1991) (quoting from King's 1967 SCLC presidential address, *Where Do We Go from Here?*).

206. *See* GLOBALIZATION AND PROGRESSIVE ECONOMIC POLICY: THE REAL CONSTRAINTS AND OPTIONS (Dean Baker et al. eds., 1980).

207. For an example of what a radical democratic planned future might look like see DEWEY, *supra* note 206, at 296–99; MARTIN CARNOY & DEREK SHEARER, ECONOMIC DEMOCRACY (1980); DANIEL SINGER, WHOSE MILLENNIUM? (1999).

208. Gregory Mantsios, *Class in America: Myths and Realities, in* RACE, CLASS, AND GENDER IN THE UNITED STATES 212 (Paula S. Rothenberg, ed.) (1998).

209. Political economist Bennett Harrison posits that income polarization is a "by-product" of the postindustrial society. *See* BENNETT HARRISON, LEAN AND MEAN: THE CHANGE LANDSCAPE OF CORPORATE POWER IN THE AGE OF FLEXIBILITY (1997).

210. *See* WOLMAN & COLAMOSCA, *supra* note 42, at 144–45 (1997).

211. *See* MICHAEL YATES, WHY UNIONS MATTER 135–40 (1998).

212. COLLECTED WORKS OF MICHAL KALECKI, CAPITALISM: BUSINESS CYCLES AND FULL EMPLOYMENT (Jerzy Osiatynski ed., 1990).

*Stephen L. Percy*

# Administrative Remedies and Legal Disputes
## Evidence on Key Controversies Underlying Implementation of the Americans with Disabilities Act

More than a decade has passed since the Americans with Disabilities Act was enacted in 1990.[1] This landmark law grew out of earlier attempts at the national and state levels to craft statutory frameworks protecting the rights and liberties of persons with disabilities.[2] With more than a decade of implementation experience behind us, an assessment of the ADA's progress in advancing the rights and opportunities of America's disabled population is apt and timely. Along these lines, this essay explores ADA enforcement from the perspective of administrative complaints that have been filed and investigated, as well as those resulting in enforcement through legal action. It also examines the legal precedents and understandings of statutory meaning that are emerging from judicial decisions in key court cases arising under the ADA. Together, these perspectives shed light on the impact of the ADA, as well as on the challenges encountered in its implementation—challenges that must be overcome for the nation to move forward in achieving the act's primary objective: "[t]o provide a clear and comprehensive national mandate for the elimination of discrimination against individuals with disabilities."[3]

## Statutory Flexibility: The Challenge and Opportunity of the ADA

It is not surprising that the federal agencies and courts are playing—and will continue to play—a significant role in implementing the Americans with Disabilities Act. While ADA supporters sought to create legislation with strong regulatory mandates to end discrimination and remove barriers to full participation in American life,[4] the overall regulatory approach of the ADA embodied two important features: *balance* and *flexibility*. Those who read the full text of the ADA will see that the statutory language does not contain a long list of specific declarations about what regulated parties must do or not do to comply with regulatory mandates. Instead, the law requires broadly defined affirmative accommodations to be taken for persons with disabilities and specifies basic operating principles that allow flexibility in attaining compliance while attempting to balance the needs of people with disabilities with the costs incurred by regulated parties.

The principles of balance and flexibility are embodied, for example, in the ADA's requirement for reasonable accommodation in employing people with disabilities.[5] The ADA's Title I stipulates that employers covered under the act must make *reasonable accommodations* to employ persons with disabilities.[6] Accommodations might include such activities as removing physical barriers or rearranging office layouts, providing specialized equipment, or reorganizing work tasks among employees. This mandate for accommodation is tempered, however, by the stipulation that accommodations are not required when the "covered entity can demonstrate that the accommodation would impose an undue hardship on the operation of the business of the covered entity."[7] The ADA provides further flexibility in determining whether and when undue hardship occurs by allowing certain factors to be weighed in this determination—for example, overall financial resources of the entity, number of employees, type of business operation, and the cost of the accommodation—without specifying a cost-based formula to be utilized.

Similar themes of flexibility and balance are found in Title III, which extends the act to providers of public accommodation (including all but small-sized purveyors of facilities and services available to the general public).[8] Parallel to the approach in Title I, this section requires entities providing services and accommodations to make changes in service delivery or to modify physical structures so that people with disabilities will not be impeded from access to or enjoyment of services or amenities. Modification in this context could mean removing physical obstacles to entry or ending policies that prevent or limit people with disability from full utilization of facilities or consumption of services.[9] Here, again, the mandate has some balance. Accommodations may not be required if they would "fundamentally alter the nature of the good, service, facility, privilege, advantage, or accommodation being offered or would result in an undue burden."[10]

The point here is that the ADA purposively does *not* seek to specifically define all mandates or answer all questions about implementation. Instead, the law challenges regulated entities and people with disabilities to be creative in finding solutions that can meet individual needs while also considering the cost or disruption experienced by the regulated parties as they perform accommodations.[11] Creativity is therefore the upside to this approach. The downside, particularly in early years prior to establishment of general understandings and administrative and legal precedent, is that case-by-case disputes can be expected to reach enforcement agencies and the federal judiciary—therefore granting administrative agencies and the courts a key role in defining the reach and breadth of disability rights mandates.

It should be noted that the statutory flexibility embodied in the ADA does not imply that the law's framers intended the ADA to be anything other than comprehensive in scope and application. To the contrary, many key definitions in the act are left open-ended. The definition of persons covered under the law, for example, is very broad. Rather than stipulating a list of disabling conditions or circumstances that would trigger legal protection under the ADA, the law's framers, drawing upon policy precedents,[12] utilized a definition that focused on conditions that impair "major life activities"—current, past, or as perceived by others.[13] This definition signals an aggressive approach to triggering protections. Thus, even though some basic operating principles of the law provide flexibility in crafting accommodations so as to balance required accommodations against the costs incurred in achieving compliance, the ADA simultaneously creates an expansive antidiscrimination mandate.

The remainder of this essay explores ADA implementation from the perspectives of the administrative agencies that investigate, mediate, and sometimes prosecute complaints of discrimination arising under ADA protection, as well as of the legal decisions and precedents that have arisen from key court decisions related to the ADA. Enforcement data and judicial findings yield insight into the types of discrimination that are being challenged through ADA protections, the individuals and entities being charged, and the resolution of discrimination charges—all of which contribute to an understanding of the real impact of the ADA and its potential to eliminate discrimination based on disability.

## Implementation of Employment Protections

One picture of ADA enforcement can be drawn through an examination of employment-related complaints under Title I of the ADA. The Equal

Employment Opportunity Commission (EEOC) is charged with primary responsibility for enforcing the employment protections for people with disabilities outlined in Title I of the ADA for private-sector entities.[14] Enforcement of employment protections for state and local governments, which is granted to the Department of Justice, is reviewed in a subsequent section of this essay.[15] The EEOC issues administrative regulations to guide implementation of Title I protections. These regulations outline the process of filing complaints when it is believed that regulated parties are not complying with the law.[16]

From the beginning of ADA enforcement of Title I in July 1992 through the end of fiscal year 1998, 108,939 charges of discrimination were filed with the EEOC.[17] Charges rose to an annual high of 19,798 in fiscal year 1995. As of 1998, about half of filed complaints were resolved with an administrative determination of "no probable cause" for a finding of discrimination. Another 34 percent of charges were classified as "administrative closures," cases where investigations were terminated for reasons such as failure to locate the charging party, charging party failing to respond to EEOC communications, charged party refusing to accept full relief, or where the case was mooted by the outcome of related litigation.[18]

The data on charges can also be examined from the perspective of merit resolutions—charges with favorable outcomes for those filing them. This category includes settlements, withdrawal of charges upon receipt of benefits, and findings of reasonable cause. Twenty-two percent of those charging discrimination received a favorable outcome. The EEOC estimates that the monetary benefits awarded through settlements and conciliation agreements total more than $211 million over the 1992–98 period.[19]

It is difficult to determine the true meaning of these numbers. One analyst has found that only a fifth of those who have filed complaints with the EEOC since the enactment of the ADA have received favorable outcomes.[20] Many unsuccessful cases, however, are closed because the charging party does not follow through (potentially as the result of a disability that makes communication difficult or a lack of confidence that a complaint will yield a successful conclusion). Other cases are abandoned after the charging party learns informally that probable cause is not likely to be found.

Further perspective on complaint assessment and resolution by the EEOC is provided in a study by Moss, Johnsen, and Ullman.[21] These authors undertook a detailed analysis of the Title I employment discrimination charges filed with the EEOC, examining employment discrimination cases by the type of disability involved. The study focused particularly

TABLE 1. Discrimination Charges Filed with the EEOC under the ADA, FY 1992–1998

| | 1992[a] | 1993 | 1994 | 1995 | 1996 | 1997 | 1998[b] | Total |
|---|---|---|---|---|---|---|---|---|
| Charges received by EEOC | 1,048 | 15,274 | 18,859 | 19,789 | 18,046 | 18,108 | 17,806 | 108,939 |
| Settlement with benefits to charging party as warranted by evidence of record | 11 (12.5%) | 422 (9.4%) | 733 (5.9%) | 811 (4.3%) | 770 (3.3%) | 1,000 (4.1%) | 1,154 (4.9%) | 4,901 (4.6%) |
| Withdrawal by charging party upon receipt of desired benefits | 7 (8.0%) | 591 (13.1%) | 1,126 (9.0%) | 1,222 (6.5%) | 1,151 (4.9%) | 888 (3.7%) | 816 (3.5%) | 5,801 (5.4%) |
| EEOC determination of reasonable cause to believe discrimination occurred | 1 (1.1%) | 106 (2.4%) | 360 (2.9%) | 474 (2.5%) | 591 (2.5%) | 1,060 (4.4%) | 1,435 (6.2%) | 4,027 (3.8%) |
| Total merit resolutions (outcome favorable to charging party) | 19 (21.6%) | 1,119 (24.9%) | 2,219 (17.7%) | 2,507 (13.3%) | 2,512 (10.7%) | 2,948 (12.2%) | 3,405 (14.7%) | 14,729 (13.8%) |
| Monetary benefits received ($ millions)[c] | 0.2 | 15.9 | 32.6 | 38.7 | 38.7 | 36.1 | 49.1 | 211.0 |
| Closed for administrative reasons (e.g., failure to locate charging party, related litigation) | 62 (70.5%) | 1,941 (43.1%) | 5,570 (44.5%) | 7,998 (42.3%) | 7,927 (33.8%) | 7,336 (30.3%) | 6,461 (27.7%) | 37,295 (34.9%) |
| EEOC determination of no reasonable cause to believe discrimination occurred | 7 (8.0%) | 1,442 (32.0%) | 4,734 (37.8%) | 8,395 (44.4%) | 13,012 (55.5%) | 13,916 (57.5%) | 13,458 (57.7%) | 54,964 (51.4%) |
| Total charges resolved | 88 | 4,502 | 12,523 | 18,900 | 23,451 | 24,200 | 23,324 | 106,988 |

Source: EEOC, Americans with Disabilities Act of 1990 (ADA) Charges FY 1992–1998, available at <http://www.eeoc.gov/stats/ada.html> (visited Feb. 20, 2000).
[a]Enforcement of ADA commenced July 26,1992.
[b]Data through Sept. 30, 1998.
[c]Benefits received through litigation are excluded.

on how people with some form of mental disability fare in the complaint resolution process.[22] The study reveals that people with mental impairments have the greatest difficulty overcoming prejudice and discrimination within the workplace—even when they possess the skills and expertise needed to perform necessary work tasks. Until recent decades, the primary treatment strategy for people with psychologically based disabilities was heavy medication or institutionalization. Even sterilization, shocking as it may seem, was practiced against people with disabilities well into the twentieth century.[23]

The empirical study by Moss and her colleagues found that mental disabilities were the second most frequently reported type of disability cited in complaints to the EEOC—suggesting that people with these disabilities understand their protections under federal law and are utilizing the enforcement mechanisms at their disposal. The authors also found only a small difference between the outcomes of complaint charges involving individuals with psychiatric disabilities and those whose complaints derived from physical disability.[24]

Another view on ADA enforcement is provided through an examination of the EEOC's litigation docket—complaints and charges that have moved to the point of legal action initiated by the EEOC in federal court. The EEOC has published a report on its litigation docket, including both active and resolved cases, from 1992 through the end of March 1998.[25] As of March 1998, the EEOC had resolved 180 court cases and was handling 98 active ones.[26] Examination of EEOC litigation data shows that within the 278 court cases, active and resolved, 470 charges of discrimination were outlined (many cases included more than 1 discriminatory charge).[27]

Table 2 presents a breakdown of the nature of discriminatory charges embodied in the EEOC cases. Discrimination related to hiring and employment status represents almost half (46 percent) of the charges presented in the cases, with charges concerning hiring and terminations being the most prominent. Legal claims that reasonable accommodations were not provided represented 20 percent of all cases. Treatment by employers—including discriminatory terms and conditions of employment, retaliation for filing discrimination complaints, harassment, and violations of confidentiality—represented another 18 percent of charges. Unlawful disability-related inquiries about employees and charges concerning allegedly discriminatory effects of disability benefits and health insurance coverage represented 9 percent and 6 percent of charges, respectively.

Examination of individual cases shows the breadth of employment situations from which discriminatory charges are emanating. The cases show

TABLE 2.    Discriminatory Charges in Active and Resolved Employment (Title 1) Cases Litigated by EEOC

| | Active | Resolved | Total |
|---|---|---|---|
| Total Cases | 75 | 144 | 219 |
| Hiring and employment status | 98 | 180 | 278 |
| | (47.8%) | (46.0%) | (46.5%) |
|   Hiring action/policies | 28 | 44 | 72 |
|   Demotion | 1 | 1 | 2 |
|   Failure to promote | 0 | 4 | 4 |
|   Termination | 41 | 86 | 127 |
|   Forced to leave | 3 | 7 | 10 |
|   Discrimination on basis of | 2 | 2 | 4 |
|     association with person with disability | | | |
| Reasonable accommodation not | 35 | 60 | 95 |
|   provided | (22.2%) | (19.2%) | (20.2%) |
| Treatment by employers | 25 | 61 | 86 |
| | (15.9%) | (19.5%) | (18.3%) |
|   Terms and conditions | 9 | 17 | 26 |
|   Retaliation | 7 | 7 | 14 |
|   Harassment/hostile work environment | 4 | 5 | 9 |
|   Limitation, segregation, classification | 1 | 9 | 10 |
|   Violation of confidentiality | 1 | 17 | 18 |
|   Inappropriate record keeping | 3 | 5 | 8 |
|   Inaccessibility in workplace | 0 | 1 | 1 |
| Disability-related inquiries | 12 | 31 | 43 |
| | (7.6%) | (9.9%) | (9.1%) |
| Benefits/health insurance coverage | 10 | 17 | 27 |
| | (6.4%) | (5.4%) | (5.7%) |
|   Disability benefits | 8 | 2 | 10 |
|   Health insurance coverage | 2 | 15 | 17 |
|     Total charges raised in litigation | 157 | 313 | 470 |

Note: The number of charges is greater than the number of cases since individual cases can have more than one charge.

Source: U.S. Equal Employment Opportunity Commission, *Docket of American with Disabilities Act (ADA) Litigation* (Washington, D.C.: EEOC, 1998). Report available on EEOC website at www.eeoc.gov.

substantial variety in the types of disabling conditions experienced by those bringing charges, including life-threatening conditions (e.g., cancer), congenitally induced disabilities, learning and attention deficit disorders, hearing and vision impairments, loss of limbs due to workplace accidents, depression, back problem or injury, and many others. The charges themselves relate to both physical and mental impairments. The types of private entities being charged also show substantial variation, ranging from small private concerns to major corporations like American Airlines,[28] General Motors,[29] Bethlehem Steel,[30] Chrysler,[31] and Federal Express.[32]

Of particular interest in these administrative cases is the wide variety of interpretations given "reasonable accommodation"—the requirement that employers take action to meet the needs of disabled workers who are "otherwise qualified" to perform relevant job responsibilities.[33] This is one of the most flexible areas of the law and accordingly has generated controversy between parties as they seek to determine the extent and nature of regulatory compliance mandated by the ADA. A review of the reasonable accommodation issues outlined in EEOC litigation demonstrates substantial variety in accommodations sought and legal settlements reached in these cases. Illustrative of the specific complaints in these cases involving charges of failure to provide reasonable accommodations in employment are the following:

Employer refused to grant charging party's request for reassignment to a different job position with less travel after company doctor imposed travel restrictions as the result of HIV/AIDS; charging party terminated. (Settlement agreement provided charging party with $63,500.)[34]

Employer failed to accommodate charging party's lumbar disk syndrome (back problem); charging party terminated. (Consent decree provided $90,000 in compensatory damages to the charging party.)[35]

Employer refused to accommodate the charging party's disability (congenitally defective left arm) by forcing her to perform nonessential typing duties. (Consent decree provided $65,000 to charging party.)[36]

Employer refused to reasonably accommodate (and then terminated) the charging party by allowing her to sit on a stool 5 to 10 minutes each hour when she became fatigued by systemic lupus. (Settlement agreement provided $75,000 in monetary relief to charging party and training for managers and employees responsible for implementing the ADA.)[37]

Employer refused to reassign the charging party to "yard work" following removal from truck driver position as the result of epileptic seizure. (Favorable jury verdict awarded charging party with more than $5 million; award amended by court order to correspond with monetary caps in the ADA.)[38]

Employer failed to accommodate charging party's carpal tunnel syndrome by refusing to let him return to work as a bus driver under a revised work schedule. (Consent decree provided charging party with $10,000 in back pay and $10,000 in compensatory damages.)[39]

Employer failed to hire and consider reasonable accommodations that would enable the charging party to perform the position in question, e.g., assigning the marginal task of answering the phone to another employee. (Consent decree provided charging party with $25,000.)[40]

These cases illustrate the variety of disabling conditions experienced by parties making charges of employment discrimination against private enterprises. They also indicate the types of accommodations the parties sought and failed to receive. While some charges of discrimination are dismissed, many, including the limited examples cited above, resulted in settlements or consent decrees providing payments to those alleging discrimination.

## Implementation of Other ADA Mandates

An examination of the cases filed by the U.S. Department of Justice (DOJ) offers another view of ADA implementation and enforcement. Under the act, the DOJ is responsible for enforcing two areas: (1) Title II—programs, services, and activities of state and local government[41] and (2) Title III—public accommodations and commercial facilities.[42] The DOJ maintains a website that reports information on settlements reached as the result of legal action brought by the DOJ against public and private-sector entities under the ADA.[43] These settlements give an indication of the types of complaints that are being filed and prosecuted under the ADA, the relative frequency of charges arising under the different titles of the act, and the types of entities being charged.[44]

Table 3 presents data on the distribution of legal actions that were filed in federal court and later settled. These actions are organized by the nature of the discrimination charge. Settlements resulting from claims under Title II, requiring state and local governments to provide programs and services that accommodate the needs of persons with disabilities, accounted for 47 percent of all settled cases. Title III, which requires accommodation by private entities, is in second place, with 44 percent of all settled cases. Finally,

TABLE 3.    Settlements in ADA Cases Initiated by the Department of Justice

| Enforcement Area | Number | Percent |
|---|---|---|
| Title I: Employment practices of state and local government | 14 | 9 |
| Title II: Programs, services, and activities of state and local governments | 72 | 47 |
| Title III: Public accommodations and commercial facilities | 67 | 44 |
| Total | 153 | 100 |

*Source:* Data on settlements provided through the Freedom of Information Act report section of the U.S. Department of Justice website located at: <http://www.usdoj.gov/crt/foia>.

9 percent of settlements involved Title I–related charges of employment discrimination by state or local government units.

Table 4 provides a breakdown of Title II–related settlements. Of the seventy-two settlements reported by the U.S. Department of Justice, 35 percent involved a complaint about the failure of state or local government to provide an interpreter, auxiliary service, or captioning to accommodate the needs of individuals with hearing impairments. About another third of settlements focused on charges related to the inaccessibility to public buildings and facilities; a quarter involved 911 emergency telephone systems that were not equipped to receive TDD communication; and 8 percent involved failure to provide other service-related accommodations (e.g., higher air transit fees for handicapped persons, treatment of persons with HIV in a hospital emergency room). The defendants in these cases represent a wide array of cities, counties, and local governing boards across the entire nation.

The DOJ's Title III–related settlements show a pattern roughly analogous to those filed under Title II (see table 5). Fifty-three percent of the Title III settlements reached between 1992 and 1998 involved restaurants, movie theaters, hotels, recreational facilities, and retail outlets that were inaccessible to persons with mobility impairments. Fifteen percent involved charges of discrimination related to failures to accommodate hearing impairments, 13 percent focused on the failure to accommodate service needs of disabled individuals (e.g., special hand controls in rental cars, refusal to allow entry to wheelchairs or motor scooters), and 7 percent involved private entities prohibiting people with disabilities from bringing their service animals (e.g., seeing-eye dogs) into their establishment. Twelve percent of the cases focused on discrimination by private vendors against individuals with HIV or AIDS, including failure to admit children

TABLE 4.   Title II–Based Settlements in ADA Cases Initiated by Department of Justice by Type of Charge Brought

| Nature of Discrimination Charge | Number | Percent |
| --- | --- | --- |
| Failure to provide interpreters, auxiliary services for hearing impaired, captioning services | 25 | 35 |
| Inaccessibility, architectural barriers prohibiting access to public facilities | 23 | 32 |
| Failure to make 911 emergency telephone systems accessible through TDD communications | 18 | 25 |
| Other failures to accommodate disability-related needs in provision of services | 6 | 8 |
| Total | 72 | 100 |

Source: Data on settlements provided through the Freedom of Information Act report section of the U.S. Department of Justice website located at <http://www.usdoj.gov/crt/foia>.

with HIV to day care programs. The range of private institutions named in the Title III settlements runs the gamut from small family-owned concerns to several prominent national companies, including Day's Inn,[45] Comfort Inn,[46] Dollar Rent A Car,[47] Budget Rent a Car,[48] Friendly's Ice Cream,[49] Shoney's Restaurants,[50] and Walt Disney World.[51]

While these data on settlements do not answer all questions about ADA enforcement, they do provide one snapshot of enforcement efforts. Across the 153 settlement agreements examined here, we see legal action taken against and settlement agreements reached with cities and counties, large and small, on several causes of discrimination against people with disabilities. We see a similar pattern of legal action and settlement by private-sector entities of all sizes and located across the nation. Thus far, the focus of discrimination charges has tended toward removal of architectural barriers and increased accessibility as well as toward provision of services and equipment to allow greater access for people with hearing impairments. Many of these settlements involved discrimination that is easily recognized and for which the remedy, such as provision of specialized services or barrier removal, is relatively easy to understand.

A smaller number of settled cases have focused on practices or policies of service delivery that unintentionally discriminate by reducing economic opportunities for people with disabilities. One interesting example involved an individual who claimed discrimination with regard to identification procedures for check cashing.[52] In this case, a private check-cashing company had a policy requiring customers to use state driver's licenses as proof of identification. The company did not accept any other

TABLE 5.    Title II–Based Settlements in ADA Cases Initiated by Department of Justice by Type of Charge Brought

| Nature of Discrimination Charge | Number | Percent |
|---|---|---|
| Inaccessibility, architectural barriers prohibiting access to public facilities | 35 | 52 |
| Failure to provide interpreters, auxiliary services for hearing impaired, captioning services | 10 | 15 |
| Failure to accommodate disability-related needs in provision of services | 9 | 13 |
| Failure to accommodate or service people with HIV or AIDS | 8 | 12 |
| Failure to allow service animals access to public facilities | 5 | 7 |
| Total | 67 | 100 |

*Source:* Data on settlements provided through the Freedom of Information Act report section of the U.S. Department of Justice website located at <http://www.usdoj.gov/crt/foia>.

forms of identification.[53] Given that medical conditions prevent some persons with disabilities from obtaining driver's licenses, the check-cashing practice was found to be discriminatory.[54] In this case, the settlement agreement stipulated that the company allow alternative means of identification in order to eliminate the discriminatory impact of the driver's license–only policy. Eliminating the discriminatory effects of policies related to routine operations remains an important objective of disability rights policy and its enforcement.

## Legal Precedents Emerging in ADA Cases

Several key court cases concerning the meaning and application of the Americans with Disabilities Act have emerged since the act was enacted in 1990. The holdings in these cases have created precedents that clarify the statutory meaning and application of ADA mandates in both the public and private sectors. The underlying issues focus mainly upon eligibility for ADA protections, the provision of reasonable accommodations, and the relationship of the ADA to disability benefit programs. The legal arguments invoked, as well as the public reaction to these decisions, highlight contemporary disputes about ADA enforcement.

### The ADA and HIV/AIDS

Controversy over who is and who is not covered by disability rights protections has raged since the first legislative protections for people with disabilities were enacted. Section 504 of the Rehabilitation Act of 1973—the pre-ADA touchstone of disability rights and immediate antecedent to the ADA—provides no definition of disability at all.[55] When the Rehabilitation Act was amended in 1974, the new version provided a definition that was ultimately included in the administrative regulations issued by the Department of Health, Education, and Welfare (HEW).[56] According to this definition, a covered person with disability is anyone who experiences a mental or physical handicap that limits one or more of life's major functions, has a record of such a handicap, or is perceived as having such a handicap.[57] Major life functions were defined as "caring for one's self, performing manual tasks, walking, seeing, hearing, speaking, breathing, learning, and working."[58]

Throughout the rule-making process, staff in HEW's Office of Civil Rights debated the question of whether various groups, including alcoholics and drug addicts, homosexuals, and elderly persons, were entitled to protections under Section 504.[59] It was decided not to include homosexuals or elderly individuals simply on the basis of sexual preference or age. Drug abuse and alcoholism were stickier issues since most health care professions characterized these conditions as mental and/or physical disorders.[60] Concerns expressed during the administrative rule-making process showed that public and private commentators objected to the extension of legal protections to alcoholics and illegal drug users. During rule making, HEW requested an interpretation from the attorney general's office on the issue of whether individuals with alcohol or drug abuse problems would be entitled to protection.[61] The attorney general replied affirmatively, causing HEW to note in an appendix to the final regulations that the "secretary therefore believes that he is without authority to exclude these conditions from the definitions."[62]

Given the nature of these disputes, it is not surprising that one of the first prominent ADA cases to move through the federal courts focused on AIDS. In 1994, Sidney Abbott visited her dentist and found that she had a cavity that needed filling. Upon disclosing that she had tested positive for HIV, the dentist refused to fill the cavity in the office. Instead, he recommended performing the necessary dental work at a nearby hospital where safety procedures would be enhanced, with the requirement that Abbott pay for the hospital costs. Abbott sued the dentist in federal court, contending that his requirement violated her rights under the ADA.[63]

The case moved through the federal court system and was eventually heard by the U.S. Supreme Court.[64] The high court ruled in a five-to-four decision that HIV was an impairment that limited an individual's ability to engage in a major life function, the eligibility definition provided in the ADA.[65] This ruling was based upon the Court's reasoning that even though HIV itself, absent outbreak of AIDS, does not interfere with *all* major functions, it does interfere with the ability to procreate—a major life function—thereby activating ADA protections.[66]

The Court went further to consider whether the dentist had acted improperly in his determination that filling the cavity in an office procedure represented an undue risk to his health and safety.[67] Lower-court decisions had looked to professional guidelines such as those of the Center for Disease Control and the American Dental Association—guidelines that indicate that it is safe to treat persons with HIV if appropriate infection controls are utilized—in order to assess the dentist's judgment that office treatment was dangerous to his health.[68] The Supreme Court disagreed with the lower-court decisions, contending that statistical likelihood, not professional guidelines, should be used to assess the appropriateness of professional treatment decisions.[69] The Court remanded the case to the appellate court to determine whether its decision on the risk to the dentist would have changed if it considered more than professional guidelines.[70] Here, we see an effort to balance the rights of the patient with the safety needs of the physician and the search for the appropriate information on which this decision should be made.

The ruling in this case also shows how answers to one question about statutory meaning can raise new, different questions that require the courts to continue their interpretive role. Advocates on behalf of people experiencing infertility saw *Abbott* as granting the people they represent—individuals who may need to undergo treatments that are exhaustive and debilitating—greater protections under the law.[71] While infertility was not the issue in *Abbott*, designating reproduction as a major life function that triggered ADA protections opened the door to expanded understanding of the reach of law.

### ADA Protections for Prisoners

Another area of dispute concerning enforcement of the Americans with Disabilities Act has been whether individuals incarcerated in prison are entitled to protections under the act. In a 1997 California case, federal judges heard a class action suit by disabled prisoners charging the prison with inadequate emergency escape procedures, an inaccessible vocational education process, and work opportunities that prevented them from earning sentence reduction credits.[72] In a case the following year, the Supreme Court was asked to consider whether an individual convicted and about to be confined by the state has the same right to choice of incarceration regardless of physical disability.[73] Because of hypertension, the plaintiff was ruled ineligible for a boot camp program that would have resulted in a significantly shortened period of incarceration.[74] These cases reveal a view among the federal courts that the limitations on prisoners' rights and opportunities within the penal system do not establish a legal basis for excluding incarcerated individuals from ADA protections.[75]

## The ADA and Disability Benefits

Some very recent cases arising under the ADA concern how the act relates to statutes governing health insurance and disability benefits. One of these cases, *Cleveland v. Policy Management Systems,* focused on the relationship between the ADA and Social Security disability benefits.[76] The question in this case was whether receipt of disability benefits under Social Security creates a presumption that the employee is not able to work and is therefore not covered by the ADA. The case followed from a lawsuit brought by a woman who received disability benefits following a stroke and was subsequently dismissed by her employer.[77] She sued the employer arguing that her termination represented discrimination under the ADA.[78] At the time of her suit, federal courts had reached mixed rulings in similar cases, with some holding that receipt of disability benefits represents a determination that a recipient is not a "qualified individual with a disability" entitled to coverage under the ADA.[79]

The Supreme Court held in *Cleveland* that despite what could be seen as a conflict in the plaintiff's simultaneously receiving SSDI benefits and seeking protection under the ADA, the two claims are not inherently in conflict. Instead, the Court held that it would be possible in some circumstances for an SSDI claim and an ADA claim to "comfortably exist side by side."[80] Nevertheless, in some cases the two claims may be in conflict, meaning that the condition triggering receipt of SSDI benefits may prevent an individual from being able to perform the job in question, even with reasonable accommodation. In such a case the ADA would afford no protection. For the Court, then, the question of an inherent conflict in receiving disability benefits, SSDI, and pursuit of ADA protections is a matter for investigation and potential legal action by either side. Receipt of SSDI, however, does not prevent the beneficiary from pursuing an ADA claim.

## The ADA and Damages under Title II

Critics of the ADA reserved some of their strongest words and actions for the clauses of the law that provided for award of damages. Critics worried that awards for damages would break the banks of private firms and deplete the treasuries of state and local governments. The issue of damages was directly addressed in a case heard before the Ninth Circuit Court of Appeals concerning the requirement that local governments make programs and services accessible.[81] In *Ferguson v. City of Phoenix,* the plaintiff had difficulty communicating with the City of Phoenix's 911 emergency telephone system. The particular 911 system used at the time did not recognize the signal from Ferguson's TDD, causing the report of a theft in progress to get a low priority for police response.[82] The plaintiff charged that the city's ineffective 911 system resulted in the theft of his truck, entitling him to compensatory damages from the city.[83] The Ninth Circuit determined that there was no evidence to suggest that the city acted with deliberate indifference or lack of appropriate training, and therefore, the city was not required to pay damages.[84] The decision, hailed as a "victory for municipalities,"[85] upheld the decision of the lower court and signaled that damages are not available under Title II of the ADA without proof of discriminatory intent.[86]

## Correctable Disabilities and the ADA

Another question addressed during the Supreme Court's 1998–99 term concerned whether the ADA provides protections to individuals who have "correctable" disabilities. These cases concerned (1) pilots who were denied employment by an airline because of nearsightedness even though their vision was corrected with contact lenses,[87] (2) a truck mechanic who lost his job because of high blood pressure that was controllable through medication,[88] and (3) a one-eyed truck driver terminated by his employer.[89] In all three cases the Court's holdings limited the reach of the ADA and narrowed the class of individuals eligible for protection under this civil rights legislation. In effect, the Court largely eliminated protections for individuals whose disabilities are correctable through medical or corrective devices.

The Court's reasoning in these cases is best illustrated in the majority opinion in *Sutton v. United Airlines,* written by Justice Sandra Day O'Connor.[90] Justice O'Connor noted three provisions of the ADA that supported the Court's conclusion that individuals with remedial conditions are not disabled under the meaning of the law, and therefore are not entitled to

ADA protections. First, she noted that the law's definition of disability—a condition that "substantially limits one or more of the major life activities"[91]—is expressed in the "present indicative verb form."[92] Thus, she reasoned that the law was intended to protect persons with a present substantial limitation and not those with a potential or hypothetical limitation; thus, a limitation that is corrected is no longer "presently" a disability.[93] Second, the law requires that people be assessed on their individual circumstances and not as members of a group that is affected in a particular way. Evaluating an individual's condition in its uncorrected form as opposed to its actual status, in the Court's view, would create a system where the individual would often be treated as a member of a group having similar impairments—rather than as a person whose situation should be assessed on an individualized basis.[94] And, third, in the preamble findings to the ADA, Congress noted that some forty-three million Americans have one or more disabilities.[95] While the source of this assertion was not documented, Justice O'Connor noted that the number of individuals who wear glasses or who have some other correctable problem would be closer to 160 million.[96] For O'Connor, this difference in numbers indicated that Congress did not intend for the ADA to provide coverage to individuals whose impairments are easily correctable through medication or devices.[97]

The rulings in *Sutton*, *Murphy*, and *Albertson's*—and their underlying legal rationale—is quite disturbing to the drafters of the ADA and to those who seek expansive, rather than limited, coverage and protection for people with disabilities. Professor Chai Feldblum of Georgetown Law School— a drafter of the original ADA language—responded to the Court's rulings by stating that these decisions "create the absurd result of a person being disabled enough to be fired from a job, but not disabled enough to challenge the firing."[98] Despite the fact that in each case the disabling condition did represent a limitation of a major life function (sight, blood circulation), and that the conditions, even when corrected, led to job termination, the Court did not see ADA protections as warranted.

### The ADA and Learning Disabilities

Discussion about learning disabilities has become increasingly contentious as schools become increasingly involved in assessing the learning capacities and disabilities of school-aged children. This issue has entered the ADA arena through several cases involving athletes with learning disabilities who were denied eligibility to compete in NCAA sports.[99] In one case, a University of Washington football player was denied eligibility to play football by

NCAA rules concerning core academic requirements.[100] The NCAA rules state that remedial or special education courses taught below the school's regular instructional level (regardless of course level) do not satisfy the core education requirements. In a victory for the athlete, a Washington district court issued a preliminary injunction in 1996, reinstating the player.[101] Other cases remain active, and the federal courts have yet to address the key questions of whether the NCAA is covered by the public accommodations requirements of Title III and whether the education core requirements, by failing to accommodate educational programs for people with learning disabilities, constitute discrimination against athletes who experience learning disabilities.

## ADA Implementation and Backlash

Public reactions to these wide-ranging court decisions provide a final perspective on ADA implementation. These mostly negative reactions demonstrate a range of perspectives on the breadth of the law, concerns (and sometimes misconceptions) about ambiguity and potential liabilities associated with the ADA, and worries that the accommodation requirement will prove too burdensome. Sidney Abbott's challenge to her dentist's policy for treating her as the result of her HIV status—and the Supreme Court's affirmation of her discrimination claim—generated substantial public reaction.[102] Many people and organizations, most notably advocates for people with disabilities, applauded the decision by the nation's highest court, a decision they credited with establishing the breadth of ADA coverage. One writer saw *Abbott* as a victory and wake-up call for all parties covered by the ADA:

> Employers, landlords and public officials in the country take note: The Americans with Disabilities Act is a significant civil rights statute. Our highest court has sent a signal to those who admit to their discriminatory behavior while arguing that their offensive acts are rational. Treating people differently because of their disabilities leaves one on shaky ground, and the courts will be applying the Americans with Disabilities Act expansively to eliminate offensive acts and penalize the offenders.[103]

The medical establishment, representing those most directly affected by the *Abbott* decision, also voiced support for the Court's opinion. Writing in the *New England Journal of Medicine,* George J. Annas averred that the "application of the law to HIV infection, in the context of continuing stigmatization and discrimination in the health care setting, has now been properly affirmed by the Supreme Court. This decision comports with the ethical principles of the medical and dental professions and with the use of universal precautions."[104] Similarly, a legal analysis of the Supreme Court decision held that "baseless fears or beliefs, even those of healthcare professionals, will not be sufficient to justify discriminatory treatment. Nor will good faith protect those who rely on poor science, from liability under the ADA."[105]

Other reactions to *Abbott* have been more critical. Some commentators view the decision, and the ADA as a whole, as yet another instance of expansive, ill-advised federal regulatory mandates on the private sector.[106] These criticisms parallel those made about other federal regulatory programs such as environmental protection, affirmative action, and occupational safety programs. Typical of this critical perspective is an article in the *Economist* that cited *Abbott* and other Supreme Court decisions in the 1997–98 term as "greatly extending the scope of antidiscrimination laws in a way that will not only increase the burdens on employers, but could well turn the American workplace into the most highly regulated in the world."[107] Similar concerns about antidiscrimination measures harming the competitiveness of American business can be traced as far back as rulemaking efforts for Section 504 of the Rehabilitation Act and the legislative debates on the ADA in 1989 and 1990.[108]

A second line of criticism focuses on skepticism about the breadth of ADA protections and a concern that minor impairments with little adverse impact will generate an overload of mandated accommodations. In this vein, an article appeared shortly after *Bragdon* in *U.S. News and World Report* about a firefighter named Jeffrey Ola who challenged the decision his county's fire department not to hire him as a paramedic on the basis of his hearing impairment.[109] According to the article, Ola never considered himself disabled and was able, despite his hearing loss, to study for and successfully beat out sixty-five other applicants for the position. His only obstacle was a strict departmental policy that normal hearing was required for the paramedic's job. The article concluded that "it turns out that the clearest beneficiaries [of the ADA] have not been the severely disabled but a much larger group of people who, like Ola, have relatively minor impairments. For better or for worse, the ADA has greatly expanded the definition of disability to include chronic and hidden problems."[110] This is an interesting example, for while the author uses a critical tone in the case of Jeffrey Ola, whose "minor impairment" nonetheless triggered ADA protections, advocates see the case as an important victory. For if Ola was successful in beating out others and was otherwise capable or performing the paramedics job, then his only obstacle to employment was a hearing policy that was not appropriately related to job performance. The case thus pointed out how existing policies can work to discriminate.

*Abbott*'s critics often claim that the case "opened the door" to expanded protections to people with disabilities and to new, likely excessive burdens on regulated parties, especially private-sector entities. The chief counsel for the U.S. Chamber of Commerce, for example, argued that the case "just throws the door wide open."[111] The director of the Cato Institute's Center for Constitutional Studies contended that "[w]e like the doors to be opened by consent, not by the force of law."[112] The greatest fear of opening the door is that enforcement will entail expansive complaints and massive accommodation costs.

The compliance cost issue is relevant not only to the ADA but to companion disability rights laws such as the Individuals with Disabilities Education Act (IDEA), which guarantees a "free and appropriate public education" to students with disabilities.[113] A Supreme Court decision in March 1999 held that the IDEA required the Cedar Rapids Community School District to provide a trained aid to monitor the needs of a quadriplegic boy who was dependent on a respirator.[114] Students who need special care during the school day, therefore, are entitled to that care at public expense. The cost issue was evident in this case in the dissenting opinion filed by Justice Clarence Thomas and joined by Anthony M. Kennedy, which argued that the interpretation of the majority opinion in the case "blindsides unwary states with fiscal obligations that they could not have anticipated."[115]

A third dimension of public reaction to *Abbott* and the ADA relates to the prejudicial views and misunderstandings that still surround HIV and AIDS. While a *Washington Post* staff writer saw *Abbott* as positive evidence of progress in dealing with the deadly disease, intoning that "the ruling signified just how far the country has come in the past decade in coping with the worst epidemic of modern times,"[116] other reporters and writers saw danger in the decision. An article in *Human Events,* for example, argued that "in the historic battle between the deadly AIDS virus and American doctors, the Supreme Court of the United States has taken the side of the virus. . . . All bloods, according to the court, are equal—regardless of what deadly diseases they may or may not carry."[117] Social and political controversy surrounds the AIDS crisis, even if prejudice has abated somewhat over the past decade. The reaction to *Abbott,* coupled with the EEOC and DOJ litigation, suggests that AIDS-related disputes will continue as a significant issue in ADA enforcement.

## Assessment and Challenges

The empirical evidence presented in this article paints a limited picture of ADA enforcement. This evidence suggests that a wide variety of people with disabilities who experience a diverse array of disabling conditions have utilized the protections of ADA to fight discrimination. Individuals whose charges of discrimination have been credited have received damages or have had their complaint otherwise addressed. Yet despite this evidence, our picture of ADA enforcement and accomplishments remains substantially incomplete. We have as yet no measure or understanding of such key issues as how many individuals with disabilities experience discrimination, how many know of ADA protections, and how many are unwilling or incapable of using the ADA to redress the discrimination they encounter. Until we can better answer these questions—vast questions given the number of people experiencing mental or physical disability and the number of private and public-sector entities regulated by the ADA  we will not be able to discern, with any confidence, how effective the ADA is in eliminating discrimination based on disability.

The evidence examined in this essay suggests that complaints and enforcement in the area of employment will remain active for some time to come. Controversies about the extent of coverage for different disabilities will undoubtedly be manifest, as will disagreements about the extent and nature of reasonable accommodations in employment that are mandated by the ADA. Some question of whether the national government's failure to provide funding to assist in the provision of employment accommodations or to target relief to subgroups with the most substantial difficulties impairs the overall effectiveness of the law.[118] The following assessment of the effectiveness of ADA protections in protecting the employment opportunities of people with disabilities sums up well the current situation:

> It may be the case that both sides have overestimated the potential impact of the ADA. Employers have overestimated the costs and difficulties of complying with the law, and people with disabilities have overestimated the ability of a civil rights act to significantly alter employment rates and circumstances.[119]

In the context of requirements for reasonable accommodation to the services and facilities offered by state and local governments, as well as by private enterprises, the challenge is getting the word out that people with disabilities have the rights to accommodations that provide them with the capacity to consume and enjoy services and programs. There are thousands upon thousands of governments and businesses regulated by Titles II and III of the ADA, and hundreds of complaints have already been filed under these titles. It will likely be some time, however, before these regulated entities, particularly the full array of businesses, will achieve compliance.

Finally, evidence of political backlash against the ADA is not unexpected. Controversy has surrounded all civil rights legislation. Discrimination based upon disability is grounded in many causal factors, including misperceptions about the origins, impacts, and accommodation needs of different forms of disability, as well as fear of the unknown, stereotypes about the capabilities of people with disabilities, and ideological perspectives that see a limited role for government in addressing discrimination and mandating accommodations to ensure civil rights. Overcoming these factors takes time, willingness to file complaints and charges when discrimination is encountered, and efforts to enhance public understanding of disability and the importance of civil rights enforcement for the large segment of the American population that experiences denial of access or other forms of discrimination on this basis. These remain significant but not insurmountable challenges, as we seek to realize full rights and equal opportunities for disabled Americans.

NOTES

1. Pub. L. No. 101–336, 104 Stat. 337 (1990) (codified as amended at 42 U.S.C. §§ 12101–12213 (1994)).

2. *See, e.g.,* Stephen L. Percy, Disability, Civil Rights and Public Policy: The Politics of Implementation (1989); Richard K. Scotch, From Goodwill to Civil Rights: Transforming Federal Disability Policy (1984); Robert Katzmann, Institutional Disability: The Saga of Transportation Policy for the Disabled (1986); and Stephen L. Percy, Disability Rights Mandates: Federal and State Compliance with Employment Protections and Architectural Barrier Removal (1989).

3. 42 U.S.C. § 12101(b)(1) (1994).

4. *See, e.g.,* National Council on the Handicapped, On the Threshold of Independence (1998).

5. *See* 42 U.S.C. § 12111(8) (1994) (defining "qualified individual with a disability").

6. *See id.*

7. *Id.* at § 12111(9).

8. *Id.* at §§ 12181–12189.

9. *See id.* at § 12182(a).

10. *Id.* at § 12182(b)(2)(A)(iii).

11. *See* Stephen L. Percy, *Challenges and Dilemmas in Implementing the ADA: Lessons and Achievements in the First Decade,* POL. STUD. J. (forthcoming 2000) (discussing creative approaches to at once meeting and balancing individuals' and regulated parties' needs).

12. *See* Robert J. Burgdorf Jr., *The Americans with Disabilities Act: Analysis and Interpretation of a Second Generation Civil Rights Statute,* 26 HARV. C.R.-C.L. L. REV. 441–45 (1991).

13. 42 U.S.C. § 12102 (1994); *see also* Burgdorf, *supra* note 12, at 447–49.

14. *See* 42 U.S.C. § 12134 (1994).

15. *See supra* notes 44–56 and accompanying text.

16. 29 C.F.R. § 1630 (1998).

17. U.S. Equal Employment Opportunity Comm'n, *Americans with Disabilities Act of 1990 (ADA) Charges, FY 1992 FY 1998* (1998) (last modified Jan. 12, 2000), <http://www.eeoc.gov/stats/ada-charges.html >. Complaint receipts represent the total number of charge receipts filed. Individuals may list more than one charge within a complaint. *Id.*

18. *Id.*

19. *Id.* This figure does not count benefits received through litigation.

20. Nancy Mudrick, *Employment Discrimination Laws for Disability: Utilization and Outcome,* 549 ANNALS AM. ACAD. POL. & SOC. SCI. 69 (1997).

21. Kathryn Moss et al., *Assessing Employment Discrimination Charges Filed by Individuals with Psychiatric Disabilities Under the Americans with Disabilities Act,* 9 J. DISABILITY POL'Y STUD. 81–105 (1998).

22. *See id.*

23. *See* Robert L. Burgdorf Jr. & Marcia Pearce Burgdorf, *The Wicked Witch Is Almost Dead: Buck v. Bell and the Sterilization of Handicapped Persons,* 50 TEMP. L. REV. 995–1033 (1977).

24. *See* Moss et al., *supra* note 21, at 81–105.

25. U.S. Equal Employment Opportunity Comm'n, *Docket of Americans with Disabilities Act (ADA) Litigation* (1998) (visited Feb. 15, 2000) <http://www.eeoc.gov/docs/ada98.txt>.

26. *Id.*

27. *Id.*

28. *EEOC v. American Airlines,* Civ. A. No. 98–463-A (E.D. Va.).

29. *EEOC v. Add-Staff, Inc.,* Civ. A. No. 96–70840 (E.D Mich.).

30. *EEOC v. Bethlehem Steel Corp.,* Civ. A. No. B96–1469 (D. Md.).

31. *EEOC v. Chrysler Corp.,* 917 F. Supp. 1164 (E.D. Mich. 1997).

32. *EEOC v. Federal Express Corp.,* Civ. A. No. PJM 95–3850 (D. Md.).

33. *See* 42 U.S.C. § 12112(b)(5) (1994).

34. *EEOC v. Allied Signal Aerospace,* Civ. A. No 92–2776 (WGB) (D. N.J.).

35. *EEOC v. Ameripol Synpol Corp.,* Civ. A. No. 95-CV-349 (E.D. Tex.).

36. *EEOC v. AMS Properties, Inc.,* Civ. A. No. 95-WY-1585 (D. Colo.).

37. *EEOC v. Bloomingdale's, Inc.*, Civ. A. No. 4–95–507 (D. Minn.).

38. *EEOC v. Complete Auto Transit, Inc.*, Civ. A. No. 95–73427 (E.D. Mich.).

39. *EEOC v. Greyhound Lines*, Civ. A. No. 95-C-652 (E.D. Wis.).

40. *EEOC v. Pomeroy Investments, Inc., d/b/a Marie Callender's*, Civ. A. No. 97–2556 (C.D. Cal.).

41. 42 U.S.C. § 12134 (1994).

42. *Id.* at § 12186(b).

43. Statistical information about and synopses of the settlement agreements are available at the EEOC website (visited Feb. 16, 2000), <http://www.eeoc.gov /docs/ada98.txt>. Many of the settlement and consent agreements themselves are available online at the DOJ's website (visited Feb. 18, 2000), <http://www.usdoj.gov /crt/ada/ settlemt.htm>.

44. *See id.*

45. *See, e.g.*, Settlement Letter from Days Inn of Port Allen, Louisiana, to DOJ Civil Rights Division (Sep. 12, 1996) (visited Feb. 16, 2000), <http://www.usdoj.gov/crt/foia/dila1.txt>. This and other settlement agreements are available on the DOJ website (visited Feb. 16, 2000), <http://www.usdoj./cr t/ada.settlemt.htm.> [hereinafter DOJ Settlements].

46. Settlement Agreement between the United States and Comfort Inn (Sep. 12, 1996), DOJ Settlements, *supra* note 45.

47. Settlement Agreement between the United States and Dollar Rent a Car (Jan. 4, 1995), DOJ Settlements, *supra* note 45.

48. Settlement Agreement between the United States and Budget Rent A Car Systems (July 3, 1997), DOJ Settlements, *supra* note 45.

49. Settlement Agreement between the United States and Friendly Ice Cream Corp. (Jan. 5, 1997), DOJ Settlements, *supra* note 45.

50. Settlement Agreement between the United States and Shoney's Restaurants (June 11, 1997), DOJ Settlements, *supra* note 45.

51. Settlement Agreement between the United States and Walt Disney World (Jan. 17, 1997), DOJ Settlements, *supra* note 45.

52. *See* Settlement Agreement between United States and Marquis Video, DOJ Settlements, *supra* note 45.

53. *See id.*

54. *See id.*

55. *See* Pub. L. No. 93–112, § 504, 87 Stat. 355, 3394 (1973) (codified as amended at 29 U.S.C. § 705 (defining "handicapped" person as someone with "a physical or mental disability which for such individual constitutes or results in a substantial handicap to employment").

56. *See* Pub. L. No. 93–516, 88 Stat. 1617, 1619 (1974) (codified as amended at 29 U.S.C. § 794 (1994)); 45 C.F.R. § 84.1. It is interesting to note that it took HEW four years (from 1973 to 1977) to promulgate the administrative regulations for Section 504 of the Rehabilitation Act of 1973. The brief generic language of the statute provided little guidance for action, and the mandates, as developed by HEW, caused substantial negative reaction. *See generally* RICHARD K. SCOTCH, FROM GOODWILL TO CIVIL RIGHTS: TRANSFORMING FEDERAL DISABILITY POLICY (1984) (presenting an excellent overview of the rule-making process).

57. 42 C.F.R. § 84.3.

58.  *Id.*

59.  42 Fed. Reg. § 22686.

60.  *See id.*

61.  *See id.*

62.  *See id.*

63.  Abbott v. Bragdon, 912 F. Supp. 580 (D. Me. 1995), *aff'd,* 107 F.3d 934 (1st Cir. 1997), *vacated in part and remanded in part,* Bragdon v. Abbott, 524 U.S. 624 (1998). Following the Supreme Court's 1998 holding, the case was remanded to the First Circuit on the direct threat issue, and the court affirmed the grant of summary judgment. 163 F.3d 87 (1st Cir. 1998). The Supreme Court declined Dr. Bragdon's subsequent petition for certiorari. Bragdon v. Abbott, 119 S.Ct. 185 (1999).

64.  524 U.S. 624 (1998). For additional discussion about the *Bragdon* litigation, see George J. Annas, *Protecting Patients from Discrimination—the Americans with Disabilities Act and HIV Infection,* New Eng. J. Med., 1255–59 (Oct. 1998).

65.  524 U.S. at 641.

66.  *Id.*

67.  *Id.* at 648–55.

68.  *Id.* at 650–51.

69.  *Id.* at 646–50.

70.  *Id.* at 649–54.

71.  *See* Esther B. Fein, *AIDS Virus Case Opens Door for Infertile,* N.Y. Times, July 5, 1998, at 6.

72.  Armstrong v. Wilson, 124 F.3d 1019 (9th Cir., 1997).

73.  Pennsylvania Dep't of Corrections v. Yeskey, 524 U.S. 206, 209 (1998).

74.  *Id.*

75.  *Id.* at 1956.

76.  Cleveland v. Policy Management Sys., 526 U.S. 795 (1999).

77.  *Id.* at 972–73.

78.  *Id.*

79.  *Id.* at 973.

80.  *Id.* at 975.

81.  Ferguson v. City of Phoenix, 157 F.3d 668 (9th Cir. 1998).

82.  *Id.* at 671.

83.  *Id.*

84.  *Id.*

85.  *See Americans with Disabilities Act: Ferguson v. City of Phoenix,* Nation's Cities Wkly., Oct. 19, 1998, at 12.

86.  157 F.3d at 674.

87.  Sutton v. United Airlines, Inc., 527 U.S. 471, 119 S. Ct. 2139 (1999)

88.  Murphy v. United Parcel Serv., Inc., 527 U.S. 516, 119 S. Ct. 2133 (1999).

89.  Albertson's, Inc. v. Kirkingburg, 527 U.S. 555. 119 S. Ct. 2162 (1999).

90.  Sutton, 527 U.S. at 475.

91.  *Id.* at 478 (citing 42 U.S.C. § 12102(2)(A) (1994)).

92.  *Id.*

93.  *Id.*

94.  *Id.* at 483–84.

95.  42 U.S.C. § 12101(a)(1) (1994).

96. Sutton, 527 U.S. at 487.

97. *Id.*

98. Linda Greenhouse, *High Court Limits Who Is Protected by Disability Law,* N.Y. TIMES, June 23, 1999, at 1.

99. *See* Butler v. NCAA, 1996 WL 1058233 (W.D. Wash.); Ganden v. NCAA, 1996 WL 68000 (N.D. Ill.); Bowers v. NCAA, 9 F. Supp. 2d 460 (1998).

100. *Butler,* 1996 WL 1058233.

101. *Id.* at 6.

102. *See, e.g., Annas, supra* note 64.

103. James J. Weisman, *Teeth in the ADA: The Supreme Court in a Narrow Split Ruled HIV a Disability in the Case of the Dental Checkup,* WE MAG., Sept.–Oct. 1998, at 114.

104. George J. Annas, *Protecting Patients from Discrimination—the Americans with Disabilities Act and HIV Infection,* 339 NEW ENG. J. MED., 17 , 1259.

105. Zita Lazzarini, *The Americans with Disabilities Act After Bragdon v. Abbott: HIV Infection, Other Disabilities, and Access to Care,* 25 HUMAN RIGHTS: J. SECT. INDIV. RIGHTS & RESPONSIBILITIES AM. BAR ASSOC. 4, 15 (fall 1998).

106. *See, e.g., Men, Women, Work, and Law: An Even More Dangerous Mixture Than Before, Thanks to the Supreme Court,* 347 ECONOMIST, July 4, 1998.

107. *See id.* at 21.

108. *See* STEPHEN L PERCY, DISABILITY, CIVIL RIGHTS, AND PUBLIC POLICY: THE POLITICS OF IMPLEMENTATION (1989).

109. *See* Joseph P. Shapiro, *The Americans with Minor Disabilities Act: The Surprising Beneficiaries of the Law,* 125 U.S. NEWS & WORLD REP., July 6, 1998, at 41. The article discussed the settlement reached in *United States v. Metropolitan Gov't of Nashville & Davidson County,* Civ. A. No. 97–264 (M.D. Tenn.), DOJ Settlements, *supra* note 45.

110. *See* Shapiro, *supra* note 109, at 41.

111. Peter T. Kilborn, *Wide Impact Is Seen for Ruling on H.I.V.,* N.Y. TIMES, July 27, 1998, at 1.

112. *Id.*

113. Individuals with Disabilities Education Act, 20 U.S.C. § 1415(b)(1) (1994).

114. Cedar Rapids Community Sch. Dist. v. Garrett F., 526 U.S. 66, 119 S.Ct. 992 (1999).

115. *Id.* at 85.

116. Justin Gillis, *Ruling Shows How Far Nation Has Come on Epidemic,* WASH. POST, June 36, 1998, at A16.

117. *Court Gives Virus Equal Rights,* 54 HUMAN EVENTS, July 10, 1998, at 1.

118. *See, e.g.,* Marjorie L. Baldwin, *Can the ADA Achieve Its Employment Goals?* 549 ANNALS ACAD. POL. & SOC. SCI., Jan. 1997, at 37–52.

119. Mudrick, *supra* note 20, at 70.

*Ruth Colker*

# The Death of Section 504

The passage of the Americans with Disabilities Act[1] (ADA) was a significant and positive development for the law of disability discrimination. The ADA strengthened the rights that already existed under Section 504 of the Rehabilitation Act of 1973[2] by extending those rights to the private sector.[3] Because Section 504 and the Individuals with Disabilities Education Act[4] already provided protection for students with disabilities,[5] the ADA's primary impact has been on the law of employment and accessibility.[6]

In theory, the ADA should have had little impact on institutions already covered by Section 504 other than to increase publicity about the existence of the rights of individuals with disabilities. Section 504 was the model for drafting the ADA;[7] the similarities are particularly striking with regard to coverage of the public sector.[8] The Section 504 regulations often became the text of the ADA itself. Codifying these preexisting rights certainly could have had the effect of increasing voluntary compliance with these rights. The nature of the rights, themselves, however, should have been largely unchanged. In fact, Congress expressly dictated that the preexisting rights under Section 504 should be the "floor" in determining the meaning of the ADA.[9]

In this essay, I shall argue that the passage of the ADA had an unexpected consequence–it resulted in the narrowing of the rights that had been understood to exist under Section 504.[10] Section 504 covered two broad areas of the law—the law of employment for individuals employed by entities receiving federal financial assistance and the law of education for students attending primary, secondary, or higher education. The effect on the law of employment, which I discuss in the next section, has been immediate and dramatic. The effect on the law of education, which I will discuss subsequently, cannot yet be fully documented; however, recent decisions suggest that those rights may also soon be limited. Thus, I will argue that passage of the ADA has resulted in the demise, if not the death, of Section 504.

The Supreme Court's decision in *Trustees of the University of Alabama v. Garrett*[11] makes the phenomenon I examine here even more significant. It is ironic indeed that passage of the ADA may well have led to the substantial dilution of the preexisting rights under Section 504, while Title I of the ADA has been found unconstitutional insofar as it permits private suits for damages against state employers.

## The Law of Employment

In two previous articles, I reported appellate outcome statistics for ADA employment discrimination cases.[12] Table 1 reports my ADA data from January 1994 through July 30, 1999.[13]

These data reflect a strong prodefendant trend for appellate outcomes in employment cases that are available on Westlaw. Since the appellate courts began to hear employment discrimination cases under the ADA, defendants have had successful outcomes in 86.5 percent of the cases.[14] This figure does not mean that defendants, in fact, are winning 86.5 percent of all ADA employment discrimination cases. It merely means that defendants are prevailing in 86.5 percent of ADA appellate, employment discrimination cases that are available on Westlaw for the time period under investigation. At a minimum, it suggests that the plaintiff bar is overpredicting their chance of success on appeal, because they are expending financial resources to appeal cases that have a limited chance of success. The appellate courts, therefore, seem to evaluate their cases more negatively than plaintiffs expect.

Many explanations can be offered for the prodefendant trend in the ADA data, and I have considered such explanations in previous articles. One way to understand this data is to say that plaintiffs' lawyers have acted irrationally—that they have made decisions to appeal cases out of a false sense of potential success. Because most lawyers take ADA cases on a contingency fee basis, it makes little sense for a lawyer to pursue meritless litigation on appeal. One would expect that economic forces would cause plaintiffs' lawyers to make more conservative judgments on appeal, so that the plaintiff success rate would come closer to the 50 percent figure that should prevail in a rational system of litigation.

It is unlikely that plaintiffs' lawyers have deliberately miscalculated their chance of success. Thus, one might ask what factors may be causing them to overpredict their chance of success on appeal. One factor may be a relatively successful experience under another, similar statute. Hence, in a previous article, I looked at Section 504 data.[15] Plaintiff's lawyers' success rate on appeal in employment discrimination cases[16] brought under Section 504[17] was approximately 35 percent on the eve of the effective date of ADA

**TABLE 1.    ADA Employment Cases**

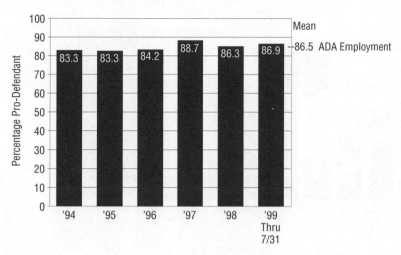

| Date | Pro-Defendant Outcome/ All Cases | Percentage of Pro-Defendant Outcome |
|------|----------|----------|
| 1994 | 5 of 6 | 83.3 |
| 1995 | 35 of 42 | 83.3 |
| 1996 | 96 of 114 | 84.2 |
| 1997 | 158 of 178 | 88.7 |
| 1998 | 189 of 219 | 86.3 |
| 1999 | 140 of 161 | 86.9 |
| All Cases | 623 of 720 | 86.5 |

Title I. The 35 percent figure is certainly closer to what one would expect under a rational economic model. When plaintiffs' lawyers took those insights from Section 504 to ADA litigation, they experienced a much lower success rate. In other words, the judicial response to their ADA cases was worse than they would have expected given their Section 504 experience. Thus, higher success rates under Section 504 may have caused lawyers to overpredict their success rate in ADA litigation in the early years of the interpretation of that statute.[18]

In this essay, I would like to explore that hypothesis from a somewhat different vantage point—to ask how the passage of the ADA affected judicial outcomes under Section 504. As table 2 reflects, the ADA failure rate seeped into Section 504 litigation beginning in 1994.

Although the overall figure is 79 percent prodefendant outcome, the statistics change significantly before and after 1994, as reflected in table 3.

TABLE 2.   § 504 Employment Cases

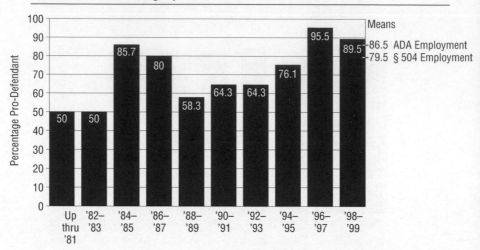

| Date | Pro-Defendant Outcome/ All Cases | Percentage of Pro-Defendant Outcome |
|---|---|---|
| Before 1982 | 2 of 4 | 50.0 |
| 1982–83 | 4 of 8 | 50.0 |
| 1984–85 | 6 of 7 | 85.7 |
| 1986–87 | 8 of 10 | 80.0 |
| 1988–89 | 7 of 12 | 58.3 |
| 1990–91 | 18 of 28 | 64.3 |
| 1992–93 | 18 of 28 | 64.3 |
| 1994–95 | 35 of 46 | 76.1 |
| 1996–97 | 42 of 44 | 95.4 |
| 1998–99 | 77 of 86 | 89.5 |
| § 504 employment cases (all) | 217 of 273 | 79.5 |
| ADA employment cases (all) | 623 of 720 | 86.5 |

After 1994, the Section 504 employment decisions have virtually the same outcome as ADA employment decisions. The defendant success rate under Section 504 rose 23 percent after the appellate courts began deciding ADA employment discrimination cases.

These results are statistically significant at the 0.001 level in a Pearson chi-square test.[19] In other words, a significant factor in predicting appellate outcome under Section 504 is whether the appeal was decided before or after 1994.

These statistics also reveal that the volume of Section 504 appellate liti-

**TABLE 3.    § 504 Employment Cases: 1994 Split**

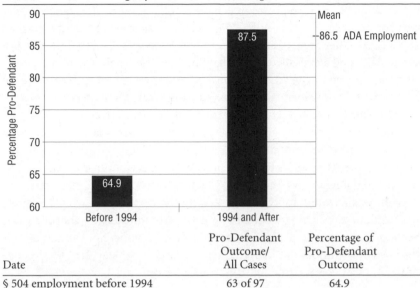

| Date | Pro-Defendant Outcome/ All Cases | Percentage of Pro-Defendant Outcome |
|---|---|---|
| § 504 employment before 1994 | 63 of 97 | 64.9 |
| § 504 employment 1994–99 | 154 of 176 | 87.5 |
| ADA employment 1994–7/31/1999 | 623 of 720 | 86.5 |

gation increased substantially when the ADA was enacted. There are more Section 504 decisions decided by the appellate courts and made available on Westlaw from 1994 to 1998 than there were from 1988 to 1994.[20] I attribute that increase, in part, to the publicity received regarding disability discrimination matters preceding and following the passage of the ADA. Although Section 504 cases increase in number beginning in 1990, the change in judicial outcome does not occur until 1994, when the courts were also first faced with ADA lawsuits.

I can imagine four ways to explain the drop-off in plaintiffs' success rate following 1994: (1) the defense bar became more organized and thoughtful in its litigation strategy, now that it had a larger volume of cases to defend under Section 504 and the ADA; (2) while the appellate courts were initially relatively sympathetic to Section 504 claims when they typically involved educational discrimination, they became less sympathetic as the volume increased and the type of claim increasingly involved employment matters; (3) some new lawyers entered the plaintiff bar to litigate ADA and Section 504 cases, and some of these lawyers litigated these cases poorly;[21] and (4) the Section 504 case law at the appellate level finally adjusted itself in light of prodefendant interpretations of the statute by the Supreme Court.[22]

Irrespective of *why* this pattern emerged, an important transition takes place. While Section 504 cases may have stood a reasonable chance of success on appeal for plaintiffs until 1994, those chances diminished significantly after 1994. Moreover, I am willing to speculate that the passage of the ADA had a causal effect on that change. The result, I would argue, is that the passage of the ADA had an important collateral consequence on Section 504. It transformed Section 504 from a relatively successful statute for plaintiffs to a relatively unsuccessful statute. This effect, I would argue, did not just occur for employment discrimination claims. Instead, it occurred for all Section 504 claims, including claims of educational discrimination that have historically predominated Section 504 claims. The passage of the ADA, one might say, was the death knell to Section 504.

This result would appear to be exactly the opposite of what Congress intended, because Congress stated quite clearly in the ADA that the prior Section 504 rules of law were supposed to be the floor, not the ceiling, for the rules of law under the ADA. In fact, however, it appears that the passage of the ADA pulled the rug out from under Section 504.

## Education Cases

### The Statistics

Although the ADA is primarily known for its impact on the law of employment, Section 504 is particularly well known for its impact on the law of education, in particular higher education. Although the IDEA is the primary regulator of the law of primary education, Section 504 is the primary regulator of the law of higher education. In the statistics presented above, I have documented the ADA's effect on the law of employment under Section 504. Now, I would like to document the effect it has had on the law of education, or the effect that it may soon have.

Education discrimination claims at the appellate level have been somewhat more successful than employment discrimination claims. Further, the ADA's effect on these cases is not as clear as with the employment cases. Nonetheless, I believe we can safely predict that passage of the ADA will have an adverse effect on Section 504 employment cases.

Tables 4 and 5 document the Section 504 education cases.

Defendant's success rate in Section 504 education cases was somewhat lower than it was under Section 504 employment cases (68 percent in education area as compared with 79 percent in employment area). However,

**TABLE 4.    § 504 Education Cases**

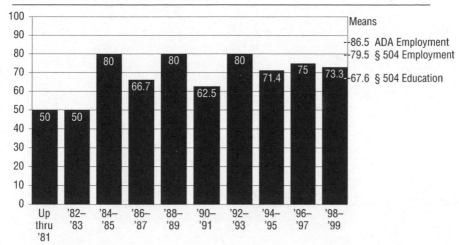

| Date | Pro-Defendant Outcome/ All Cases | Percentage of Pro-Defendant Outcome |
|---|---|---|
| Before 1982 | 4 of 8 | 50.0 |
| 1982–83 | 5 of 10 | 50.0 |
| 1984–85 | 4 of 5 | 80.0 |
| 1986–87 | 2 of 3 | 66.7 |
| 1988–89 | 4 of 5 | 80.0 |
| 1990–91 | 5 of 8 | 62.5 |
| 1992–93 | 4 of 5 | 80.0 |
| 1994–95 | 5 of 7 | 71.4 |
| 1996–97 | 6 of 8 | 75.0 |
| 1998–99 | 11 of 15 | 73.3 |
| § 504 education cases (all) | 50 of 74 | 67.6 |
| § 504 employment cases (all) | 217 of 273 | 79.5 |
| ADA employment cases (all) | 623 of 720 | 86.5 |

the figures after 1994 for defendant success rate are higher than for the period before 1994. Table 5 reflects those statistics.

Unlike the employment cases, this difference based on time is not statistically significant. Nonetheless, as I will discuss below, I believe we can expect to see a statistically significant difference in the future if the existing trend expands in the next several years.

Table 6 compares all the statistics.

This final table reflects that ADA and Section 504 employment cases are currently receiving the same judicial results. This result is not surprising,

TABLE 5.    § 504 Education Cases: 1994 Split

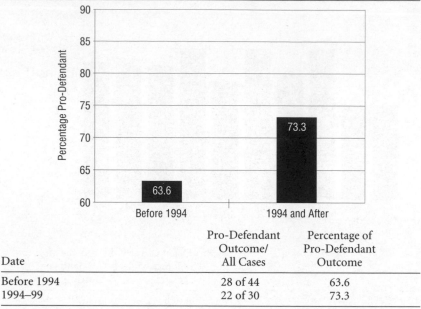

| Date | Pro-Defendant Outcome/ All Cases | Percentage of Pro-Defendant Outcome |
|---|---|---|
| Before 1994 | 28 of 44 | 63.6 |
| 1994–99 | 22 of 30 | 73.3 |

because most Section 504 cases are filed under both the ADA and Section 504. Moreover, my previous research found that whether the defendant was public or private was not a significant factor in predicting appellate outcome. Education cases have become less successful since the passage of the ADA, but those cases are still more successful than employment cases.

Although Section 504 cases involving education issues are not significantly more prodefendant since the passage of the ADA, such a trend may be on the horizon, because a significant number of those cases involve individuals with a particularly contentious disability—a learning disability. Of the seventy-eight cases in my database, thirteen involved individuals with learning disabilities.[23] Of those thirteen cases, eight were decided before the ADA became effective. Of those eight cases, three were successful. Of the remaining five cases, which were decided after the ADA became effective, one was successful. These are obviously small numbers, but an examination of the case law suggests that cases involving learning disabilities have a much more limited chance of success today than they did in 1992. In none of the thirteen cases decided before 1992 did the court question whether the plaintiff was disabled.

TABLE 6.    Comparison of ADA and § 504 Cases

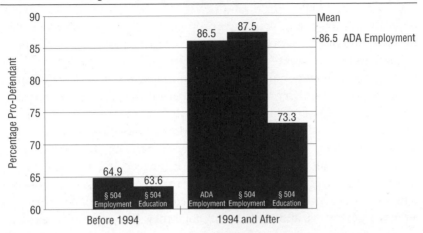

| Date | Pro-Defendant Outcome/ All Cases | Percentage of Pro-Defendant Outcome |
|---|---|---|
| Before 1994 ADA | 0 of 0 | 0 |
| Before 1994 § 504 employment | 63 of 97 | 64.9 |
| Before 1994 § 504 education | 28 of 44 | 63.6 |
| 1994–7/31/1999 ADA employment | 623 of 720 | 86.5 |
| 1994–99 § 504 employment | 154 of 176 | 87.5 |
| 1994–99 § 504 education | 22 of 30 | 73.3 |

A recent decision by the Second Circuit in *Bartlett v. New York State Board of Law Examiners*,[24] however, makes it clear that that strategy is now available and may sometimes be successful. Plaintiff Marilyn Bartlett had been diagnosed with dyslexia, a learning disability. There seems little doubt from the record that Bartlett is a very poor reader, especially for someone with both a Ph.D. in Educational Administration from New York University and a law degree from Vermont Law School. In comparison with the general population, she scored around the thirtieth percentile on one measure of reading but scored between the first and fourth percentiles when compared to college freshmen. Under the applicable ADA regulations, the court insisted that she be compared with the general population, not college freshmen or graduate students. This requirement stems from the Department of Justice's regulations implementing the ADA.[25] Although the Supreme Court in *Sutton v. United Air Lines, Inc.*[26] found that no federal agency had been given authority to define the term *disability,* every court is accepting the validity of the regulation requiring individuals with disabilities to be compared with the general population, rather than with the group with which they are competing for education or employment. In fact, there is little inherent logic in these regulations because, on the one hand, they require individuals to be compared to the general population in determining whether they are disabled in the major life activity of reading but permit them to be compared to individuals of equal training, skills, and abilities to determine if they are disabled in the major life activity of working. Education, of course, is a necessity to many jobs (such as the one sought by Bartlett—being a lawyer). The result of this reasoning is that the learning disabled student who has attained accommodations under the IDEA (which does not contain this set of requirements) may stop receiving accommodations upon admission to college and graduate school if their IDEA-sponsored education was reasonably successful.

When the ADA was enacted, commentators predicted that it would be of particular benefit to students with learning disabilities who were pursuing higher education. One commentator argued:

> Students may have more opportunity for successful academic accommodation claims as a result of recent cases and laws. However, perhaps the most important aspect of the Rehabilitation Act and the ADA related to academic accommodations is that both laws provide students with important tools—tools that will be useful to them in dialogue with their respective colleges and universities. . . . [S]tudents with disabilities should enter colleges and universities knowing that the law provides protection against discrimination. The law may not allow students to receive every accommodation they believe that they deserve, but it provides them with a place to begin the dialogue.[27]

In fact, passage of the ADA may hinder discussion about accommodations, because the discussion will now focus on whether the individual is even disabled.

## Implications

As one commentator has noted, "Today's generation of students is the first to have benefited from the Individuals with Disabilities Act . . . during both primary and secondary education. . . . [S]tudents entering colleges and universities today have progressed through an educational system in which they received necessary accommodations and services as a matter of course."[28] Students with what the IDEA calls "specific learning disabilities" are unquestionably covered by the IDEA.

Decisions involving professional examinations in both law and medicine, however, have begun to question whether individuals with learning disabilities should be able to benefit from the ADA or Section 504. Because these high-achieving individuals are being compared with the "general population," they are increasingly finding it difficult to demonstrate that they are substantially limited as compared with the norm. The ADA's mitigating measures decision is being applied to this area of the law, in some ways undercutting the achievements of the IDEA. Because these students have been taught ways to self-accommodate their underlying difficulties in reading or communicating, they are being taken out of the definition of disability. The result is that they are being left to sink or swim under a new set of rules.

One might justify this set of decisions by saying that Section 504 and the ADA were not intended to be crutches for the "barely disabled" who can learn over time to self-accommodate. But these decisions take us down a dangerous slippery slope. Boston University has already shown itself willing to challenge whether individuals diagnosed as learning disabled are entitled to accommodation.[29] Other universities may become more aggressive in questioning their responsibility to learning disabled students.

Unless the IDEA is amended, it is unlikely that these decisions will affect the law of primary or secondary education (although certainly there is a move afoot to withdraw services from that community). What will it mean for society if students with learning disabilities fail to receive accommodations after twelfth grade? Given the increasing importance of higher education for employment, this could have a dramatic effect on the already high unemployment rate in the disability community.

I understand that some people might welcome that direction in our laws, because they are skeptical of the ease with which middle-class children can be diagnosed with learning disabilities to receive accommodations.[30] The solution, however, should not be to take away these services from middle-class children but to extend these services to more poor children. It is hard to see how withdrawing money from one group of children who are having trouble learning to read solves any aspect of America's educational crisis.[31]

## Conclusion

One imagines the following conversation taking place on the eve of passage of the ADA:

> *Member of Congress:* I am willing to vote for the passage of the ADA, but I must warn you that passage of the ADA will significantly harm litigation outcomes under Section 504. The chances of a plaintiff prevailing on appeal will plummet by a factor of two.
>
> *First member of disability rights community:* No thanks. I'm not interested in a statute that will raise false hopes while eroding the rights we have worked so hard to obtain.
>
> *Second member of disability rights community:* I refuse to proceed from such a pessimistic outlook. Maybe we will see such consequences in the early years following passage of the ADA. But with efforts to explain the importance of these rights, we can overcome those problems over time. In the long run, we will have a strong Section 504 and ADA.
>
> *Member of Congress:* So what should I do? Should I wait for a better political and judicial climate or seize the opportunity at hand despite the short-term consequences? Can we be certain those short-term consequences will ever be reversed? Or will ADA's last legacy be the death, not just the wounding, of Section 504?

The positive news for the disability civil rights community is that the ADA has not yet killed the law of education under Section 504, although it has had an arguably negative impact on the law of employment under Section 504.[32] There is reason to believe, however, that the narrowing of the law of higher education for students with learning disabilities is around the corner. We may soon have a generation of students educated with the assistance of the IDEA who are left to sink or swim in postsecondary education.

NOTES

    1.  42 U.S.C. § 12101–12213 (1994).

    2.  29 U.S.C. § 794 (1994).

    3.  *See, e.g.,* Ronald D. Wenkart, *The Americans with Disabilities Act and Its Impact on Public Education,* 82 ED. LAW. REP. 291, 291 (1993) ("It is expected that the Act will have its greatest impact on the private sector, since the provisions of the ADA are patterned after the provisions of section 504 of the Rehabilitation Act of

1973, which prohibits discrimination against the handicapped by agencies receiving federal financial assistance.").

4. 20 U.S.C. §§ 1401–1485 (1994 & Supp. IV 1998) (formerly known as the Education of All Handicapped Children Act).

5. The IDEA requires states that accept federal funding for their educational programs (as virtually all do) to ensure that all children with disabilities receive a "free appropriate public education (FAPE)" in the least restrictive environment possible. The IDEA governs all children with disabilities who require special education services, and are therefore classified as "educationally disabled." A child may have a disability within the meaning of Section 504 yet not be covered by the IDEA because the child is not in need of special education services. For example, a child who uses a wheelchair may have no difficulties in learning associated with her disability but cannot gain access to the building without improvements in accessibility. The accessibility requirements would be governed by Section 504 rather than the IDEA.

6. In an earlier database that I constructed of all ADA appellate cases, I found that employment discrimination cases constituted 76 percent of my database. *See* Ruth Colker, *The Americans with Disabilities Act: A Windfall for Defendants,* 34 HARV. C.R.-C.L. L. REV. 99, 100 n.7 (1999) [hereafter *"Windfall"*]. Although I have not been able to document much litigation under ADA Title III (which involves accessibility matters), it is clear that many private and public institutions have been modified to increase their accessibility. For a discussion of ADA Title III, *see generally* Ruth Colker, *ADA Title III: A Fragile Compromise,* 21 BERKELEY J. EMP. & LAB. L. 377 (2000) [hereafter *"Fragile Compromise"*].

7. *See* Colker, *Windfall, supra* note 6 at 134–35.

8. Whereas the ADA states, "Subject to the provisions of this subchapter, no qualified individual with a disability shall, by reason of such disability, be excluded from participation in or be denied the benefits of the services, programs, or activities of a public entity, or be subjected to discrimination by any such entity," 42 U.S.C. § 12132, the Rehabilitation Act states, "No otherwise qualified individual with a disability . . . shall, solely by reason of her or his disability, be excluded from the participation in, be denied the benefits of, or be subjected to discrimination under any program or activity receiving Federal financial assistance . . ." 29 U.S.C. § 794(a). The only important difference in language is that Section 504 has the "solely" requirement that is absent from the ADA. The omission of the "solely" language should make the ADA broader than Section 504 with respect to determinations that discrimination has taken place.

9. *See* 42 U.S.C. § 12201 (a) ("Except as otherwise provided in this chapter, nothing in this chapter shall be construed to apply a lesser standard than the standards applied under title V of the Rehabilitation Act of 1973 (29 U.S.C. 790 et seq.) or the regulations issued by Federal agencies pursuant to such title.")

10. This essay will not discuss the effect that the Eleventh Amendment decisions may have on the ADA and Section 504. But one could argue that passage of the ADA heightened people's sensitivities to the regulation of state and local government and is causing courts for the first time to question the constitutionality of Section 504 under the spending power. *See, e.g.,* Jim C. v. Arkansas Dep't of Educ., 197 F.3d 958 (8th Cir. 1999) (granting rehearing en banc on spending clause issue in

Section 504 case); Amos v. Maryland Dep't of Pub. Safety and Correctional Servs., 178 F.3d 212 (4th Cir.), *rehearing en banc granted, judgment vacated* (Dec. 28, 1999).

11. 531 U. S. 356, 121 S.Ct. 955 (2001).

12. *See* Colker, *Windfall, supra* note 6; Ruth Colker, *Winning and Losing Under the Americans with Disabilities Act,* 02 OHIO ST. L. J. 239 (2001) [hereafter "*Winning and Losing*"]. This data reflects appellate cases decided during the applicable time period that are available on Westlaw. It does *not* reflect trial court decisions and does not reflect appellate decisions which are not made available to the public. I discuss the selection bias that results from this data set in my two previous articles, cited above.

13. The ADA became effective two years after passage; the first appellate cases were decided in 1994. My database only reflects decisions through July 30, 1999.

14. I define a successful outcome for a defendant as the affirmance of a pro-defendant outcome at trial or the reversal of a pro-plaintiff outcome at trial. The affirmance of a pro-defendant outcome at trial results in a clear victory for the defendant unless the case is appealed to the Supreme Court. It is, of course, possible that a reversal of a pro-plaintiff trial court outcome on appeal will ultimately result in the plaintiff winning (again) on remand. Nonetheless, I should note that the overwhelming majority of my pro-defendant appellate outcomes involve affirmances of pro-defendant trial court outcomes. In an earlier article, for example, I reported that of the 621 cases which I defined as a pro-defendant appellate outcome, 594 (95.6 percent) of those cases were affirmances of pro-defendant trial court outcomes. See Colker, *Winning and Losing, supra* note 12. If anything, my definition of pro-defendant outcome understates defendant's success rate because my definition of pro-plaintiff outcome included affirmances of pro-plaintiff trial court outcomes as well as reversals of pro-defendant trial court outcomes. Of the 99 cases I reported in a previous article, which were pro-plaintiff appellate outcomes, only eighteen (18 percent) of those cases were affirmances of pro-plaintiff trial court outcomes. The remaining cases were reversals of pro-defendant trial court outcomes. It is quite possible that the plaintiff will ultimately lose on remand in the eighty-one cases in which the appellate court reversed a dismissal or summary judgment decision at the trial court level.

15. See Colker, *Winning and Losing, supra* note 12.

16. Section 504 cases can be brought against any entity receiving federal financial assistance. They are not limited to issues of employment discrimination. In fact, my subjective impression is that most section 504 cases brought before 1994 involved issues of educational discrimination.

17. I have also included section 501 and 503 employment discrimination cases in the database although the overwhelming majority of the cases are brought under Section 504.

18. Many other explanations are also possible to explain this pattern over time. Some of these explanations include: (1) the defense bar may have become increasingly sophisticated in handling disability discrimination claims thereby mounting a stronger defense on appeal, (2) the judiciary may have grown increasingly conservative or hostile to ADA claims, (3) plaintiffs may have been overly emboldened by the passage of the ADA and pursued frivolous claims, and (4) pro se plaintiffs may not be responding to the economic forces that affect private litigation. By focusing

on one explanation in this essay, I do not mean to discount these other explanations. Their cumulative effect may explain the results that I have discovered.

19. The statistics were analyzed under SPSS version 9.0.

20. My research assistants were not able to find any Section 504 cases in the appellate courts prior to 1988 that involved issues of employment discrimination. One factor causing this result may be that Westlaw has become more inclusive in the cases it reports and the courts of appeals have become more inclusive in the cases they make available to Westlaw.

21. *See* Jeffrey A. Van Detta & Dan R. Gallipeau, Ph.D., *Judges and Juries: Why Are So Many ADA Plaintiffs Losing Summary Judgment Motions, and Why Would They Fare Better Before a Jury? A Response to Professor Colker,* 19 REV. LITIGATION 505, 517 (2000) ("Many ADA cases founder because counsel for plaintiffs have not prepared the minimum factual record necessary to provide the jury with a basis to conclude that the ADA protects their clients.").

22. Although there has been a lot of publicity about the pro-defendant decisions rendered by the Supreme Court under the ADA, comparatively little attention has been focused on the fact that the Supreme Court has also consistently interpreted Section 504 in a pro-defendant manner. Of the seventeen Section 504 cases heard by the Supreme Court between 1979 and 1996, only two of them resulted in a pro-plaintiff holding. *See* Consolidated Rail Corporation v. Darrone, 465 U.S. 624 (1984) (holding that an action for employment discrimination against an individual with a disability may be maintained even if the federal aid the defendant receives is not for employment purposes); School Board of Nassau County v. Arline, 480 U.S. 273 (1987) (holding that contagious diseases can be covered under Section 504 as a disability). Although four of the seventeen cases cannot be readily classified as pro-plaintiff or pro-plaintiff, eleven of the decisions rendered in this time period were clearly pro-defendant. *See* Southeastern Community College v. Davis, 442 U.S. 397 (1979) (holding that nursing program could lawfully fail to admit Ms. Davis into its program due to her hearing impairment); Community Television of Southern California v. Gottfried, 459 U.S. 498 (1982) (Section 504 does not impose new enforcement obligations on the FCC to consider disability accessibility issues in license renewal applications); Pennhurst State Schools and Hospitals v. Halderman, 465 U.S. 89 (1984) (finding no Section 504 violation in treatment of patients at state hospital); Irving Independent School District v. Texas, 468 U.S. 883 (1984) (finding that Section 504 could not be used as a basis to attain attorney's fees in case involving discrimination in violation of the Education of the Handicapped Act); Alexander v. Choate, 469 U.S. 287 (1985) (Tennessee found not to violate Section 504 in its treatment of Medicaid patients); Atascadero State Hospital v. Scanlon, 473 U.S. 234 (1985) (finding that Congress failed to use the necessary unequivocal language necessary to abrogate the Eleventh Amendment so that plaintiff could not obtain requested relief); Bowen v. American Hospital Association, 476 U.S. 610 (1986) (invalidating rules promulgated under Section 504 to protect infants with disabilities); United States Department of Transportation v. Paralyzed Veterans of America, 477 U.S. 597 (1986) (holding that commercial airlines are not the recipients of federal funding due to airport operators or government control of the air traffic control system); Traynor v. Turnage, 485 U.S. 535 (1988) (permitting VA to distinguish between veterans who are and are not alcoholics in

rendering treatment decisions); Lane v. Pena, 518 U.S. 187 (1996) (holding that Congress had not waived the federal government's sovereign immunity under Section 504 with respect to awards of monetary damages). Many of these decisions did not directly relate to issues of employment discrimination. Hence, they may not have had a major impact on lower courts rendering employment discrimination decisions under Section 504. Moreover, one of the pro-plaintiff cases—*Arline*—did have a significant impact on Section 504 employment discrimination cases. Hence, it is possible that this record had only a minimal impact on the lower courts until the appellate courts and the Supreme Court followed these decisions with strong, pro-defendant decisions under the ADA.

23.  *See* Miener v. Missouri, 673 F.2d 969 (8th Cir. 1980) (pro-plaintiff); Smith v. Special School Dist. No. 1, 184 F.3d 764 (8th Cir. 1983) (pro-defendant); Sellers v. School Bd. of Manassas, 141 F.3d 524 (4th Cir. 1984) (pro-defendant); Zukle v. Regents of the Univ. of Calif., 166 F.3d 1041 (9th Cir. 1986) (pro-defendant); Ridgewood Bd. of Educ. v. N.E., 172 F.3d 238 (3rd Cir. 1986) (pro-plaintiff); Wong v. Regents of Univ. of Calif., 192 F.3d 807 (9th Cir. 1989) (pro-plaintiff); Weber v. Cranston School Committee, 212 F.3d 41 (1st Cir. 1990) (pro-defendant); Wynne v. Tufts, 976 F.2d 791 (1st Cir. 1992) (pro-defendant); Pottgen v. Missouri State HSAA, 40 F.3d 926 (8th Cir. 1994) (pro-defendant); Mallett v. Marquette Univ., 65 F.3d 170 (7th Cir. 1995) (pro-defendant); Sandison v. Michigan HSAA, 64 F.3d 1026 (6th Cir. 1995) (pro-defendant); Susan N. v. Wilson School Dist., 70 F.3d 751 (3rd Cir. 1995) (pro-plaintiff); Powell v. Defore, 699 F.3d 1078 (11th Cir. 2000) (pro-defendant)

24.  *See* Bartlett v. New York State Bd. of Law Examiners, 226 F3d 69 (2d Cir. Aug. 30, 2000) (remanding for determination of whether plaintiff, who has a learning disability, is disabled for the purposes of Section 504 and the ADA). On remand, the district court held in favor of the plaintiff. *See* Bartlett v. New York State Bd. of Law Examiners, 2001 WL 930792 (S.D.N.Y. Aug. 15, 2001). The state is not appealing this decision.

25.  *See* 28 C.F.R. Pt. 35, App. A, § 35.104 (1999) ("A person is considered an individual with a disability . . . when the individual's important life activities are restricted as to the conditions, manner, or duration under which they can be performed in comparison to most people.")

26.  527 U.S. 471 (1999).

27.  Claire E. McCusker, *The Americans with Disabilities Act: Its Potential for Expanding the Scope of Reasonable Academic Accommodations,* 21 J. C. & U.L. 619, 641 (1995).

28.  McCusker, *Id.* at 620.

29.  *See* Guckenberger v. Boston University, 974 F. Supp. 106 (D. Mass. 1997). *See also* Wynne v. Tufts Univ. School of Medicine, 932 F.2d 19 (1st Cir. 1991) (*en banc*) (successful challenge to Tufts University refusal to accommodate plaintiff's disability by altering its testing methods).

30.  See MARK KELMAN & GILLIAN LESTER, JUMPING THE QUEUE (1997).

31.  Professor Kelman and Lester's argument ignores the relevance that school financing has to the equity problem. It may be the case that many middle class children are obtaining assistance under the IDEA by receiving intervention services at their local public school. That assistance, however, is largely funded by their local school district and, in no way, affects the intervention services received by children

in poor school districts. Poor and middle-class children are simply not competing for the same educational dollar in states in which property taxes are primarily funding education. Although it may be proper to criticize the financing of education through property taxes as inequitable to poor children, it seems inappropriate to blame middle-class children who are learning disabled for those inequities.

32. In April, 2001, the Supreme Court decided Alexander v. Sandoval, 121 S.Ct. 1511 (2001). It is too early to predict what effect that decision may have on the enforcement of Section 504; however, it is possible that private rights of actions to enforce Section 504 may be seriously curtailed based on the *Sandoval* decision. Anecdotally, I do know that attorneys are rethinking their litigation strategies in light of the *Sandoval* decision.

*Linda Hamilton Krieger*

# Sociolegal Backlash

Many of the articles in this book were presented in earlier form at a two-day symposium on public, judicial, and media responses to the Americans with Disabilities Act held at the University of California at Berkeley in the winter of 1999. At different points in the proceedings, various participants suggested that, at least at this point in its history, the disability rights movement may be overrelying on the power of law to effect social change.[1] This notion provoked a great deal of discussion, and no small measure of consternation from other participants, who rejoined that the right to assert a legal claim to access had transformed disabled people's individual and collective self-conceptions and their relationship to society. Law, in this view, had brought the movement a long, long way.

This difference in perspective notwithstanding, there was broad-based agreement that, in many critical respects, implementation of the Americans with Disabilities Act was not unfolding as its supporters had planned. Whether decrying the crabbed constructions of the ADA in federal judicial decisions or excavating derisive media portrayals of the act's beneficiaries and enforcers, symposium presenters, commenters, and audience participants repeatedly lamented, "They just don't get it."

The notion that the disability rights movement may be overrelying on the power of law to transform culture, and disability activists' frustrated observations that people outside the disability community "just don't get" the ADA, may point in the same direction. Both suggest that the act, at least as its drafters conceived it, got too far ahead of most people's ability to understand the social and moral vision on which it was premised.

Curiously, one of the more obscure definitions of *backlash* metaphorically describes precisely such a condition. The *Webster's Third New International Dictionary* defines the word, among other ways, as "a snarl in that part of a fishing line which is wound on the spool, caused by overrunning of the spool." The image here is one of a fishing reel that has been overcast—that has gotten ahead of itself—and has for that reason become entangled. Backlash, this image suggests, has something to do with one part of a process or mechanism getting too far ahead of another.

In this essay, I offer an account of backlash premised on this image and situate that account within a larger theoretical model of sociolegal change and retrenchment. My central premise is simple: backlash is about the relationship between a legal regime enacted to effect social change and the system of preexisting norms and institutionalized practices into which it is introduced. Specifically, backlash tends to emerge when the application of a transformative legal regime generates outcomes that diverge too sharply from entrenched norms and institutions to which influential segments of the relevant population retain a strong, conscious allegiance. In some situations, these norms and institutions may be those directly targeted by the new law. In such a case, normative conflict is inevitable. In other situations however, transformative law may have collateral effects, conflicting with norms and institutions that the law's promoters did not aim to destabilize. In either case, preventing backlash, or reckoning with it when it emerges, requires careful attention to *existing* patterns of normative commitment, and to *existing* institutionalized practices and social meaning systems, not merely attention to the *aspirational* norms, institutions, and understandings that the new law seeks to reify.

My inquiry comprises three parts. The first explores various foundational concepts and situates my project within related areas of theoretical inquiry. It goes on to posit a preliminary theoretical model of sociolegal change and retrenchment, and to examine how elements of that model explain certain aspects of public, media, and judicial responses to the Americans with Disabilities Act. The second part proposes a specific definition of backlash and, through the use of two case studies, distinguishes backlash from other forms of sociolegal retrenchment, in terms of both manifestations and causal antecedents. The final section deepens this analysis of causal antecedents and applies that analysis to the ADA.

## Conceptual Foundations: Laws, Norms, and Institutions

In attempting to understand the relationship between law and the larger society of which it is a part, it is useful to distinguish between laws designed to enforce existing social norms and laws enacted to displace or transform them. Similarly, it is important to distinguish between laws that reinforce established institutions and social meaning systems and laws designed to destabilize, subvert, and ultimately reconstruct them. Laws function quite differently, and the threats to their effective enforcement vary significantly, in these two contexts. Before elaborating this thesis, or exploring its relationship to the concept of backlash generally or to reactions to the ADA in particular, various foundational terms, concepts, and principles must be explored.

Consider first the relationship between formal legal rules and informal social norms. Formal law, whether found in statutes, administrative regulations, constitutions, or cases, represents only one broad class of restraint imposing limits on acceptable behavior. In any society having a formal legal system, legal rules exist within a larger system of informal social norms. By social norms, I mean those standards of conduct to which people conform their behavior not because the law requires it, but because conformity is conditioned by subtle or overt forms of positive or negative social sanction.

Informal social norms not only constrain our conduct in relation to others, they also shape our expectations about how others will behave toward us. We generally expect other people to comply with the major social norms associated with a particular context. Violation, either by oneself or by another, generates a kind of "normative dissonance,"[2] a state that, like its cognitive cousin, creates an unpleasant sensation that people generally attempt to reduce. Through these processes of conditioning, dissonance creation, and efforts to reduce dissonance, social norms come to function like preferences and can usefully be viewed as preferences in connection with attempts to understand or predict attitudes, behavior, judgment, and choice.

Of course, formal law and informal social norms are not mutually independent. Social norms both shape and are shaped by formal law. In most situations, formal laws, such as those prohibiting murder or theft, reflect and are designed to enforce consensus social norms. In these contexts, a lawmaker's primary task is to translate nuanced, amorphous, often context-dependent informal norms into clear, precise legal rules that can be applied consistently across diverse contexts.[3] Although this task can be challenging and may be executed more or less artfully, formal law and informal social norms that closely mirror each other are apt to be mutually reinforcing. In such situations, formal law is likely to be viewed as legitimate by most influential social actors, and is unlikely to be met with widespread attempts at evasion, subversion, or outright rollback. For ease of expression, I will refer to formal legal rules of this type—that is, those that reflect and seek to enforce informal consensus norms—as *normal law*.

However, formal law is sometimes enacted by constituencies wishing to displace established social norms. Law of this sort, which I will refer to as *transformative law,* can emerge from a variety of sociopolitical contexts.

Most relevant to our present inquiry is a kind of transformative law that emerges from normatively diverse societies, in which some interest group or coalition succeeds in enacting reformist laws aimed at changing social norms it perceives as unjust or otherwise undesirable. Civil rights laws in general, and the Americans with Disabilities Act in particular, can be understood in this way, as one among many species of transformative law.

Just as formal legal initiatives can be more or less consistent with established social norms, they can be more or less congruent with established institutions. I use the term *institution* here in a specific sense, not as a synonym for *organization*, but as the term is used in the new institutionalism in sociology and organization theory. An institution in this sense comprises a web of interrelated norms, social meanings, implicit expectancies, and other "taken for granted" aspects of reality, which operate as largely invisible background rules in social interaction and construal.[4]

For example, a stop sign is an institution, as well as an object, in that it symbolizes and evokes an entire set of norms, expectancies, and social meanings. These include rules about what actually constitutes a "stop" (consider in this regard the "California stop"—arguably an institution unto itself), or rules about who has the right of way when cars on perpendicular trajectories stop at about the same time. The institution "stop sign" also includes a whole set of expectancies—"scripts" about what may happen to drivers who violate stop sign rules in particular contexts. "Stop sign" carries with it a set of social meanings reflected, for example, in the spontaneous judgments made about drivers who run stop signs, or the different judgments made about drivers who slow but do not quite stop (the "California stop," again).

The norms constituting an institution are likely to include various rules of exemption, imparting social meanings that would not be obvious to an "institutional outsider." Consider in this regard the quite different attributions made when an ambulance or fire engine runs a stop sign, as opposed to a car full of teenage boys.

While the stop sign might seem a trivial example of an institution, it effectively illustrates an important point. All social interaction is mediated by taken-for-granted background rules, which structure social perception, communication, and interpretation and create an impression—even if false—of shared meaning and experience. As we will see, any formal law designed to alter patterns of social action must contend with institutions and with their constitutive patterns of expectancy, action, and interpretation. The promoters of any formal legal regime that fails to take such institutions into account are apt to find themselves swimming perpetually upstream against a powerful alignment of normative, interpretive, and attitudinal currents.

This conceptual foundation set, we can return to the project of categorizing formal law in terms of its relationship to underlying norms and institutionalized practices. Just as a simple instance of transformative law may be devised to displace a discrete social norm, a more comprehensive legal regime may be deployed in an effort to destabilize, subvert, and reconstitute an entire set of interrelated institutions. Various devices can be brought to bear in pursuit of this end.

First, transformative law may challenge preexisting consensus definitions of particular categories or concepts, and by statute, regulation, or judicial decision attempt to redefine, or "reinstitutionalize" them with a different set of constituent social meanings, values, and normative principles. The Americans with Disabilities Act uses this device, for example, when it defines a person with a disability not only as a "person with an impairment that substantially limits one or more major life activities"— which is how most people would reflexively define the disabled state—but also as a person who has a *record* of an impairment, or who is *perceived* as having an impairment.[5] Through this definition, the ADA constitutes the disability classification not only in terms of the internal attributes of the arguably disabled individual, but also in terms of external, "disabling" attributes of the attitudinal environment in which that person must function. "Disability," under this conception, resides as much in the institutional environment and in the attitudes of nondisabled persons as in the characteristics of a person with an impairment.

In similar fashion, the ADA seeks to reinstitutionalize the concept of employment qualification. It defines a "qualified" person with a disability not merely in terms of a person's ability to perform the functions of a particular job *as she finds it,* but in terms of her ability to perform the job's *essential* functions *with or without reasonable accommodation.*[6] In this way, the ADA rejects the notion that a disabled person is "unqualified" if she can not function effectively in the "world as it is." Rather, she can legitimately be classified as unqualified only if she would be unable to function effectively in the "world as it could be," after reasonable environmental adaptation.

In recasting the concept of qualification in this way, the ADA's drafters sought to transform the institution of disability by locating responsibility for disablement not only in a person's impairment, but also in disabling attitudinal or structural environments. Under such a construction, the concept of disability takes on new social meaning. It is not merely a container holding tragedy, or occasion for pity, charity, or exemption from the

ordinary obligations attending membership in society. The concept of disability now also, or to a certain extent instead, contains rights to and societal responsibility for making enabling environmental adaptations. The
ADA was in this way crafted to replace the old impairment model of disability with a sociopolitical approach.

Just as transformative law may be designed to subvert and reconstruct
relevant institutionalized categories, it may also be deployed to displace
institutionalized patterns of inference and action. In the most extreme
cases, a transformative legal regime may even strive to displace patterns of
inference and action that, at least among certain constituencies, are so far
taken for granted as to seem not only permissible, but normative—deriving
from common sense, and responding to the natural order of things.

In this regard, consider the direct threat defense, set out in ADA Section
103.[7] Under Section 103, an employer who wishes for safety reasons to
exclude a person with a disability from a particular job must satisfy a much
more exacting standard than most employers would apply on their own.
The substance of that standard is spelled out in administrative regulations
issued by the Equal Employment Opportunity Commission, pursuant to a
congressional delegation of interpretive authority contained in ADA Section 106.[8]

Direct Threat means a significant risk of substantial harm to the
health or safety of the individual or others that cannot be eliminated
or reduced by reasonable accommodation. The determination than
an individual poses a "direct threat" shall be made on an individualized assessment of the individual's present ability to safely perform
the essential functions of the job. This assessment shall be based on a
*reasonable medical judgment* that relies on the *most current medical
knowledge* and/or on the *best available objective evidence*. In determining whether an individual would pose a direct threat, the factors to be
considered include:

(1)  The duration of the risk;
(2)  The nature and severity of the potential harm;
(3)  The likelihood that the potential harm will occur; and
(4)  The imminence of the potential harm.[9]

Consider the many norms and institutions implicated by the ADA's
direct threat standard. First, there are norms of prudential risk management, conveyed by such aphorisms as "Better safe than sorry," and "A

stitch in time saves nine." Over time, these norms have been institutionalized into the legal constructs of "foreseeable risk" and "the reasonable
man" (now, the more inclusive "reasonable person"). However objectively
small a particular risk might be, if it actually materializes and causes harm,
it is apt be viewed after the fact as having been "foreseeable."[10] One who
fails *ex ante* to recognize and take steps to avoid a foreseeable risk is not
likely to be viewed *ex post* as having acted with reasonable care.

We can expect hindsight bias of this sort to operate even more powerfully where a specific type of risk is associated in popular myth or stereotype
with members of a stigmatized group.[11] So, for example, if mental illness is
associated with violence, a person with a mental illness is apt to be viewed
as posing an elevated risk of future violence. If that person later does behave
violently, his behavior will probably be viewed as having been more foreseeable than it would have been absent his mental illness. The nondiscrimination and direct threat provisions of the ADA prohibit precisely this type
of "risk management by heuristic," creating a powerful tension between
compliance with the statute on the one hand and popular (read, "irrational") approaches to risk on the other.

The nature of the tension between direct threat analysis and heuristic
approaches to risk management becomes even more evident when one
considers the "reasonably prudent person" of American tort law. The reasonably prudent person is not really reasonably prudent at all. She is perfect—vigilant, prescient, swift to neutralize every conceivable risk.
Through this lens, an employer who hires or retains an employee who,
because of mental illness, is irrationally assumed to be dangerous will likely
not be viewed as having been reasonably prudent. If the ADA is seen as dic-
tating such a person's hiring or retention, it will be viewed as violating
"common sense," as a cartoon that appeared in the *Richmond Times-Dispatch*[12] shortly after publication of the EEOC *Guidance on Psychiatric Disabilities and the ADA,* so vividly reflects.

As the cartoon reveals, a formal legal rule that requires a scientific
approach to risk assessment in situations where people are not accustomed
to seeing it applied is apt to violate popular conceptions of common sense.
Unfortunately, as those who work in public health, risk management, and
environmental policy can attest, rational scientific and irrational "common
sense" approaches to risk often wildly diverge.

In requiring a less stereotype-driven and more scientific approach to risk
analysis, the ADA's direct threat provisions challenge a number of inter-
connected institutions bearing on risk assessment and management. The
judgment of a company doctor, for example, long accorded broad discre-

Reprinted with permission. Brookins, 1997, *Richmond Times Dispatch.*

tion in determining who could "safely" be employed in particular jobs, can be delegitimated under the ADA if his or her opinion is not based on "the most current medical knowledge."[13] The act directly prohibits preoffer fitness-for-duty exams and the use of blanket "medical standards," lists of medical conditions once used to exclude affected applicants from particular jobs without individualized inquiry.[14] The company doctor, the eligibility physical, and medical standards are easily recognizable institutions with long histories of application across diverse organizational fields.[15] The Americans with Disabilities Act was designed by its drafters to destabilize and reconstitute these institutions, along with other taken-for-granted aspects of reality bound up in popular assumptions about the relationship between disability and risk. In this respect, the ADA provides an almost perfect example of transformative law.

Of course, the formal displacement of an entrenched network of social norms and institutions by a transformative legal regime does not guarantee that network's immediate, or even eventual, de facto displacement. Through a variety of mechanisms, established norms and institutions can be expected to resist displacement by new formal legal rules. To the extent that these resistance efforts succeed, transformative law becomes what we might refer to as "captured law."

Consider the many threats posed by traditional norms and institutions to the effective enforcement of laws designed to uplift historically subordinated groups. In the case of criminal laws, or civil laws as to which there exists no effective private right of action, law enforcement officials, whose loyalties often lie with the traditional normative system, may be unwilling to enforce the new formal legal rules. Where a victim's complaint is required to initiate formal legal proceedings, social pressures, expressed as either subtle or blatant social boycotts and reprisals, may make resort to the new legal protections too costly. Similar social pressures may constrain the willingness of witnesses to cooperate with the new legal order, resulting in the suppression of evidence needed for successful prosecution of a theoretically viable claim.

Effective implementation of transformative law may be further constrained by resource imbalances between those who seek to mobilize or enforce the new legal rules and those who seek to avoid liability under them. In the context of "normal" criminal law, where the state acts to enforce dominant social norms, prosecutors are likely to occupy positions of greater power and are apt to possess greater resources than the strata of defendants they prosecute. Where transformative law challenges or contradicts traditional social norms, the opposite situation often obtains. Transformative law is often mobilized by social "outsiders" against social "insiders." When challenged under a transformative legal regime, these insider defendants are often better able than their outsider opponents to exploit the law's soft spots. They are therefore often able to restrict the law's application, both to themselves individually and more broadly, as a function of judicial precedent.

The operation of subtle cognitive and motivational biases that distort social perception and judgment may further constrain the implementation of transformative law. The mechanisms through which social stereotypes and other institutionalized expectancies, social group allegiances, and subjective conceptions of fairness bias the evaluation of evidence are all well documented in the relevant social science literature.[16]

Other subtle processes can also foil the displacement of entrenched social norms and institutions. Law does not exercise a direct effect on individuals. The space between formal legal constraints and individual action is occupied by organizational structures and social relationships, and by the many social norms and institutions produced and monitored by those structures and relationships. As formal law is filtered through these mediating norms and institutions, it is interpreted, constituted, and reenacted in ways that tend to reflect and reify them.

For example, legal sociologist Lauren Edelman and her colleagues have shown that over time, Title VII's civil rights protections have tended to be interpreted by organizational complaint handlers as generalized rules of fairness, bearing increasingly less resemblance to the antiracist, antisexist political ideologies from which they emerged.[17] As Edelman observes, formal law is initially ambiguous and acquires specific meaning only after professional and organizational communities have constructed definitions of violation and compliance.[18]

Not surprisingly, this interpretive process is powerfully influenced by the taken-for-granted background rules represented by norms, institutionalized practices, and related social meaning systems. Sometimes, these interpretive processes work from the top down, as organizational actors interpret and voluntarily comply with the indeterminate legal standards contained in legislation, regulations, or lawyer advice. Other construal processes, through which norms, institutions, and social meaning systems influence law, operate from the bottom up. Complex statutory regimes contain many ambiguous provisions requiring judicial and/or administrative construction. Judges and administrative officials, whose conscious or unconscious allegiances often lie with traditional rather than transformative normative and institutional systems, may powerfully constrain the new law's full implementation by way of statutory interpretation and implementation.

Judges and administrative officials can, of course, deliberately exploit loopholes or ambiguities in the law, thereby systematically limiting its sphere of application or attenuating its requirements. But the process of capture through construal need not be animated by deliberate efforts to undermine a transformative law's effectiveness. Biased judicial or administrative construal can result from far more subtle mechanisms through which entrenched norms and institutionalized practices, operating as taken-for-granted background rules, systematically skew the interpretations of transformative legal rules so that those rules increasingly come to resemble the normative and institutional systems they were intended to displace. Eventually, if these interpretive biases operate unconstrained, the new transformative law may provide a vehicle for the reassertion and relegitimation of the very norms and institutions it was designed to undermine.[19]

The U.S. Supreme Court's April 2002 decision in *US Airways, Inc. v. Barnett*[20] provides an almost perfect illustration of this relegitimation process. In *US Airways,* the Court was asked to determine whether assigning a disabled employee to a vacant position in order to accommodate his or her disability would be *per se* "unreasonable" if another employee would otherwise be entitled to the position under the terms of a seniority system. At least in broad segments of the American labor market, there are few work-place institutions as well-entrenched and as broadly viewed as normative as the bona fide seniority system. In fact, except for the ADA, all federal employment discrimination statutes, including Title VII of the Civil Rights Act of 1964, the Age Discrimination in Employment Act, and the Equal Pay Act, contain an explicit, statutory defense for bona fide seniority systems.[21]

That no equivalent seniority system defense appears in the text of the ADA is not an accident. The ADA's drafters and legislative sponsors left it out on purpose, in large measure, seniority systems, virtually always established by nondisabled constituencies, were viewed as part of the problem the ADA was designed to address. Both the House and the Senate Committees conducting hearings on the bills that would become the ADA made clear that they were aware of title VII's bona fide seniority system defense and had expressly chosen not to include such a provision in the ADA.[22] The Ninth Circuit, in its *en banc* decision in *US Airways,* had recognized this. Following the approach prescribed by the House and Senate Committee Reports, the *en banc* panel had ruled that the existence of a seniority system should be considered merely as one factor among many in determining whether reassignment to a vacant position would constitute an undue hardship in any particular case.[23] Thus, the Ninth Circuit decision implicitly recognized that seniority systems, like other institutionalized practices, can operate to exclude people with disabilities from employment opportunities and, for this reason, must, like other "soft" structural barriers, be scrutinized for their discriminatory effects.

But despite the absence of any textual basis for an ADA seniority system defense, and despite clear legislative history evincing Congress' deliberate departure from the approach taken in other civil rights legislation, the Supreme Court in *US Airways* held that an employer's showing in an ADA case that a requested accommodation conflicts with seniority rules will ordinarily be sufficient to establish that the accommodation is *per se* unreasonable.[24] Moreover, concluded the Court, such a showing will ordinarily entitle the employer to summary judgment, that is, to a ruling in its favor as a matter of law, without a trial.[25]

In reaching this conclusion, the Court constructs a starkly tautological argument: An accommodation is not "reasonable" under the ADA, the Court states, unless that accommodation "seems reasonable on its face, *i.e.,* ordinarily or in the run of cases."[26] On its face, the Court continued, it seems unreasonable to let a request for accommodation trump a seniority system. Why? Because employees expect assignments to be made by seniority, and because "we can find nothing in the statute that suggests Congress intended to undermine seniority systems in this way.[27] In other words, the Court concludes in *US Airways* that seniority systems, so long as they are *bona fide*, can not be considered discriminatory because the institution of seniority is so firmly entrenched in American labor markets. The Court simply finds it impossible, plain statutory text and legislative history notwithstanding, to understand something so unquestionably normative as a seniority system to be "part of the problem" the ADA was designed to address. The ADA's drafters and legislative promoters may have meant to destabilize the institution of seniority, but in *US Airways,* the Supreme Court uses the ADA to relegitimate it.

Before bringing backlash into this analysis, let me organize the ideas explored thus far by describing them and their relationship to each other in graphic form. Figure 2 depicts a model of sociolegal change and retrenchment that incorporates the concepts of normal law, transformative law, and captured law, and illustrates the interactions between formal law and the sociocultural environment in which it functions and evolves.

At the upper left-hand corner of figure 2, we begin with an established normative and institutional framework. This framework corresponds with and in a sense includes the system of formal legal rules and procedures referred to earlier as normal law.

Moving across the top of figure 1 from left to right, we find an established normative and institutional system destabilized by a variety of social, political, and cultural forces that press for normative and institutional change. These forces include political speech and expressive action, formal political initiatives, artistic representations, media accounts, and critical accounts by academics and other intellectuals. Through these and other devices, participants in sociopolitical movements attempt to transform—and to a greater or lesser extent may succeed in transforming—entrenched social norms, social meaning systems, and institutionalized practices. As the traditional normative and institutional system is destabilized, one may also observe incremental changes in normal law, or the proliferation of expressed dissent by influential legal decision-makers.

Three aspects of this process require consideration at this juncture. First, even if forces militating for social change succeed in enacting a transformative legal regime, traditional norms and institutions do not vanish overnight. As earlier described, transformative law often emerges out of normatively heterogeneous societies. In such societies, no one normative or institutional system exercises exclusive sway. Thus, in most situations in

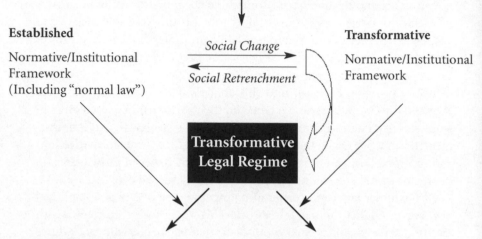

**Speech & Expressive Action**
**Cultural Representations**
**Media Accounts**
**Incremental Destabilization of Normal Law**
**Intellectual Trends, Theoretical Accounts**

**Established**

Normative/Institutional
Framework
(Including "normal law")

*Social Change*

*Social Retrenchment*

**Transformative**

Normative/Institutional
Framework

**Transformative
Legal Regime**

**Socio-Legal Retrenchment**

*Re-Assertion of Established
Normative/Institutional Framework
("Capture")*

Under-Enforcement by Gov't Agencies
"Top-Down" Endogeneity Effects:
　Institution-Perpetuating Construction
　by Organizational Complaint Handlers
Beneficiary Lack of Access to Legal
　Resources
Fact-Finder Bias
"Bottom-Up" Endogeneity Effects:
　Institution-Perpetuating Constructions
　of Law by Courts +/ or Administrative
　Agencies
Reassertion-Relegitimation of Pre-
　existing Norms through the New Law

**Socio-Legal Change**

*Reinforcement of Transformative
Normative/Institutional
Framework*

Appropriate Enforcement by Gov't Agencies
"Top-Down" Endogeneity Effects:
　Institution-Transforming Constructions
　of Law by Organizational Complaint
　Handlers
Beneficiary Access to Legal Resources
"Bottom-Up" Endogeneity Effects:
　Institution Transforming Constructions of
　Law by Courts +/or Administrative
　Agencies
Reification of Transformative Institutional
　Reconstructions
Legitimation of Transformative Norms
Dissemination of Transformative Social
　Meanings

FIGURE 1.　Processes of sociolegal change and retrenchment

which social change efforts are under way, pressures for social retrenchment vie with emerging pressures for social change. This norm competition does not end with the enactment of a transformative legal regime.

A second point is closely related to the first. Transformative legal regimes can emerge at earlier or later stages of a social justice struggle. In this regard, it is useful to contrast the Civil Rights Act of 1964 with both Section 504 of the Rehabilitation Act of 1973 and the Americans with Disabilities Act.

The Civil Rights Act of 1964 was passed after many years of well-publicized struggle for racial justice. The Montgomery bus boycott began in the spring of 1955.[28] The Little Rock Nine entered Central High School in the fall of 1957, following Arkansas governor Orval Eugene Faubus's infamous threat that blood would run in the streets if black students attempted to enter the school. It was February 1960 when four young black students from North Carolina A&T sat down at a white's only lunch counter at the Woolworth's in Greensboro, North Carolina. The same year also saw the beginning of the Freedom Rides, which continued into 1961. In 1963, pictures of Bull Connor's police dogs ripping at civil rights demonstrators and of members of the Birmingham Fire Department turning fire hoses on black children found their way onto the front pages of newspapers around the world. The same year also produced Martin Luther King's "Letter from the Birmingham Jail," the March on Washington, and King's "I Have a Dream" speech. In short, by the time the Civil Rights Act finally passed, it was supported by a powerful and well-publicized movement for social change, whose major tenets and aspirations had already garnered widespread sociocultural support.[29]

Disability rights legislation sits at almost the opposite end of a continuum in this regard. Although there was certainly a disability rights movement in the United States during the 1970s and 1980s, it was neither as broad-based nor as well disseminated into popular consciousness as the black civil rights movement of the 1950s and 1960s, or the women's movement of the 1970s. As a result, neither Section 504 of the Rehabilitation Act of 1973 nor the Americans with Disabilities Act was supported by a broad-based popular understanding of the injustices faced by disabled people, the nature of their continuing struggle for inclusion and equality, or the particular theory of equality that informed the statutes' many ambiguous provisions.

As Richard Scotch has documented,[30] Section 504 of the Rehabilitation Act of 1973, which prohibits disability discrimination by federal agencies, federal contractors, and recipients of federal funding, was not enacted in response to a broad social movement for disability rights, or even through the efforts of particular disability rights lobbyists or activists. Rather, the section was included in the Rehabilitation Act based on the spontaneous impulse of a small group of congressional staffers who were familiar with Title IX, which prohibits sex discrimination in education, but who had virtually no experience with or knowledge of disability issues.[31] No hearings were held on Section 504, and congressional staffers could not even remember exactly who among them had suggested adding the nondiscrimination section to the overall bill.[32]

According to Scotch, members of Congress who voted on the Rehabilitation Act were either unaware of the section's existence or interpreted it simply as "little more than a platitude."[33] As economist Edward Berkowitz characterized the situation, "It would not be an overstatement to say that Section 504 was enacted into law with no public comment or debate."[34]

The same cannot be said, however, about the process leading up to final adoption of the Section 504 implementing regulations. Those regulations were drafted by a small group of Senate aides, Department of Health, Education, and Welfare (HEW) staffers, and disability rights advocates. The proposed regulations, both in their definition of disability and in their incorporation of a reasonable accommodation duty, were based on a social or civil rights model of disability rather than on the older impairment model that underlies the disability provisions of the Social Security Act.[35] After their publication for comment, the proposed Section 504 regulations drew a great deal of fire. The Ford administration left office in 1976 without adopting them,[36] and after assuming his position in the new Carter administration, HEW secretary Joseph Califano was similarly negatively inclined.[37]

The best-publicized episode of disability rights activism emerged from the struggle to implement the Section 504 regulations. On April 5, 1977, disability activists staged sit-ins and demonstrations in nine HEW offices around the country. While most dissipated within twenty-four hours, the occupation of HEW's regional office in San Francisco lasted twenty-five days and received a good deal of national media attention.[38] It ended on April 28, 1977, when, four years after the law's passage, Secretary Califano signed the regulations.[39]

The 1988 Deaf student uprising at Gallaudet University in Washington, D.C., was also relatively well publicized, at least in major metropolitan areas. In the 184 years since its founding by Thomas Hopkins Gallaudet, a Congregationalist minister, and Laurent Clerc, a Deaf educator, the federally chartered university had never had a Deaf president.[40] In August 1987, when President Jerry Lee announced his intention to resign, Gallaudet students and alumni demanded that his successor be Deaf. When the board of trustees instead selected Elisabeth Zinser, a hearing candidate for the position who did not even know American Sign Language, Gallaudet students and alumni exploded in protest. Zinser never set foot on the Gallaudet campus. She resigned without taking office and was succeeded by King Jordan, Gallaudet's first Deaf president.

As Joseph Shapiro's account reflects, disability rights activism in the 1970s and 1980s centered primarily in the San Francisco Bay Area and Washington, D.C. In the years between adoption of the Section 504 regulations in 1977 and passage of the ADA in 1990, relatively few well-publicized actions took place outside of those two areas.[41] One salient exception, a widely publicized action protesting inaccessible public transit in Detroit, Michigan, ended in public relations disaster, when at the last minute invited participant Rosa Parks withdrew from the event and issued a scathing open letter chastising the action's organizers for their "aggressive" tactics.[42]

A final burst of well-publicized disability rights activism took place as the ADA was being marked up in the House Energy and Commerce Committee in March 1990. Early that month, demonstrators organized by American Disabled for Accessible Public Transit (ADAPT) converged on Washington, D.C., for an action that came to be known as the Wheels of Justice March. The event began with a rally at the White House, during which the crowd was addressed by White House counsel C. Boydon Gray, an enthusiastic supporter of the Americans with Disabilities Act. After the rally, demonstrators marched to the Capitol. There, as ADAPT's Mike Auberger spoke from his wheelchair about the grim symbolism of the inaccessible building, three dozen ADAPT activists cast themselves out of their wheelchairs and commenced a "crawl-up," during which they dragged themselves hand over hand up the eighty-three marble steps leading to the Capitol's front entrance. The action concluded the next day, with a noisy occupation of the Capitol rotunda.[43]

Despite this and other efforts to educate the public about the physical and attitudinal obstacles confronting people with disabilities, by the time the ADA was passed in the summer of 1990, few people understood what the law provided, why it was important, or what core values and ideals should guide its implementation. Indeed, a nationwide poll conducted in 1991 by Harris Associates revealed that only 18 percent of those questioned were even aware of the law's existence.[44] Sixteen percent of respondents—just 2 percent fewer than knew about the ADA—reported feeling anger because "people with disabilities are an inconvenience."[45]

In short, by the time the ADA was passed, relatively little popular consciousness-raising around disability issues had taken place. Few Americans outside a relatively small circle were familiar with the notion that the obstacles confronting persons with disabilities stemmed as much from attitudinal and physical barriers as from impairments as such. Without question, the fact that many influential legal actors, including numerous senators, congressional representatives, and Bush administration officials were, by virtue of their own situations or their connections to family members with disabilities, sympathetic to the proposed legislation. But in a sense this relatively ready access to influential power exacted a price from the disability rights movement after the ADA was signed into law. Most people, including the federal judges who would interpret and apply the new statute, simply did not understand the theoretical constructs, social meaning systems, and core principles on which the disability rights movement, the Section 504 regulations, and the ADA were based. As the ADA case law developed, and as representations of the ADA emerged in the media, outmoded but still broadly disseminated understandings of disability powerfully shaped the act's implementation and popular reception. In short, people "just don't get" the ADA because they have never come to understand, let alone accept, the social, theoretical, and moral visions on which it was premised.

A transformative normative and institutional framework developed as part of a social justice movement rarely represents a complete break with the traditional normative and institutional system from which it emerged. In fact, social justice movements often draw upon a core subset of deeply rooted values, myths, and symbols and attempt to link the movement's agenda to the aspirations these values, myths, and symbols express. These aspirational constructs, which we might refer to as *legacy values,* serve in a sense as transitional objects, linking the new normative framework to valued elements of the larger society's sociopolitical self-conception. The ultimate success of a social justice movement, I suggest, depends in large measure on its ability to integrate legacy values into the new transformative normative and institutional framework it proposes, and to keep the close relationship between the two salient.

In summary, transformative law often emerges when a reformist group or coalition seeks to harness the power of law to advance its program of normative and institutional change. Transformative law may take the form of a major statutory initiative, like Title VII of the Civil Rights Act of 1964, or it may emerge through judicial action in response to a major constitutional crisis, as in *Brown v. Board of Education.*[46] In other situations, it may emerge from common-law developments alone, as occurred for example in the landmark cases establishing a cause of action for strict liability for man-ufacturing defects.[47] Indeed, one might define "judicial activism" as the manifest willingness of appellate court judges to participate in the produc-tion of transformative law.

But as figure 2 suggests, the enactment of a new statutory regime or the issuance of a major judicial decision is not a sociolegal telos; it is merely one part of a larger process. The influence of social and cultural forces on for-mal legal rules does not end with the passage of legislation or the judicial pronouncement of a new legal rule. On the contrary, as figure 2 indicates, both the entrenched/traditional and the emerging/transformative norma-tive and institutional frameworks exert pressure on the interpretation and elaboration of formal law, as it is reenacted in its application to concrete sit-uations. To the extent that reformist influences (represented by the dotted arrow moving from upper right to lower left on the right-hand side of figure 2) predominate in the implementation process, transformative law will be elaborated and applied in ways that reinforce transformative norms and institutional reconstructions. In these situations, one can begin to see manifestations of sociolegal change.

However, as the dotted arrow appearing on the upper left side of figure 2 indicates, the traditional normative/institutional framework does not simply disappear. Rather, it continues to shape the legal environment as the transformative legal regime is interpreted, elaborated, and applied. To the extent that sociolegal actors continue to be influenced by traditional norms, social meaning systems, and institutionalized practices, the con-strual, elaboration, and reenactment of transformative law will move pro-gressively in the direction of sociolegal capture. Capture, then, can usefully be understood as the subtle reassertion of preexisting norms, social mean-ings, and institutionalized practices into a formal legal regime intended by its promoters to displace them.

## Sociolegal Backlash

The process of sociolegal capture is often subtle and accretive, and it can occur even if legal actors do not consciously or deliberately set out to undermine the reformist norms embedded in a transformative legal regime. Indeed, capture can occur even if a large majority of influential sociolegal actors embrace key aspects of the transformative normative framework. In backlash, however, opponents of the new legal regime explicitly reject one or more of its key elements, and ground that rejection in open assertions of the *normative superiority* of preexisting sociolegal institutions.

Because in the case of backlash, efforts to subvert or delegitimate the new legal regime are overt and based on explicitly normative grounds, a number of additional features, which I will refer to as *backlash effects,* begin to emerge. These include the following phenomena, not ordinarily present in simple sociolegal capture contexts.

Explicit attacks on the moral desert of the new regime's beneficiaries; often accompanied by

> Attempts to limit the class benefited by the new legal regime, based explicitly on asserted differences in the desert status of different beneficiary subgroups
>
> Parades of horribles—claims, often supported by vivid anecdotes, that application of the new legal rules is systematically resulting in unfair, absurd, or otherwise normatively undesirable outcomes

Rhetorical attacks on and other attempts to delegitimate law enforcement agents and agencies; often accompanied by

> Derisive humor leveled at the law and at those who mobilize and seek to enforce it
>
> Opinion cascades: sudden, large-scale shifts in manifest willingness to publicly express support for or opposition to a particular law, policy, group, activity, or principle
>
> Calls for, or concrete efforts directed at achieving, outright rollback of transformative legal norms
>
> Other assertions of the normative superiority of the preexisting social, legal, and institutional framework

It might be helpful at this juncture to consider two cases illustrating the admittedly fuzzy but still discernible line between capture and backlash. The contrast I propose here is between the legal framework represented by Title VII of the Civil Rights Act of 1964 and the network of norms and institutions implicated by preferential forms of affirmative action.

The disparate treatment aspects of Title VII have not been subjected to backlash, as I am defining that concept here. Since the mid-1960s, few influential social actors have expressed normative opposition to the antidiscrimination principle. Even when Title VII plaintiffs lose their cases, their motives or moral desert are rarely attacked in either judicial opinions or mainstream media commentaries. It is virtually impossible to find cartoons lampooning Title VII in mainstream newspapers or news magazines. Even those who oppose Title VII on economic efficiency grounds[48] profess support for its central normative principles and goals; they simply contend that regulation is not the best way to achieve them. Few influential social actors advocate, or I would suggest even secretly wish for, a return to the pre–Title VII patterns of race, sex, and national origin discrimination.

Finally, it would also be hard to argue with the proposition that, at least in substantial measure, Title VII has had significant transformative effects. Official, separate job classifications, union locals, and lines of progression for whites and nonwhites; separate pay and benefits scales for men and women; sex-specific help-wanted ads in newspapers—these were all commonplace in 1963 and are all virtually unheard of today.

On the other hand, in recent years, Title VII has undeniably been subject to sociolegal capture, at least in certain significant respects. Over the course of the 1980s and 1990s, courts progressively heightened standards of proof for plaintiffs asserting Title VII claims.[49] The class action standards contained in Rule 23 of the Federal Rules of Civil Procedure have been interpreted and applied in ways that have made it increasingly difficult to certify employment discrimination class actions.[50] This in turn has made hiring and promotion discrimination harder to redress in a systematic way. Over time, courts have interposed a variety of other substantive, procedural, and evidentiary obstacles, making successful prosecution of individual and class-based discrimination cases more difficult.[51]

Institutionalized practices like word-of-mouth recruitment and non-posting of job openings, once routinely invalidated as discriminatory, have been upheld with increasing frequency, treated by federal judges not as part of the problem of racial injustice, but simply as part of "the common nature of things."[52] Although disparate impact theory, first endorsed by the Supreme Court in 1971,[53] seemed poised to displace a broad range of employment-related institutions, in subsequent years the requirements attending its successful mobilization were increasingly tightened and its sphere of permissible application progressively constricted, sharply circumscribing its transformative effect.[54]

These and other restrictive developments, however, have progressed against a backdrop of proclaimed allegiance to nondiscrimination norms.

Even during the Reagan administration, as Equal Employment Opportunity Commission (EEOC) officials all but shut down the commission's systemic discrimination enforcement operations and issued new policies prohibiting commission attorneys from invoking the statute's most powerful remedies, they continued to express firm commitment to antidiscrimination principles and vigorous law enforcement.[55] As Lauren Edelman has demonstrated, even as business organizations found ways to insulate their established practices from Title VII's transformative effects, they systematically constructed and displayed symbolic indicia of compliance, thus signaling their support for the statute's basic normative principles.[56] The antiracist, antisexist ideology undergirding Title VII was not explicitly denounced by organizational actors. Rather, it was gradually transmuted into basic principles of procedural fairness, which were familiar and relatively nonthreatening to high-level managers and human resources professionals.[57] In these and other ways, processes of sociolegal capture functioned covertly, as the transformative strength of the nondiscrimination principle was increasingly diluted and its dictates recast to harmonize with rather than destabilize entrenched institutions and social meaning systems.

The response to affirmative action, on the other hand, provides a paradigmatic illustration of sociolegal backlash. Opposition to affirmative action is often based explicitly on assertions that "colorblind" or "merit-based" allocation regimes are normatively superior to selection systems incorporating gender- or race-based preferences.[58] Both popular and scholarly accounts, often supported by vivid anecdotes, assert that affirmative action programs benefit the unworthy at the expense of the worthy, undermine important values and traditions, and systematically result in unfair, perverse, and otherwise undesirable outcomes.[59] Candidates for public office who support affirmative action policies have been subjected to blistering rhetorical attacks. These are perhaps best exemplified by the derisive labeling of Lani Guinier as a "quota queen" by those opposing her nomination to head the Civil Rights Division of the Justice Department in 1993.[60] Eventually, affirmative action programs were targeted for outright rollback in the courts,[61] in Congress,[62] and in legislative initiatives or public referenda in a number of states.[63] Many of these efforts were successful, the most notable being the issuance of the Fifth Circuit's decision in *Hopwood v. Texas*[64] and the passage of Proposition 209 by the California electorate in 1996. In short, one finds in responses to affirmative action virtually all of the elements of sociolegal backlash, as that construct was earlier defined.

Although backlash can be distinguished from simple sociolegal capture, it would be a mistake in my view to make too much of the distinctions between them. Backlash and capture emerge from similar conditions, specifically, where the normative and institutional foundations of a transformative legal regime diverge too sharply from the system of informal social norms and institutionalized practices into which the new regime was introduced. Moreover, preventing backlash or capture from occurring, or reckoning with them once they do emerge, requires attention to similar elements.

Rather than conceiving of backlash and other forms of sociolegal retrenchment as discrete phenomena, it is more useful to think in terms of the relative presence or absence of backlash effects within broader trends toward sociolegal change or retrenchment. To be sure, as distinguished from other manifestations of sociolegal capture, backlash effects are more overt, more characterized by confrontational rhetoric, and more squarely based on claims to the moral superiority of traditional normative and institutional arrangements. But few situations, I suggest, will represent "pure" cases of either backlash or capture. More commonly, elements of each will diverge or overlap in various ways, in response to social factors and forces far too complex to reliably specify.

These cautions aside, it is nonetheless useful to draw a distinction between backlash and other, more subtle forms of sociolegal retrenchment. By virtue of their directness and their reliance on explicit moral claims, backlash effects can help social change activists identify, in a way mere capture often can not, the precise areas of strain between a transformative legal regime and the system of existing normative and institutional commitments into which that regime is being introduced. Carefully attributing the causes of backlash or the reasons why backlash was averted in a particular case can help social change activists develop curative or prophylactic strategies. It is to the question of causation that our attention now turns.

## Sociolegal Backlash: A Causal Account

Specifying the causal antecedents of even a simple social phenomenon is an ambitious and essentially empirical endeavor, so let me say at the outset that my effort here to posit a causal model of sociolegal backlash is necessarily tentative and conjectural. That point conceded, I offer the following general principles as a framework for understanding why, as a general matter, backlash effects emerge, and why they have emerged in response to the Americans with Disabilities Act.

At its core, backlash is about the relationship between a transformative legal regime and the traditional social norms and institutionalized practices it implicates. Specifically, backlash can be expected to occur when the application of a transformative legal regime generates outcomes that conflict with norms and institutions to which influential segments of the relevant populace retain strong conscious allegiance.

Vulnerability to backlash increases, I suggest, if a transformative legal regime is normatively ambiguous or opaque. Normative ambiguity results when a law's moral underpinnings are ill defined or conflict with related norms, or if the law's practical effects diverge from the moral principles on which it was rhetorically premised. Normative opacity results when a transformative law expresses the social, theoretical, or moral vision of an insular subgroup that managed to enact the law, but has failed to disseminate its vision more broadly and has therefore lost control over the law's interpretation and application. Because the broader polity does not understand the moral vision on which the new legal regime is based, the new regime appears to lack normative foundation and thus becomes more vulnerable to sociolegal capture in general, and to backlash effects more specifically.

In the discussion that follows, I examine these ideas and relate them to the ADA. First, I examine a case in which backlash emerged but ultimately failed to derail a particular agenda for sociolegal change. I then attempt to extract from this examination various factors that might help explain the case's counterintuitive outcome and contrast those factors with features of the ADA. Using the ADA as a case in point, I then explore the notion that backlash results from dissonance between the norms advanced by a transformative legal regime and entrenched patterns of normative and institutional commitment into which the new regime is injected. Finally, I argue that the ADA is in certain key respects normatively ambiguous and opaque, as those terms were earlier defined, and demonstrate how this normative ambiguity and opacity have increased the Act's vulnerability to retrenchment and backlash effects.

## Backlash without Retrenchment: The Santa Cruz Appearance Ordinance

In 1993, the Santa Cruz City Council approved an ordinance that banned, among other things, discrimination based on personal appearance.[65] Outside of Santa Cruz, reactions to the ordinance were scathingly negative, reflecting many of the backlash effects earlier described. Media coverage was blistering, characterized by derisive humor aimed at the law, its promoters, and its presumed beneficiaries.

Examples of this coverage are far too numerous to catalog. The following treatment by the *Washington Times,* however, was typical:

Out in Santa Cruz, Calif., the weirdos are on the march double time. The City Council is considering enacting a law that would forbid discrimination on the basis of personal appearance. As a result, every geek in the country seems to be flying, flapping, crawling or hopping into town to squeak and gibber in support of the measure. If it passes next month, the city's population may soon resemble nothing so much as the cast of a 1950's drive-in horror movie . . . One "victim" of "lookism" . . . is 22 year old Cooper Hazen. His contribution to funny-lookingness is his insistence upon wearing a half-inch post in his tongue. His employer at a local psychiatric hospital gave him the heave-ho when he recently discovered this practice. . . . "Thith ith wha gah me thired," confirmed Mr. Hazen to an Associated Press reporter, protruding his tongue with its attachments.[66]

Media coverage like this broadly reflected the familiar "parades of horribles," offering vivid examples of the absurd outcomes the law would supposedly compel. One particularly interesting example of this effect appeared in the *Los Angeles Times:*

Here's a little common-sense test:

Imagine you run a small Jewish deli and you have an opening for a checkout cashier. In walks an applicant with a swastika tattooed prominently on his arm. Do you hire him?

Pretend you own a fast-food restaurant in a predominantly black neighborhood and you need a short-order cook. The most technically qualified person seeking the job is a skinhead fond of wearing a T-shirt emblazoned with the words "White Power." Does he get the job?

Now let's say you're a newspaper editor looking for someone to cover the police beat. An experienced professional journalist wants the job, but he shows up for the interview wearing a dress. Does he get a chance to be our ace crime reporter?

If you live and work in the California cities of Santa Cruz or San Francisco, the answer to all three of these questions had better be yes or you could be in for serious trouble.[67]

Although a number of interesting things can be said about the Santa Cruz ordinance, three observations are particularly significant for our purposes here. First, despite the fact that the ordinance, its promoters, its beneficiaries, and the town of Santa Cruz itself were subjected to widespread, withering ridicule from as far away as Malaysia,[68] the law has apparently never been targeted for repeal. Furthermore, it appears to be operating precisely as its promoters intended, providing a legally enforceable claim to nondiscriminatory treatment in employment, housing, and public accommodations for persons stigmatized by their weight, sexual orientation, gender, or physical attributes.[69]

The second point may help account for the first. The ordinance was first proposed and successfully passed through one of two required city council votes in January 1992. The second vote, which had been scheduled for the following February 11, was postponed in response to the firestorm of negative media coverage and opposition to the ordinance from the Santa Cruz business community. Between the first vote and the second, which was eventually held on May 28, the law was redrafted to narrow the particular aspects of self-presentation it would protect. These revisions eliminated protection for most purposeful changes in personal appearance, such as tattoos and body piercings.

The final provisions of the 1992 ordinance are now codified as part of the Santa Cruz Municipal Code.[70] Section 9.83.010 of the code prohibits discrimination based on age, race, color, creed, religion, national origin, ancestry, disability, marital status, sex, gender, sexual orientation, height, weight or *physical characteristic,* as opposed to physical appearance. "Physical characteristic" is defined in the following way:

> "Physical characteristic" shall mean a bodily condition or bodily characteristic of any person which is from birth, accident, or disease, or from any natural physical development, or any other event outside the control of that person including individual physical mannerisms. Physical characteristic shall not relate to those situations where a bodily condition or characteristic will present a danger to the health, welfare or safety of any individual.[71]

These changes circumscribed the class of people who would be able to invoke the law's protection, but did not by any means exclude all classes of individuals whose inclusion had subjected the ordinance to ridicule. "Out" were people with objectionable body piercings, tattoos, or wild hairstyles. Still "in" were fat people, transsexuals, people who had physical disfigurements or were simply considered "ugly," effeminate men, and others with mannerisms that could be characterized as "outside their control."[72]

One final feature of the Santa Cruz ordinance merits consideration. Under Municipal Code Section 9.83.120, a person claiming to be aggrieved under the law must file a complaint with a city official, who then selects three mediators from a predetermined list. Each party strikes one of the three and is then required to work informally with the remaining mediator to resolve the dispute. As the ordinance provides, "The objective of the mediation process shall be to achieve resolution of the complaint of discrimination by way of an understanding and mutual agreement between the parties. It shall not be to assign liability or fault."[73] If mediation fails, the complainant can file a civil action in any court of competent jurisdiction. As of the writing of this article, however, there were no published decisions interpreting, applying, or even mentioning the law.[74]

Three aspects of this case suggest conditions under which sociolegal retrenchment is more or less likely to occur. First, the ordinance applied only to the City of Santa Cruz—a relatively small and insular jurisdiction. As a result, it does not much matter what opinion-makers or other influential actors in St. Petersburg, Florida, Washington, D.C., Los Angeles, or Malaysia think of the ordinance. Similarly, it does not much matter whether people outside of the law's relatively homogenous compliance community understand, let alone embrace, the norms and values that underlie it. *The community from which the ordinance emerged coextends with the community empowered to interpret and apply it.*

This contrasts sharply with the Americans with Disabilities Act and the Section 504 Regulations on which the ADA was modeled. As earlier described, both were drafted by a relatively insular group of disability activists, joined in the case of the ADA by a small sympathetic group of legislative and administrative officials who understood the sociopolitical model of disability and sought to reify it through federal legislative and regulatory power. But few people outside of this relatively small circle, including the federal judges empowered to interpret the ADA, understand the social model of disability or adhere to the norms, values, and interpretive perspectives it was designed to advance. This situation, I suggest, dramatically increases the ADA's vulnerability to capture and backlash effects.

In contrast to the ADA, a second feature of the Santa Cruz ordinance may have protected it from sociolegal retrenchment. As earlier described, the Santa Cruz law is enforced primarily through mediation, rather than through litigation. As a consequence, disputants and their advocates, rather than judges or other professional legal decision makers, are the agents empowered to "reenact" the law, that is, to infuse it with meaning and apply it to specific disputes. Mediation, much more than litigation, I suggest, encourages disputants to develop an intersubjective understanding of the norms and values implicated by their dispute, and of the relationship of those norms and values to their particular situation. Because they are required to listen to one another, participants in mediation will at least be exposed to each other's normative perspective and to the social meanings each ascribes to the law's technical terms. Consequently, mediated outcomes are less likely than litigated outcomes to turn on technicalities or fine parsings of statutory language. This reduces the influence of many of the mechanisms of sociolegal retrenchment that have so powerfully limited the transformative potential of the ADA.

Finally, in contrast to Section 504 or the ADA, the Santa Cruz ordinance was fully debated, and the major normative objections generated by its earlier versions thoroughly aired by an engaged public, before the law was passed.[75] By eliminating from protection people who had purposefully changed their appearance by, for example, tattooing or body piercing, and by clarifying the right of employers to enforce consensus norms of dress, grooming, and personal hygiene, the law's promoters accomplished a number things. The first is obvious: they reduced the ability of opponents to discredit the ordinance with plausible "parades of horribles" or with humorous depictions of the "absurd" results a literal application of the ordinance might effect.

In addition, by subjecting the ordinance to intense public scrutiny, debate, and eventual modification, its promoters achieved something far more significant. They uncovered a set of core normative principles underlying the new law, connected those principles to key legacy values, and recrafted the statute to ensure that the norms and values the statute was *asserted* to advance were in fact the norms and values that the ordinance would advance *in practice.*

The legacy value most clearly reflected by the modified ordinance can be captured in a familiar aphorism: "You can't (and by implication, should not) judge a book by its cover." Many people stigmatize and discriminate against fat people, people with cosmetic disfigurements, and those simply considered "ugly." But most, if pressed, would admit that they should not. The Santa Cruz ordinance then, despite its nonconventionality, is actually anchored in a deeply entrenched traditional norm that most of us learned as young children. What makes the ordinance transformative, of course, is that it extends the canopy of that norm over traditionally unsheltered groups, like effeminate men, whose "cover" was traditionally, and in most parts of the country is still, seen as revealing some-thing defective about "the book."

In sum, certain features characterizing the Santa Cruz ordinance, absent in connection with the ADA, may have helped protect it from sociolegal retrenchment. First, the community out of which the ordinance emerged coextends with the community empowered to reenact it through interpre-tation and application. Second, before the law was passed, its normative underpinnings were clarified and its connection with legacy and other con-sensus values strengthened. Finally, the law's enforcement mechanisms limit opportunities for construction and application by technically ori-ented legal decision makers and encourage lay disputants to develop mutu-ally acceptable interpretations of the law through dialogue about norms, values, and subjective social meanings. In this way, informal consciousness raising becomes an integral element of the law's enforcement. Ongoing sociocultural change and the law's reenactment through interpretation and application remain closely linked.

### Reasonable Accommodation, Disability Status, and the Social Psychology of Distributive Justice

If, as I have suggested, backlash emerges when the elements of a transfor-mative legal regime conflict with norms and institutions to which influen-tial sociolegal actors retain strong, conscious allegiance, the question arises, precisely what elements of the ADA conflict with preexisting norms and institutionalized practices? Earlier in this article, I described the tension between the direct threat provisions of the Americans with Disabilities Act and a set of entrenched norms and institutionalized practices relating to the management of certain types of perceived workplace risk. The relationship between that tension and the emergence of anti-ADA backlash effects is systematically explored in the article by Vicki Laden and Greg Schwartz appearing earlier in this volume. Laden and Schwartz's analysis highlights one salient example of the type of dissonance between a transformative legal regime and an entrenched set of norms and institutions that generates sociolegal retrenchment and accompanying backlash effects. Here, I explore a second example, by examining how the ADA, under the broad and flexible definition of disability advocated by its proponents, effects out-comes that conflict with a powerful system of entrenched social norms and institutions relating to distributive justice.

At the outset, I should explain why, in examining the Americans with Disabilities Act, I would be discussing distributive justice at all. Harlan

Hahn has persuasively argued[76] that the ADA is not about distributive justice at all; it is about corrective justice. The nondisabled majority simply has trouble understanding this, Hahn maintains, because its members are so inured to the prejudice against the disabled manifested in the built physical environment. Professor Hahn's point is extremely well taken, especially in relation to certain disabilities and corresponding accommodations. Admittedly, a legal mandate compelling a private or public entity to make its buildings physically accessible to persons with mobility impairments has distributive implications. There is only so much money to spend. But such a mandate also provides an easily recognizable correction to an earlier decision by that entity, whether conscious or simply uncaring, to minimize costs at a stigmatized group's expense.

However, it is harder to argue persuasively that accommodation lacks distributive justice implications where the disability category is broad or contested. For example, requiring an employer to allocate a private office to a relatively new, not particularly productive employee diagnosed with attention deficit disorder instead of to a high-seniority, very productive employee who is simply fed up with noise and a lack of privacy has little intuitive connection with corrective justice principles. Its distributive fairness implications, on the other hand, are viscerally clear.

The extent to which the ADA will be seen as having distributive as opposed to corrective justice implications will vary, I suggest, with a set of identifiable factors. These include

The nature of the disability in question (prototypic versus non-prototypic);

The nature of the discrimination involved (disparate treatment versus failure to accommodate);

The nature of the accommodation, if any, at issue (available to everyone, like a curb cut, versus "zero-sum," like a shift assignment; and

The conceptual frame through which disability policy issues are viewed (impairment/social welfarist frame versus social/civil rights frame).

More to the point, whether justified or not, people evidently *view* the ADA as distributing benefits to persons permitted to invoke its protection. This perspective is clearly reflected in newspaper commentaries responsive to the Supreme Court's 1999 definition-of-disability cases.[77] While the following excerpts represent but a tiny fraction of similar expressions of opinion, they amply illustrate my point.

Consider first a statement by former National Public Radio reporter John Hockenberry, now a syndicated columnist and lecturer on disability issues.

> Rather than fixing a specific problem with a specific set of changes, the proponents of the Americans with Disabilities Act have decided to induce change through a series of lawsuits, encouraging people to think of disability as *a non-specific cache of misery redeemable for a compensatory benefit.*[78]

The notion that the ADA is primarily about the allocation of material benefits and privileged treatment, can be seen in the following two excerpts as well:

> The professionally disabled . . . have consistently promoted the expansion of the definition of who is to be included among the disabled and entitled to its protection and benefits. They ignore that *many people want to be seen as disabled when there is a material reward for being defined in this way.* . . . These spokespersons forget that when they demand that everyone be entitled to protection under the ADA, no one will be protected. Worse, those with severe disabilities will be pushed out of the way by those people with minimal or non-existent disabilities who are often in a stronger position physically and financially *to sustain a fight for privilege.*[79]

> [I]f some disabilities were not easily and largely correctable, they conceivably could be used as *legal tickets to employment* even if they entailed some unacceptable risk to others.[80]

The idea that disability status is contested because it has distributive implications is of course nothing new. Exploring the definition of disability under the Social Security Act, Deborah Stone in *The Disabled State*[81] argued that the disability category is controversial precisely because it is used to resolve issues of distributive justice.

As Stone observes, virtually all societies have two parallel distribution systems—a primary or default system, and a secondary system based on need. In most modern contexts, the primary or default distribution system is based on work. Under that system, outputs, or distributions to an individual, correspond with inputs from that individual—that is, from work.[82]

In the modern welfare state, Stone maintains, disability status can entail political privilege as well as social stigma. It can entail privilege because it functions as an administrative status, permitting those who hold it to be excused from participation in the work-based system and to enter the need-based one. Disability status may also provide exemption from other burdens and obligations generally viewed as undesirable, such as military service, debt, even potential criminal liability. As Stone concludes, "Disability programs are political precisely because they allocate these privileges . . . the fight is about privilege rather than handicap or stigma."[83]

In certain situations, being classified as "disabled" within the meaning of the Americans with Disabilities Act can be seen as functioning in a similar way. Such classification removes an individual from an employer's default system of obligation and entitlement and places her in a parallel system, which in certain circumstances is reasonably viewed as more desirable. For example, absent a disability designation, an employee has no right to force her employer to engage in a good faith, interactive process to resolve disputes over job duties, shift assignments, or other aspects of work organization. The ADA imposes such an obligation on employers in relation to requests for accommodation by disabled employees.

Consider a second example: absent a formal learning disability diagnosis, a person who simply works slowly or has difficulty concentrating will not be entitled to extra time on otherwise time-limited educational or licensing examinations.[84] As Mark Kelman and Gillian Lester point out, under current disability discrimination laws, some, but not all, students whose performance fails to meet their or others' expectations receive beneficial entitlements that other students do not receive, but from which they too might benefit.[85] It is hard to argue with the proposition that such a system has significant distributive effects, and that these may shape people's attitudes toward the system itself.

We know a good deal about the factors mediating people's perceptions of distributive justice, and about the rules people apply in assessing the fairness of distributive allocations.[86] The earliest and most widely studied of these rules is the equity principle, which posits that outcomes, or distributions, should be proportional to inputs, or contributions. Within social psychology, equity theory was first developed to explain workers' reactions to wages and promotions,[87] and was later extended in an attempt to explain perceptions of fairness in such far-flung contexts as intimate social relationships,[88] affirmative action,[89] and the division of household chores.[90] By the late 1970s, equity theory had developed into a general psychological theory of justice, broadly used to explain subjective perceptions of distributive fairness across a wide variety of interaction contexts.[91]

Problems associated with this broad, cross-contextual extension quickly emerged as studies yielded results contradicting the theory's predictions. These findings lent empirical support to a theoretical model posited by Morton Deutsch, who suggested that people apply different distributive justice rules in different contexts, depending in part on interaction goals. These distribution rules, according to Deutsch, include the principles of equitable allocation (distributions proportional to relative contributions), equal allocation (equal distributions regardless of contribution), and allocation based on need.[92]

Subsequent research supported both Deutsch's insight that people prefer different distribution rules in different social contexts and his claim that this choice has something to do with interaction goals.[93] This literature reveals certain consistent patterns. In the context of economic relations, including those in the workplace, people tend to apply equity principles,[94] particularly where productivity goals are salient.[95] Where civil rights are implicated, or in other situations where the most important goal is the fostering of harmonious social relationships, people tend to perceive equal distributions as being most fair.[96] Need-based distributions are rarely favored outside a narrow band of contexts, including situations involving close personal relationships, such as those existing within the family, situations where humanitarian social norms have been activated, or where the primary goal being pursued is the fostering of individual development or welfare.[97]

Additional factors appear to influence whether or not people view the application of a particular allocation rule as fair. Edna and Uriel Foa suggest that the nature of the resource being allocated also influences the choice of distribution rule.[98] Preferences for particular rules may vary, for example, according to whether the resource being allocated is perceived as scarce or easily subject to depletion.[99] Other research indicates that the nature of the relationship between the people involved exerts a powerful effect on the choice of an allocation rule.[100] In general, this research shows that closer relationships, such as those existing within the family, are associated with equality or need-based allocations, more distant relationships with equity-based distribution. Other research demonstrates an ideology effect, with conservatives generally supporting equity-based allocations, and liberals generally preferring allocations based on the principle of equality.[101]

Allocation rules can usefully be understood as a type of social norm.

They are acquired, and they function, in much the same way.[102] Just as people care when important social norms are violated, they care when resource allocation decisions violate the contextually appropriate distribution rule. If we want to understand why many people see the reasonable accommodation provisions of the Americans with Disabilities Act and other disability rights statutes as unfair, it makes sense at least to consider the situation from a distributive justice perspective. ADA Title I may be viewed as unfair because it requires the selective application of a need-based allocation principle *in the workplace*—a context in which most people, whether liberal or conservative, do not expect it to apply.

Because it is a needs-based allocation rule, the ADA's reasonable accommodation provisions conflict with both the equity principle, which conservatives and those most concerned with productivity are likely to favor, and the principle of equal allocations, which liberals and those most concerned with fostering harmonious social relationships are apt to support. In the workplace, both productivity and the fostering of harmonious social relationships represent centrally important, highly salient social interaction goals. And while it perhaps would not be so in a truly good world, the promotion of workers' individual, personal welfare is not generally treated as a significant workplace priority.

Accordingly, it is not surprising that most people expect workplace distributions to be governed by some combination of equity and equality principles, rather than in accordance with need. Furthermore, if workplace allocations *are* to be based on need, it is hard to justify a system that considers only certain types of need at the expense of others that might reasonably be viewed as equally pressing.

This problem is exacerbated, I suggest, by the civil rights model of disability itself. Claiming a *right* to a *needs-based allocation* generates powerful normative dissonance, because where political rights are implicated, people expect allocations to be based on the principle of equality, under which everyone is treated the same.[103] Because need-based allocation is viewed as the "wrong" distribution rule to apply in a civil or political rights context, a demand for accommodation, couched in the rhetoric of rights, is viewed by many as "attempting to have it both ways." This viewpoint is vividly illustrated in the following example of news commentary responsive to the Court's summer 1999 definition of disability decisions mentioned earlier in this section:

> Many advocates [for the disabled] . . . see little conflict between demanding that the disabled be treated like everyone else, while

insisting that more physical and mental problems be labeled disabilities, *entitling people to special treatment.*[104]

The problem is harder still in situations involving "invisible" impairments, or conditions that are not viewed as "disabilities" within popular understandings of the disability category. As earlier described, needs-based allocation regimes tend to be viewed as fair in only a narrow band of contexts. In addition to degree of social closeness and interaction goals, three factors can be expected to influence whether people view needs-based distribution as just. These include the nature and extent of the need, the need's distinctiveness, and the causes to which the need is attributed.

An expansive definition of disability can be expected to generate problems on each of these three dimensions. Consider first the problem of "invisible" disabilities, such as cancer, lupus, or many forms of mental illness. Under the medical privacy provisions of the ADA,[105] employers are generally prohibited from disclosing medical information about an employee to his or her peers. As a result, coworkers may know (or suspect) that a particular employee is receiving an accommodation, and may know that he would not be receiving this benefit under equity or equality-based distribution principles, but they might not be permitted to know why the employee is being accorded this "special" treatment. In such situations, coworkers will be unable to evaluate either the nature or extent of the need, and will thus be less likely to view a needs-based distribution as fair. The broad and indeterminate nature of the ADA's definition of disability creates problems on the dimension of distinctiveness as well. Under ADA Section 3, a "person with a disability" is defined in the following way:

Disability. The term "disability" means, with respect to an individual:

(A) a physical or mental impairment that substantially limits one or more of the major life activities of such individual;
(B) a record of such an impairment; or
(C) being regarded as having such an impairment.[106]

Consider the definition under subsection A. Whether a particular individual is deemed a "person with a disability" will depend on how the relevant legal decision maker answers three questions: (1) what qualifies as an "impairment"? (2) what constitutes a "major life activity"? and (3) at what point does a limitation become "substantial"? Application of this highly technical and indeterminate definition of disability will not necessarily generate outcomes matching popular conceptions of either what disability means, or whether a particular claimant would be properly included in the disability category.

"Persons with disabilities" can usefully be viewed as a fuzzy set, that is, a category with no clear boundaries separating members from nonmembers. Fuzzy set theory, initially posited by Berkeley computer scientist Lofti Zadeh,[107] reflects Wittgenstein's earlier observation that, unlike formal theoretical categories, natural categories are indeterminate, in that not all objects viewed as members of a category will possess all of the attributes associated with category membership.[108] The concept of the fuzzy set can usefully be applied in attempting to understand the nature of socially constructed categories, like "the disabled."

Cognitive psychologists Nancy Cantor and Walter Mischel were among the first to apply fuzzy set theory to social categories,[109] and to connect it to the work of Berkeley psychologist Eleanor Rosch. Rosch suggests that natural categories are organized around prototypical category exemplars, which provide the "best" examples of the category, with less prototypical members forming a surrounding network or continuum.[110] This model, especially when considered in conjunction with Zadeh's and Wittgenstein's insights, suggests that judgments of category membership will have a probabilistic quality. The more a candidate for category membership diverges from the category's prototypical exemplars, the lower the probability it will be viewed as a member of the category.

It is reasonable to assume that people view "disability" as distinctive. But the farther a particular claimant's condition diverges from prototypical exemplars of the disability category, the less likely it is that the condition will be recognized as a "disability." If the claimant's condition is not recognized as a disability, people are less likely to view the resulting need as distinctive. If the claimant's condition is not viewed as distinctive, people are less likely to view it as justifying needs-based allocation, especially at others' expense. This analysis suggests that once ADA coverage extends beyond a relatively distinct set of prototypic disabilities associated with an accompanying set of "accommodation schemas,"[111] the law is placed at greater risk of violating established norms governing distributive allocation.

Finally, a substantial body of research indicates that patterns of causal attribution powerfully affect both people's willingness to help a stigmatized other[112] and their support for needs-based distributions in general.[113] This research shows that people are generally less willing to help and less supportive of needs-based distributions if they view stigmatized claimants as responsible for their own predicament. This effect is accentuated by conditions of perceived resource scarcity,[114] the nature of the stigma,[115] and the political orientation of the person making the fairness judgment.[116]

Taken as a whole, this research suggests that people would respond more positively to the reasonable accommodation provisions of the ADA if the class being benefited and the resources being allocated satisfied certain criteria. To maximize public acceptance, the protected class would be narrowly defined. It would, in the language of ADA Section 2, actually comprise "a discrete and insular minority,"[117] whose need for accommodation was both clear and distinctive. Under this approach, both the term "impairment" and the phrase "substantially limit one or more major life activities" would be narrowly construed.

Viewed from a public-acceptance-of-accommodation perspective, the "best" ADA protected class definition would include only those persons with prototypic disabilities, whose social inclusion could be achieved through the use of prototypic accommodations that could readily become institutionalized. It would exclude persons popularly viewed as "responsible for their own predicament." The ADA's drafters must have recognized the rhetorical power of this concept, as the act's findings and purposes section characterizes individuals with disabilities as having being subordinated "based on characteristics that are beyond [their] control."[118]

Disability activists cannot solve these public acceptance problems, however, by simply acceding to the narrow definition of disability presently characterizing judicial interpretations of the ADA. Defining disability in this narrow way frustrates other policy goals that the act's drafters sought to achieve. Moreover, it violates central tenets of the social model of disability upon which the act was premised. In short, concessions that might facilitate public acceptance of one set of policy goals would substantially frustrate the achievement of others.

The ADA was designed to advance two distinct equality projects. People within the disability rights movement view those two projects as thoroughly consistent and compatible, but those outside the movement tend to see them as contradictory and mutually exclusive.

The first of these two projects, which we might refer to as the ADA's "anti-disparate-treatment project" is unambiguously corrective in nature. It prohibits covered entities from discriminating against persons with disabilities in much the same way that the Age Discrimination in Employment Act[119] prohibits discrimination against those over forty. The ADA's anti-disparate-treatment project strongly resembles other similar contemporary projects, such as those undertaken by Title VII, or the Reconstruction Era civil rights acts. As compared to equivalent provisions in those statutes, the anti-disparate-treatment provisions of the ADA forbid similar types of conduct, are grounded in similar norms and values, and share common theoretical and doctrinal frameworks.

Sociologist Richard Scotch refers to the ADA's anti-disparate-treatment project as requiring the removal of "attitudinal barriers" to the full participation of disabled individuals in social, economic, political, and cultural life.[120] These attitudinal barriers include the following sorts of things:

> Social discomfort generated by being in the presence of a person with a stigatizing physical or mental condition, leading to a desire for social and/or physical distance

> Myths and stereotypes about the attributes, abilities, or other characteristics of people with various kinds of stigmatizing physical or mental conditions

> Fears, more or less realistic, but often inflated, about the risks associated with allowing persons with disabilities to perform certain job functions or to be present in the employment context at all

> Concerns, realistic or unrealistic, that persons with certain physical or mental conditions, or having a record of certain physical or mental conditions are at greater risk of future injury or incapacitation, or will be more expensive to insure under medical or other benefit plans, in comparison with other employees not so affected

It is important to note that the social ills targeted by the ADA's anti-disparate-treatment project can occur not only when the target of discriminatory treatment has an actual impairment, but whenever a target person has a stigmatized visible or labeled condition that causes no functional impairment at all. If one interprets the ADA's definition of disability narrowly, as the federal courts have done, mental or physical conditions that result in impairment only because of the biased attitudes of others remain uncovered. This is clearly not what the ADA's drafters intended.

The ADA's second project, which we might refer to as its "structural equality project," differs from the first in significant respects. This project seeks to eliminate barriers to the inclusion of people who *do* have impairments and are disabled not only by attitudes but also by disabling features of the institutional environment. This second project can be interpreted through a corrective justice lens, but it often has significant redistributive implications.

It is important to recognize that in attempting to address both attitudinal and structural barriers, the ADA targets two quite separate types of disadvantagement. It is also important to note that if we examine these two projects closely, we find that they generate considerably different problems that call for inconsistent solutions.

Consider first the definition of the class protected by the ADA, and the relationship of that definition to the specific behavior the statute prohibits or requires and to the norms and values inspiring those prohibitions and requirements. If, as is plainly the case, the statute's drafters intended the ADA to prohibit disparate treatment based on derogating myths and stereotypes, social discomfort effects, or statistical discrimination[121] against persons with stigmatizing physical or mental conditions, the definition of disability should be designed to track patterns of social stigma, irrespective of the presence or absence of actual impairment. It makes little sense to define a disparate treatment class according to the presence or absence of impairment, because people who are not impaired but nonetheless have stigmatizing mental or physical conditions are equally likely to be subjected to the wrong targeted by the statute's disparate treatment provisions. Anyone who, absent statutorily sufficient justification, is subjected to disparate treatment on the basis of a past, present, or imagined mental or physical condition should be entitled to protection of this sort. Accordingly, achievement of the ADA's anti-disparate-treatment project requires a broad definition of disability, geared as much to patterns of stigma as to the presence or absence of actual impairment.

Precisely the opposite approach to the definition of disability, however, would advance the ADA's structural equality project. The ADA's reasonable accommodation provisions often have distributive implications. People's reactions to needs-based distribution regimes can be expected to turn in large measure on perceived characteristics of the class benefiting from the redistribution it prescribes. For a redistributive scheme to be palatable, claimants' needs must be clear, distinctive, stable, and attributable to causes outside their control. In short, to maximize public acceptance of the ADA's reasonable accommodation and disparate impact provisions, the protected class would be limited to those having severe, visible impairments that clearly distinguish them from the general population.

This results in normative incoherence. The class definition that would best cohere with the normative impulses underlying the ADA's structural equality project would frustrate its anti-disparate-treatment agenda. Conversely, the class definition that would best advance the act's anti-disparate-treatment project renders its structural equality project normatively objectionable to large segments of the American public.

To make matters worse, I suggest, large segments of the public, including many judges and media programmers, completely fail to understand the ADA's anti-disparate-treatment agenda. They do not understand that the ADA, even with its redistributive reasonable accommodation provisions, is an antidiscrimination statute, not a social welfare benefits program like Social Security disability, which seeks to provide a safety net for the nonworking disabled.

One consequence of this confusion is that people tend to assume that the ADA should cover only those with the most severe disabilities. The view that the ADA should benefit only those with severe impairments is clearly reflected in a post-*Sutton* editorial in the *Chicago Tribune,* which asserted:

> The ADA was meant to protect people with disabilities—not everyone with a physical ailment or flaw. . . . This distinction is akin to welfare programs that offer financial aid to people in actual poverty but not people who are also in need but slightly above the poverty line.[122]

This excerpt, and many others reflecting a similar perspective, support Matthew Diller's claim, developed earlier in this volume, that the ADA's definition of disability has come under such powerful narrowing pressure because people do not understand that the ADA is an antidiscrimination statute rather than an entitlement program. Indeed, as if attempting to prove Professor Diller's point, media commentary following the Supreme Court's definition of disability cases revealed a shocking lack of understanding that the plaintiffs in those cases were seeking not some sort of entitlement benefit under the ADA, but rather freedom from *unjustified disparate treatment.* Such claims might be lost on the merits, but the plaintiffs in those cases were simply never permitted to litigate them.

One editorial reflected on *Sutton v. United Airlines, Inc.,*[123] in the following terms: "Had the justices ruled the other way, it would have made it impossible for employers to set reasonable physical standards for certain jobs."[124] This is just wrong. Even if the *Sutton* plaintiffs, whose myopic vision was corrected with glasses, had been found to be "persons with disabilities" within the meaning of the ADA, United might well have justified their exclusion under the act's direct threat defense. Putting the policy to that test would have meant confronting the key *normative* issue presented by the case—was United's exclusionary rule a product of irrational myths and stereotypes about corrected myopia, a condition obviously stigmatized within the airline piloting field, or was the policy justified under a reasoned analysis of the risks involved? By deciding the case on the issue of statutory coverage, the *Sutton* Court simply dodged the important normative questions it presented.

It makes sense to exclude persons with corrected impairments from redistributive entitlement programs, like the Social Security disability system. One might even make a creditable argument that persons without present impairments should be excluded from the reasonable accommodation provisions of the ADA. But excluding people with mental or physical defects that do not result in present impairment from protection against disparate treatment ignores the pernicious effects of stigma.

For some combination of reasons, media pundits and federal judges alike have had difficulty understanding the concept of stigma, let alone grasping how it should inform interpretation of the ADA. From a media standpoint, perhaps the clearest example of this can be found in an editorial in the *Plain Dealer,* lauding the Supreme Court's Summer 1999 decisions in *Sutton,*[125] *Kirkingburg,*[126] and *Murphy:*[127]

> The broad reading of the ADA demanded by the near-sighted, *one-eyed,* and hypertensive plaintiffs in the cases that went before the court would have made a mess of litigation. Worse, it would make a mockery of the statute's intent: to prohibit discrimination against the 43 million Americans whose disabilities "substantially limit one or more . . . major life activities" but do not affect their ability to do a particular job.[128]

The very fact that the editorialist would derisively refer to plaintiff Kirkingburg as "one-eyed" and then contrast him with those who are "able to do a particular job" proves the point plaintiff Kirkingburg made but ultimately lost: people with mitigated physical defects may be stigmatized and discriminated against even if their defect does not result in actual impairment. Accordingly, it makes little sense to limit ADA protection against disparate treatment to those with actual, present, or past impairments or with conditions regarded by defendants as impairments.

With the welcome exception of the Supreme Court's decision in *Olmstead v. L.C.,*[129] federal judges interpreting the ADA appear strangely oblivious to the problem of stigma or to the role the ADA's drafters expected it to play in the act's implementation. The best example of this phenomenon appears in the Seventh Circuit's opinion in *Vande Zande v. State of Wisconsin Department of Administration.*[130] Plaintiff Lori Vande Zande, a paraplegic who used a wheelchair, argued that the sink in the employee lounge should have been lowered, at a cost of around two hundred dollars, so that she could reach it from her wheelchair. The defendant argued that this would not be a *reasonable* accommodation: Vande Zande could simply use the sink in the bathroom. Vande Zande opposed this solution on the ground that requiring her to use a bathroom sink when nondisabled employees could use the sink in the kitchenette stigmatized her as different and inferior. Stated Judge Posner in response:

> [W]e do not think an employer has a duty to expend even modest amounts of money to bring about an absolute identity in working conditions between disabled and non-disabled workers. The creation of such a duty would be the inevitable consequence of deeming a failure to achieve identical conditions "stigmatizing." *That is merely an epithet.*[131]

Whatever one may think about the ultimate merits of the *Vande Zande* case, stigma is *not* "merely an epithet." That a federal circuit court judge could characterize the concept in this way gives substance to Professor Hahn's claim that the ADA's crabbed interpretation derives in substantial part from judges' failure to understand the connection between stigma, structural exclusion, and discrimination in the disability rights context.

A second stark example of this "stigma disconnect" can be found in another Seventh Circuit case, *Christian v. St. Anthony Medical Center, Inc.*,[132] in which Judge Posner wrote:

> Suppose that the plaintiff had a skin disease that was unsightly and also very expensive to treat, but neither the disease itself nor the treatment for it would interfere with her work. And suppose her employer fired her nevertheless, either because he was revolted by her disfigured appearance or because the welfare plan that he had set up for his employees was unfunded and he didn't want to incur the expense of the treatment that she required. *Either way he would not be guilty of disability discrimination.*[133]

The court justifies this result on the ground that, although the hypothetical plaintiff's disfigurement was a physical condition, it was not an impairment, and therefore not a "disability" within the meaning of the ADA because it did not, in fact, disable her. She was, after all, able to work.

One can reach this conclusion only by ignoring the role played by attitudinal barriers—stigma—in *producing disability*. Judge Posner's hypothetical plaintiff is indeed disabled, but it is not her condition that disables her. She is disabled by the attitudes of others in her social environment. As Professor Hahn suggests, cases like *Christian v. St. Anthony Medial Center* indeed reflect a startling incomprehension of the social model of disability on which the ADA and other disability rights statutes were based.

As I have suggested throughout this article, the norms, theoretical constructions, and social meanings that underpin the Americans with Disabilities Act have not diffused into popular or judicial legal consciousness. They are somehow "opaque" to those empowered to reenact the ADA through statutory interpretation and application to particular disputes. Generating the political power to enact transformative legislation is, of course, important to any social justice movement. But ultimately, it is the power to control popular discourse and to influence popular understanding of the law, its theoretical underpinnings and normative aspirations, that determines whether it will ultimately effect the social transformation its promoters sought to achieve.

The success of any law designed to transform social norms and institutionalized practices that disadvantage members of subordinated groups turns at least in part on how that law performs on the following dimensions:

1. Can the behavior the law prohibits or requires be described with sufficient precision to avoid creating conditions of severe normative ambiguity?
2. Is the connection between the conduct prohibited or required by the law and the norms and values the law is designed to further clear and strong? Are those norms and values understood and shared by a large enough segment of the affected polity to give the new law "normative legs"?
3. Is the protected class defined in a way that makes clear to its beneficiary and compliance communities precisely who is entitled to the law's protection?
4. Do the contours of the protected class bear a clear and rational relationship to *(a)* the specific conduct the law prohibits or requires; and *(b)* the normative goals and values the law was enacted to further?

The negative reception the ADA is receiving, described in the many articles appearing earlier in this volume, stems at least in part from problems the act has encountered along these four dimensions. The ADA is an extremely complex statute, incorporating many vague standards requiring the case-by-case balancing of underspecified factors. This complexity and underspecification, I suggest, has created a legal environment characterized by intense uncertainty, which has in turn engendered hostility toward the act, its enforcers, and its beneficiaries. Too many influential sociolegal actors simply do not understand the social and moral vision that animates the ADA. Furthermore, the act itself is too complex, its standards too ambiguous and underspecified, to be normatively self-enforcing. In short, the ADA is normatively ambiguous and opaque, and this has increased its vulnerability to sociolegal retrenchment and backlash effects.

## Conclusion

One of the hazards of social justice advocacy is that activists can begin to confuse the question, "How do we think people *should* react to a particular argument, case, or claim?" with the question, "How can we realistically *expect* people to react to that argument, case, or claim?" No matter how frustrating, careful attention to the second question is critical to the success of any social justice initiative.

When law is used as a tool for effecting social change, its architects and promoters within a social justice movement must ask and satisfactorily answer a series of critically important questions: What norms and institutions does the new law seek to displace or transform? Has the process of normative change proceeded to the point that the new law will receive adequate support, or has that aspect of the movement that focuses on enacting transformative legal rules "overspun" itself relative to the pace and momentum of sociocultural change? What norms and institutions not actually targeted by the new law will it implicate or infringe upon? Are people—not just the ill-meaning or thoughtless, but the well-meaning and thoughtful as well—likely to resist interference with these "collateral" norms and values? And finally, how can the new law be structured and implemented so as to adhere to the greatest extent possible with broadly accepted, if yet unrealized, aspirations, values, and ideals?

Any transformative legal regime that fails to reckon successfully with these questions is unlikely to fulfill its architects' expectations. Misunderstood, misconstrued, or directly perceived as illegitimate, it will eventually yield to the mechanisms of sociolegal retrenchment, of which backlash is simply the most conspicuous type.

NOTES

1. *See, e.g.,* Michael Wald, *Comment: Moving Forward, Some Thoughts on Strategies,* 21 BERKELEY J. EMP. & LAB. L. 472 (2000).

2. I draw here on Festinger's concept of cognitive dissonance. *See* LEON FESTINGER, A THEORY OF COGNITIVE DISSONANCE (1957).

3. In connection with this process, see Paul Bohannan, *The Differing Realms of the Law,* 67 AMERICAN ANTHROPOLOGIST, 33, 35–36 (elaborating a theory of "double institutionalization" of social norms when incorporated into formal legal rules).

4. This definition is not drawn from any particular source, but synthesizes definitions and descriptions of the concept of "institution" reflected in various places. *See, e.g.,* Victor Nee & Paul Ingram, *Embeddedness and Beyond: Institutions, Exchange, and Social Science, in* THE NEW INSTITUTIONALISM IN SOCIOLOGY 19 (Mary C. Brinton & Victor Nee eds., 1998) (describing institutions as "webs of interrelated rules and norms that govern social relationships and set formal and informal constraints on actors' 'choice sets'"); HOWARD GARFINKEL, STUDIES IN ETHNOMETHODOLOGY 76 (1967) (describing institutions as background rules that function as the "socially-sanctioned-facts-of-life-in-society-that-any-bona-fide-member-of-society-knows"); PETER L. BERGER & THOMAS LUCKMANN, THE SOCIAL CONSTRUCTION OF REALITY 44, 54 (1967) (characterizing institutions as taken-for-granted patterns of action that transmute subjective meanings into apparently objective "facticities").

5. 42 U.S.C. § 12102(2) (1994).

6. Section 101(8) of the ADA provides in relevant part, "The term 'qualified individual with a disability' means an individual with a disability who, with or without reasonable accommodation, can perform the essential functions of the employment position that such individual holds or desires." 42 U.S.C. § 12111(8).

7. 42 U.S.C. § 12113(b) (1994).

8. *Id.* at § 12116.

9. 29 C.F.R. § 1630.2(r) (emphasis added).

10. This tendency is generally referred to as "hindsight bias." The seminal paper describing the bias is Baruch Fischhoff, *Hindsight [not = ] Foresight: The Effect of Outcome Knowledge on Judgment Under Uncertainty,* 1 J. EXP. PSYCH. 288 (1975). For more recent treatments, see generally Jay J. Christensen-Szalanski & Cynthia Fobian Willham, *The Hindsight Bias: A Meta-analysis,* 48 ORG. BEHAV. & HUMAN DECISION PROCESSES 147 (1991) (reviewing relevant research). For an application of hindsight bias theory to legal adjudication processes, see Jeffrey J. Rachlinski, *A Positive Psychological Theory of Judging in Hindsight,* 65 U. CHI. L. REV. 571 (1998) (arguing that jurors' hindsight bias in effect converts negligence-based liability regimes into systems of quasi-strict liability).

11. For a helpful overview of cognitive biases influencing risk perception, see Paul Slovic et al., *Facts Versus Fears: Understanding Perceived Risk, in* JUDGMENT UNDER UNCERTAINTY: HEURISTICS AND BIASES 465 (Daniel Kahneman et al. eds., 1982).

12. Brookins, RICHMOND TIMES-DISPATCH, May 1997. Reprinted with permission.

13. 29 C.F.R. § 1630.2(r).

14. *See* 42 U.S.C. § 12112(d) (prohibition on preemployment medical examinations and inquiries).

15. I use the term *organizational field* to indicate "a collection of organizations that, in the aggregate, constitute a recognized area of institutional life." Paul J. DiMaggio & Walter W. Powell, *The Iron Cage Revisited: Institutional Isomorphism and Collective Rationality in Organizational Fields, in* PAUL J. DiMAGGIO & WALTER W. POWELL, THE NEW INSTITUTIONALISM IN ORGANIZATIONAL ANALYSIS 65 (1991). So, for example, civil service employment in many different states and localities might constitute an organizational field, as would employment in related skilled trades, or specific industries.

16. For examples, see, e.g., TOM R. TYLER ET AL., SOCIAL JUSTICE IN A DIVERSE SOCIETY 53–54 (1997) (effect of subjective perceptions of justice on evaluation of social information); Linda Hamilton Krieger, *Civil Rights Perestroika: Intergroup Relations After Affirmative Action,* 86 CAL. L. REV. 1251, 1327–29 (1998) (effects of attribution bias on civil rights adjudications); Jody Armour, *Stereotypes and Prejudice: Helping Legal Decisionmakers Break the Prejudice Habit,* 83 CAL. L. REV. 733 (1995) (effect of social stereotypes on jury decision making); Albert Moore, *Trial by Schema: Cognitive Filters in the Courtroom,* 37 UCLA L. REV. 273 (1989) (sources of cognitive bias, broadly conceived, in jury decision making).

17. Lauren Edelman et al., *Employers' Handling of Discrimination Complaints: The Transformation of Rights in the Workplace,* 27 LAW & SOC. REV. 497 (1993).

18. *Id.*

19. Lauren Edelman and her collaborators have referred to this phenomenon as reflecting the "endogeneity" of law. Edelman et al., *supra* note 17, at 407; Lauren B. Edelman, *Constructed Legalities: Socio-Legal Fields and the Endogeneity of Law, in* BENDING THE BARS OF THE IRON CAGE: INSTITUTIONAL DYNAMICS AND PROCESSES (Walter W. Powell & Daniel L. Jones eds., 2000).

20. 122 S. Ct. 1516 (2002).

21. title VII's bona fide seniority system defense appears at 42 U.S.C. §2000e–2 (h). The ADEA analog appears at 29 U.S.C. §623(f), and the EPA analog at 29 U.S.C. §206(d)(1).

22. H.R. Rep. No. 101–485, pt. 2, p. 65, 68 (1990), U.S. Code Cong. & Admin. News 1990, pp. 303, 345, 350 (stating that the existence of a collectively bargained protection for seniority would not be determinative of whether an accommodation was "reasonable" within the meaning of the ADA); S. Rep. No. 101–16, p. 32 (1989) (same).

23. Barnett v. US Airways, 228 F.3d 1105 (2000).

24. 122 S. Ct. at 1525.

25. 122 S. Ct. at 1525.

26. 122 S. Ct. at 1523.

27. 122 S. Ct. at 1524.

28. Historical references to the civil rights movement of the 1950s and 1960s are taken from DAVID J. CARROW, BEARING THE CROSS: MARTIN LUTHER KING, JR. AND THE SOUTHERN CHRISTIAN LEADERSHIP CONFERENCE (1988).

29. For a comprehensive discussion of this point, see generally Michael J. Klarman, *Brown, Racial Change, and the Civil Rights Movement,* 80 VA. L. REV. 7 (1994).

30. RICHARD SCOTCH, FROM GOOD WILL TO CIVIL RIGHTS (1984).

31. *See id.* at 139–41.

32. *Id.* at 51–52, 54.

33. *Id.* at 54.

34. EDWARD D. BERKOWITZ, DISABLED POLICY: AMERICA'S PROGRAMS FOR THE HANDICAPPED 212 (1987).

35. *See* SCOTCH, *supra* note 22, at 143–45.

36. *Id.* at 112; *see also* JOSEPH CALIFANO, GOVERNING AMERICA 259 (1982).

37. *See* SCOTCH, *supra* note 22, at 145.

38. *See id.; see also* JOSEPH P. SHAPIRO, NO PITY: PEOPLE WITH DISABILITIES FORGING A NEW CIVIL RIGHTS MOVEMENT 66–69 (1993).

39. *Id.* at 69.

40. *Id.* at 74.

41. I do not mean to imply that disability rights activism was not occurring in other locations. Such a claim would be patently incorrect. For example, American Disabled for Accessible Public Transit (ADAPT), founded in 1983, conducted numerous civil disobedience actions around the country during the 1980s and 1990s, agitating for accessible public transit facilities. For a description of ADAPT's efforts in this regard, see SHAPIRO, *supra* note 30, at 128–29.

42. *Id.* at 128.

43. For a description of the Wheels of Justice action, see *id.* at 130–36.

44. *Public Attitudes Toward People with Disabilities,* conducted for the National Organization on Disability by Louis Harris and Associates, Inc. (1991), cited in SHAPIRO, *supra* note 30, at 328–29.

45. *Id.*

46. 347 U.S. 483 (1954).

47. *See, e.g.,* Henningsen v. Bloomfield Motors, Inc., 32 N.J. 358, 161 A.2d 69 (1960) (holding both manufacturer of a defective automobile and the dealer who sold it liable for product defect on a strict liability theory); Heaton v. Ford Motor Co., 248 Or. 467, 435 P.2d 806 (1967) (same). *See generally* Page Keeton, *Product Liability—Some Observations About Allocation of Risks,* 64 MICH. L. REV. 1329 (1966) (describing judicial development of doctrine of strict liability in tort for defective products).

48. *See, e.g.,* RICHARD EPSTEIN, FORBIDDEN GROUNDS: THE CASE AGAINST EMPLOYMENT DISCRIMINATION LAWS (1992) (opposing antidiscrimination regulation on economic efficiency grounds).

49. Between 1973, when the Supreme Court decided *McDonnell Douglas Corp. v. Green,* 411 U.S. 792, and 1981, when it decided *Texas Dept. of Community Affairs v. Burdine,* 450 U.S. 248, courts divided on whether the burden that shifted after plaintiff established a prima facie case was a burden of proof, or merely a burden of producing evidence of a legitimate, nondiscriminatory reason. In *Burdine,* the Court decided that issue in defendants' favor, but stated that the plaintiff could carry her ultimate burden of proving that the defendant's proffered reason was pretextual either directly, by showing that discrimination more likely motivated its action, or indirectly, by establishing that its proffered reason was "unworthy of proof." 450 U.S. 248 at 255 n.10. As a practical matter, that standard was further narrowed in *St. Mary's Honor Ctr. v. Hicks,* 509 U.S. 502 (1993), in which the Supreme

Court held that establishing pretext did not, as a matter of law, entitle the plaintiff to judgment.

50. *See, e.g.*, East Texas Motor Freight Sys. v. Rodriguez, 431 U.S. 395 (1977) (questioning "across the board" approach to class actions previously permitted in Title VII cases); General Telephone Co. v. Falcon, 457 U.S. 147 (1982) (rejecting "across the board" approach outright).

51. Although a systematic discussion of these various devices is beyond the scope of this article, one example is the "same actor inference," now an accepted feature of Title VII disparate treatment doctrine in most federal circuits. For an analysis of the same actor inference, see Krieger, *supra* note 16, at 1310, 1314 (1998).

52. *Compare* Domingo v. New England Fish Co., 727 F.2d 1429, 1435–36 (9th Cir. 1975) (finding word-of-mouth hiring discriminatory because of its tendency to perpetuate the all-white composition of the employer's workforce) *and* NAACP v. Evergreen, 693 F.2d 1367, 1369 (11th Cir. 1982) (same) *with* EEOC v. Consolidated Serv. Sys. 989 F.2d 233, 235–36 (7th Cir. 1993) (holding that word-of-mouth recruitment does not violate Title VII under a disparate treatment theory; it was the most cost-effective method of recruitment and there was no evidence of invidious bias against any underrepresented group) *and* EEOC v. Chicago Miniature Lamp Works, 947 F.2d 292, 298–99 (7th Cir. 1991) (refusing to apply disparate impact theory in case challenging word-of-mouth recruitment practices).

53. Griggs v. Duke Power Co., 401 U.S. 424 (1971).

54. *See, e.g.*, Wards Cove Packing Co. v. Atonio, 490 U.S. 642, 650 (1989) (requiring showing of disparate impact to be based on statistics limited to qualified persons in the relevant labor market); EEOC v. Chicago Miniature Lamp Works, *supra* note 44, at 298–99 (refusing to apply disparate impact theory in case challenging word-of-mouth recruitment practices); Pegues v. Mississippi State Employment Serv., 699 F.2d 760, 766–67 (5th Cir. 1983), *cert. denied,* 464 U.S. 991 (1983) (imposing strict requirement regarding proof of causation in disparate impact cases); Carroll v. Sears, Roebuck & Co., 708 F.2d 183, 189 (5th Cir. 1983) (refusing to apply disparate impact theory to challenge a test that was only one of many factors considered in making hiring decisions).

55. Two informative treatments of Title VII enforcement by the EEOC during the Reagan years addressing these and other issues include David L. Rose, *Twenty-Five Years Later: Where Do We Stand on Equal Employment Opportunity Law Enforcement?* 42 VAND. L. REV. 1121 (1989), and Eleanor Holmes Norton, *Equal Employment Law: Crisis in Interpretation: Survival Against the Odds,* 62 TULANE L. REV. 681 (1988).

56. *See* Lauren Edelman, *Legal Ambiguity and Symbolic Structures: Organizational Mediation of Law,* 97 AMER. J. SOCIOL. 1531 (1992) (discussing the organizational construction of symbolic indicia of compliance with antidiscrimination laws).

57. *See generally* Lauren Edelman et al., *supra* note 17.

58. *See, e.g.*, SHELBY STEELE, THE CONTENT OF OUR CHARACTER (1990); SHELBY STEELE, A DREAM DEFERRED: THE SECOND BETRAYAL OF BLACK FREEDOM IN AMERICA (1998); V. Dion Haynes, *Called "Blasphemy," Spot Won't Run: King Speech in GOP Ad Sparks Furor,* CHI. TRIB., Oct. 25, 1996 (describing argument

advanced by Ward Connerly to the effect that merit-based decision-making systems are needed to "bring the races together").

59. *See, e.g.,* Dee Ann Durbin, *Debaters Take Their Shots on Prop. 209: U.C. Regent, Attorney Vie over Affirmative Action,* SAN DIEGO UNION-TRIB., Oct. 9, 1996 (describing anecdote regarding a white male student denied admission to U.C. San Diego Medical School, used in debate by U.C. Regent Ward Connerly); Jeff Howard & Ray Hammond, *Rumors of Inferiority: The Hidden Obstacles to Black Success,* NEW REPUBLIC 17 (Sept. 1985) (positing that affirmative action creates a debilitating sense of self-doubt in beneficiaries).

60. The "quota queen" label originated with a piece in the *Wall Street Journal* bearing the headline "Clinton's Quota Queens." The piece was authored by Clint Bolick, a former Justice Department attorney and aide to William Bradford Reynolds, Chief of the Civil Rights Division during the Reagan administration. *See* Linda Feldman, *Failure to Combat Labels Sunk Justice Nominee,* CHRISTIAN SCI. MONITOR, June 7, 1993, at 4 (stating that "it was Mr. Bolick who fired the first salvo—a column in the Wall Street Journal titled 'Clinton's Quota Queens'—after Ms. Guinier's nomination was announced April 29").

Both print and broadcast media coverage of the Guinier nomination regularly repeated the slur, to the point that it became emblematic of the Guinier affair. As one article noted, "[T]he fatal error, Guinier's supporters say, was the White House's failure to counter the 'quota queen' epithet, which worked its way into other media and into the Zeitgeist." *See id.* For examples of the label's use in the broadcast media, see, e.g., *All Things Considered* (National Public Radio Broadcast, June 2, 1993); *see also* Catherine Crier & Bernard Shaw, *Controversial Guinier Nomination Hits Senate* (CNN Broadcast of *Inside Politics,* June 2, 1993, transcript 345).

President Clinton withdrew the Guinier nomination on June 3, 1993. *See Clinton Drops Guinier as Choice for Civil Rights Post; Avoids a Fight over Writings on Race,* FACTS ON FILE WORLD NEWS DIG., June 10, 1993, at 422, A2.

61. *See, e.g.,* Piscataway Township Board of Ed. v. Taxman, 91 F.3d 1547 (3d Cir. 1996) (en banc), *cert. granted,* 521 U.S. 1117 (1997), *cert. dismissed,* 522 U.S. 1010 (1997); Hopwood v. Texas, 84 F.3d 720, *cert. denied,* 518 U.S. 1033 (1996); Adarand Constructors v. Pena, 515 U.S. 200 (1995).

62. *See, e.g.,* Civil Rights Restoration Act of 1997, S. 46 105th Cong. (1997) (introduced, but not passed); Civil Rights Act of 1997, H.R. 1909, 105th Cong. (1997) (introduced, but not passed); Racial and Gender Preference Reform Act, H.R. 2079, 105th Cong. (1997) (introduced, but not passed).

63. For a discussion of various such initiatives contemporaneous with California's Proposition 209, see Linda Hamilton Krieger, *Civil Rights Perestroika, supra* note 16 at 1255 n.10.

64. 21 F.3d 603 (5th Cir. 1994) (holding that law school may not use race as a factor in admissions, despite the goal of improving diversity and remedying past discrimination), *reh'g en banc denied,* 84 F.3d 720, *cert. denied,* 518 U.S. 1033.

65. SANTA CRUZ, CAL., ORDINANCE 92–11 (Apr. 28, 1992).

66. *Santa Cruz' Weirdocracy,* WASH. TIMES, Jan. 21, 1992, at F2.

67. Joseph Farah, *Job Bias Law Takes a Walk in Purple Zone; Some Cities May Prohibit Discrimination in Hiring on the Basis of Appearance,* L.A. TIMES, February 7, 1993, at 5.

68. *See* Shukor Rahman, *Looks Still Count,* NEW STRAITS TIMES (Malaysia), Sep. 12, 1997, at 8. The NEW STRAITS TIMES article described the ordinance as follows: "In 1992, Santa Cruz, a coastal town about 120 km south of San Francisco, imposed an unprecedented ban on discrimination in employment and housing based on a person's looks. The law, believed to be the most far-reaching 'anti-lookism' statute in the US, protects not only 'ugly' people but also the fat, skinny, short, toothless and anyone else with abnormal physical traits."

69. So, for example, in 1995, the Body Image Task Force used the Santa Cruz ordinance to negotiate an agreement with theater companies United Artists and the Harris Group to install a certain number of extra wide seats in newly constructed theaters so as to accommodate fat moviegoers. *See Large Moviegoers Demand Large Seats,* NEWS & RECORD (Greensboro, N.C.), Feb. 17, 1995, at W2; Leah Garchik, *Room with a View,* SAN FRAN. CHRON., Feb. 8, 1995, at F8.

70. SANTA CRUZ, CAL., CODE § 9.83 ("Prohibition against Discriminating").

71. SANTA CRUZ, CAL. CODE § 9.83.020(13). Discrimination based on "personal appearance" is prohibited only in housing. Section 21.01.010 of the code provides:

It shall be unlawful for any person having the right to rent or lease any housing accommodation to discriminate against any person on the basis of race, color, creed, religion, national origin, ancestry, disability, marital status, sex, sexual orientation, personal appearance, pregnancy or tenancy of a minor child except as provided for by state law.

"Personal appearance" is not defined.

72. *See id.*

73. *See id.* at § 9.83.120.

74. This was the case as of a LEXIS search performed June 18, 2001.

75. It is not my intention to imply that this sort of debate and statutory tailoring was completely absent from the process leading up to the enactment of the act. ADA Section 508, now codified at 42 U.S.C. § 12209, for example, explicitly excludes transvestitism from the definition of disability. Section 511 explicitly exempts other controversial conditions as well. 42 U.S.C. § 12211. However, the inclusion of mental disabilities, and the broad, flexible definition of disability set out in ADA Section 3, left ample room for normative ambiguity and dissension.

76. *See, e.g.,* Harlan Hahn, *Civil Rights for Disabled Americans: The Foundations of a Political Agenda, in* IMAGES OF THE DISABLED/DISABLING IMAGES 281 (A. Gartner & T. Joe eds., 1987); Harlan Hahn, *Toward a Politics of Disability: Definition, Disciplines, and Politics, in* 22 SOC. SCI. J. 87 (1985); Harlan Hahn, *Reconceptualizing Disability: A Political Science Perspective,* 48 REHABILITATION LITERATURE 362 (1984) (positing a civil rights model of disability premised on corrective justice principles).

77. These include *Sutton v. United Airlines, Inc.,* 527 U.S. 471, 119 S. Ct. 2139 (1999) (corrective lenses and myopia), *Murphy v. United Parcel Serv., Inc.,* 527 U.S. 516, 119 S. Ct. 2133 (1999) (hypertension controlled by medication), and *Albertson's, Inc. v. Kirkingburg,* 527 U.S. 555, 119 S. Ct. 2162 (1999) (monocular vision).

78. John Hockenberry, *Disability Games,* N.Y. TIMES, June 29, 1999, at 19 (emphasis added).

79. Bill Bolt, *Commentary: Ruling Is a Blow to the Disabled but It's Also an Opportunity*, L.A. TIMES, June 27, 1999, at 5 (emphasis added).

80. *Wise Ruling on Disability Law*, DENVER ROCKY MOUNTAIN NEWS, June 25, 1999, at 52A (emphasis added).

81. DEBORAH STONE, THE DISABLED STATE (1984).

82. Of course, this is not always the case. Principles other than work at times function as the applicable distribution rule. Veteran status, for example, or seniority, or in the case of preferential affirmative action programs, racial, ethnic, or gender characteristics, may also function as distribution rules. In any event, when need will be permitted to trump any other applicable distribution rules is a critical question in virtually any society, whatever its default distribution system might be.

83. STONE, *supra* note 73, at 28.

84. For a thorough and sharply critical analysis of the distributive justice implications of disability discrimination laws in the educational context, see MARK KELMAN & GILLIAN LESTER, JUMPING THE QUEUE: AN INQUIRY INTO THE LEGAL TREATMENT OF STUDENTS WITH LEARNING DISABILITIES (1997).

85. *See id.*

86. For a comprehensive review of research on subjective perceptions of distributive justice, see TOM R. TYLER ET AL., *supra* note 16, at 45–74. It should be noted that virtually all of this research was conducted in the United States. Because conceptions of justice are socially constructed, the study's findings should not be generalized to other countries or cultures.

87. For examples of this early work, see J. S. Adams & W. B. Rosenbaum, *The Relationship of Worker Productivity to Cognitive Dissonance About Wage Inequities*, 46 J. OF APPLIED PSYCHOL. 161 (1962); J. S. Adams, *Inequity in Social Exchange, in* 2 ADVANCES IN EXPERIMENTAL SOC. PSYCHOLOGY 267 (Leonard Berkowitz ed., 1965).

88. *See, e.g.,* E. Hatfield & J. Traupmann, *Intimate Relationships: A Perspective from Equity Theory, in* PERSONAL RELATIONSHIPS (S. Duck & R. Gilmour eds., 1981); E. Hatfield et al., *Equity Theory and Intimate Relationships, in* SOCIAL EXCHANGE IN DEVELOPING RELATIONSHIPS (R. L. Burgess & T. I Huston eds., 1979).

89. *See, e.g.,* Rupert Barnes Nacoste, *Sources of Stigma: Analyzing the Psychology of Affirmative Action*, 12 LAW AND POL'Y 175 (1990) (exploring implications of equity theory for the affirmative action debate).

90. J. M. Steil & B. A. Turetsky, *Is Equal Better? The Relationship Between Marital Equality and Psychological Symptomatology, in* FAMILY PROCESSES AND PROBLEMS: SOCIAL PSYCHOLOGICAL ASPECTS (S. Oskamp ed., 1987).

91. The classic statement of this view can be found in E. WALSTER ET AL., EQUITY: THEORY AND RESEARCH (1978).

92. *See* MORTON DEUTSCH, DISTRIBUTIVE JUSTICE (1985).

93. *See generally* T. R. TYLER ET AL., *supra* note 16 at 56–60; *see also* Elizabeth A. Mannix et al., *Equity, Equality, or Need? The Effects of Organizational Culture on the Allocation of Benefits and Burdens*, 63 ORGANIZATIONAL BEHAVIOR AND HUMAN DECISION PROCESSES 276 (1995) (business managers base allocations on equity when productivity goals are salient and on equality when pursuing interpersonal harmony within the workplace); GEROLD MIKULA, JUSTICE AND SOCIAL INTERACTION 177–79, 187–88 (1980) (discussing the interaction goals furthered by differing distributive allocation rules).

94. *See, e.g.,* Jerald Greenberg, *Equity and Workplace Status: A Field Experiment,* 73 J. OF APPLIED PSYCHOL. 606 (1988) (demonstrating, in an employment rather than a lab setting, that subjects adjust outputs to match distributions as predicted by equity theory). *See generally* T. R. TYLER ET AL., *supra* note 16, at 57, 59 (reviewing research).

95. *See* Edith Barrett-Howard & Tom R. Tyler, *Procedural Justice as a Criterion in Allocations Decisions,* 50 J. PERSONALITY AND SOC. PSYCHOL. 296 (1986) (people who view productivity as a goal are more likely to use equity as a justice standard.); E. A. Mannix et al., *supra* note 85 (showing association between productivity versus social harmony goal orientation and choice of distribution rule).

96. *See, e.g.,* Tom R. Tyler, *Justice in the Political Arena, in* THE SENSE OF INJUSTICE: SOC. PSYCHOL. PERSPECTIVES 192–93, 194–97 (Robert Folger ed., 1984) (reviewing research indicating that people prefer allocation according to the principle of equality in the context of political rights); Tom R. Tyler & Eugene Griffin, *The Influence of Decision Makers' Goals on Their Concerns About Procedural Justice,* 21 J. OF APPLIED SOC. PSYCHOL. 1629 (1991) (demonstrating difference in allocation preferences depending on whether decision makers were more concerned about promoting positive interpersonal relations or enhancing productivity); E. Barrett-Howard & T. R. Tyler, *supra* note 87 (illustrating that those who view social harmony as a goal are more likely to choose equality as applicable distribution rule); E. A. Mannix et al., *supra* note 85 (same).

97. DEUTSCH, *supra* note 84, at 146–47; MIKULA, *supra* note 85 at 187–88; Lerner, Miller, & Holmes 1976 (Need is likely to be the operative distribution principle within the family, where the legitimate needs of the various members tend to determine distribution, regardless of the members' relative contributions); Prentice & Crosby 1987 (In work settings, judgments of deservingness are governed by equity principles, but at home, deservingness is judged according to need).

98. Edna. B. Foa & Uriel G. Foa, *Resource Theory of Social Exchange, in* CONTEMPORARY TOPICS IN SOCIAL PSYCHOLOGY (John W. Thibaut et al. eds., 1976) (early explication of resource theory). For a more comprehensive discussion of resource theory, see RESOURCE THEORY: EXPLORATIONS AND APPLICATIONS (Uriel G. Foa et al. eds., 1993) (reviewing theory and research).

99. *See* T. R. TYLER ET AL., *supra* note 16, at 61.

100. *See* A. P. Fiske, *The Four Elementary Forms of Sociality: Framework for a Unified Theory of Social Relations,* 99 PSYCHOL. REV. 689 (1992) (differentiating between allocation rules applied in four types of relationships, including communal sharing, authority ranking, equality matching, and market pricing); G. Mikula et al., *What People Regard as Unjust: Types and Structures of Everyday Experiences of Injustice,* 20 EUROPEAN J. OF SOC. PSYCHOL. 133 (1990) (arguing that relationship type matters more than interaction goal); E. Barrett-Howard & T. R. Tyler, *supra* note 87, at 206 (1986) (showing that the nature of relationship influences both the interaction goals pursued and the allocation rules preferred); Morton Deutsch, *Interdependence and Psychological Orientation, in* COOPERATION & HELPING BEHAVIOR (V. J. Delilega & J. Grzelak eds., 1982) (arguing that the extent of interdependence between participants to the interaction influences choice of distribution rule); H. Lamm & E. Keyser, *The Allocation of Monetary Gain and Loss Following Dyadic Performance: The Weight Given to Effort and Ability Under Conditions of*

*Low and High Intra-Dyadic Attraction,* 8 EUROPEAN J. OF SOC. PSYCHOL. 275 (1978) (illustrating that the nature of relationship influences choice of equity versus need as applicable distribution rule).

101. *See* L. J. Skitka & P. E. Tetlock, *Allocating Scarce Resources: A Contingency Model of Distributive Justice,* 28 J. OF EXPERIMENTAL SOCIAL PSYCHOL. 491 (1992); K. Rasinski, *What's Fair Is Fair . . . Or Is It? Value Differences Underlying Public Views About Social Justice,* 53 J. PERSON. & SOC. PSYCHOL. 201 (1987).

102. For a discussion of the development of context-dependent allocation rule awareness in young children, see C. Sigelman & K. Waitzman, *The Development of Distributive Justice Orientations: Contextual Influences on Children's Resource Allocations,* 62 CHILD DEVELOPMENT 1367 (1991) (discussing children's developing awareness of the socially sanctioned allocation rules applicable in differing social contexts).

103. For a review of research supporting this proposition, see Tyler, *supra* note 88, at 192–97.

104. Robert J. Samuelson, *Dilemmas of Disability,* WASH. POST, June 30, 1999, at A3.

105. 42 U.S.C. § 12112(d)(3)(B) (1994).

106. 42 U.S.C. § 12102(2) (1994).

107. Lofti Zadeh's seminal paper on the subject of "fuzzy sets" is *Fuzzy Sets,* 8 INFORMATION AND CONTROL 338 (1965). For additional overviews of fuzzy set theory and its applications, see generally Lofti A. Zadeh, FUZZY SETS AND THEIR APPLICATIONS TO COGNITIVE AND DECISION PROCESSES (King-Sun Fu et al. eds., 1975); Lofti A. Zadeh, FUZZY SETS AND APPLICATIONS: SELECTED PAPERS (Ronald R. Yager ed., 1987).

108. Ludwig Wittgenstein, PHILOSOPHICAL INVESTIGATIONS 232 (G.E.M. Anscombe trans., 1953).

109. Nancy Cantor & Walter Mischel, *Prototypes in Person Perception, in* 12 ADVANCES IN EXPERIMENTAL SOCIAL PSYCHOL. 3, 8–13 (Leonard Berkowitz ed., 1979).

110. Eleanor Rosch et al., *Basic Objects in Natural Categories,* 8 COGNITIVE PSYCHOL. 382 (1976); Eleanor Rosch, *Cognitive Reference Points,* 1 COGNITIVE PSYCHOL. 532 (1975).

111. I use the phrase "accommodation schema" in the sense that disabled parking spaces, curb cuts, and larger bathroom stalls in public restrooms have become readily recognized, or "scripted" accommodations for paraplegia or other mobility disorders. Allowing guide dogs (but not other dogs) in public accommodations, for example, is a prototypical accommodation for the corresponding prototypical disability of blindness. One way at looking at the question of "prototypical" versus "nonprototypical" accommodations is to recognize that certain accommodations are becoming "institutionalized," as that concept was defined above.

112. Much of the empirical work in this area has been conducted by Bernard Weiner and his colleagues. *See, e.g.,* Bernard Weiner, *On Perceiving the Other as Responsible, in* NEBRASKA SYMPOSIUM ON MOTIVATION 165 (Richard Dienstbier et al. eds., 1990) (discussing importance of attribution-based perceived controllability on reactions to stigmas and willingness to help); Bernard Weiner & Raymond P. Perry, *An Attributional Analysis of Reactions to Stigmas,* 55 J. PERSONALITY & SOC.

PSYCHOL. 738 (1988) (examining perceived controllability and stability of physically vs. mentally based stigmas and assessing effect of controllabilty/stability judgments on pity, anger, and willingness to help).

113. *See* Linda J. Skitka & Philip E. Tetlock, *Allocating Scarce Resources: A Contingency Model of Distributive Justice,* 28 J. OF EXPERIMENTAL SOCIAL PSYCHOLOGY 491 (1992) (demonstrating effect of attribution of need, political ideology, and perceived resource scarcity of reactions to need-based distribution).

114. *See id.*

115. For example, people are generally less willing to help targets with stigmatizing mental impairments than stigmatizing physical impairments. The effect appears to be mediated by people's beliefs about the controllability and stability of mental/behavioral versus physical conditions.

116. *See* Linda J. Skitka & Philip E. Tetlock, *Providing Public Assistance: Cognitive and Motivational Processes Underlying Liberal and Conservative Policy Preferences,* 65 J. PERSONALITY & SOC. PSYCHOLOGY 1205 (1993) (demonstrating mediating effect of ideology on attribution of need and reactions to need-based resource allocation under conditions of perceived scarcity and nonscarcity).

117. ADA Section 2(a)(7) provides:

> [I]ndividuals with disabilities are a discrete and insular minority who have been faced with restrictions and limitations, subjected to a history of purposeful unequal treatment, and relegated to a position of political powerlessness in our society, based on characteristics that are beyond the control of such individuals and resulting from stereotypic assumptions not truly indicative of the individual ability of such individuals to participate in, and contribute to, society.

42 U.S.C. § 12101(a)(7) (1999).

118. *Id.*

119. Age Discrimination in Employment Amendments of 1996, 29 U.S.C. § 621.

120. SCOTCH, *supra* note 22.

121. "Statistical discrimination" is the kind of discrimination that results from the use of group status as a proxy for decision-relevant traits. So, for example, the exclusion of all individuals with a history of a particular medical condition, on the rational ground that they present an elevated risk of future injury or incapacitation, is a form of statistical discrimination.

122. CHI. TRIB., June 24, 1999, at 28.

123. 527 U.S. 471, 119 S. Ct. 2139 (1999) (holding that corrected myopia does not constitute a disability within the meaning of the ADA).

124. *Defining Disability,* INDIANAPOLIS STAR, June 25, 1999, at A18.

125. 119 S. Ct. 2139 (1999).

126. Albertson's v. Kirkingburg, 527 U.S. 555, 119 S. Ct. 2162 (1999) (holding that monocular vision is not a disability within the meaning of the ADA).

127. Murphy v. United Parcel Serv., Inc., 527 U.S. 516, 119 S. Ct. 2133 (1999) (holding that hypertension controlled with medication is not a disability within the meaning of the ADA).

128. *Blowing Away a Legislative Fog: High Court Injects a Welcome Dose of Com-*

*mon Sense into the Americans with Disabilities Act,* PLAIN DEALER, June 25, 1999, at 8B (emphasis added).

129.  527 U.S. 581, 119 S. Ct. 2176 (1999) (ADA Title II held to require states, under certain circumstances, to provide persons with mental disabilities with community-based treatment rather than placement in an institution).

130.  44 F.3d 538 (7th Cir. 1995).

131.  44 F.3d at 545 (emphasis added).

132.  117 F.3d 1051 (7th Cir. 1997), *cert. denied,* 523 U.S. 1022 (1998).

133.  *Id.* at 1053.

# Contributors

**Ruth Colker, J.D.** holds the Heck-Faust Memorial Chair in Constitutional Law at the Ohio State University College of Law. She has written extensively on the Americans with Disabilities Act and is coauthor of a leading casebook on disability law. Recent publications include *Winning and Losing under the ADA, ADA Title III: A Fragile Compromise, The Americans with Disabilities Act: A Windfall for Defendants,* THE LAW OF DISABILITY DISCRIMINATION, 3d ed. (with Bonnie P. Tucker), and AMERICAN LAW IN THE AGE OF HYPERCAPITALISM: THE WORKER, THE FAMILY, AND THE STATE .

**Lennard J. Davis, Ph.D.** is Professor of English and Professor of Disability Studies and Human Development at the University of Illinois, Chicago. Professor Davis has written extensively in both deaf studies and disability studies, and is the editor of the DISABILITY STUDIES READER. Other recent publications include MY SENSE OF SILENCE: MEMOIR OF A CHILDHOOD WITH DEAFNESS, and ENFORCING NORMALCY: DISABILITY, DEAFNESS, AND THE BODY. He has also edited a collection of his parents' correspondence, entitled, "SHALL I SAY A KISS?": COURTSHIP LETTERS OF A DEAF COUPLE, 1936–1938. His newest book is *Bending Over Backwards: Disability, Dismodernism, and Other Difficult Positions.*

**Matthew Diller, J.D.** is Professor of Law at Fordham University School of Law. Professor Diller has written extensively in the areas of disability policy, focusing on the intersection of disability issues with public benefits policy. His recent publications include *Dissonant Disability Policies: The Tensions between the Americans with Disabilities Act and Federal Disability Benefit Programs; Entitlement and Exclusion: The Role of Disability in the Social Welfare System* and *The Revolution in Welfare Administration: Rules, Discretion, and Entrepreneurial Government.*

**Harlan Hahn, Ph.D.** is Professor of Political Science at the University of Southern California and has written extensively on disability policy. Major disability-related publications include *Disabled Policy: America's Programs for the Handicapped, The Politics of Physical Differences: Disability and Dis-*

*crimination,* THE ISSUE OF EQUALITY: EUROPEAN PERCEPTIONS OF EMPLOYMENT FOR DISABLED PERSONS; and *Disability and Rehabilitation Policy.*

**Linda Hamilton Krieger, J.D.** is a former civil rights lawyer and is now Professor of Law at the University of California, Berkeley, School of Law and Codirector of the Center for the Study of Law and the Workplace. Her research interests center on antidiscrimination law and social cognition theory. Recent publications include *Civil Rights Perestroika: Intergroup Relations after Affirmative Action* and *The Content of Our Categories: A Cognitive Bias Approach to Discrimination and Equal Employment Opportunity.*

**Vicki A. Laden, J.D.** is a former public health policy researcher and Human Genome Project Fellow. She is now a lawyer in Oakland, California, where her practice centers on labor and employment law.

**Wendy E. Parmet, J.D.** is a disability rights lawyer and Professor of Law at the Northeastern University School of Law. Professor Parmet represented plaintiff Sidney Abbott in the 1998 Supreme Court case of *Bragdon v. Abbott,* and she writes extensively on disability law. Recent publications include *Positively Disabled: The Relationship between the Definition of Disability and Rights under the ADA* (with Patricia Illingworth) and *Individual Rights and Class Discrimination: The Fallacy of an Individualized Analysis of Disability.*

**Stephen L. Percy, Ph.D.** is Professor of Political Science and Director of the Center for Urban Initiatives and Research at the University of Wisconsin, Milwaukee. His major research interests include disability policy and implementation, urban politics, and urban service delivery. Professor Percy's recent publications include DISABILITY, CIVIL RIGHTS, AND PUBLIC POLICY: THE POLITICS OF IMPLEMENTATION; Challenges and Dilemmas in Implementing the ADA: Lessons and Achievements in the First Decade; and Disability Policy in the United States: Policy Evolution in an Intergovernmental System.

**Marta Russell** is an independent journalist who focuses on the socioeconomic dimensions of disability. She is the author of BEYOND RAMPS: DISABILITY AT THE END OF THE SOCIAL CONTRACT. She has published in the Journal of Disability Policy Studies, Disability and Society, Monthly Review, and The Review of Radical Economics. Her commentaries have appeared in the Los Angeles Times, the San Diego Union Tribune, the Austin Statesman, and many other newspapers. She writes a monthly column for 2Net.

**Kay Schriner, Ph.D.** is on the faculty of the School of Social Work at the University of Arkansas. Professor Schriner was the founding editor of the *Journal of Disability Policy Studies,* was a presidential appointee to the President's Committee on the Employment of People with Disabilities, and was awarded a Distinguished Switzer Fellowship by the National Institute on Disability and Rehabilitation Research. Dr. Schriner's research interests include the political participation of people with disabilities. Recent publications include *Creating the Disabled Citizen: How Massachusetts Disenfranchised People under Guardianship, Democratic Dilemmas: Notes on the ADA and Voting Rights of People with Disabilities,* and *Drawing the Competency Line: Insanity and Idiocy in American Suffrage.*

**Gregory Schwartz, J.D.** is a civil rights lawyer practicing in San Francisco. His practice centers primarily on employment discrimination law.

**Richard K. Scotch, Ph.D.** is Professor of Sociology and Political Economy in the School of Social Sciences at the University of Texas, Dallas. He is past president of the Society for Disability Studies and served on the Committee on Disability Studies in the Twenty-first Century organized by the National Institute of Disability and Rehabilitation Research. Some of his major publications include FROM GOOD WILL TO CIVIL RIGHTS: TRANSFORMING FEDERAL DISABILITY POLICY, DISABILITY PROTESTS: CONTENTIOUS POLITICS, 1970–1999 (with Sharon Barnartt), and *Disability as Human Variation: Implications for Policy* (with Kay Schriner).

**Anita Silvers, Ph.D.** is Professor of Philosophy at San Francisco State University. She has written extensively on justice and disability policy with a focus on the intersections between gender studies and disability. Some of her major publications include *The Double Edge of Convention: Disability Rights in Sports and Education* (with David Wasserman); *Disability and Biotechnology* (with Ari Satz); *The Rights of People with Disabilities; Reconciling Equality to Difference: Caring [F]or Justice for People with Disabilities; Reprising Women's Disability: Feminist Identity Strategy and Disability Rights;* DISABILITY, DIFFERENCE, DISCRIMINATION (with Mary Mahowald and David Wasserman); and AMERICANS WITH DISABILITIES: IMPLICATIONS OF THE LAW FOR INDIVIDUALS AND INSTITUTIONS (with Leslie Francis).

**Michael Ashley Stein, J.D., Ph.D.** is a lawyer and legal historian, and is Assistant Professor at the College of William and Mary School of Law. He is a former civil litigator and president of the National Disabled Bar Association. His recent publications include *Empirical Implications of Title I, Labor Markets Rationality and Workers with Disabilities,* and *Employing*

*People with Disabilities: Some Cautionary Thoughts for a Second Generation Civil Rights Statute.* During 2001–2002, he served as the National Institute on Disability Rehabilitation and Research Switzer Research Fellow.

# Index